THE INDUSTRIAL DIET

THE INDUSTRIAL DIET

THE DEGRADATION OF FOOD
AND THE STRUGGLE FOR HEALTHY EATING

Anthony Winson

NEW YORK UNIVERSITY PRESS
Washington Square, New York

First published in the U.S.A. in 2014 by
NEW YORK UNIVERSITY PRESS
Washington Square
New York, NY 10003
www.nyupress.org

First published in Canada by
UBC PRESS
The University of British Columbia
2029 West Mall, Vancouver, BC, V6T 1Z2

Library of Congress Cataloging-in-Publication Data

Winson, Anthony.
The industrial diet : the degradation of food and the struggle for healthy eating /
Anthony Winson.
pages cm
Includes bibliographical references and index.
ISBN 978-1-4798-6279-5 (pb : alk. paper)
1. Diet. 2. Nutrition. 3. Food supply – Health aspects. 4. Food industry and trade –
Health aspects. 5. Industrialization – Health aspects. I. Title.
RA784.W656 2014
613.2–dc23
2013011874

New York University Press books are printed on acid-free paper,
and their binding materials are chosen for strength and durability.
We strive to use environmentally responsible suppliers and materials
to the greatest extent possible in publishing our books.
10 9 8 7 6 5 4 3 2 1

Printed and bound in Canada by Friesens

CONTENTS

Figures and Tables

Figures

TABLES

ACKNOWLEDGMENTS

A S IS INEVITABLE IN WRITING a book of this nature, I owe numerous debts of gratitude. Particular thanks are due to the research
assistants I have had over the years: Chris Valequet, Lea Gallaugher, Alexandra
Dao, Myra Leydon, Tala El Ashkar, Ursula Abramczyk, and Shawna Holmes.
The assistance of Melisa Luymes at the last stages of producing the book is
most appreciated.

During the fieldwork phase of this project, the staff of Marin Organic in
California were especially helpful, particularly Helge Hellborg and Scott
Davidson, as were the staff at Food Share in Toronto, including Debbie Field
and Lori Nikkel. Discussions with Nick Saul of the Stop Community Food
Centre were valuable as well. In Guelph, Bruce Holub helped me understand
the issues surrounding trans fats while Rong Tsao provided valuable information on research about phytochemicals in food.

The interdisciplinary scholarly community that comes together for the
annual meetings of the Canadian Association for Food Studies and the Agriculture, Food and Human Values Society provided valuable venues to discuss
and gain feedback on the numerous ideas found in this book. The University
of Guelph provided financial support and a research leave, which were critical
for the book's completion.

At UBC Press, a great debt is owed to Peter Milroy for his original, and
sustained, enthusiasm for my book project. I also wish to thank Darcy

Cullen for her enthusiasm and many diligent efforts as my editor and Lesley Erickson, who was so conscientious about production details.

Sustaining such a long project is not possible without the support of friends and loved ones. My Wednesday night partners in crime – Hans, Thanasis, Glen, and Dave – provided levity when needed. To Mari, my thanks for useful discussions on issues of nutrition; and to Wady, your interest and spirited discussions along the way helped keep me going. My son, Devin, has had an engaged interest in this project, for which I am most thankful. Finally, for all her efforts reading early drafts, her critical comments and suggestions, and her emotional support during the ups and downs of this project, I owe Anita a very special debt of thanks.

THE INDUSTRIAL DIET

INTRODUCTION

THIS BOOK IS NOT SO MUCH about food as it is about what food has become. It is about the forces – socio-economic, technological, and ultimately political – that have reshaped food into edible commodities that too often subvert our well-being and promote disease instead of nourishing us. It seeks to appreciate how it is that the amorphous entity that is the "food industry" has been enormously successful not only in transforming food but also, more importantly, in constructing and diffusing an industrial mass diet. This diet is remarkably homogeneous in certain respects, and one can make a strong case that it impinges, to a greater or lesser degree, on the health of billions of human beings today.

The industrialization of food over the last 150 years or so has had a number of profound consequences. Among them, the nutritional degradation of food has been one of the most salient, if one of the least studied and understood. This book explores the key processes that have degraded food in the industrial era and the potent forces that have promoted an industrial mass diet that has come to supplant pre-existing diets in the developed, and now the developing, world. It also considers the variety of health consequences that are increasingly associated with this mass diet. Finally, this book considers the emerging resistance to the industrialization of food, in particular the incredibly promising struggle for healthy food environments, and the challenge it poses to "business as usual" in the food business.

Using a term such as "industrial mass diet" is a matter that bears further examination, if only because some may balk at its usage. Do we not live in a world of incredible dietary diversity, where globalized markets have made the culinary delights and traditions of faraway places available to us whenever we desire? The obvious answer is, to some degree at least, yes: those with sufficient disposable income do appear to. But in today's complicated world, answers are never so straightforward. There is a political-economic reality that stands between eaters and food. This reality must be examined carefully before we can begin to understand the food environments around us.

A diversity of foods certainly does exist, but for most this is a bit of a sham. Underlying this apparent diversity is an organized ensemble of edible commodities, typically processed to a greater or lesser extent, that are aggressively marketed now on a global basis to literally billions of eaters. These commodities are largely controlled by a remarkably small number of economic agents – corporations, to be more precise – that have a powerful vested interest in *not* letting what you or I eat for breakfast, lunch, supper, and snacks be simply a random act of the average human imagination. Far from it. But I am perhaps getting a bit ahead of myself. My arguments and evidence to win over skeptical readers, or at least challenge their cherished beliefs, shall unfold soon enough.

WHAT THIS BOOK DOES AND DOES NOT DO

A part of my agenda here is to explore, however briefly, some of the profound changes that have shaped human food environments and, in the process, changed diets and nutritional possibilities and, ultimately, health outcomes over long periods and in diverse places on the planet. I believe that the exploration of food environments must be grounded in the material reality of the times, and in the social structures and resultant power relationships that play their role in determining who will eat what, and how much.

Inevitably with such a vast topic, we will have to pick and choose where we focus our attention, in terms of both time and place. When I touch on the revolutionary change that occurred when humans embraced the domestication of plants and animals – the Neolithic Revolution – I consider evidence from diverse regions around the globe. However, given that my main emphasis is on more contemporary times and a preliminary exploration of what I term the "industrial diet," much of the focus of this book is on the nation that gave birth to it, the United States, and the food business based there that continues to promulgate this mass diet on an increasingly global level. The industrial diet could easily be termed the "American diet," so powerful has the influence of the American food industry been in shaping it.

Other countries, notably Canada and other now developed nations, receive some attention as I cover the historical development of this mass diet. When I turn to the globalization of this diet in more recent years, I broaden the geographical scope of my analysis considerably. Numerous regions in the global South are brought into the discussion at this point to illustrate what I consider to be important dietary trends in that part of the world. It should be emphasized, nevertheless, that I do not pretend to have captured, in any comprehensive sense, the rich reality of food environments in the global South. Each country, and indeed many regions within countries, has rich culinary traditions that predate the contemporary onslaught of industrial foods. Careful local studies will ultimately be necessary to yield further insights into the outcome of the confrontation of traditional local diets and an imported mass diet shaped by corporate imperatives.

In my discussion, I also consider food environments and diets in the exceedingly long period in which the human species existed before recorded human history. This period before the Neolithic Revolution, dating back to our Paleolithic origins, is the topic of much controversy and research. Nevertheless, there is a good argument to be made that this long period of human existence provided the environmental contexts that shaped the unique genetic makeup humans have today. And part of this genetic inheritance presumably determines what foods we thrive upon and also, by extension, the kinds of foods we might ingest that will undermine our health and shorten our lives.

I begin with some broad questions. I consider, for example, whether there is a particular diet for which we are most suited given our evolutionary development. Most species have a very narrow dietary niche upon which they depend. Some, like humans, seem to survive on a fairly broad range of animal- and plant-based foods. Our omnivorous traits have no doubt helped us to become as incredibly numerous as we are. But does that mean we can achieve our optimal health by eating just about anything? Few, other than teenagers, would argue that. In fact, with chronic disease becoming so prevalent in developed countries, medical and nutritional scientists, among others, are becoming more and more critical of many of the so-called foods that we now eat, and some have advanced the thesis that our present-day diets are radically discordant with what we had evolved to thrive on over millennia.

Another question I consider is what the emergence of large human communities, with complex stratifications and multiple inequalities, meant for human food environments and our health and well-being. How have they changed over the millennia, and in particular, what are the more recent transformations, and their consequences, in the era of industrial capitalism? It is the latter to which I devote most of my attention, particularly what Eric Hobsbawm has termed the "long twentieth century," when so many drastic shifts in the quality and quantity of food production, in the processing and technology of food, and in the distribution of food occurred.

WHAT INFLUENCED THE WRITING OF THIS BOOK?

The subject of food has become, in a sense, a crucible in which ideas, values, and political projects of varying provenance interact, and out of which exciting new intellectual orientations are emerging. Among the influences on this book are, of course, the often sparkling insights and wisdom of numerous authors who have sought to explore the intertwined worlds of agriculture, food, food processing and preparation, culinary arts, and the modern industry devoted to the selling of food. In years past, the slow food movement has encouraged us to think about what we are losing, from a cultural and culinary perspective, as we allow industrial foods free rein in our food environments.[1] At the same time, students of the food system have documented and critically analyzed the metamorphosis of the organic food movement to its present state, comprising a multi-billion-dollar sector of modern agriculture that is still rapidly expanding.[2] Concern with the fate of millions of smallholding farmers in the poorest countries of the world has galvanized activists to promote a fair trade system for an expanding number of foods produced there in an effort to inject an element of equity into an increasingly inequitable global economy. This phenomenon too has inspired careful scrutiny.[3]

More recently, the intense interest in relocalizing food systems has brought into focus questions of the sustainability of a food system built upon global sourcing that is so completely petroleum dependent and damaging to the environment.[4] It has also spawned a growing "buy local" movement that is spreading well beyond the individual actions of citizen/consumers to encompass an ever larger number of independent restaurant operators and even the beginnings of a "buy in" on the part of large retail food chains. I would also note the important contributions of those seeking to bring to the fore the issue of animal welfare and the tragedy that factory farming represents for several warm-blooded animal species upon which we choose to depend for our subsistence.[5] To this upwelling of interest in what have been called alternative agricultural and food movements, I would add an incipient movement organized around the struggle for healthy eating. Underlying the latter is a phenomenon that is reaching global dimensions, and which has played an important role in propelling this book project forward: the crisis in what medical and nutritional scientists term "overweight and obesity."

A CRISIS IN SEARCH OF AN EXPLANATION

Having a long-term interest in agriculture and food, and in the food business, I was both intrigued and disturbed by what was emerging as a veritable tectonic shift in the human physical condition. For the first time in the history of our species, the majority of adults in certain societies, and surprising proportions of children and youth there, was becoming what we have come to term "overweight" and "obese." Up until fairly recent times, in most if not all societies, this condition was almost entirely the fate of a very small pampered elite. To be obese was a marker of high status, privilege, and, often, power and influence. Now, its sociological significance is more complicated, and it has emerged as a mass phenomenon. In any case, as Tim Lang and Michael Heasman have remarked in their prescient book *Food Wars,* "Obesity is the *leitmotif* for the modern food age."[6]

By the late 1990s, if not before, medical and nutritional scientists were amassing ever more detailed evidence of the likely health outcomes this phenomenon would produce as well. As the US government's recently released report on dietary guidelines for Americans points out, approximately one-third of Americans are now clinically obese, and when those simply overweight are included in the count, the numbers encompass some 72 percent of women and 64 percent of men. No longer attempting to sugar-coat this reality, the authorities behind these guidelines note starkly that "such a high prevalence ... leads to a much higher risk of premature death and many serious disorders."[7]

One important aspect that spurred my desire to study this phenomenon was the contrast between the rigour with which medical and nutritional science could document overweight and obesity in society – and, increasingly, the negative health outcomes as well – and the rather pathetic analysis of the root causes of this situation – its etiology, to use the standard medical term. To be fair, scientists in these fields have played a leading role in bringing into sharper focus, for both governments and the general public, the extent of population-wide weight gain that is occurring in one society after another. Such research has also mapped out the increasingly global dimensions of this issue. So too has it provided an expanding body of evidence that overweight and obesity has serious related-disease impacts, or co-morbidities, that dramatically affect one's quality of life in later years. Moreover, we now have more evidence than ever that obesity is correlated with early mortality.[8] In addition to this research, studies in these fields have alerted us to the deleterious impacts of several core components of the contemporary industrial diet – notably, added sweeteners, sodium, and certain types of fats.

As for explaining the obesity crisis, I believe it is mistaken to expect the natural sciences to yield significant results. For some time, a popular medical explanation relied on what was basically a mechanical input/output model. One study in a prominent science journal some years ago was tellingly titled "Obesity in Britain: Gluttony or Sloth?" Too many nutrients going in and not enough energy expended. The result: the balance needed for stable weights was upset. The solution proposed was both remarkably simplistic and entirely focused on individual responsibility: eat less and/or move more. These kinds of explanations are still heard among prominent medical authorities.

Much was written about the so-called thrifty gene as well, the idea that with food scarcity and starvation over millennia, through the process of natural selection, nature had favoured humans, who had genetically evolved to rapidly put on weight when food was abundant. Now that food was abundant as never before, our genes were working against us.

These were interesting and satisfying explanations, as long as one did not think about the issue too deeply. What could not be easily accounted for by these kinds of explanations of why so many humans were rapidly getting larger was why this is happening only now – and so quickly. Certainly, this is what intrigued me. With a background in research on agriculture and the food-processing and retailing business, I gradually became convinced that the tools of the natural sciences – medical, nutritional, or otherwise – were not going to be the appropriate ones for understanding what is, at the most fundamental level, a social, economic, and political problem. A genuine understanding of the root causes of this issue and *real* solutions to what has become a first-order health problem, as opposed to damage-control measures, lie largely outside the realm of natural science. This is despite the never-ceasing interest of pharmaceutical corporations to find the magic bullet for obesity, and the willingness of authorities to funnel prodigious amounts of funding to natural scientists seeking remedies for it.

If the medical and nutritional sciences do not have the tools to understand the forces producing this crisis, nor the solutions needed to confront it, then who does? As a social scientist, I am strongly inclined to believe real understanding lies with the social, rather than natural, sciences. But have social science contributions made significant progress here? An answer to this inevitably gets somewhat complicated. Today, a good deal of the literature in this area is dominated by writers who see the obesity crisis as overblown and as, essentially, a social construct. Some have argued that the predominant measure of obesity, the body mass index (BMI), is flawed and not reliable. Although there is a small element of truth to this assertion,[9] it hardly justifies dismissing population-wide weight gains out of hand. More significantly, some authors have argued that it is a crisis constructed largely by specific vested interests in society that benefit from the increasing medicalization of this condition and the prominence it has achieved in the mass media. Pharmaceutical companies and medical specialists are prime examples of benefactors in this view.

Aligned with, and often underpinning, some social science approaches to the contemporary phenomenon of obesity is the critique of nutritionism. Gyorgy Scrinis's essay "On the Ideology of Nutritionism" has been particularly influential in this regard, although the term predates it.[10] Scrinis charges nutritional science with various kinds of reductionism with respect to food: the reduction of foods and diets to their effects on bodily health; the reductive focus on individual foods in isolation from other foods, diets, and broader factors; and (and most importantly for him) the reductive focus of nutritional science on nutrient composition as the principal means for evaluating the quality of foods and their relationship to physical health.[11] In addition, Scrinis argues that nutritionism, with this focus on health, undermines other equally important modes of understanding and engaging with food. Although it is not possible to treat this issue in real depth here, this critique does bear on my analysis.

I am in substantial agreement with the critique of nutritionism to the extent that the reductionist tendencies inherent in it are being exploited by the food industry to promote dubious claims about nutritionally enhanced "functional foods" and highly processed products with nutrients identified by nutritional science as beneficial. Moreover, its proponents argue that the ideology of nutritionism has promoted widespread confusion among the lay public about healthy eating more generally. There is no doubt considerable truth to this.

On the other hand, reductionist thinking, and practice, is hardly the sole domain of nutritional science. I would contend that other approaches that arguably are a good deal more influential than nutritional science with the general public are even more reductionist. For example, the contemporary phenomenon of the celebrity chef and the food programs featuring them tend to be almost wholly focused on the *sensory* qualities of the meals being prepared, regardless of the fact that these meals very often use manifestly unhealthy ingredients and are prepared in unhealthy ways solely to maximize visual and sensory appeal, when they need not be (e.g., food is fried when it could be baked with much less fat). This sensory reductionism, in other words, reigns supreme in the hedonistic culture promoted in such widely viewed programs. Indeed, it is the exception (think Jamie Oliver) and not the rule that a celebrity chef pays attention to the health of the audience, even though it is perfectly possible to prepare delightful meals with ingredients that enhance, rather than damage, the health of those who consume them. Healthful cooking and sensory pleasure are incompatible only to those with a limited culinary imagination.

My fear about the critique of nutritionism is that those who embrace it may tend to throw out the baby with the bathwater, as the saying goes. Food should have sensory appeal, and it should serve as a catalyst for social engagement and cultural regeneration, to be sure, as Scrinis implies. But it is also meant to nurture us physically, and when it increasingly does not, we ought to pay attention to why this is so. In part, I tend to believe that we can better understand why what we eat is undoing our health by understanding something about the ways that whole foods have been degraded, why they have been degraded, and what the effects of this on our health are likely to be.

An overarching theme that orients this book is that between food producers and eaters lies a political-economic reality that shapes the food system and food environments within it. One of the main keys to understanding the contemporary crisis of obesity and elaborating effective strategies to overcome it is, therefore, understanding the forces that structure our food economy. This is the domain of political-economic analysis. Beyond this, however, is the need to better understand how people confront, adapt, or resist these forces as they go about their lives. These concerns with structure and agency lie at the heart of much social science today, of course, and I believe it is the tools of social science that hold the most promise for successfully understanding the global obesity crisis – and, I might add, that they are the most effective tools to aid those who might want to confront this crisis.

There is also one factor that may ultimately force society to finally undertake a genuinely critical appraisal of the causes of population-wide weight gain and obesity, and also of a host of chronic diseases, some of which are closely related to obesity. This is the astounding cost to society that chronic disease represents, and the increasing evidence that diet is a key determining factor. Indeed, this cost threatens to financially debilitate the state and seriously drain resources from pressing societal needs other than health care. Obesity-related chronic diseases are going to become staggeringly expensive. Two examples from the United States are instructive. The cost of cardiovascular disease, now the leading cause of death in that country and elsewhere, is projected by the American Heart Association to triple by 2030 to $800 billion annually. Type 2 diabetes, a largely preventable disease, is expected to afflict half of all Americans by 2020 and cost $500 billion annually.[12] Yes, these almost unbelievable estimates refer to *annual* costs, hard as this may be to comprehend.

A More Global Perspective

These are the concerns that initially inspired my interest in the subject matter of this book. Other factors have shaped my views and analysis over the longer term and have instilled an intense interest in the developing world. Some of my most salient experiences date back to the late 1970s and early 1980s, when I began my adult travels in Mexico, Central America, and South America. At a time when a one-star hotel was a rarely afforded luxury, the daily search for sustenance led me to many new culinary discoveries and, it must be added, the hard realization that pathogenic bacteria in food and drink are something to be taken very seriously.

As curiosity-driven wanderings turned into more focused and disciplined graduate and later postgraduate field research, I gained an appreciation for (what some call) "food environments" that radically departed from what had then become the North American norm – the procurement of food from supermarket chain stores filled with processed edible products, or from another type of chain store operation, the ubiquitous fast-food outlet.

The countries I travelled through and lived in at that time were, in fact, in the early transitional stage of what had become, in the developed world, a much more corporate-controlled food system. The early supermarkets I visited in Mexico and Costa Rica – for they did exist there some thirty years ago – were small, poorly organized affairs selling mostly canned and packaged foods that (to me at least) were largely unappealing. Produce sections were largely stocked with a limited range of fruits and vegetables of questionable quality, usually much inferior to produce that could be had at the open-air market a few blocks away. The same was true of meat and fish. And yet, they were attracting a sizable and largely middle-class clientele, whether because of a perceived convenience (they were usually open at night, whereas markets were not, and some had ample free parking), or a desire to emulate a North American lifestyle, or likely both. As for fast food, it was also becoming established, attracting a small clientele that was drawn largely from the emerging middle class and was eager to emulate American ways. But outlets were few, and in Central America only to be found in the capital cities.

A stint of fieldwork in Nicaragua a few years later, during the early years of the Sandinista revolution, brought me into contact with the "popular kitchens" of that era. These were largely open-air eating establishments where, buffet style, one could select from a large variety of meats, fish, vegetables, and starches served from immense steaming cauldrons. Food was plentiful, notably varied, nutritious, and cheap enough to allow local people of modest means to afford a sizable noontime meal. Although there was one McDonald's outlet in the capital city, Managua, it was expensive by local standards and attracted only those of some affluence, many of whom travelled, often frequently, to the United States.

Around the same time (mid-1980s), I visited a country somewhat larger and more prosperous, and more developed, than tiny Nicaragua. My sojourn in Ecuador, in the Andean region of South America, brought me into contact with researchers from various disciplines, including nutritionists examining the diets of urban workers. They talked about a rapid dietary transition they were witnessing among this group of urban working poor. I was both surprised and disturbed to hear that the prominent elements of this new diet were white bread and Coca-Cola.

In an important sense, these experiences challenged the prevalent "truths" of that time, truths that have stayed with us. By this I'm referring to the strongly held notion that part of the benefit coming from "development" is to leave behind an impoverished and meagre diet and embrace new opportunities of dietary variety and ample nutrition. In real terms, then, it was the promised shift from the monotony of rice and beans every day to a richer and more satisfying diet replete with meat on a regular basis and access to all the products of the modern food system. As with most received wisdom, there no doubt was some element of truth to it, but also a good deal of falsehood, and it involved the failure to understand something much more complex that was happening. As diets were changing, there would be winners and losers – the losers in this case being the new impoverished urban working class. And as we shall see, even those we might call winners would find that the new diet offered by the industrial food system would have a definite downside for their health.

As we are better aware today, food environments have been transformed again and again, sometimes in incredibly profound ways. The food environments I encountered in my travels through Central and South America in the 1970s and 1980s had been shaped, in fact, by several centuries of colonial conquest, epidemic disease, plunder, and exploitation. Indeed, we know that the agricultural and dietary traditions predating the pre-colonial era had survived the shock of conquest in some forms. Then again, after 1850, upon achieving independence from colonial masters, these new nations found themselves reinserted into the expanding worldwide economy as landed elites, and wealthy *parvenus* began to invest heavily in export crops such as coffee for mass consumption in Europe, which was then being radically transformed by industrial capitalism. This momentous historical transition dramatically reshaped social structures in the countryside.[13] I spent the first part of my academic career, in fact, documenting this process in parts of Central America and elsewhere. But this transition must have also had profound effects on local food environments and the dietary regimen of the mass of the labouring population. We know much more today about how this process changed agrarian social structure, however, than we know about its repercussions for the food environment, diet, and the nutritional outcomes for the populations affected.

Amid all this relatively recent attention to food, it is somewhat remarkable that so little attention has been given to the very essence of what makes food so important to us: its provision (but increasingly non-provision) of the very nutrients that sustain our existence. This book, with its focus on the degradation of diets and the emergent struggle for healthy eating, aims to encourage a reflection on the state of the food environments around us, as well as interest in and engagement with realistic and innovative strategies that can lead to a healthier future for the broad mass of the population.

PART 1

FOOD ENVIRONMENTS FROM PALAEOLITHIC TIMES

THERE IS A STILL LARGELY unwritten history of human diets that pre-date the industrial era. It is true that fascinating histories of food have been compiled, and more in-depth work has been done on diets and cuisines in limited geographical zones in very specific historical eras. Some of these studies prove useful in distinguishing very broad trends in nutritional outcomes over very long periods, as does the concept of dietary regimes as a tool to help understand these trends.

Diets have always reflected the material conditions under which humans have existed at a given point in time. By this I refer to the opportunities and constraints dictated by the environments they inhabit, and the advantages that are provided by a given level of technological development. In this regard, we can speak of the advantages for food procurement and preparation provided by the development of stone weapons and cutting tools in prehistoric times and the advantages that came with metal weapons, implements, and vessels during the Iron and Bronze Ages of human technological development.

With the low levels of technology that characterized hunting and gathering during the Stone Age, environmental conditions were all-important. If local edible plants and wild game were becoming scarce, Stone Age technologies were not going to be able to delay the urgent necessity of searching for lands where foods were more abundant. With limited abilities to carry quantities of food any distance or to store foods, diets would have had to reflect the immediate environment and the richness or scarcity of foods it contained. It is worth reflecting on the fact that the diets of our hunting and gathering past were the diets that have shaped us as a species for the great majority of our existence.

The gradual domestication of some plant and animal species that has been termed the "Neolithic Revolution" opened up a completely new chapter for the human species. Increasingly, it meant that beyond environmental conditions, specific social and economic arrangements as well as the structures of political domination, regulation, and control were becoming ever more significant in determining who ate what. Humans were taking on a more sedentary existence, and more and more of them were living in close proximity to each other, in ever larger settlements that were taking on decidedly stratified characteristics. Contemporary research supports the hypothesis that with social stratification came differential access to foods, and diets began to calcify along hierarchical lines.

It is at this point that it becomes possible to speak of dietary regimes. The concept of dietary regimes recognizes that, since the Neolithic Revolution, diets are no longer simply a reflection of what nature has to offer at any given point in time. Diets for more and more people of evolving hierarchical societies are increasingly social constructs, wherein, in addition to cultural and religious practices, technological development and power relationships within communities take on increasing potency. Diets have and no doubt always will reflect, to some degree, individual human preferences and idiosyncrasies, but, in a more important way, they exhibit certain common features at a given place and point in time. Dietary regime is a construct meant to capture the commonalities in dietary experience and to help us understand why they exist and the specific issues or contradictions that characterize a society's dietary arrangements.

The concept of dietary regimes owes much to the food-regime approach that revived the interdisciplinary study of agriculture, markets, and the state in the modern industrial era. These interlinked themes were, of course, very much at the core of the classical political-economic works of Adam Smith, David Ricardo, John Stuart Mill, and Karl Marx. The food-regime approach has produced verdant discussions and debates over the last two decades or so. It has not been particularly strong on shedding light on the nature, determinants, and contradictions of mass diets, however. For this reason, it is useful to consider dietary regimes as a necessary complementary conceptual approach.

CHAPTER ONE

BETWEEN PRODUCERS AND EATERS

SHAPING MASS DIETS

A NEW CONCEPT OF DIETARY regimes can help us understand the relationship between the food system as it has evolved in the modern era and diet and health, and it can help us understand the manifold implications of the industrialization of food, most notably how this industrialization is implicated in the global obesity issue confronting us.

This industrialization of food cannot be reduced to the way food has been changed by industrial agriculture and manufacturing processes over the past century or so. This is, of course, part of the story, but only part of it. The industrialization of food has also entailed the production of a mass diet that is very much part of the entire process; indeed, it is central to its reproduction over time. If there is a strong case for arguing that this reality is not well captured by the medical and nutritional sciences in their efforts to understand this crisis, have the social sciences fared much better? A good part of the social science approach to issues of obesity, diet, and nutrition has been to take a cautionary and critical approach and to both contest the medicalization of obesity and critique the rise of what has been called "nutritionism." I note in the Introduction my areas of agreement and skepticism regarding this line of thinking. However, there is another literature within the interdisciplinary study of food and agriculture in the social sciences that has laid important foundations for understanding the relationship between the food system, diet, and health outcomes, and this is the literature on food regimes, a concept that has seen renewed interest of late. Although a conceptual innovation in the area of food, diet, and health is needed beyond what the concept of food regimes has offered, I believe the concept of dietary regimes, as I develop it here, complements the food-regime approach. But first, what do I mean by "dietary regimes"?

A DIETARY REGIME APPROACH

There are several concepts that can be useful in understanding the complex and dynamic reality of food and the constitution of what we might call mass diets, or the kinds of foods that are habitually eaten in a given community, region, or wider society. The overarching conceptual term that I use to orient the discussion throughout the book is that of "dietary regimes." What do I mean by this concept, and how will it be used? In answering this question, it is useful to step back for a minute to consider separately the terms "diet" and "regime."

"Diet" is a term most commonly used today to indicate a food regimen one follows, usually to promote weight loss or because of some specific health concern. But the term has long meant something of a broader nature, such as "food and drink regularly provided or consumed," or "the usual food and drink of a person or animal," to quote two standard dictionary meanings of the term.[1] In focusing on the more recent transformations of food environments, I am exploring nothing more or less than how changes came about to the foods and beverages usually consumed by broad masses of people within particular societies.

At the most basic level, the term "regime" may denote the conditions under which a scientific or industrial process takes place. In its origins, the term "regime" is laden with meanings of a system of political rule, and its earlier usage was often more explicitly political, as in reference to the *ancien régime* in Europe of the eighteenth century. Although contemporary usage is more eclectic, my use of the term retains a political dimension.

The concept of dietary regimes as employed here is a conceptual tool to draw attention to the fact that diets are ultimately social and political projects and have been even before recorded time. As such, diets reflect the material conditions of a particular society, and specific social and economic arrangements, as well as the structures of political domination, regulation, and control. I am most concerned to examine the period when industrial capitalism began what has amounted to a massive reshaping of the world, and especially the last 150 years. Nevertheless, it is worthwhile considering previous dietary regimes, if only to throw into relief what is unique about more recent dietary arrangements.

FROM FOOD REGIMES TO DIETARY REGIMES

Students of the interdisciplinary study of agriculture and food within the social sciences and humanities may think of the food-regime approach and wonder what relation exists between dietary regimes and the former. The food-regime approach offers a macro-political-economic analysis of the global food system over different historical epochs. The concept of food regimes was introduced by Harriet Friedmann and Philip McMichael more than twenty years ago to explore the unique role of agriculture in the development of the world capitalist economy and the evolution and trajectory of the state system.[2]

The food-regime approach has garnered considerable interest, and criticism, over the intervening years and has received renewed attention more recently.[3] Bringing forward insights of the French regulationist school of political economy,[4] the concept of food regimes highlighted two interrelated processes: (1) the development of a system of independent, liberal nation states and (2) the industrialization of agriculture and food. More recently, Hugh Campbell and Jane Dixon have summarized what the food-regime approach consists of:

> The "food regime" is a historically significant cluster of global scale food relationships that contributed to stabilizing and underwriting a period of growth in global capitalism. A food regime comprised of a series of relationships, often enshrined in rule-making and enforcing institutions (including imperial/national policy, trade policy, institutional forms of land use/farming, company regulation, commodity complexes, labour relations, consumption relations in the industrial core) ... These relationships coalesced to form a stable pattern of accumulation (historical conjuncture) over a period of time, before then destabilizing and moving into disjuncture and crisis.[5]

Why do we need a concept of dietary regimes, and would not the food-regime approach serve our needs? My answer to this is that food regimes offer a very useful conceptual tool to help us think through the relationship between capital and the nation state, and the specific features of the global food trade, and their respective roles and influences at different points in time in restructuring agriculture. However, the approach was not developed to explore the dietary and nutritional dimension of food commodity systems. We need another conceptual tool to explore these matters, a tool that can be complimentary to the conceptual apparatus of the food-regime approach but that has its own emphases and temporal demarcations. Nevertheless, I think it is useful as we map out the concept of dietary regimes to see where the distinct food regimes as outlined by Friedmann and McMichael can help us clarify the forces and relationships underlying dietary arrangements in different historical periods.

The concept of dietary regimes is a tool with which we may build upon the insights of the food-regime approach to better understand the constitution, reproduction, crisis, and transformation of mass diets. In principle, I do not see why the concept cannot be extended back into history to earlier, precapitalist systems of production, although, as with the analysis of food regimes, I develop here the concept of dietary regimes primarily to explore the capitalist food economy.

If food regimes can be seen to constitute a foundation upon which dietary regimes are organized, one cannot, I would argue, be reduced to the other. In what follows, I outline a schema of dietary regimes that can orient our thinking of broad-based eating patterns and the conditions that determine these. The schema is cast at a very general level, meant to capture only the most broad-based characteristics of dietary arrangements. It is meant to deny neither the complexity of diets nor the effects of a host of factors that may mean that diets in specific places and points in time may diverge rather substantially from those features that broadly define a particular regime.

My particular focus is with dietary regimes characteristic of the industrial era and up until the present day. It makes sense to call these industrial dietary regimes, as the industrialization of food is the central motif of this period, and indeed continues to be, despite the increasing complexity of the contemporary food system.

DIETARY REGIMES OF EARLY AGRARIAN SOCIETIES

The Neolithic Revolution, entailing the domestication of numerous plant and animal species for human usage, was a pivotal process in the evolution of the human species. Beginning some eight to ten thousand years ago and spanning a considerable period, diets for the mass of humanity changed, and rather substantially. Before this fundamental change for the human species, there was an exceptionally long period (in terms of our natural history as a distinct species) when hunting and gathering activities of one sort or another made human existence possible. The so-called Palaeolithic diets of this period lie beyond the scope of any discussion of dietary regimes, but they may in fact provide us with a very useful benchmark – as diets that we evolved as a species to thrive on – to gauge contemporary diets and understand their impacts upon health.

The impact of the Neolithic Revolution on diet was twofold. First, the contents of diet began to change as a few cultivated grains came to replace animal protein and wild plants in the diets of many. Second, as humans replaced foraging with agriculture to meet their subsistence needs, there arose the possibility for ever greater sedentary settlements, urbanization, technological advancement, and long-distance trade. With this, diets took on a class character, as emergent social hierarchies gradually structured who got what.

The dietary regimes of early agrarian societies, or so the sporadic evidence of them would suggest, were dominated by a grain-gruel diet for the great majority, with considerably more dietary diversity for elites as social inequalities became much more marked. This dietary divergence had certain health outcomes as well. There is evidence that agriculture intensified under the pressures of maintaining large standing armies and satisfying the needs of larger numbers of urbanized people. Historians have suggested that in the Mediterranean region, where wheat was a staple, diets changed somewhat with the disintegration of the Roman Empire and the influence of the Germanic peoples and their customs from the north. Nevertheless, a grain-gruel regimen supplemented by an array of vegetables, herbs, and products from wild areas, as well as the occasional inclusion of meat in the diet, would likely have been the lot for the great majority.

Far-reaching changes in diet were to come after the so-called voyages of discovery that opened up the New World for Europeans. What Crosby termed the "Columbian Exchange" entailed the transfer of a variety of plants and domestic animal species to the western hemisphere, along with devastating European diseases.[6] On the other hand, New World crops, especially the potato and maize, are credited with allowing for an unprecedented population expansion in Europe.[7]

From the end of the fifteenth century until approximately the latter part of the eighteenth century, then, diets in much of Europe and the New World may be said to be in a state of flux as an uneven transition to a more decid-edly industrial food economy based on the factory system slowly began to take shape, first in Britain and later with much vigour in the United States. During this time, the emergence of agrarian capitalism in Britain and then elsewhere produced tremendous dislocation among the rural population, while the standards of living of large masses of people in the British Isles and in parts of continental Europe, especially eastern Europe, went into decline – and with it the quality of their foods. The far-reaching social disruptions occasioned by this development opened the door much wider to the use of the potato in particular, and later sugar, in the diets of growing masses of European peoples.

It was during the period of agrarian capitalism that the unity of produc-tion and consumption in the rural domestic unit was increasingly disrupted, and indeed fundamentally torn asunder in the English context, by the thirst of powerful landowners for more lucrative opportunities. This initially took the form of the displacement of the rural folk and the transformation of their lands, as well as the land historically held in the commons, into sheep pas-ture. For the rural majority, the loss of control over the means of gaining a material subsistence that this dispossession entailed meant an increasing loss of control over diet also.

THE FIRST INDUSTRIAL DIETARY REGIME, 1870-1949

Capitalism as an economic system found its beginnings more than two hun-dred years ago with the mass production of commodities in a factory system using labour free of feudal encumbrances, a development that according to a classical treatment of the subject, really set in after 1760 in Britain, the first country to employ such a system on a large scale.[8] Initially, factory produc-tion was centred on commodities such as textiles; with the exception of sugar production (which although processed on a large scale was associated with slavery for a long time), it was only considerably later that factory production came to characterize the production of food.

It has been argued by some that the industrialization of the food economy did not occur until after the Second World War, which, others have argued, inaugurated an era of "durable" foods.[9] In fact, we can discern the emer-gence of a truly industrial dietary regime by the latter third of the nineteenth century. The foundations for this were significant technological changes in agricultural production and the establishment of new relationships between agriculture and industry. The period 1870 to 1949 has been termed the "first food regime" and is defined in part by a dramatic upsurge in exports of wheat and meat from new settler nations – the United States, Canada, Australia, and New Zealand – to Europe.[10] As various authors have argued,[11] a central dimension of these settler nations was the establishment of specialized commercial family-farming units that controlled land sufficient to allow for the accumulation of surplus that could be used to purchase productive inputs (principally horse-drawn farm implements initially) and consumption goods. Once tariff protection for industry had been established in these settler societies, purchases of these goods from local manufacturing enterprises became much more attractive, and this was a major stimulus to the first phase of industrialization in these countries. The other side of the coin was the development of markets for more differentiated local farm production as an urban working class rapidly expanded in the settler economies themselves.[12] These newly independent settler states, with their increasingly integrated agriculture and industry, come to form the model for integrated nation states of the twentieth century.[13] Among them, the United States was, of course, pre-eminent.

How were these developments relevant to the formation of the first industrial dietary regime? As with the formation of food regimes in the capitalist era, developments in the United States were central to the formation of the industrial diet that later came to transform food environments worldwide. The development of integrated internal markets in the United States augured well for those entrepreneurs intent on establishing business enterprises that could manufacture a growing range of processed foodstuffs.

The emergence of the first industrial dietary regime is perhaps no better illustrated than by the flour-milling industry. In fact, the milling companies of North America producing wheat flour played a pioneering role in the transformation of food production from a small-scale artisanal type of operation to modern factory methods (see Chapter 4). I see the industrialization of flour milling as lying at the core of the first industrial dietary regime, which is the reason it makes sense to establish the beginnings of this regime with the switch to industrial milling, which happened in the 1870s and afterward in the United States.

Small-scale milling operations, typically water-powered, were an essential part of the foundation of early proto-industry in North America. A confluence of factors, including the possibility of opening up the west to wheat farming, the availability of new hard wheat varieties that grew best there and the new milling technology needed to successfully process them, rapid urbanization, the consolidation of a national market with the construction of an extensive network of railroads, and the expanding print media, to name some of the key ones, spurred the industrialization of milling on a large scale after 1870 or so.

With the advent of new sifting and roller-milling technology, wheat flour was transformed from a relatively perishable product produced in small-scale mills and suitable only for local and regional markets to a relatively durable food commodity that could be stored for considerable periods and marketed on a much larger scale, using some of the emergent mass advertising opportunities that the print media offered by the latter part of the nineteenth century. Wheat flour became a pioneering branded commodity by the late nineteenth century, then, even before the iconic Coca-Cola did around the turn of that century, and was sold on a regional and then national scale by large milling companies based in milling capitals such as Minneapolis, St. Louis, Buffalo, and Toronto.

Despite recent claims that the industrialization of food began with the spread of the fast-food industry after the Second World War,[14] it in fact began much earlier, and so too did the impact of this industrialization on diet. In addition to flour milling, the other main sectors emblematic of this first phase of the industrialization of food were the meat-packing, ready-to-eat breakfast cereal, and canning industries.

The canning industry was a pillar of the emergent industrial dietary regime at this time. The tin can for preserving food had been developed in Europe during the time of Napoleon I and was to come into widespread use to provision the troops during the American Civil War more than half a century later. Already by 1870, the canning industry was sizeable enough to be listed separately in the US census of that year. By that time, something in the order of 30 million cans of food were being processed annually in the United States and at prices that placed this product within the reach of consumers of humble means. As a US government bulletin dated 1893 noted, though no doubt with some hyperbole,

> Preserved food has been a great democratic factor, and has nearly obliterated one of the old lines of demarcation between the poor and the wealthy. Vegetables out of season are no longer a luxury of the rich ... In the American grocery – pineapples from Singapore, salmon from British Colombia, fruit from California, peas from France, okra from Louisiana, sweet corn from New York, string beans

from Scotland, mutton from Australia, sardines from Italy, stand side by side on the shelves.[15]

Canning technologies were slowly being perfected and by the first decades of the twentieth century had advanced sufficiently to make large canning factories possible. It took only the innovations of an entrepreneur like H.J. Heinz to harness the technologies already established with the new marketing technologies and begin producing industrially processed fruits and vegetables on what was, in historical terms, a very large scale.

It was Marx who argued that the concentration and centralization of capital was one of the hallmarks of capitalism as an economic system,[16] and this was nowhere more true than in the industrial canning sector. In Canada, the firm that became Dominion Canners extensively bought up and consolidated fruit and vegetable canners in a process of horizontal integration, until it had become, by the 1930s, the largest canning operation in the British Empire. Canned fruits and vegetables, jams, preserves, pickles, and the like were being produced on a mass scale for national markets decades before the Second World War, in other words.[17]

The case of the ready-to-eat breakfast cereal industry is another clear-cut example of the early dietary transformation that constituted the advent of the industrial diet. Packaged hot-cereal breakfast products were being marketed in national print media by the 1890s in the United States.[18] Shortly after the turn of the nineteenth century, a new industry centred on experiments with a grain-based breakfast food designed to be eaten cold gathered momentum, notably in Battle Creek, Michigan. This new type of product was shaped, cooked, dried, and packaged by the manufacturer.

What made the impact of these products revolutionary, in dietary terms, was not the technological innovations so much as the marketing innovations. Taking their cue from earlier efforts of the flour-milling industry to brand what had once been an undifferentiated commodity – flour – breakfast cereal entrepreneurs such as C.W. Post and the Kellogg brothers used the emerging technologies of mass marketing to create nationally branded products in the very early decades of the twentieth century, products that were soon marketed nationwide in the United States and not long afterward in Canada as well. In the minds of consumers, these products were no longer run-of-the-mill food commodities such as oatmeal but, rather, differentiated through extra processing and, particularly, extraordinary expenditures (for the time) on advertising as qualitatively distinct and superior. Thus, their manufacturers could command higher prices. As the food historian Harvey Levenstein has noted about the impact of this on the eating patterns of Americans: "The entrepreneurs of the breakfast food industry ... almost singlehandedly destroyed the traditional American breakfast."[19]

The remarkable success of the new breakfast cereal entrepreneurs was a harbinger of early dietary change, as had been the success of the concentrated flour-milling companies some decades earlier with their highly processed "patented" refined white branded flours. Both of these developments signified the expanded consumption in the American diet of a nutritionally degraded grain food that, via processing, was now largely devoid of the essential B vitamins, iron, calcium, and fibre that had previously been present in flour produced by simpler stone-grinding technology. Moreover, as research many decades later was to indicate, these edible products were also unhealthy because of the rapidity with which they provoke a spike in blood sugar in the human body. The high glycemic effect of this food was enhanced, it was later demonstrated, by the specific type of processing the grain underwent in the factory.[20]

Mass Marketing and the "Normalization" of Industrial Diets

The industrial diet cannot be reduced to the transformation of foodstuffs in a factory system. For an industrial mass diet to really become established, it required the development and refinement of the phenomenon we have come to call mass marketing. The food and beverage industry took a leading role in the establishment of mass marketing in the modern age and continues to be heavily reliant on advertising. Food and beverage entrepreneurs, in the United States in particular, seized the opportunities offered by emergent mass communication technologies (newspapers, mass magazines, and, later, radio) in the late nineteenth and early twentieth centuries, first with industrial flours and shortly after with carbonated beverages and ready-to-eat breakfast cereals. A few of those entrepreneurs who took the big chances with new and expensive promotional strategies in the new media reaped extraordinary benefits. They were able to marry the explosive productive potential of the factory system for producing food products with strategies that dramatically boosted the demand for their products. The limited liability companies they pioneered came to dominate food environments for generations to come.

What made processed industrial foods a "diet" was the fact that the products of that system were also widely adopted as suitable foods. For this to happen, such products had to be in a sense normalized, because they were in no way a normal part of food environments up to that time. Early mass advertising campaigns were crucial in this regard in that they made novel processed foodstuffs acceptable, indeed desirable, by trading on promises of convenience and time saving, on claims to purity, and on suggestions that the consumption of certain products would confer social status.

In the end, a diet that in another context might be considered a radical and disturbing departure from traditional foods was made socially acceptable, even desirable. Far from this being in any sense a "natural" process, the normalization of an industrial mass diet was a social process firmly rooted in the prevailing political economy. It was more or less consciously orchestrated by particular entrepreneurs willing to take sizable risks with their money, but always with a view to maximizing returns on their investments. For a few it paid off very handsomely. Among the significant consequences of this historically momentous turn to industrial edible commodities was the degradation of the nutritional value of available foodstuffs and, as becomes much more evident late in the twentieth century, the incredible growth of a wide range of nutrient-poor products, or what I term "pseudo foods," that come to pollute the food environments of developed countries and, more and more, countries of the global South as well. Not until the first decade of the twenty-first century, however, do the health-damaging consequences of this situation come to be appreciated, and only to a limited extent even then.[21]

The state's role in this, beyond its not insignificant involvement in establishing and maintaining tariff protections for various industries, is less prominent in the first dietary regime. An exception was the passing of the pure foods law under the Roosevelt government in 1906, which arguably put the entire food-processing industry on a sounder footing for the longer term by curtailing some of the more egregious practices of food processors that threatened to undermine public acceptance of industrial foods. The law prescribed penalties for misbranding and adulteration, required removal and destruction at the manufacturer's expense of goods that were in violation of the law, and required publication of convictions.

On the nutritional front, I would argue that all these developments had negative implications for vitamin intakes and the quality of fats being consumed, and promoted excessive sugar and sodium consumption. Data on the disappearance of food in the US food supply provide some, albeit crude, support for this argument. Per capita consumption of sugar and sweeteners, already high by 1909, when data of this kind were first collected, increased some 23 percent over roughly the first half of the century (see Table 1.1).

TABLE 1.1

Food content of the US food supply, pounds per capita, 1909-96

Food group	1909-13	1947-49	1982-86	1992-96	1909-13 to 1992-96 (% change)
Meat	172	176	181	191	11
Cheese	5	10	22	27	440
Fats and oils	41	46	65	71	73
Grain products	291	171	153	192	−34
Sugar and sweeteners	91	114	125	147	62

NOTE: Numbers are rounded.

SOURCE: Anthony Winson, "Bringing Political Economy into the Debate on the Obesity Epidemic," *Agriculture and Human Values* 21, 4 (Winter 2004): 303. Adapted from S.O. Welsh and R.M. Marston, "Review of Trends in Food Use in the United States, 1909 to 1980," *Journal of the American Dietetic Association* 81 (1982): 120-25; and Judith Jones Putnam and Anne E. Allshouse, *Statistical Bulletin*, no. 965, April 1999, Economic Research Service, US Department of Agriculture, 196.

Consumption of grain products diminishes significantly over this period, however, while per capita consumption of fats and oils increases a modest 10 percent. This change is not accompanied by any dramatic shifts to more per capita meat consumption, contradicting the widespread belief that dramatic shifts to more meat in the diet occurs as societies develop and become wealthier. Meat consumption, it turns out, was already high, in the United States at least, by the turn of the nineteenth century. On the other hand, cheese consumption doubles in this period. These data indicate little, however, about changes in the quality of fats and oils consumed, nor do we have information on sodium consumption, although I believe it likely increased because of the dramatic rise in the consumption of canned meats and vegetables.

The extent to which a population embraced an industrial diet in this period would have been highly variable among the most economically advanced countries. It was most thoroughly embraced in the United States, but even there residues of what might be termed a more "artisanal" diet no doubt persisted, at least up until the Second World War. Nevertheless, food historians argue that even farm families more and more emulated urban diets, and that housewives, by the 1930s, were more likely to follow mass-based media culinary advice than traditional family wisdom of cooking.[22]

The Great Depression of the 1930s provided a strong test of the degree to which the industrial diet had become entrenched. Despite the dramatic decline in average incomes and unemployment rates reaching 30 percent, the consumption of processed foods showed great resilience. An initial decline in the consumption of processed products in the first years of the Depression did occur, though Levenstein notes that the increasingly concentrated packers and processors were able to significantly lower prices to consumers by forcing agricultural producers to accept much lower prices for farm products. The same held true for the dairy industry.[23] Although processor revenues declined, the volume of their production barely changed, and even saw substantial increases. American consumers were eating 50 percent more canned fruits and vegetables by the end of the decade than they were at the beginning, and processed-meat consumption also rose despite hard economic times. Soft drink consumption was another area of growth in the midst of the Depression.

Levenstein argues that technological changes in transportation, preserving, and distribution increasingly liberated Americans from the hold that seasonality and geographical variability had had on diet since the beginning of time.[24] Vegetables and fruits that had been only seasonally and regionally available were now stocked year-round in processed form, and to some extent fresh as well. With this development, diets lost much of their regional flavour, taking on a more homogeneous national dimension.

THE SECOND INDUSTRIAL DIETARY REGIME, 1950-80

How does the second industrial diet regime differ from the first? To answer this question, I borrow insights from the food regime theorists. Friedmann and McMichael argued more than twenty years ago that the period after the Second World War constituted a qualitatively different food regime than that which preceded it. It did so because of key changes that had occurred. One of these was the intensification of agriculture in the advanced capitalist countries, along with the deepening intra-sectoral integration of agriculture across international borders. They argued that agriculture had become an industrial sector as food increasingly shifted from final use to processed (even durable) products.[25]

A second feature of the second food regime, they argue, was the appearance of strong state protectionism in the developed world, along with the consolidation of the nation-state system in the global South and the emergence of a fervent developmentalism in the South that coincided with American geopolitical interests in finding external markets for surplus wheat. Cheap imported American wheat fit the agenda of poor countries that sought low-cost food to boost industrialization. As Friedmann and McMichael argued, cheap American grain led to the displacement of traditional foods, rather than their commodification.[26]

A third feature of this food regime was the transnational restructuring of agricultural sectors. With agricultural intensification, specific crops and livestock were integrated into agro-food chains dominated at both the input and processing ends by ever more concentrated corporations, a phenomenon I have examined elsewhere in depth in the Canadian context.[27]

It was argued that, with this intensification in the second food regime, agricultural products have shifted more and more from final use to inputs for manufactured foods. Friedmann and McMichael see the durable foods complex and the intensive meat complex as the central foci of this intensification and integration process. Indeed, beef is argued to be the "symbolic centre" of the postwar diet.[28]

What about Diets?

Can we infer that this transformation of the production and processing spheres of the agro-food complex brought about, in turn, a transformation in diets? The relationship between food regimes, so conceived, and the outcomes for mass diets has not been well studied, but it is problematic to say that the first food regime gave shape to one form of mass diet, whereas the second food regime gave shape to another form of mass diet. There was no simple correspondence between food regimes as demarcated in the literature and the dietary regimes I discuss here. Nevertheless, these important changes at the level of production processes could be expected to have an impact in some form on the industrial diet that had already emerged.

If we consider the second food regime, it is clear that the period after the Second World War and until the mid-1970s had much to do with corporate competition, the concentration of capital, and the ever-present pressures to drive down costs and improve profitability. In the dietary realm, however, it served more to continue and intensify a diet *that had already been given form and developed in a previous period.* In other words, dietary regimes and food regimes were and are related but did and do not overlap in any simple fashion.

As noted above, evidence points to the much earlier establishment of so-called durable foods than envisioned in the food-regime approach. As for the argument that beef becomes the "symbolic centre" of the postwar diet, I also noted above the impact of the breakfast food industry in replacing a largely meat-based breakfast with breakfast based on refined-grain flour. Actually, in the United States, both beef and pork were consumed in greater quantities around the turn of the nineteenth century than was the case in later decades. This turned around only after the Second World War, and only for a limited time, and red meat consumption in the United States and Canada has steadily fallen since the 1970s, to be replaced with poultry meat consumption.[29] This is not to say that the so-called beef complex, involving the international integration of a soy- and corn-based-feed corporate complex with beef production was not emblematic of the second food regime, for it undoubtedly was.

The argument that the second food regime incorporated a marked intensification in food production in newly developing meat-feed complexes is, I believe, also reflected in the dietary realm, with the intensification of the industrial diet in the post–Second World War era. Before considering the case for the intensification of the industrial diet, it is useful to explore further what the industrialization of food has entailed from a nutritional standpoint, for it is especially the health impact of industrial diets that makes their investigation so critical.

Degradation of Food and the Industrial Diet

The industrialization of food within the context of for-profit economic organization entailed three broad and interrelated processes that together have had the net effect of degrading food from a nutritional standpoint: (1) simplification, (2) adulteration, and (3) speed-up of agricultural and transformative (processing) activities. These processes, together with the advent of mass marketing and the various corporate strategies that comprise what I refer to as "spatial colonization" gave shape to the industrial diet. This mass diet might just as well be called the "American diet" because it was food companies originating principally in the United States that led the way in promoting a variety of new processed edible commodities, and also new ways of preparing and marketing food and drink that have been encapsulated by the term "fast food." Now, more than a hundred years after its emergence in the mills of Minneapolis, the slaughterhouses of Chicago, and the cereal factories of

Battle Creek, this diet has taken on truly global dimensions, and American food and beverage corporations still play a leading role in it.

The real significance today of the industrial dietary regime is that it was to transform food environments with a suite of aggressively promoted, nutritionally compromised edible products that are themselves the outcome of an ensemble of agricultural and food technology processes, and marketing machinery. What, then, is involved with the three processes I argue to be at the root of the degradation of food with the advent of industrial dietary regimes?

By "simplification" I am referring to the reduction in the biological diversity available to us in our food environments. This simplification is very likely having profound nutritional impacts. Simplification is favoured in our food system for several reasons. In agriculture, it entails a drastic reduction in varieties available for a whole range of fruits, vegetables, and grains. This varietal reduction has occurred for reasons of cosmetic appearance, and especially in the quest to promote the durability of edible commodities and thereby reduce spoilage. It has also occurred because of the demands of industrial processes such as mechanical harvesting, processes that have nothing to do with nutrition but everything to do with savings on labour costs. In the processing sphere, simplification reduces the biological richness of food in order to enhance durability and therefore storability of the end products, and also to save on labour costs. The case of the flour-milling industry is an excellent example of this: extraction methods for producing flour introduced after 1870 radically reduced its vitamins, minerals, and fibre – vital nutritional components of grain.

By "adulteration" I am referring to a set of systematic practices that essentially adulterate much of the food we eat, which in the end compromises the nutritional integrity of the food. My use of the term "adulteration" differs from the current conventional use of the term by nutritionists. Nevertheless, the adulteration practices I focus on have much the same underlying causes as traditional forms of adulteration going back through the ages. Principally, adulteration is a means of cheapening the cost of producing an edible product, with the added motivation today of the desire to make cheap food more palatable.

Sugar, fat, and salt, notably hydrogenated fats, are key components added to manufactured foods, and I term these "macro-adulterants." To these we should add the sophisticated chemical additives that are ubiquitous in processed food. The purpose of macro-adulterants in the contemporary food system is twofold: they increase the palatability of foods, and they reduce costs for manufacturers by producing shelf-stable, semi-durable edible consumer goods. Consumers get the benefit of convenience, as well as perceived flavour and texture enhancement, but at a cost to their health. The use of macro-adulterants is particularly prominent in the meal offerings of chain restaurant and fast-food operations. Indeed, as Eric Schlosser has remarked about the chemical food additives used in the fast-food business, their role is to impart tastes to cheaply produced processed edible products so that they may successfully mimic more expensive whole foods.[30]

By "speed-up of agricultural and transformative (processing) activities," I am referring to the systemic preference for processes that reduce the amount of time necessary for capital to be employed in the process of production until a profit is realized – in other words, the turnover time of capital. The shorter the turnover time of capital invested, the quicker this capital and the surplus capital created can be profitably reinvested in a new round of production, and the greater the accumulated profits over a specific period. The importance of this within the sphere of food production was noted by Mann and Dickinson several decades ago.[31]

Efforts to speed up the turnover time of capital can be illustrated by practices in the beef industry. Reducing the time it takes to raise beef cattle from birth to market in this branch of the food system include the selection of specific breeds noted for rapid fat deposition, the use of hormone implants to speed growth, and the use of industrial corn-based feeding regimes and feedlots to "fatten" cattle in the later stage of their short lives. The nutritional outcomes of this process include animals with excessive amounts of saturated fats and an unhealthy balance of "good" and "bad" fats compared with similar animals fed the grasses they evolved to thrive on; changes in the vitamin composition of the meat; and the promotion of pathogenic bacteria.

These processes come to have real purchase in society when the edible products that result from them come to dominate food environments. This brings us back to the discussion of the intensification of the industrial diet, which happened in the decades after the Second World War.

Intensification

Ultimately, intensification of the industrial diet involved the increasing per capita consumption of the suite of nutritionally compromised products that make up this diet. How did this occur? Underlying the possibility of intensification were fundamental technological and sociological changes in society.

The experience of the Second World War provided some of the initial conditions for intensification. Household economies were dramatically disorganized by the war, with men away from the home in the armed forces and many women away from the home working in the armaments industries. Despite shortages in foodstuffs for the general population, particular food and beverage manufacturers used their political contacts to advance their products aggressively to the men and women under arms – a captive market. Of particular note in this regard were the Coca-Cola Company and the Hershey chocolate company, which had great success in accessing American army canteens and military food environments more generally, and in getting the troops accustomed to consuming the snack foods and beverages they produced. On the home front, busy working wives were marketed to by food manufacturers with a growing suite of "time-saving" products.

Among the technological changes, none was likely more profound than the spread of the use of the automobile and the massive state-sponsored highway projects that made car culture possible. With the automobile and the advent of suburban life dependent upon it, the conditions were ripe for the dramatic expansion of fast-food enterprises, which had actually emerged in the pre-war era, but in highly urbanized settings rather than the suburban milieu that absorbed much of the demographic growth after the Second World War. Fast-food corporations were responsible for inventing their own products, of course. At the same time, they aggressively promoted other nationally branded, nutrient-poor edible products, such as soft drinks, to complement their proprietary meal offerings.

Of the changes more sociological, among the most significant from a dietary standpoint was the decline in the proportion of the on-farm population since the early years of the twentieth century, and the absolute decline in the number of farm families after the 1940s, in both the United States and Canada. Although family farms in North America had been heavily integrated into markets almost from their beginnings, ready access to the land meant a certain amount of food provisioning had been characteristic of farm life. Once this tie to the land was broken, families had to buy most of their food and were from that point on more and more vulnerable to the dietary influences of the food industry.

Another sociological change of major proportion was the movement of women out of the home and into the workforce, with all the attendant claims this had on time previously devoted to culinary tasks, once almost the exclusive domain of women in the home. I am referring to middle-class women in particular, given that working-class women had been in the workforce since the dawn of the industrial era. This development, which came after much of the rural to urban shift, was prefigured by the experience of many women during the war years. Although social pressures on women in the immediate postwar years prompted many to return to the domestic domain, the generation of women coming of age in the 1960s is another story altogether. The move of this generation into the workforce opened the door in a dramatic way to the restaurant industry in its various forms, and particularly to the fast-food chain restaurant corporations that came to dominate this sector of the economy. It also opened the door to a plethora of convenience foods, many of which were and continue to be nutritionally compromised.[32] Indeed, television was the new preferred outlet for advertising these convenience foods, and no one watching television in the late 1950s and 1960s could escape the barrage of advertisements for products such as Duncan Hines and Betty Crocker cake mixes and assorted other high-sugar desserts that came out of a box.

The idea that industrial foods in the diet of North Americans intensified in the immediate postwar period is supported by evidence of processed fruit

FIGURE 1.1

Consumption of processed foods by country, 1945-70

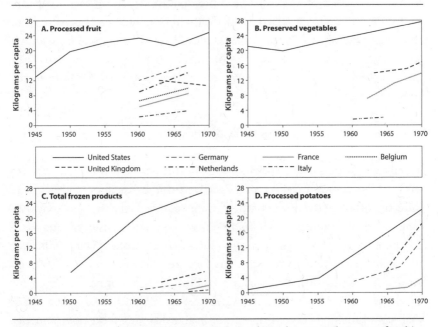

SOURCE: Organisation for Economic Co-operation and Development, *The Impact of Multinational Enterprises on National Scientific and Technical Capacities: Food Industry* (Paris: OECD, 1979), 118.

and vegetable consumption (see Figure 1.1). Already by the end of the war, American consumption of processed fruit and vegetable products had reached levels that were not to be seen in a number of European countries for another thirty years. In the United States, canned fruit and vegetable consumption was to continue to climb so that it was approximately double the 1945 level by 1970. Consumption of novel processed foods such as frozen vegetables and processed potatoes, mainly french fries, was to soar from minimal amounts postwar to over fifty pounds per person per year by 1970.[33]

Some of these products, notably several frozen processed vegetable products, arguably had clear nutritional benefits to the extent that they preserved higher levels of nutrients than traditional canned processed products, and also made nutritious foods more readily available to those who could afford refrigerators and freezers. Many other processed products had more dubious benefits, particularly when they came in the form of "fast food" and "convenience food," the consumption of which exploded in this period. Nutrient-poor snack foods saw a dramatic increase at this time, with sweetened beverages and salty snacks being especially prominent vectors for the increase in sugars and dangerous fats in the diet. Recent research has confirmed that these two products are, indeed, the most obesogenic, or obesity promoting, of the various products in the contemporary American diet.[34] Fat consumption per capita increased dramatically, in fact, by some 41 percent from the end of the war to the early 1980s in the United States, while sugar and sweetener consumption, already high, rose another 10 percent over that period (see Table 1.1). These trends would continue, and even intensify, in the years after 1980.

Spatial Colonization

The intensification of the industrial diet in this period was not due only to the ever more powerful reach of mass advertising by the food and beverage industry, although the power of this cannot be underestimated. It also was an outcome of the processors' ability to secure the physical visibility and availability of the processed edible commodities they controlled. The significance of corporate strategies toward this goal became evident to me only through an in-depth study of the role of supermarkets in promoting nutrient-poor edible products.[35] I felt these strategies needed to be captured by a concept that would highlight their importance in transforming food environments, and so I use the term "spatial colonization" to capture how processors and supermarket chain stores, largely working together, manage to promote the consumption of nutrient-poor edible commodities more generally. These nutrient-poor edible commodities, as it turns out, tend to be among the most profitable edible products sold today. The concept of spatial colonization can also help us understand the impact of fast-food chain outlets on contemporary diets; it can help us understand how the reality of differential profits, corporate concentration, market power in the food system, and mass advertising come to affect the geography of critically important food environments and, most notably, the prominence of nutrient-poor edible commodities within them.

With the rise of the variety of political-economic changes associated with the neo-liberal era post-1980, might we expect significant changes of a dietary nature to emerge? My view is that this has very much been the case. It is tempting to consider this most recent phase of the industrial food economy as basically an extension on a truly global scale of what had already come into existence in North America. Nevertheless, it can be argued that the quantitative extension of the American diet in the most recent period amounts to a dramatic qualitative change in the eating experiences, and subsequent health outcomes, of whole new populations across the globe. The corporate organizations undergirding this change have themselves been transformed in their quest to position themselves favourably in globalized markets. For these reasons, it seems reasonable to consider the era from roughly the 1980s onward as a distinct dietary regime.

THE THIRD INDUSTRIAL DIETARY REGIME:
GLOBALIZATION AND RESISTANCE POST-1980

The neo-liberal era emerges in the 1970s in important respects, but the impact of this event in terms of dietary regimes is not really seen until some years later. Certain countries in the global South that were heavily influenced by American economic interests, such as Mexico and those of Central America, experienced an early dietary transformation, at least in the most urbanized areas. Although any definitive assessment awaits further research, it is reasonable to argue that really significant dietary impacts of the spreading neo-liberal policy environment in developing countries did not really become evident for at least another decade or so.

The period of the 1990s onward is unique in several ways. It may not have been characterized by a fundamental change in the basic features of the industrial diet that had been established previously in the developed countries, but certain features of it were exacerbated there, such as the super-sizing phenomenon, the spatial colonization of nutrient-poor products into new food environments (e.g., institutions in the public domain, such as schools and hospitals), and the intensification of this colonization in more traditional food environments.[36]

In the developed world and beyond (more about this later), the post-1990 era witnessed the rapid emergence of chronic disease linked to dietary causes in broad sectors of the population. This event, in addition to the impact of diet, has likely been exacerbated by the various lethargy-promoting technologies that have come to dominate activities at work and in the leisure realm. What is now referred to as the "obesity epidemic" was the most visible manifestation of the problem, and, in recent years, a steady stream of scientific studies has provided an ever clearer picture of the multi-dimensional health impacts of overweight and obesity.[37] It is in the neo-liberal era, then, that the century-long process of industrialization of the food system and the degradation of food that characterized this process appear to have particularly devastating consequences for human health. I note above some of the likely reasons this has emerged in the current dietary regime, but the relationship between this dietary regime and the extraordinary rise in obesity and its associated diseases around the globe is a research subject that still has unresolved questions.

In the developing world, truly dramatic changes in diets have characterized the post-1990 scene. Here again, seismic shifts of a sociological nature have opened the door to powerful corporate actors with a strong vested interest in shifting mass diets in this geographical context. Foremost among these are accelerating rural to urban migration on a massive scale. Increasing disposable income among the emerging middle classes in many countries has been crucial. In the realm of political economy, the opening up of domestic markets via neo-liberal reforms in much of the developing world in the 1980s and 1990s paved the way for transnational food corporations to establish major beachheads in contexts where their presence had once been minimal, thanks to tariff barriers and the like.

Vectors of Change

Dietary change in the developing world has at least three important vectors. One is the transformation of food retailing that has taken place, and continues to do so, in Latin America, Asia, and, more recently, Africa. Supermarket chain stores are the main agents of this transformation, and increasingly these chain operations are under the control of global corpora-tions.[38] Supermarkets are a key vector because they are a conduit for a whole suite of nutrient-poor products into the diets of their customers, much as they were in the developed world. Another related retail phenomenon is the convenience chain store, and together these two are helping to rapidly fa-cilitate the proliferation of nutrient-poor edible commodities throughout the global South.

The second vector has been transnational fast-food corporations and, to a lesser extent, copycat local variants. These fast-food operations have colonized food environments in many developed countries, but in recent years it is China and India that have received the lion's share of investments by such firms. Among these corporations, two stand out. McDonald's Corporation and Yum! Brands – which controls KFC, Taco Bell, and Pizza Hut restaurants – are the most substantial players at the global level in the fast-food realm.[39]

A third vector can be seen to be the actions of transnational snack food manufacturers. These firms are either specialized almost exclusively in the area of snack foods, or else snack foods are an important division of a larger food-processing corporation. Snack food companies are among the largest of the global food and beverage companies, and they have some of the largest advertising budgets as well. PepsiCo and Coca-Cola are major players in this category, while Nestlé and Kraft constitute prime examples of conglomerate food firms with very large snack food and confectionery divisions that have a global presence.

As food environments are being transformed in the global South, the health impacts are becoming more and more visible. Populous countries such as China and Indonesia have rates of increase in overweight and obesity matching those countries in the developed world with the highest rates. A recent study led by Barry Popkin of women aged twenty to forty-nine shows that the prevalence of overweight exceeds underweight among women in dozens of poorer societies, in both urban and rural areas.[40] Among young children in China in the ten years after 1989, the prevalence of overweight doubled, while the prevalence of obesity increased about ten times.[41]

Not surprisingly, the incidence of chronic disease associated with dra-matic weight gain is rising rapidly in the developing world. In the developed world outside the United States, where the American food and beverage companies have had a longer existence, as in Japan, the incidence of type 2 diabetes among school-aged children increased ten times in the twenty years after 1976. Now we are witnessing a rapid development of the same phenom-enon in developing countries such as Thailand and India, and those of the

Middle East, sub-Saharan Africa, and Southeast Asia.[42] Although it is no doubt true that weight gain and attendant chronic disease in these societies cannot be wholly ascribed to the transformation of their diets occasioned by the actions of foreign food and beverage corporations, there is considerable evidence that their impact is greater and more thoroughgoing than commonly appreciated.

Transnational Dominance, the State, and the Politics of Resistance

As with food regimes, the state's role when it comes to dietary regimes can be seen as contradictory. This is true even with earlier dietary regimes. In the period from roughly 1870 to the 1930s, the state is typically conceived as being non-interventionist, in accordance with the laissez-faire political-economic model that dominated this era. Nevertheless, even in the United States, the most laissez-faire of nations at the time, the state was forced to be responsive to an upwelling of public agitation and concern and in 1906 passed the Pure Food and Drugs Act, following along a path fashioned by European governments somewhat earlier.

In the dialectic of the time, public agitation by women's organizations and consumer groups had been building as a response to the growing evidence of abuses by increasingly monopolistic purveyors of foods and drugs in the closing years of the nineteenth century. The 1906 publication of Upton Sinclair's *The Jungle*, a fictionalized account of the unfair labour practices and outrageously unsanitary conditions of the plants owned by the Chicago meat-packing consortium, the latter notably influential in fanning the flames of public outrage. Once President Roosevelt's staff had confirmed that actual conditions were even worse than Sinclair's account indicated, Roosevelt decided to get ahead of the wave – some would argue opportunistically – and use his influence to force through legislation, despite strong resistance from industrial interests.[43]

The present era has some resonance with events of this earlier time. Governments are once again reluctant to intervene in the economy because of the hegemony of neo-liberal ideology and the force of legislation passed in many countries proscribing state intervention as such. As Friedmann and McMichael argued some time ago with respect to food regimes, the shift in the current era is "from the state to capital as the dominant structuring force."[44]

Nevertheless, corporate consolidation in the sphere of the agro-food system during earlier decades had brought this sector unprecedented power to transform food environments in the interests of profit making. Profit making, it turns out, has not proven synonymous with the advancement of nutritional health, nor environmental sustainability or food safety. Resistance to the globalized industrial food system fostered by transnational food and beverage companies has progressively come to the fore in numerous forms that have more recently been characterized as alternative agriculture and food movements.[45] Whether it be attempts to relocalize food, preserve heritage foods and culinary traditions, or, notably, reassert public control over what vulnerable populations such as children and youth are eating, the current impetus to resist the corporate food model has yet to run its course.

The threats to public health posed by contemporary food environments has an impact over a much longer term than did the toxic adulterants and lack of basic sanitation that characterized the food system of a century ago. The threats of today, nevertheless, are proving just as deadly in the end. Recognition of the magnitude of these threats, and in particular the financial burdens they pose to state budgets, has begun to have traction at the political level. Most dramatic in its response has been that of the British government, which has been motivated to move relatively decisively to curtail the most egregious of the business practices of the corporate food and beverage companies by banning their advertising on programs oriented to children and youth. Interventions to eliminate nutrient-poor processed food in schools have also been implemented. By 2009, Spain was considering similar legislation, but also extending its reach to include the prohibition of celebrities promoting fast food to children and the use of toys to entice children to eat fast food.[46]

Elsewhere, nations have been much slower to intervene, and it has been left to lower-level state structures to react. Where this is also absent, forms of public resistance and action to encourage healthy eating have been the most visible forms of food system change. Food has once again become very much politicized, as it was in the Progressive Era of the United States. The corporate forces that stand behind the diffusion and intensification of the industrial diet continue to expand their influence in the global South at the same time as this diet and its corporate backers are under increasing attack in the developed world. The third industrial dietary regime is proving to be ever more unstable, even while capital in the food sector seeks to re-establish a new equilibrium.

The key question may be whether a new corporate equilibrium will supersede various streams of resistance to the industrial diet, or whether this resistance will be successful in transforming food environments in significant and lasting ways. To date, popular struggles concerning food have had some limited successes in promoting healthy eating, particularly in the key institutional sphere of the schools. Public pressure has resulted in bans of health-debilitating products such as soft drinks in entire school districts in certain US jurisdictions, for example, and several Canadian provinces have embarked on a thoroughgoing revision of their dietary guidelines for schools, with the goal of eliminating nutrient-poor products from school food environments.

On the other hand, the forces that produced the industrial diet over the last century still overwhelmingly dominate food environments, and they show strong signs of rethinking their business models in order to meet contemporary threats. One example is the efforts of the global leaders in the soft drink and salty snack businesses, Coca-Cola and PepsiCo, to reposition their brands via the purchase of companies associated with the marketing of "healthier" edible products and juices, products that would likely be considered acceptable as guidelines and legislation governing school food environments become more restrictive. On the other hand, although corporate purveyors of snack foods and fast food are prevented from pushing their products in school environments in some jurisdictions, they have not been prevented from colonizing food environments adjacent to schools and thereby hanging onto the youthful consumer they have so assiduously cultivated.[47]

To what extent, then, do these new forms of resistance challenge the corporate-dominated food system? To what extent can they be co-opted by it? These are issues I explore in the last chapter. I do believe, however, that, in the developed world at least, it is only the incipient struggle for healthy eating that has any real possibility of challenging fundamentally the existing corporate food model.[48] In some limited ways and in certain places, it already has done so.

The provision of truly healthy diets based on minimally processed whole foods for the broad mass of the population is something the forces underpinning the current industrial dietary regime are not likely to be able to co-opt and absorb. Indeed, their profit-based model is premised largely on the provision of the nutritionally compromised products that are essentially the antithesis of what the struggle for healthy eating is trying to achieve. This is not to say that what Dixon refers to as the "nutritionalization" of the food economy is not accelerating in the developed world in particular as food corporations capitalize on often limited scientific evidence of the purported benefits of specific nutrients to produce highly profitable "nutriceuticals" and food products with purportedly enhanced health benefits.[49] This is a practice enabled by pliant state deregulation on what processors can claim about their products.[50] The power of the corporate food system is that, while it profits from the degradation of diets more generally, it can also profit from those consumers wishing to resist this trend via changes to their consumption habits.

Needless to say, the struggle for healthy food environments has little to do with so-called nutritionally enhanced novel edible products. In its most progressive manifestations, it is the fight for a society in which all community residents can obtain a safe, culturally acceptable, health-enhancing diet via a sustainable food system that maximizes community self-reliance and social justice, a situation that some have argued is best captured by the concept of community food security.

CHAPTER TWO

DISCORDANT DIETS,
UNHEALTHY PEOPLE

Modernity's double punishment is to make us both age
prematurely and to live longer.

—Nassim Nicholas Taleb, *The Bed of Procrustes*[1]

Food processing procedures were developed, particularly following
the Industrial Revolution, which allowed for quantitative and
qualitative food and nutrient combinations that had not previously
been encountered over the course of hominin evolution.

—Loren Cordain and colleagues, "Origins and
Evolution of the Western Diet"[2]

INDUSTRIAL FOODS HAVE EVOLVED for more than a century and have per-
meated the lives of people in developed countries for many decades. Not
surprisingly, it is difficult to gain a perspective on them, but this is exactly
what it is necessary to do. For although humans are living longer than ever
before in developed countries, ever greater numbers of people are manifestly
unhealthy, and mounting evidence suggests that the upcoming generations
may live shorter lives than their parents.

Fortunately, a body of literature has emerged that allows us to gain some
needed perspective on today's industrial diet. It is the product of the work of

specialists in nutrition, archaeology, anthropology, and medical science who have attempted to understand the evolution of the diet of modern humans over an exceedingly long period, and more specifically, to gain insights into what humans evolved to thrive on, in nutritional terms, over what was by far the greatest span of our existence. This research dovetails rather nicely with a good deal of recent research in the areas of nutritional and medical science on the health impacts of major components of the industrial diet.

PALAEOLITHIC DIETS

If we compare humans to other animal species known to have been around for several hundred million years – sharks or jellyfish, for example – it becomes evident that we have had a relatively brief existence in evolutionary terms. For the great part of our evolution as a species, we followed a hunting and gathering lifestyle, and the foods we ate and evolved to thrive upon were the product of that mode of existence. As much as we may believe we have evolved culturally and technologically since our beginnings, physiologically we are much the same as we were over that very long period that preceded the advent of agriculture. Knowledge of the kinds of foods people ate for the greater part of our existence as a species may indeed hold the key to understanding what is wrong with what we are eating today. It is the Palaeolithic diet that I am speaking about here, and some background to it is in order.

The genus *Homo*, of which modern humans (*Homo sapiens sapiens*) are the last surviving species, can be traced back several million years, whereas anatomically modern humans are thought to have emerged between 150,000 and 200,000 years ago (though the earliest date is forever being pushed back as new discoveries come to light). For a very long period, then, earlier hominin species gained their subsistence via the hunting and gathering of food, and even modern humans have spent less than 10 percent of their existence with a dietary regime shaped in some way by foods gained through the cultivation of plants and domestication of animals – the Neolithic Revolution. Moreover, in the relatively brief period since the Neolithic Revolution, up until very recently, most humans led a rural existence and therefore were close enough to natural areas to supplement their diets in important ways with wild foods of plant and animal origin. Looked at another way, approximately one hundred thousand generations of humans existed by hunting and gathering, five hundred generations have survived as agriculturalists, and only about ten have existed since the Industrial Revolution, and less than a handful since the full industrialization of our diets.[3]

When looked at through the lens of our total time on planet Earth as a distinct species, roughly 150,000 to 200,000 years (and perhaps significantly longer), it is clear that we have had an exceedingly short period to adjust to processed foods deriving from the Industrial Revolution; their presence in our diets comprises less than 0.1 percent of our existence if we consider that such foods really only made an impact over the last hundred years or so. We have had even less time to adjust physiologically to the onset of sedentary work *and* leisure that is now so widespread in the developed countries and increasingly beyond them. Indeed, it is remarkable that it is difficult to think of more than a handful of commonly held jobs that require any degree of physical effort. At the same time as sedentary work and leisure overtakes our lives, diets in developed countries and now the developing countries have become even more energy-dense and yet degraded in a number of essential ways. In this evolving scenario, it would indeed be exceedingly surprising if dramatic negative health outcomes had *not* been the result.

And what about these diets that nourished so much of our existence? Recent research of the earlier hominin species, and in particular *Homo erectus*, which is thought to have come into existence at least 1.89 million years ago and to have survived as a species some 1 million years,[4] suggests an increased variability in the diet of this hominin species, in comparison with the great apes. A key development seems to be the incorporation of meat into the diet and a move away from crude vegetable matter such as leaves. This is indicated by evidence that early hominins were using stone tools to process animal meat beginning more than 2 million years ago, that is, even before the emergence of *Homo erectus*.[5] Indeed, it has been posited by different scientific authorities on these matters that meat consumption was a response to changing ecological conditions in Africa, and that the consumption of meat created a feedback loop, as the high-protein meat diet allowed for larger brains, while the hunting of animals led to a division of labour, more complex social systems, and the selection for even greater intelligence over time.[6]

Anthropologists have supplemented the fossil records with careful studies of hunting and gathering peoples from around the world who have survived into the modern era. We have this to add to our knowledge of diets as they existed, and in a few cases still exist, before people took on a more settled livelihood that came with the cultivation of plants and the raising of livestock for food. It had previously been thought that the diets of human foragers were typically 60 to 70 percent plant-based, but more recent analysis of diets

among contemporary hunting and gathering groups indicates the importance of animal-based protein, which is now believed to constitute the majority of the calorie intake of such peoples.[7] This supports findings derived from
analysis of fossil evidence from Palaeolithic peoples, including Neanderthal
people, which also indicates a high animal-protein content in their diets.[8]

Overall, it is thought that early tool development likely also increased
the range of plants that could be recovered and eaten by early humans.[9]
Compared with the earliest human species and primates, *Homo erectus* and
later human species appear to have evolved a greater versatility in adapting
to foods produced by a wide variety of ecological situations,[10] a trait no doubt
central to the longer-term survival of modern humans. Although it has
been pointed out that it would be wrong-headed to argue for any unitary
Palaeolithic diet, nevertheless there is evidence that the diets in this formative
phase of human evolution exhibited important nutritional characteristics
that since have been lost.[11] What would these be?

Palaeolithic diets were significantly different from what most people eat
today in several important respects. First of all, they were different in content.
They would have been rich in a wide variety of edible plants, including nuts,
tubers, and an array of wild fruits and berries when available. As noted above,
there is good evidence that this was supplemented by a broad variety of animal protein, from shellfish and sea foods to insects and small and large wild
animals. However, this animal protein would have differed in its nutritional
quality in important ways from the majority of animal proteins produced
under an industrial system of confinement agriculture that are presently
consumed.

So, what was *absent* from the diets of Palaeolithic peoples? For one, there
was an absence of any significant contribution of grains to the diet and the
refined flours derived from grains, which were not cultivated, processed, and
eaten until very recently in evolutionary terms. There was also the absence
of dairy products of any kind, as well as the relative absence of sweeteners in
the diet, which although now abundant were in Palaeolithic times limited
to the occasional consumption of sweet fruits and honey where and when
available.

Palaeolithic diets were also different because of the absence of food-
processing technology, which, especially since the Industrial Revolution, has
radically altered many whole foods, including the nutritional content of
grain-derived flours with modern flour-milling and extrusion technologies,
matters I discuss in depth later. These technologies have degraded the nutritional content of grains by removing the bran and the germ. By removing

the fibre content of the grain and changing the molecular structure of the food (via extrusion technologies), these technologies also produce products that act to raise blood sugar levels much more rapidly than other whole foods, or even whole-grain flours, ever did.[12]

In the case of vegetable oils used for food processing and margarines, the introduction of a process that hydrogenates vegetable oil to make it more shelf-stable and solid at room temperature has introduced novel but dangerous trans fats into the diet. In the case of sweeteners, their dramatically increased consumption, plus the widespread use of genetically engineered high-fructose corn syrup, has increased the ingestion of fructose in the diet, which is believed to play a significant role in producing insulin resistance in humans and thereby to contribute to the exploding incidence of diabetes globally. It has also been argued that such technology has divorced the nutritional attributes of foods from their sensory attributes and thereby impairs or prevents cues associated with appetite and satiety from playing their traditional roles.[13]

In addition, Palaeolithic diets, and diets for most of the period since, differ radically from contemporary diets because they were not skewed by the powerful monetary incentives provided by the prevailing economic system. Within this system, despite nutritional knowledge having advanced to historically unprecedented levels, narrowly defined priorities for economic efficiency and profitability have taken precedence over any other factors, including nutritional health, in determining diets. This reality heavily influences what kinds of foods are produced and promoted in most food environments today. It has been convincingly argued that this reality has even seriously distorted the advice and practice of many nutritionists and dietitians, whose professional associations and publishing venues have developed an unhealthy dependence on the food industry.[14]

Diets today are radically different from what they had been for most of our evolutionary existence, then, because they differ in content and in the way foods are processed, and also because of the distorting incentives produced by the prevailing political economy.

THE EVOLUTIONARY DISCORDANCE THESIS

For a long time, the popular view has been that the rise of agriculture assured humanity a more stable and richer diet than that of hunter and gatherer societies, along with the health benefits that would come from this, but in more recent times there has been growing evidence to challenge this view. This evidence is both from the developing archeological record and ethnographic evidence gleaned by anthropologists from a host of hunting and gathering societies over more than one hundred years. It suggests that the shift to agriculture had an impact on human nutrition in significant ways, as it marked a clear change in the content of human diets and the introduction of novel foods. Moreover, as this evidence indicates, the rise of agriculture tended to be associated with a noticeable deterioration in diet, which in turn provoked negative health-related outcomes, from dental disease to overall shorter stature, all of which can indicate severe dietary deficiencies.

As advocates of the so-called discordance thesis have forcefully argued, agriculture and the domestication of plants and animals associated with it involved the increasing consumption of foods for which the human genome was not well adapted, producing an evolutionary discordance between humans and their food environments. The desire to understand more about foods that humans evolved to thrive upon sparked interest in Palaeolithic nutrition. For a little more than twenty years, a growing group of scientists from various disciplinary domains have worked together to consider the relationship between diets that characterized our Palaeolithic past and the development of a host of chronic diseases that characterize more and more contemporary societies.

S. Boyd Eaton at Atlanta's Emory University is credited with having gotten the ball rolling with an article titled "Palaeolithic Nutrition," published in a 1985 issue of the prestigious *New England Journal of Medicine*.[15] The premise of this influential article was relatively simple but had far-reaching implications. It was that "our genes determine our nutritional needs, [and] our genes were shaped by selective pressures of our Palaeolithic environment, including the foods our ancient ancestors ate ... Understanding what they ate is essential for understanding what we should eat today to improve our health."[16] Out of this work has emerged the discordance thesis, which essentially posits a disconnect between the ancient human genome and contemporary food environments. This has been summarized as follows:

> There is growing awareness that the profound environmental changes (e.g., in diet and other lifestyle conditions) that began with the introduction of agriculture and animal husbandry 10,000 years ago occurred too recently on an evolutionary time scale for the human

genome to adapt. In conjunction with this discordance between our ancient, genetically determined biology and the nutritional, cultural, and activity patterns in contemporary Western populations, many of the so-called diseases of civilization have emerged.[17]

Although a few of the "diseases of civilization," or what are now more often referred to as "chronic diseases," are commonly believed to be heavily influenced by a single dietary cause (e.g., saturated fats and heart disease, salt and hypertension), the advocates of the discordance thesis argue that Western diets impact health in a much broader manner. The host of diseases they link to contemporary diets include cardiovascular disease; hypertension; stroke; osteoporosis; gastrointestinal tract and other cancers; asthma; diverticulitis; chronic constipation; and diseases of insulin resistance, including type 2 diabetes, to mention only some of the most serious. As Loren Cordain and his co-authors put it, "Evidence gleaned over the past 3 decades now indicates that virtually all so-called diseases of civilization have multi factorial dietary elements that underlie their etiology."[18]

It was in an important study published in 2005 that Cordain and his co-authors elaborated on the significance of this discordance for the production of a host of chronic diseases that afflicts a growing proportion of the planet's population.[19] Their argument has considerable resonance with the ideas I advance in this book and, indeed, it has inspired a number of lines of thought pursued here.

The evolutionary discordance thesis owes a debt to Darwin's theory of natural selection. As Cordain and his co-authors argue,

> Evolution acting through natural selection represents an on-going interaction between a species' genome and its environment over the course of multiple generations ... When environmental conditions permanently change, evolutionary discordance arises between a species' genome and its environment ... This evolutionary discordance manifests itself phenotypically as disease, increased morbidity and mortality, and reduced reproductive success.[20]

The corollary of this argument, as it pertains to our current dietary dilemmas, is that even though the shift to foods that we were not adapted to occurred from five to ten thousand years ago, on an evolutionary time scale, they have occurred too recently for the human genome to adapt successfully, and therefore this shift is responsible for many of what have been called "the diseases of civilization."

Today, wherever the industrial diet dominates, which means much of the developed world and increasingly urban areas of developing countries, humans are consuming the great majority of their energy needs via foods that lie outside what humans ate for most of their existence. These products include those derived from milk and cereal grains, refined sweeteners, refined vegetable oils, and alcohol; together, they are estimated to make up over 70 percent of the total daily energy consumed by those living in the United States.[21] The percentage for other societies in which the industrial diet has sway should not be expected to differ markedly. This contemporary diet also includes an extraordinary amount of sodium compared with the diet of Palaeolithic people, most of which is added to processed foods. Excess sodium consumption figures considerably in our present-day disease burden as well.[22]

However, it may be overstating the case to suggest that no evolutionary adaption has occurred to the novel foods that came with the Neolithic Revolution. For example, recent research indicates that although humans initially were likely similar to their primate cousins in lacking the amylase enzyme necessary for the digestion of high-starch diets, populations in some parts of the world eventually adapted to the higher-starch diets that came with the Neolithic Revolution: their saliva contains the greater amount of amylase necessary to digest such foods.[23] Similarly, although humans typically stop producing the enzyme lactase in their small intestine after childhood, making the digestion of lactose in milk very difficult, over time, populations associated with the development of pastoralism have exhibited a lactase persistence that allows them to digest milk into adulthood.

In addition to genetic adaption, humans learned to make certain plant and animal products more digestible through processing, as with the cooking of legumes, and the adding of bacterial lactase to milk, as with yoghurt.[24] Cultural adaptions have assisted the expansion of dietary variety, in other words. Nevertheless, varying degrees of intolerance to high-gluten grains such as wheat, for example, is being recognized by the medical science literature on celiac disease. The prevalence of this disease, which is associated with several negative health outcomes, including autoimmune disease, is generally recognized to be approximately one in a hundred in North American and European populations. This prevalence is much higher among populations with certain conditions, such as iron-deficiency anemia. It is also recognized that the condition is under-reported.[25]

SWEETENERS, HIGH-GLYCEMIC FOODS, AND HEALTH IMPACTS

In the first decades of the post–Second World War period, much of the advice of health authorities as it pertained to sweeteners was largely focused on the role that products with added cane sugar had in producing tooth decay. More recent times have seen much renewed interest in sweeteners, but this time the concern has been about much more than the possibility of rotten teeth. The rapid rise of overweight and obesity to the status of a first-order public health concern has stimulated intense debate over both its likely health consequences and the root causes of this historically unprecedented increase in weight gain. It is notable that despite the ready availability of low- or no-fat food options in our supermarkets for many years now, and evidence that overall fat intake has decreased, at least in the United States, the incidence of overweight and obesity has continued to increase.[26] Dramatic increases in obesity among children and youth are especially disturbing (see Figure 2.1).

To some extent, the advent of new high-fat products in our diet, such as ice-cream desserts and processed-cheese products, has likely mitigated the health benefits of declining red meat consumption and low-fat food options.

FIGURE 2.1
Incidence of childhood and teenage obesity rates in the United States, post-1960

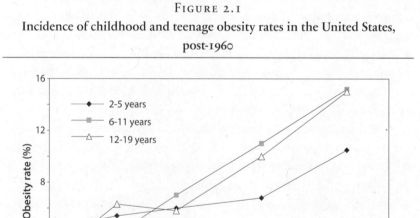

SOURCE: Urban Design Lab, Earth Institute, Colombia University, 2007, based on data from Centres for Disease Control and Prevention, National Health and Nutrition Examination Survey.

However, the role of the increasing consumption of various sweeteners in our diet warrants much more attention. Indeed, the World Health Organization's statement in 2003 that obesity and overweight had "reached epidemic proportions globally" argues that the key causes, along with reduced physical activity, were "the increased consumption of energy-dense foods high in saturated fats and sugars."[27]

It has been estimated that the proportion of complex carbohydrates (derived from consumption of grains, fruits, and vegetables) versus simple carbohydrates (largely derived from sweeteners) has shifted dramatically over the twentieth century, from 68 percent complex versus 32 percent simple in the first decade of the century to 47 percent complex versus 53 percent simple by 1980.[28] This change is largely the result of the increasing consumption of sweeteners since 1900. What are the health impacts of sweetener consumption, then?

Sweetener consumption is linked to two related disorders that pose traumatic health and financial implications for many societies: obesity and what has been termed the "metabolic syndrome." The latter, which has also been labelled "syndrome X," refers to a group of related health problems that together increase the risk of developing diabetes and coronary heart disease. These problems include insulin resistance, along with one or more of: glucose intolerance, overweight, abnormal blood fats (high LDL cholesterol or high triglycerides), and high blood pressure.[29] The evidence linking this disorder with our contemporary diet, and with our lifestyle more generally, is substantial. That is ultimately a good news story because it means that something can be done about it.

Not long ago, diabetes was relatively rare and practically invisible to those not afflicted with the genetic disorder characterized by an inability to produce insulin sufficient to regulate blood sugar (glucose) levels. Today, this type of diabetes, or type 1 diabetes, has been dramatically augmented by the accelerated incidence of type 2 diabetes. Previously called "adult-onset diabetes," type 2 diabetes is characterized by insulin levels higher than those in non-diabetics, but in conjunction with the phenomenon of insulin resistance (more on this later).

The complications of diabetes include retinopathy, which may result in blindness; the possibility of kidney failure; ulceration of the feet; neurological conditions; coronary heart disease; and stroke. The dramatic increase in the incidence of diabetes is due to the increase in type 2 diabetes. Not long ago, this disease was associated primarily with aging adults; now it is increasing dramatically among children and youth as well.[30]

In the United States, a leading journal of public health notes that diabetes there has become an epidemic. One in every twelve adult Americans has been diagnosed with diabetes, and for every two adults diagnosed with the disease there is one with undiagnosed diabetes.[31] It was conservatively estimated in 2002 that the costs of treating diagnosed diabetes in that country were approximately $132 billion.[32]

In Canada's most populated province, Ontario, the prevalence of diabetes doubled between 1995 and 2005, from 6.49 to 10.54 percent of the provincial population.[33] Globally, predictions indicate that by 2030, 350 million people will have diabetes, with the majority in India and China, thus constituting a major global epidemic disease of this century.[34]

The link between diabetes and sugar intake can be seen as indirect: although it was once thought that sugar intake was directly linked to diabetes, it is now known that the causes of the disease are more complex. However, the ever greater intake of sugar is surely a factor in the rising incidence of overweight and obesity, and excess weight gain and type 2 diabetes are known to be correlated. As one authority argues, "A totally consistent observation in prospective as well as cross-sectional studies is the striking association between T2DM [type 2 diabetes mellitus] and increasing obesity, particularly when the excess body fat is centrally distributed."[35]

High-Glycemic Foods

One outcome of the industrial diet is regular ingestion of historically unprecedented amounts of refined sweeteners. In the less than two hundred years since 1800, annual per capita consumption of sugar exploded from about four pounds annually to almost one hundred pounds annually. Many processed food products today lead to high glucose levels in our blood, levels that are thought to be well beyond those the human organism evolved to handle.[36] A 2000 book authored by Jack Chellem, Burton Berkson, and Melissa Smith describes the outcomes:

> You overdose on highly refined, rapidly digested carbohydrates and sugars – all of which are quickly converted to glucose. Because large amounts of glucose are toxic to the kidneys and other organs, the pancreas responds by releasing large amounts of insulin to lower the glucose levels. The insulin moves glucose into cells, where it is either burned for energy or stored as fat (triglyceride in adipose cells).

In some people, the pancreas can compensate for a number of years by secreting more and more insulin. These people will appear to be "normoglycemic" – that is, will maintain normal glucose levels and not become overtly diabetic.

In time, though, the body's ability to deal with all this glucose wears out. When people keep consuming large quantities of refined carbohydrates and sugars year after year, skeletal muscle cells (that is, the muscles that wrap around your bones and where most glucose/insulin activity occurs) start to become overwhelmed by all of the insulin, and they start to respond to the insulin much more sluggishly.

Meanwhile, the pancreas keeps receiving signals that glucose levels are high, so it further ratchets up insulin production. The more insulin that's released, the less effective it becomes, and the more resistant to insulin the body's cells become.

Aggravating the situation, insulin also promotes the formation of fat, technically known as *lipogenesis* ... Ultimately, both glucose and insulin levels remain elevated – a virtual prescription for Syndrome X, diabetes, and heart disease.[37]

The Glycemic Index

The discordance thesis argues that what has evolved as the contemporary North American diet involves a dramatic increase in the consumption of foods that are categorized as high-glycemic-index foods: foods that are quickly digested and rapidly converted into glucose in our body. The glycemic index was developed about three decades ago to assist with the control of diabetes.[38] Its use has not been without controversy, but significant research supports its efficacy as a tool for understanding the health consequences of certain foods in our diet.[39]

A food's glycemic index refers to its ability to raise blood glucose levels after being consumed. Foods that are rapidly absorbed or transformed metabolically into glucose in our bodies are considered high-glycemic foods.[40] Although there exists some scientific controversy over this concept and the related concept of glycemic load, there is sufficient evidence to support the relationship of high-glycemic edible products to insulin resistance and the onset of diabetes, and also increased risk of coronary heart disease.[41] In fact, a joint committee of the United Nations Food and Agricultural Organization and the World Health Organization has endorsed the use of the glycemic index as a method for classifying carbohydrate-rich foods. It has also recommended that the glycemic index (GI) values of foods be used in conjunction with information about food composition to guide food choices. Australia has incorporated this concept into its official dietary recommendations, and a trademark certification program is in place that puts the GI values on food labels.[42]

The industrial diet, characterized as it is by copious use of sweeteners and refined flours, is replete with high-glycemic edible products. Perhaps most notorious in this regard are the processed breakfast foods that came to define breakfasts on an ever greater global basis by the late twentieth century. Table 2.1 shows the high-glycemic nature of many widely available and consumed breakfast products.

Glycemic Load

With the glycemic index, glucose equals 100. A food such as pizza has a glycemic index (GI) value of 86, an apple, a GI value of 55.[43] Complementing the glycemic index is the calculation of the glycemic load of foods. This allows one to take into account that while foods have differing glycemic index rankings, the actual quantity of carbohydrate they contain differs as well. The glycemic load of a food is calculated as the GI value times its carbohydrate content, as measured in grams. In the case of an apple, for example, although it has a GI value of 55, its actual glycemic load is only 12, because of the presence of considerable fibre, water, and other elements that reduce its glycemic impact. Pizza, on the other hand, has a very high GI value of 86, and its glycemic load is calculated at 68, indicating that its potential to raise blood sugar levels is much higher than an equal quantity of fruit, such as an apple.

Foods that spike blood glucose trigger insulin release in the body, and consumption of these foods on a regular basis is thought to result in sustained high blood sugar levels, or chronic hyperglycemia. The decreasing effectiveness of insulin in removing excess blood sugar from our blood (insulin resistance) can and does have serious health consequences, among which may be type 2 diabetes.

The food industry's development of a multitude of processed foods made from refined flours with virtually all the fibre removed is responsible for some of the dramatic increase in the glycemic load of our diets. Many breakfast cereals, baked goods, bread products, and the like fit this description, but so too do other foods, including white rice, which has the bran coating removed

TABLE 2.1

Glycemic index/load of major ready-to-eat breakfast cereals
(serving size = 30 grams)

Brand, 1998	Market share, 2000	Glycemic index (pure glucose = 100)	Glycemic load
Cheerios (General Mills Canada)	4.9	74	15
Froot Loops (Kellogg Australia)	1.8	69±9	18
Total (General Mills Canada)	1.9	76	17
Rice Krispies (Kellogg Canada)	1.9	76	22
Corn Flakes (Kellogg USA), mean of 5 studies	2.4	81±3	21
CornPops (Kellogg Australia)	1.8	80±4	
Crunchy Nut Corn Flakes (Kellogg Australia)	0.2	72±4	17
Golden Grahams (General Mills Canada)	1.1	71	18
Cocoa Krispies (Kellogg Australia), mean of 2 studies	–	77	
Special K (Kellogg USA)	1.6	69±5	14
Grape-Nuts (Kraft Foods USA)	0.8	75±6	16
Frosted Flakes, sugar-coated cornflakes (Kellogg Australia) – now Frosties	4.6	55	15
Rice Chex (General Mills Canada)	0.8	89	23
Crispix (Kellogg Canada)	0.9	87	22
Raisin Bran (Kellogg USA)	2.8	61±5	12
Life (Quaker Oats Canada)	1.3	66	15
Corn Chex (General Mills Canada)	0.6	83	21

SOURCE: Kaye Foster-Powell, Susanna H.A. Holt, and Janette C. Brand-Miller, "International Table of Glycemic Index and Glycemic Load Values," *American Journal of Clinical Nutrition* 76, 1 (2002): 5-56.

via processing and is among the foods highest on the glycemic index. In addition to refining technologies, the glycemic load of our diets has been exacerbated by the extraordinary increases in added sweeteners to our diets over the last 150 years or so, in developed countries and increasingly in the global South as well.

Why Who Does the Cooking or Processing Matters

Pseudo foods tend to be notoriously high-glycemic products, for reasons that are not readily obvious. In Chapter 4, I discuss the technological revolution in flour processing in the nineteenth century that allowed processors to remove the bran from rice, wheat, and corn. This process, in addition to depleting the grain of most of its essential vitamins and minerals, renders the end products more easily digestible and therefore more prone to spike insulin levels on consumption than whole-grain flours with the bran present. The role of technology in raising the glycemic index of foods did not end with flour milling, however. In the twentieth century, breakfast cereal and snack food manufacturers began to incorporate innovations in the cooking end of the process of transforming whole grains into novel edible commodities. These cooking innovations have apparently had their own role to play in producing high-glycemic foods.

In the 1980s, researchers at the University of Sydney found evidence that factory cooking methods had different consequences for our body than did conventional cooking methods. They noted that the food industry had invented methods of extrusion cooking, explosion pressurization, and "instantization" that made use of extreme temperatures and pressures, and repeated wetting and drying methods that in the end produced substantial changes to the structures of the starch molecules of the flour being processed.[44]

These researchers found evidence that these factory cooking methods increased the speed by which such products are digested by producing a hydration of the starch granules, a process called gelatinization, and "changes in chemical nature or disruption of the granule structure of the starch."[45] They believe that these industrial cooking processes act to increase the availability of the starch in these foods to the enzyme amylase, which is excreted by our pancreas into the small intestine and serves to digest carbohydrates.

The cooking and processing of grains by industrial food manufacturers is quite unlike any normal cooking procedure people would be familiar with in their homes:

> Extrusion puffers are designed to compress the dough and heat it to more than 100 degrees C. so that water in the extrudate suddenly bursts into steam as the extrudate emerges from the die. The dough then expands, becomes cellular and porous, and finally sets due to cooling and drying. Most snack products including corn chips are produced by low or high pressure extrusion with or without frying ...

In contrast, conventional cooking methods such as boiling involve less physical disruption and only moderate heat, and are therefore less likely to cause starch damage or complete gelatinization.[46]

Over the last one hundred or more years, then, large numbers of humans have regularly ingested carbohydrates that are foreign to our evolved digestive systems, in a double sense. First, a large proportion of the carbohydrates consumed are deprived of the naturally occurring fibre via the industrial roller-milling process first brought in during the late nineteenth century. Second, over the twentieth century, corporate food processors, such as breakfast cereal manufacturers seeking novel products that could be sold on the basis of their convenience, invented new cooking and processing procedures that further changed the nature of whole foods (grains). These changes had the effect of even further spiking blood sugar levels upon consumption. For our body, in other words, these types of edible products are adulterants and serve to exacerbate the glycemic impact of a high level of sweetener ingestion. When we think of sweeteners as a macro-adulterant, then, it should be kept in mind that many snack food products of the American diet that may not be sweetened at all (although some are, as in the case of pre-sweetened breakfast cereals) could and probably should be considered as macro-adulterants as well (see Chapter 8).

Sweeteners and Fructose Overdose

Corn-based sweeteners, as opposed to the traditional cane and beet sugar that were the predominant sweeteners in European diets in the nineteenth and the first two-thirds of the twentieth century, may be more directly related to diabetes, or so the most recent research on the topic would indicate. To appreciate this, we have to look at the veritable revolution in the food industry's use of sweeteners since the 1970s, with particular attention paid to the role of fructose and the now-dominant sweetener in our food environment, high-fructose corn syrup.

Fructose is a simple sugar found in foods such as honey and fruits, but it is also a major component of the dominant sweeteners in our current food system, including cane sugar, and especially high-fructose corn syrup, which by 2008 accounted for about 40 percent of sweeteners available for consumption in the United States.[47] The editorial of a recent issue of a leading American journal of nutritional science focuses on the growing evidence linking fructose to the metabolic syndrome and diabetes. It notes that fructose consumption has quadrupled since the early 1900s, and consumption has accelerated since the introduction of high-fructose corn syrup approximately three decades ago. As the authors of this editorial note, "Experimental studies in animals have shown that fructose can induce most features of the metabolic syndrome, including insulin resistance, elevated triglycerides, abdominal obesity, elevated blood pressure, inflammation, ... micro vascular disease ... renal injury and fatty liver."[48] Recent studies have shown that in humans, the consumption of large amounts of fructose can rapidly produce insulin resistance and raises triglycerides in the blood and blood pressure after eating, more than either starch or glucose.[49]

One further disturbing finding is that fructose consumption is associated with weight gain because it does not appear to trigger the endocrine signals that are involved with feelings of satiety and long-term energy balance in the same way that glucose does.[50] This may explain why, beginning in 2001, studies have found an association between consumption of soft drinks (sweetened with high-fructose corn syrup) and obesity in children.[51] In the period from 1965 to 1996, the per capita daily soft drink consumption for boys aged eleven to eighteen rose from 179 to 520 grams, and from 148 to 337 grams for girls in the United States.[52] This trend of rising soft drink consumption has characterized other developed societies also, including Canada, where it increased some 50 percent between 1985 and 1999. Soft drink manufacturers, with ongoing aggressive advertising aimed at the youth market, have managed to displace milk consumption and expand their markets (see Figure 2.2).

FATS AND HEALTH

Contemporary diets are characterized, it is argued, by a significant shift in the quality of the fats being consumed. The theory of evolutionary discordance argues that science has demonstrated that it is not so much the quantity of fats consumed but the type of fats being consumed that are so deleterious to our health. Specifically, increasing quantities of damaging saturated fats and trans fats are being consumed. The reasons for this are multiple, but two salient causes are the confinement agriculture system that demands corn-based feeds to rapidly grow livestock for markets, and the use of hydrogenated fats by the baking industry to increase shelf life and other commercial qualities of the products it produces. The first raises the saturated fat content of the meats produced and alters the fat profile of the meat in other ways as well;

FIGURE 2.2
Trends in per capita food consumption in Canada, 1935-99

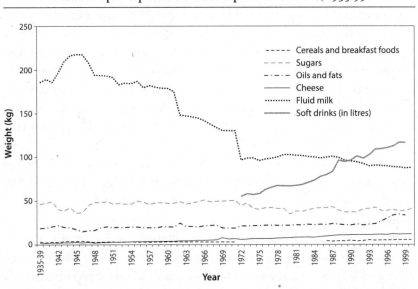

SOURCE: Statistics Canada, "Per Capita Disappearance of Major Food Groups," summary tables (various years), *Food Consumption in Canada, Part II* (Ottawa: Statistics Canada, 2001).

the second creates trans fats; and both have been demonstrated to be injurious to health.

By the 1970s, fats had become much more of a target for health authorities than previously, and fat avoidance was to become a preferred strategy among that segment of the population concerned with health issues. Fat consumption among Americans had increased substantially over the twentieth century, from about 125 grams per day to about 160 grams per day by the mid-1970s. So too had coronary heart disease (CHD), which by then accounted for approximately one-half of American deaths, with cancer a distant second cause of death.[53] Although the relationship between diet and CHD was not clear, the results of large-scale epidemiologic studies in the United States indicated by the 1970s that a relationship existed between high rates of blood cholesterol levels and a greater incidence of CHD. Moreover, saturated fats were known to increase blood cholesterol.[54] The strong correlation between percentage of energy derived from saturated fats and CHD was given more support by an important seven-country study coordinated by American scientist Ancel Keys and begun several decades ago.[55]

Advice to reduce intake of foods high in saturated fats, in particular red meats and dairy products high in butter fat, seemed to be prudent. There is evidence that the public has heeded these warnings to some extent. Not only have lower-fat options been a growth segment for food manufacturers over the years but substantial shifts in meat consumption, away from red meats highest in saturated fats and toward leaner meats and poultry in particular, have occurred. Red meat consumption in Canada in the mid-1970s was at about sixty kilograms per person annually; it has since declined to less than forty-five kilograms per person annually by 2006. Meanwhile, poultry consumption increased some 85 percent over the same period, to about thirty-seven kilograms per person annually.[56] Similar trends have occurred in other industrialized societies. The food industry, for its part, has been happy to respond to these concerns about fat, rushing to launch products in many categories that could be advertised as low-fat or no-fat options.

With respect to dairy products, the consumption of full-fat milk has declined dramatically over the years, but the same cannot be said for all high-fat dairy products. In fact, cheese consumption has become a significant route for saturated fats to continue to characterize the North American diet. Cheese consumption in the United States had tripled from the period immediately following the Second World War to the 1990s; in Canada it has tripled since the 1970s.[57] At the same time, ice cream products, notoriously high in saturated fats (and sweeteners), have increased quite dramatically as well.

We might expect to see a change in coronary disease rates with this marked change in the dietary intake of saturated fats with shifting meat-consumption patterns. This has in fact occurred. For example, a six-country study in 1999 of trends in CHD in men aged forty to sixty-nine found that in rich countries with previously high rates of death from CHD, including the United States, Finland, England, and New Zealand, rates of CHD declined significantly, from between five and six hundred deaths per 100,000 in 1970 to approximately three hundred deaths per 100,000 in 1999.[58] Nevertheless, these rates are still dramatically higher than those that prevail in countries with radically different dietary traditions, such as Japan, where the rate of CHD in males of the same age group was under fifty per 100,000 in 1999, or one-sixth the American rate.[59]

These dramatically lower rates of fatal coronary disease for Japanese men compared with their North American counterparts, and the lower rates that prevail among men in southern European countries as well (notably France, but also Spain, Portugal, and Italy), put the lie to any simplistic notions that mortality due to CHD is just one of the "diseases of affluence." Societies can be affluent and yet not suffer the damaging rate of CHD that prevails in North America. The fact that Japanese who leave Japan to live in the United States soon come to exhibit rates of CHD similar to those of US-born citizens strongly suggests how important the role of diet and lifestyle factors can be.[60]

Later (in Chapter 6) I explore the notion that the trend for saturated fat consumption to increase over time cannot be understood without considering the role of confined animal feeding operations, or factory farms, and the corn-based feeds they use in shaping the fat profiles of the animals we raise for meat. Had North Americans been able to maintain high levels of beef consumption by eating only grass-fed animals, that is, cattle eating what they evolved to eat, the ratio of "bad" fats to "good" fats in the diet would have undoubtedly been rather different. How different, however, is inevitably also a factor of the relative role of other unhealthy foods in the diet. In this regard, despite some gains that have been made in reducing saturated fat intake via consumption of meat and some dairy products high in saturated fats, these fats continue to prevail in our food environments at dangerous levels.

Trans Fats: The Industrial Facilitators

A considerable amount of scientific effort has gone into discovering the dangers inherent in a diet high in saturated fats. Nevertheless, as far as fats go, saturated fats have been shown to be considerably less lethal than another kind of fat that is largely a product of the food industry. These trans fatty acids, or trans fats, have been under scrutiny by nutritional scientists for many years. Yet, despite concern for their impact on human health voiced more than two decades ago in Canada, little was done to reduce their use in the food industry.[61]

By adding extra hydrogen atoms in place of the double bonds between carbon atoms in the fat molecule, a process that requires heating of the fat in the presence of hydrogen and a catalyst such as nickel, the physical characteristics of the fat can be significantly changed. In technical terms, this process increases the saturation of the fatty acids in the oil by reducing the number of double bonds and thereby raising the melting point of the fat. This newly created fat is solid at room temperature, something that is not characteristic of the polyunsaturated or monounsaturated fats that these new fats are made from. Products made from this artificial fat resist oxidation and are not as susceptible to spoilage or damage from sunlight as those made from unaltered fats. As such they are valued by manufacturers, and possibly by consumers as well (think peanut butter), for the consistency and spreadability they impart to the product.[62] From the point of view of food manufacturers, this translates into products that will last longer on the shelf under a greater variety of conditions. This also appeals to retailers, who can store these products for much longer periods without risk of their going rancid.

There are other reasons manufacturers have been keen to use trans fats in their products. For many years, medical authorities have warned about the dangers of saturated fats and cholesterol, and hydrogenated oils are made from vegetable oils that are free of saturated fats and cholesterol. By using trans fats, processors had marketing ammunition to influence consumers concerned about cholesterol and heart disease.[63]

This benefit for the food industry does not carry through for the consumer of these products in terms of its health impacts, however. Indeed, it is quite the contrary. As an artificially created substance, trans fats are not something our body is designed to process. Trans fats have been implicated in promoting cardiovascular disease, and there has been concern about the possible detrimental effects they may have on infant development.[64] Although there are still those who are skeptical that the hydrogenated fats are harmful to us, especially some in the food industry, the weight of science is on the side of those who regard trans fats to be dangerous indeed. The US-based Institute of Medicine, a division of the National Academy of Sciences, declared in its 2002 report that there are *no* safe levels of trans fats in our food and called for a reduction of them in our diet.[65]

Trans fats in our diet are largely derived from unsaturated fats formed by the partial hydrogenation of vegetable oils. There is also a relatively small amount of naturally occurring trans fats in our diet derived from meat consumption, and some research suggests that these kinds of trans fats may have beneficial effects. It is another matter with the type of trans fats produced via hydrogenation.

Trans fats produced by the industrial hydrogenation of unsaturated fats are believed to account for 2 to 3 percent of daily calories consumed in the United States.[66] This may sound like a relatively inconsequential amount of fat in the diet, but numerous studies have found a relatively small increase in the amount of trans fats in the diet to be associated with a substantial increase in adverse health outcomes.

Trans fats have been found to raise the proportion of low-density lipoproteins (LDL cholesterol, the harmful cholesterol) and decrease the proportion of high-density lipoproteins (HDL cholesterol, the beneficial cholesterol) in the blood, compared with the effect of consumption of an equal amount of saturated or unsaturated non-hydrogenated fat. Trans fats consumption has been found to also increase the ratio of total cholesterol to HDL cholesterol. This is known to be a powerful predictor of CHD risk.[67] However, the relationship between trans fats consumption and CHD is greater than would be expected from its impact on serum cholesterol.

Trans fats are also implicated in the provocation of a systemic inflammatory response in the body, which is itself believed to be related to disease. Inflammation has been found to be an important risk factor for atherosclerosis, sudden death from cardiac causes, diabetes, and heart failure.[68] Trans fats have been found to be powerful modulators of cell functions and have also been observed to affect vascular function, impairing arterial dilation.

In summing up the evidence from numerous studies examining the effects of trans fats in the diet on health, a major review article notes:

> On a per-calorie basis, *trans* fats appear to increase the risk of CHD more than any other macro-nutrient, conferring a substantially increased risk at low levels of consumption (1 to 3 percent of total energy intake). In a meta-analysis of four prospective cohort studies involving nearly 140,000 subjects, including updated analyses from the two largest studies, a 2 percent increase in energy intake from *trans* fatty acids was associated with a 23 percent increase in the incidence of CHD. *The evidence and the magnitude of adverse health effects of trans fatty acids are in fact far stronger on average than those of food contaminants or pesticide residues, which have in some cases received considerable attention.* (emphasis added)[69]

Prevalence of Trans Fats

While governments slowly respond to mounting evidence of the damage caused by trans fats, typically by requiring labels that indicate the presence of trans fats, and some manufacturers respond to growing concern by reformulating products and advertising them as trans fats–free, the reality so far is that the food system is still heavily laced with products made with these dangerous fats. One nutritional source published as recently as 2004 estimated that at the time some 40 percent of grocery products contained trans fats, including 95 percent of cookies, 80 percent of frozen breakfast foods, 75 percent of salty snacks and chips, 70 percent of cake mixes, and almost half of all cold cereals.[70] These products were adulterated with trans fats for many years presumably and over this time had compromised the health of consumers.

The Fast-Food Connection

Fast-food products have historically been a potent source of trans fats in our diets, or so early studies examining the presence of these fats in fast-food products would suggest. Recent studies corroborate that these dangerous fats are still very present in fast-food offerings around the world, but they do indicate that there is a distinct variation in the levels of these fats from country to country. For example, one notable study found that a meal of chicken nuggets and french fries purchased at McDonald's or KFC would contain from five to ten grams of trans fats if bought in the United States, the United Kingdom, Peru, South Africa, Poland, Finland, France, Italy, Norway, Spain, Sweden, Germany, or Hungary, but relatively less (one to five grams) if purchased in Portugal, Austria, the Netherlands, the Czech Republic, or Russia. In the case of KFC products, a meal of chicken nuggets and french fries could contain as much as ten to twenty-five grams of trans fats if purchased in Hungary, Poland, the Czech Republic, or Peru but considerably less in some other countries. The trans fat content of these products varied considerably by country and even by city, they noted.[71] No explanation for these differences was given, although data show that Denmark had by far the lowest levels of such fats in these fast-food products. Not coincidentally, Denmark is the one country whose government has moved proactively to ban trans fats from its food system in recent years.

More meaningful than absolute amounts of trans fats in products would be labelling information for consumers on the proportion of trans fats in various kinds of foods, compared with the total fat content. However, given that similar products can have dramatically differing amounts of trans fats, and the growing evidence that trans fats are a potent health danger in our food supply, protecting the consumer requires government action to eliminate trans fats from our food supply wherever possible. Denmark has led the way in banning trans fats from Danish food. What is remarkable is that few other governments have taken its lead.

A minor victory on this front was won in Canada when opponents of trans fats in food were able to convince the federal government that food-packaging labels should be required to list the trans fat content of the product. The federal government set up a trans fat monitoring program for two years beginning in 2007 that examined a sample of products from various food restaurant chains and supermarkets for their trans fats contents, and then posted the results on the Health Canada website. It has called for voluntary action from the food industry to reduce trans fats in margarines and oils to a maximum of 2 percent of total fat, and in other food products to a maximum of 5 percent of total fat.[72]

What has the effect of these limited interventions been? Officials in Health Canada believe it has resulted in some reduction of these artificial fats in food products sold in supermarkets and restaurant chains, as more and more manufacturers seek competitive advantage in declaring their products to be trans fats–free.[73] The data from 2008, the last date for which companies are identified, show that although retail food outlets had indeed reduced or eliminated trans fats from some of the products they sold, there still remain dangerous amounts of trans fats in other products, whether these are snack foods, bakery products, cookies, or desserts. The consuming public can avoid such products only by vigilant examination of food labels on prepackaged edible products. This is not possible with many purchases in restaurant and doughnut chain operations, however, nor even purchases from in-store bakeries in supermarkets, where no labels are required. In the end, the voluntary approach to reducing trans fats in Canada has resulted in their reduction in some areas, but from the consumer's point of view, it is a hit-and-miss approach, and therefore it is still extremely difficult to protect oneself from these damaging fats.

SODIUM UNDERMINES DIETARY HEALTH

As a recent scientific article on salt noted, a lack of sodium intake or a depletion of existing sodium in the body is incompatible with survival. Sodium is essential for various metabolic reactions and neurological processes.[74] But the body is naturally able to regulate sodium balance if our kidneys are functioning normally, and the amounts of sodium needed are far below the amounts typically consumed today. An estimated ten grams of salt are consumed per capita each day worldwide, a level that far exceeds the intakes recommended by credible nutritional authorities.

If we compare these amounts with the estimated amounts of salt consumed in Palaeolithic people's diets, which was about one to one and a half grams per day,[75] we can see how out of step contemporary consumption and contemporary dietary recommendations are compared with the salt consumption we were adapted to consume for much of our evolutionary existence. Examination of hunter and gatherer diets in the context of Papua New Guinea reinforce this conclusion that diets very low in sodium are not only possible without adverse effects but are also associated with very low incidence of diseases such as hypertension that are linked with excess sodium consumption.[76]

An important question is, How did we get into a state of excess salt consumption on such a worldwide basis? The short answer is that some, but not all, humans have apparently consumed salt on a much-increased scale since roughly the advent of agriculture and the development of sedentary human settlements. Why this is so is a matter somewhat more complicated. But as one scholarly treatment of the subject has noted, salt "is a fact of culture, rather than nature."[77] Palaeolithic people would seem to have consumed enough salt through their varied diet without needing to seek out salt to add to their food. The fact that salt became such an economic enterprise over the last few thousand years of human settled history requires explanation. Fortunately, the subject of salt has received several fascinating historical treatments as part of the emergence of commodity histories over the last several decades. These studies illuminate much about salt's history and provide useful context for the contemporary era.[78] For our purposes, I will draw out only some of the basic highlights of this complex history.

Salt, its production, and its social use is closely associated with the development of sedentary, hierarchical societies; the emergence of high cuisine; and the need to feed growing numbers of people tied to the land or forced to provide labour services through the institution of slavery. Abandonment of a hunting and gathering existence and a diet relatively high in animal protein, and with it sufficient salt for human needs, entailed substantial changes in human diets and likely a deterioration in nutrients for the majority. As cereals came to make up a significant component of daily meals, the salt intake associated with the considerable consumption of animal protein declined, and this may have stimulated an appetite for salt and therefore so too the enterprise needed to procure it.[79] Numerous histories of salt have documented the widespread nature of ancient salt works among newly sedentary civilizations, from Asia through Europe to the New World.[80]

Beyond the stimulus provided by dietary transformation, salt, it has been argued, came to provide social status and distinction among increasingly socially differentiated peoples. Samuel Adshead notes that among the ancient Celtic people, the development of social hierarchy saw the emergence of the "hall and the banquet" where the military elite entertained, and this demanded "high cooking," a cuisine out of the ordinary that required salt both as a flavouring element and as a preservative. "Salt," he writes, "prevented decay, activated latent differences in taste and created them by its uneven distribution. It thereby destroyed monotony and set up a gamut of possibilities for cooks and gourmets."[81]

A further stimulus to the appetite for salt was its early identification with health. The belief that salt had medicinal properties had roots in ancient Chinese and Indian societies, where it was seen as useful for the treatment of intestinal parasites, for the application to wounds, and for fainting due to the loss of blood. Adshead suggests that the ancient use of salt may have paralleled that of opium in China, the use of which began as a medicinal prophylaxis against malaria and tuberculosis and then eventually changed to become more of a "social accomplishment, entertainment and minimal luxury. The story of salt, one may suppose, was similar. Part of the struggle of culture against nature, a weapon of culture supplied by nature, salt became part of culture itself."[82]

Salt's preservative qualities were established by the ancient Egyptians with their elaborate mummification process and the use of a form of salt known as natron, along with resin.[83] In more recent times – from the sixteenth century onward – salt was needed to preserve vast quantities of herring, and later cod, foods that became central to the diet of European peoples. By the seventeenth century, beef preserved with salt was also becoming common, and such preserved meats became essential fare for sailors in the burgeoning navies of Europe. As Mark Kurlansky notes of the importance of the fish trade for salt consumption during this period, "Salt made it possible to get the rich bounty of the northern seas to the poor people of Europe."[84] He also argues that it led to a dramatic increase in the consumption of salt in the diet. One authority places European consumption of salt in the nineteenth century at about eighteen grams per day, whereas Swedes, who relied heavily on salted fish in their diet, were reportedly eating an incredible hundred grams per day![85] This astounding consumption of salt would presumably have been characteristic only of those regions in which preserved (not fresh) fish consumption was central to the diet and would not have been common where and when diets became more varied, as they eventually did. Nevertheless, preserved fish and meat consumption continued to some degree up to the present day and were important means by which Europeans and the peoples they influenced and subordinated became habituated to salt consumption.

The industrialization of food in the nineteenth century was another major impetus for the introduction of salt into human diets. The dramatic expansion of the vegetable and fruit canning industry in the late nineteenth and early twentieth centuries saw the increasing use of salt, and sugar, for their preservative qualities. The first mass-produced industrial convenience foods were canned foods, after all.

By the twentieth century, humans in sedentary societies in many parts of the globe had thus become accustomed to the regular dietary intake of substantial amounts of salt. Far from this being the result of some physiological need beyond a minimal level, however, this level of salt consumption appears to have clear cultural and socio-economic bases. Graham MacGregor and Hugh de Wardener cite anthropological evidence to support this conclusion. Indigenous peoples of western North America were noted to be geographically divided according to their preference for salt. Those to the north of an irregular line running roughly from the mouth of the Columbia River to the southeast toward present-day Nevada did not eat salt, whereas those tribes to the south of this line uniformly did. As MacGregor and de Wardener note, "This difference did not appear to be due to the prevalence of sea food, a meat diet or a warmer climate." It was concluded that whether or not salt was used, it was in most instances a social custom, in other words, part of the "culture."[86] Denton's comprehensive study *The Hunger for Salt* notes that a wide variety of peoples across the globe showed little inclination to use salt and typically found it distasteful when introduced to it by visitors. This included nomadic peoples such as the Inuit of North America and tribes of Siberia, the Kyrghiz of Turkestan, the Numidians of northeastern Africa, several tribal groupings of southwest Africa, and the nomadic hunting people of eastern Finland.[87]

Inducing Salt Addiction

Anthropologists have also helped us understand how people can become habituated to salt. The American anthropologist Allan Holmberg, who lived with the Siriono people of Bolivia in the 1950s, noted that they exhibited a distaste for salt when he first introduced it to them. However, "by using small quantities in cooking ... they soon developed a craving for it. In some instances, this craving (once the people had become accustomed to eating salt) has become so great as to become an important factor in establishing and maintaining friendly relations with the whites."[88] Other species closely related to humans, such as chimpanzees, have been observed to have a preference for a high-salt diet when introduced to it, even though their natural diet is very low in salt.[89] Although herbivores are attracted to natural salt deposits, probably because of the low amounts of sodium in their plant-based diet, predator species show little interest in seeking out natural salt deposits, or if they do, it would appear to be because their prey does so.

Experimental studies using animals have explored the psycho-biological mechanisms that promote excessive salt intake. This research suggests that high doses of salt in diet influences the reward pathways of the brain, the same pathways involved in drug abuse and possibly the maintenance of addiction. Because of the apparent plasticity of the central neurological system, high salt intake may thus lead to enduring changes in one's appetite for salt over the longer term, this research would suggest.[90] MacGregor and de Wardener summarize the argument for salt habituation:

> For millions of years our ancestors ate a diet that contained much less salt than it does now. The change to a high salt diet was probably due to the accidental finding that meat could be preserved by immersion in brine. There is no evidence that it was due to a sudden increase in physiological need. Primitive, unacculterated human populations, whose salt intake is near that of our ancestors, are fit and energetic. When introduced to salt they initially find it unpleasant and repulsive but easily become addicted to it.[91]

Salt and Disease

There is some long-standing evidence that elevated consumption of salt is linked to raised blood pressure, or hypertension.[92] The Intersalt study of fifty-two populations around the world found a strong association between salt consumption and blood pressure, with people still following a hunting and gathering lifestyle, from Brazil to Papua New Guinea, having by far the lowest salt consumption and also the lowest blood pressure levels.[93] Moreover, these populations did not become hypertensive as age increased, the typical pattern among populations elsewhere in the world where salt consumption is much higher.

The evidence linking high blood pressure to harm to health has been recognized for many years; indeed, it was once used by the insurance industry to deny people with hypertension coverage.[94] In particular, the condition is seen as an important predictor of the risk for stroke and a major predictor of heart attack. Hypertension is known to cause rupture or dilation of the arteries, or to create such a load on the heart that it becomes enlarged and its pumping function eventually compromised. It is known to damage the small arteries and filters in the kidneys, which leads to kidney failure. High salt consumption has been linked consistently with kidney damage in several experimental studies, for example.[95]

However, the most dramatic effect of high blood pressure is that it increases the likelihood that blood vessels will burst. The damage that results depends where it occurs, but if it is in the brain it leads to hemorrhage into the brain and typically body paralysis and possibly death. Large arteries may also be affected by high blood pressure, which causes their dilation and weakening.[96] And finally, medical scientists are finding evidence that excessive salt intake is producing organ damage over and above that which may be produced by its effect in raising blood pressure alone.[97]

The evidence confirming high blood pressure and increased likelihood of premature death has been somewhat more contested, however, despite health authorities often linking it with increased incidence of stroke and heart disease.[98] For example, a study using data from the Second National Health and Nutrition Examination Survey (NHANES II) in the United States produced evidence suggesting that lower levels of salt consumption were associated with *higher* incidence of death from cardiovascular disease. Yet, even the authors of this study note that this relationship was not observed among non-whites, the obese, or those under age fifty-five in the study sample, and that several other studies have found the opposite relationship; that is, greater salt consumption is associated with a greater likelihood of death among subjects under study. This was the case with an earlier Finnish community study and among the obese subjects of the first NHANES survey done in the United States. As well, they note that higher salt consumption was associated with more chronic heart disease among women in a Scottish study, and with higher incidence of stroke in a recent Japanese study.[99]

That the scientific evidence linking increased salt consumption to higher mortality rates is not conclusive does not mean that a relationship does not exist, of course. Studies of this nature are confounded by many difficulties, not the least of which is the culturally specific levels of salt consumption of the populations around the world from which samples are drawn. In fact, the evidence linking high salt consumption to higher incidence of death was in studies with subjects who had significantly higher levels of average salt consumption than was the case with the American study. As the authors of that study note, the positive relationship between salt consumption and mortality may be operating only where average salt consumption is high to begin with.

On the other hand, it is necessary to distinguish between early mortality and the incidence of disease. For a host of reasons, including a reduction in smoking, better treatment for high blood pressure, and, to a lesser extent, better outcomes from medical interventions,[100] there has been a significant reduction in the number of people dying from coronary heart disease and stroke in North America. Despite this, the incidence of cardiac disease, arterial disease, and advanced kidney disease has continued to climb, which indicates that the root causes of these major health problems remains unaddressed, regardless of the more effective interventions to prevent fatal outcomes from these diseases.[101]

BEYOND SWEETENERS, FATS, AND SODIUM

Considerable research on novel and excess sweeteners and fats, as well as on excess sodium, in the industrial diet lends support to the discordance thesis as a useful explanation for much chronic disease. Before I consider some criticisms of this thesis, it should be noted that the thesis argues that contemporary diets are discordant with the foods humans evolved with in several other significant ways also, some of which are open to more debate than those noted above.

Macronutrient Composition

The discordance thesis argues that contemporary diets represent a macronutrient composition (fats, carbohydrates, proteins) that diverges significantly from Palaeolithic diets, and this results in negative health outcomes. Specifically, contemporary diets are viewed as having a substantially higher carbohydrate content than protein content. It argues that higher protein intake and carbohydrate reduction has been shown to have several positive health effects. One issue here is, of course, what form higher protein consumption takes.

Micronutrient Deficiencies

In addition to macronutrient imbalances, the discordance theorists argue that our contemporary diet produces serious deficiencies of the beneficial micronutrients (minerals, phytochemicals, vitamins) that humans need to remain healthy. They note that in the US diet, over one-third of daily energy comes from vegetable oils and sweeteners, and that these are very low in essential micronutrients. Furthermore, much of the rest of the diet consists of refined grains and dairy products, which offer more nutritional value than sweeteners and oils but have lower total micronutrient values than fruits and vegetables, lean meats, and seafood, which they tend to replace in the industrial diet. This contributes to a micronutrient deficiency for many, it is argued.

Given that many foods, including pseudo foods, are now fortified with vitamins and minerals, it may be more accurate to say that the diets of some segments of the population are at risk. The most vulnerable are marginalized populations, including the poor, those living in veritable food deserts, certain Aboriginal populations, and especially those living in remote northern communities. Many children and youth, at least in North America, may also have micronutrient deficiency, given the considerable evidence that they are eating far fewer fruits and vegetables than is considered desirable.

This argument, it seems to me, is perhaps most relevant when it comes to the issue of phytochemicals. I consider in Chapter 7 evidence to suggest that the radical varietal simplification that characterizes the modern food system may be implicated in this outcome.

Acid-Base Balance

Once foods are digested and metabolized, they tend to affect the pH balance of the body, making it either more acid or base (alkaline). The pH level is a measure of the acidity or alkalinity of a substance, typically on a scale ranging from zero to fourteen, with zero being the most acidic. Our bodies make constant adjustments in tissue and fluid pH to maintain a very narrow pH range in the blood between 7.35 and 7.45. Fish, meat, shellfish, cheese, milk, cereal grains, and salt are net acid producing. Fresh fruit and vegetables, tubers, and nuts are base producing; legumes are nearly neutral.[102] Why does this matter? Cordain and his co-authors sum up the significance: "Healthy adults consuming the standard US diet sustain a chronic, low-grade pathogenic metabolic acidosis that worsens with age as kidney function declines." This is in contrast to the effect of the diets that prevailed throughout most of our evolution, which was a net base-producing diet. As these authors note, "The known health benefits of a net base-yielding diet include preventing and treating osteoporosis, age-related muscle wasting, calcium kidney stones, hypertension and exercise-induced asthma and slow[ing] the progression of age and disease related renal (kidney) insufficiency."[103] An understanding of the significance of this factor may help us understand, for instance, the apparent incongruence of the high incidence of bone-density loss with age and the development of osteoporosis among Westerners, with their dairy-rich diets, whereas Asians, who do not traditionally consume significant quantities of milk, have also had a much lower incidence of osteoporosis.[104]

Potassium-Sodium Ratio

Discordance thesis advocates argue that a diet low in potassium and high in sodium may be linked to numerous chronic illnesses, from hypertension and stroke to asthma and gastrointestinal tract cancer. A shift away from a potassium-rich diet in Palaeolithic times would have begun with the dietary narrowing that came with the advent of agriculture. Over time, the sodium content of the diet increased, at times dramatically, especially when societies had more recourse to preserved foods, as in salted fish in Europe after the fifteenth century or so. The industrialization of food has exacerbated the shift to sodium-rich diets, particularly so with the advent of modern fast foods. The increase in vegetable oil and sweetener consumption has tended to displace potassium-rich foods, it is argued, as has the increase in dairy and grains in the diet, since fruits and vegetables are four to twelve times richer in concentrations of potassium.

Fibre

Diets high in fibre are believed to lower concentrations of harmful cholesterols and may help moderate appetite and thereby reduce the intake of calories. Low-fibre diets are thought to exacerbate the incidence of various ailments, from constipation and gastric reflux to appendicitis, diverticulitis, and hiatal hernia. The shift to agriculture likely did not affect the fibre content dramatically compared with the Palaeolithic period, as a diet more dependent upon grains would have contained the fibre present in the bran of the grain, whether it be rice, wheat, rye, or barley, given milling technology until the late nineteenth century. With the industrialization of foods, this was to all change. Modern milling machinery introduced after 1870 was capable of extracting nearly all of the fibre from the grain to produce a whiter end product (flour), and even today it is estimated that 85 percent of the grains consumed in the United States are fibre-depleted refined-grain products. The fruits and vegetables displaced by the increasing consumption of refined grains contain some eight times the fibre of the latter. Other fruit and vegetable "displacers"

– dairy, refined sugars, and refined oils – contain virtually no fibre, exacerbating the effect of refined-grain consumption.

Was it the shift to agriculture alone, and the subsequent change in diet, that was responsible for the differences that archaeologists and anthropologists have noted in the health, physical stature, and physical prowess between hunting and gathering and agriculture-dependent people? Here, the evidence would indicate that the most likely answer is no, it was not the advent of agriculture alone, but rather agriculture within an evolving social context characterized by ever greater degrees of social hierarchy, a matter I explore more closely below.

ASSESSING THE DISCORDANCE THESIS

Although I believe there is much of value in the arguments offered by advocates of the discordance thesis, there are also areas of ambiguity and ongoing debate over certain nutritional matters (e.g., the purported micronutrient deficiency and acid-base imbalance with the industrial diet), as well as issues that, because of the sweep of history it covers, are not seriously confronted. First, as noted above, the matter of growing social hierarchy and power imbalances and their impact on the nutrition and health of the majority of those subject to the domination of a few is something largely overlooked.

Second, it is not clear what weight we should ultimately give to the transition to agriculture, compared with the modern era of food industrialization. The latter development gets the most attention in the sentinel article by Cordain and his co-authors referred to earlier, and I believe that this is correct. They argue, "With the advent of agriculture, novel foods were introduced as staples for which the hominin genome had little evolutionary experience. *More importantly, food processing procedures were developed, particularly following the Industrial Revolution, which allowed for quantitative and qualitative food and nutrient combinations that had not previously been encountered over the course of hominin evolution*" (emphasis added).[105]

The transition to agriculture was very partial and very drawn out, it would appear, at least for many areas of human habitation. Since agriculture became established, civilizations waxed and waned and dietary regimes flourished and declined. Although the bulk of humanity became engaged in some form of production of its means of subsistence on the land, people undoubtedly continued to supplement their diets with wild terrestrial and marine foods whenever they could for much of recorded history, until very recently. These facts would have attenuated the effects of an agricultural-based diet for many up until the last few hundred years, and even more recently for people living in rural and remote areas.

Another weakness of the discordance thesis is its lack of attention to different phases of the food economy within the industrial era. Early industrialization after 1850 or so affected the nutritional quality of grain products in particular but left untouched other foodstuffs for decades. Only later, for example, did confinement livestock and poultry raising based on a regime of corn-based feeds change the fat profile of the meat in North America, later Europe, and now the developing world. The proliferation of fast foods and snack foods starting in the mid-twentieth century helped sustain and exacerbate the trend for increasing consumption of sweeteners and refined vegetable oils and trans fats, which have become so prominent in the contemporary American diet. The retailing revolution occasioned by the proliferation of supermarket chain stores over the twentieth century, but especially after the Second World War, has had a largely unrecognized impact on dietary change as well. This revolution, which took place over some eighty years in North America, is presently dramatically changing the food retail landscape in the global South, and all in the space of less than two decades (see Chapter 11).

The processes explaining why the industrialization of the food economy has led to the proliferation of such a plethora of nutrient-poor products that undermine the health of an ever greater portion of humanity is somewhat of a black box for the discordance thesis. Nevertheless, the advocates of this thesis have rendered a major service in drawing our attention to the extraordinarily anomalous nature of much of our contemporary diet. It remains for them to explain how this came about, and what can be done about it.

It is the manifold impacts of the industrialization of food that will receive the most attention in the pages that follow. Before I delve more deeply into this matter, it is necessary to examine, if only briefly, the dietary changes that could be seen as precursors of the full industrialization of food. These changes were given stimulus by the historically unprecedented expansion of market relations and trade that accompanied the spread of agrarian capitalism and its variants in Europe, and in the New World, after the seventeenth century or so.

CHAPTER THREE

FROM NEOLITHIC
TO CAPITALIST DIETS

White bread and tea passed, in the course of a hundred years, from
the luxuries of the rich to become the hall-marks of a poverty line
diet ... Whereas they were mere adjuncts to the tables of the wealthy,
they became all too often the total diet of the poor, the irreducible
minimum beyond which lay only starvation.

—John Burnett, historian of nineteenth-century
England[1]

FOR REASONS THAT ARE NOT well understood, modern humans began
to shift from a gathering and hunting existence to one that involved
the increasing control of a select and limited number of plants and animals
for an increasing portion of their food needs. The origins of agriculture are
widely debated; indeed, the historian Felipe Fernández-Armesto notes that
thirty-eight different and competing explanations of how farming came
about have been identified in the literature.[2]

Until recently, it was supposed that humans were at one point hunter-
gatherers and at some point they switched to farming and became agriculturalists, at least in some parts of the world. It now appears that a more
complex transition occurred, as evidence emerges that, whether it was in
the Middle East, China, or the Americas, people began experimenting with

the cultivation of some types of plants while still carrying on a foraging life-style, and that this mix of subsistence strategies lasted for perhaps several thousand years. This gradual shift to agriculture now appears to have pre-dated by a good long time, at least in certain regions, the emergence of settled communities as well.[3] But there is also evidence of semi-sedentary settle-ments that appear to predate the domestication of food sources.[4]

Evidence of the earliest domestication process of plants (wheat, peas, olives) is strongest for the Fertile Crescent area of the Middle East (present-day Iraq, Syria, Lebanon, Turkey, Israel, and Jordan) and took place around 8,000 to 10,000 BC. This cultivation later spread westward through the Mediterranean into present-day western Europe, and possibly also south-westward into present-day Ethiopia.[5] Several other sites of plant domestica-tion are known, notably China (rice, millet), Meso-America (corn, beans, and squash), the Andes and Amazonia (potato and cassava), and the eastern United States (sunflower, goosefoot). Other possible sites of early plant do-mestication include the Sahel (sorghum, African rice) and West Africa (yams, palm oil).[6] These latter sites were thought to have domesticated crops much later than the Fertile Crescent, but research through new methods suggests that people began to domesticate plants in the Americas (present-day Ecuador) and China several thousand years earlier than previously thought, possibly ten to eleven thousand years ago.[7]

The domestication of a few species of large mammals, including dogs, sheep, goats, pigs, cows, horses, and water buffalo, occurred during roughly the same period, principally in Eurasia. Along with food, this domestica-tion process provided draught power to assist the shift from hunting and gathering to agriculture.

With this dramatic shift in the human food environment came other equally far-reaching technological changes, including the refining and work-ing of metal, use of the wheel, and writing. Perhaps even more important, however, is the association of sedentary human existence with the rise of social hierarchies or stratification, and the development of bureaucratic in-struments of governance, along with institutional means – early judicial systems, standing armies, naval forces, and so on – to preserve and enhance the position of those who came to dominate these expanding human com-munities. I am referring to, in other words, the emergence of class-based soci-eties, with their inherent inequities in the distribution of power and resources which, in terms of our history as a species, is a very recent phenomenon. This development, as it turns out, had profound implications for the diet of the majority as well.

SOCIAL HIERARCHY AND DIETARY DEGRADATION

The transformation of human food environments with the Neolithic Revolution and the rise of agriculture were associated with several other major developments in the way humans organized their material subsistence. None was as important as the shift to socially stratified human communities. The origins of social stratification merits a book in itself, but suffice to say that it was one particularly notable outcome of the shift humans made to more sedentary existence and the domestication of plants and animals this required as nomadic ways were gradually abandoned.

What has the emergence of social hierarchy got to do with diet? As it turns out, a good deal, or so some research would indicate. This is not surprising, one might think, given the great differences between the diet of the rich and the poorest sectors of practically any society one can think of in today's world. The benefits of the earliest forms of civilization were not equally shared either, including the benefits of agricultural activities carried out in the earliest stratified human settlements.

One field of archeology has examined the relationship between political organization and diet and nutrition. As it turns out, the analysis of ancient skeletons can yield an amazing amount of information. Archeologists look for certain markers of growth disruption, for example, and here, teeth, as the most durable element of the human skeleton, can yield important clues. A deficit of tooth enamel, and furrows or pits on the teeth, can indicate serious dietary stress. Depressed cortical bone thickness, or more typically, depressed stature, can also indicate serious dietary deficiencies. Dental analysis can yield more specific knowledge of the actual content of diets. Evidence of dental cavities, or caries, is indicative of a diet whereby enamel is destroyed by acids caused by the bacterial fermentation of carbohydrates.

Chemical analysis of bones can yield information about the dominant constituents of diet, and in particular, the relative contribution of animal versus plant foods, and even what types of plant foods were eaten (maize versus temperate grains versus succulent plants), and whether foods were marine or terrestrial based.

A final tool archeologists may be able to use to discern information about the diets and nutrition of an ancient population is demographic analysis. A high level of infant mortality may point to poor maternal nutrition, particularly if there is no reason to believe that infanticide was being practised for some reason, such as population control in a situation of limited resources.[8]

Marie Elaine Danforth has examined archeological evidence from a broad range of studies encompassing prehistoric settlements with differing levels of social hierarchy, from egalitarian communities to stratified/state-level societies that show evidence of significant differences in power, status, and prestige. In the latter, there is clear evidence of differential access to what she terms "quality dietary resources,"[9] and markedly different health outcomes for different social strata. This was generally not the case with archaic human settlements that had much more egalitarian social organization, where redistributive social mechanisms helped overcome existing inequities and ensured adequate diets for all community members; here there is little evidence of differences in diet-related negative health outcomes.

Meso-America has provided relatively rich archaeological resources to gauge the effects of early forms of social hierarchy on health. In what today is central Mexico and southern Mexico, Guatemala, and Honduras, highly stratified human societies had emerged by approximately two thousand to fifteen hundred years ago. The Mayan civilization to the south is estimated to have had five main social strata characterizing it, whereas the large city state of Teotihuacán in central Mexico is thought to have had seven main strata. In the ruins of ancient Teotihuacán, the clues provided by human remains are particularly rich. Here, evidence is especially convincing that inhabitants of what is believed to be a lower-class section of the city suffered significantly from poor nutrition, as indicated by lower stature, high levels of anaemia, and growth disruptions among juveniles, as well as high infant mortality. In the Mayan city states of Copán in modern Honduras and Tikal in the lowlands of modern Guatemala, similar evidence of poor nutrition among lower-class residents compared with members of the elite have been found.[10] Not surprisingly, there is also evidence suggesting that the diet of the elite was considerably more varied than was that of the general population.

The transformation of food environments occasioned by the transition to agricultural activities for the provision of an increasing part of the subsistence needs of human communities undoubtedly affected the nutrient intake and thus had certain health outcomes. Where wild foods were growing scarce, the domestication of certain plants may have allowed humans to continue to exist in certain regions that they otherwise would have had to leave or risk perishing. But the transition likely came at a price. For example, as the cultivation of maize replaced a more varied Palaeolithic diet for a growing portion of energy needs – estimated to account for 45 to 65 percent of daily energy requirements in one major North American site[11] – the health of all members of the community may have been compromised. Smaller stature among maize-dependent peoples has been attributed to nutrient deficiencies of a maize-based diet, for example.[12]

Social hierarchy, however, exacerbated the negative effects of this transition for the less fortunate majority, it would seem. So evidence suggests for the early city states of what is now present-day Mexico and Central America, where hierarchy had become solidified into rigid social rankings with wide gaps between the elite and the commoners, and where institutions appeared to bolster the grip of those in power. In those early societies, diets had begun to diverge markedly according to social class and status ranking, and so too did the health outcomes associated with different diets.

DIETS IN THE ANCIENT AND MEDIEVAL EUROPEAN WORLD

In the European context, Hans Teuteberg argues that the rise of the Greco-Roman empires (800 BC to AD 500) led to an intensification of agriculture centred on wheat production,[13] as the work of extending empires and maintaining large standing armies required such efforts. Nevertheless, a grain-gruel diet was the lot for the great majority of Romans, and indeed many of the other peoples in western and central Europe. This intensification was likely the experience of other areas where political elites sought to establish and maintain empires, from Asia to the New World.

Massimo Montanari has argued that the decline of the Roman Empire inaugurated a new era of growing dietary diversity, instigated by the increasing influence of Christian doctrine and the growing influence of the dietary preferences of invading Germanic tribes. Products of the forest, and meat in particular, became more acceptable for the masses, when it could be procured.[14] Christianity's contribution was to oppose the sacrificing of animals that had been widespread and, by deconsecrating meat, help turn it into an everyday food. The Germanic invasion brought with it a different food ideology, one based on exploiting the forest and uncultivated lands and a greater emphasis on meat in the diet. The era of the Middle Ages that follows was one of more dietary diversity for many, Montanari contends, than that which had prevailed during imperial Roman times.[15]

Nevertheless, for many hundreds of years, and indeed up until relatively recent times, in most parts of the world it was principally the diets of a small minority of rich and well-connected citizens that experienced growing diversity and change. For most in Europe, wheat, barley, spelt, and rye were the basis for both beer making and livestock feeding, and remained a dietary mainstay for the great majority, only occasionally supplemented with animal proteins, chiefly pork, and increasingly fish after the fifteenth century as New World cod began to find its way into European markets. Animal protein remained a privileged food of the upper class for the most part.[16] The role of religion in dictating diets cannot be forgotten either; indeed, in Russia, for example, some two hundred fasting days were noted on which meat and milk were prohibited, although the eating of fish may have been allowed.[17]

By the late Middle Ages, however, processes were underway in Europe that would disrupt long-standing dietary patterns. There is a relatively rich literature that describes dramatic changes in land tenure in various regions of continental Europe and Britain. So too is there a considerable literature about the massive increases in trade that came about as a result of the "voyages of discovery" undertaken by Europeans in the fifteenth century and afterward, as well as of the great agricultural enterprises that were established in the new lands, producing various foodstuffs for the European markets. There is much less written about how these momentous changes affected what people had to eat as a result, whether in the New World or the Old.

THE COLUMBIAN EXCHANGE, AGRARIAN CAPITALISM, AND DIETARY TRANSITION

The voyages of Columbus were not path-breaking in terms of European forays to the New World, but they *are* credited with initiating what became a broadly based exchange of edible plants and animals, technology, and people and their diseases between the Old World and the New World.[18] The impacts of this exchange were far-reaching, including in the area of diets. Alfred Crosby's comprehensive work on this process is particularly noteworthy.[19] From the New World to the Old went cacao, maize, potatoes, tomatoes, capsicum peppers, cassava, squashes and pumpkin, peanuts, and several bean varieties, along with fruits such as the pineapple, avocado, guava, and papaya. Of the animal species, the turkey was of note. Introduced into the New World were sugar cane, citrus fruits, bananas, and vegetables such as cabbage and lettuce, along with several animal species whose introduction had considerable impact, including cattle, sheep, pigs, and horses.[20]

The impact of Old World diseases, especially small pox, on the indigenous peoples of the Americas was catastrophic, leading to the collapse of an estimated 95 percent of the indigenous population in North and South America.[21]

On the other hand, New World crops, especially the potato and maize, are credited with allowing for a dramatic population expansion in Europe, an expansion that was historically unprecedented since the advent of agriculture thousands of years earlier.[22]

The rise of the great European trading companies such as the Dutch East India Company and its British counterparts, the East India Company, the North West Company, and the Hudson's Bay Company, with their exclusive rights to exploit the New World, were part and parcel of a transitional period of European economic expansion often referred to as the mercantilist era. It was an era of greatly expanded trade, which involved the lucrative commerce in edible foodstuffs, including spices, sugar, and coffee, to name only some of the most economically important. For a considerable period, it was largely the diets of the aristocracy and the emergent bourgeoisie that were affected by this trade, but this was to change with the dramatic expansion of agrarian capitalism in different locations in the Old and New Worlds. The far-reaching social disruptions occasioned by this development opened the door much wider to the use of the potato, in particular, and later sugar, in the diets of large masses of European peoples.

We are accustomed to hearing that the rise of a capitalist market-based economic system in what is now the developed world inaugurated an era of plentiful cheap food for the majority of citizens. What is interesting is that, at least for a considerable period, it did exactly the opposite. Among the first of the multitude of changes wrought by the emergence of capitalism as a distinct economic system were those transformations to agrarian economy. To date, much attention has been paid to this agrarian reorganization and its impacts on peasant and yeoman producers, the creation of a rural proletariat, the impetus it provided for rural to urban migration, the rise of the modern city, the creation of global commodity markets, and so on. Less attention has been given to its role in the early reshaping of food environments and the effects this may have had on the nutritional dimension of diets for the broad mass of society.

The onset of the modern capitalist era, by numerous accounts, ushered in a time of nutritional distress. Indeed, studies from England, France, Scandinavia, and more recently Scotland indicate a general dietary decline for much of the rural population between the fifteenth and sixteenth centuries and between the seventeenth and eighteenth centuries, as meat, cheese, and milk consumption became less common, replaced by increased eating of grains and, later, potatoes. This was the period when market relations were becoming more widespread, of course, and industrial capitalism was rapidly developing in the English context.

Jean Louis Flandrin provides evidence from across Europe to indicate the direction of this trend:

> In Berlin the average per capita daily meat consumption at the end of the nineteenth century had dropped to less than a quarter of a pound compared with three pounds in 1397 (a twelvefold decrease). In Naples in 1770, 21,800 head of cattle were slaughtered to feed a population of roughly 400,000, whereas two centuries earlier some 30,000 head had been slaughtered to feed a population of roughly 200,000 (a threefold decrease). [In France] the amount of meat allocated to each farmworker fell from 40 kilograms (88 pounds) to just 20 kilograms (44 pounds) after 1583.[23]

Good evidence on the health impacts related to nutritional deficiencies as diets deteriorated during this period is difficult to come by. Flandrin does note, however, that data on the stature of army recruits in different European armies, as well as data on adolescents in London and German adults, indicate that heights generally decreased in the eighteenth and nineteenth centuries compared with earlier centuries.

What were the immediate causes of this dietary decline? Unfortunately, few have examined the impact of the massive structural changes in the agrarian sphere (which has been well studied) on diets. With respect to the former process, the agonizing history of the "clearances" that were part of the Agrarian Revolution in England is perhaps best known and studied. There, the resurgent landlord class appropriated the common lands upon which rural folk depended for much of their subsistence for generations, forced off the land entirely the numerous class of yeoman farmers, and caused a general displacement of masses of rural folk to urban slums of the burgeoning industrial areas of the northwest of England.[24]

On the European continent, landlords to the northeast pursued a different course than their English counterparts. In Prussia, the opening of a lucrative export market for grains saw landlords there revive harsh feudal-like obligations on local peasant farmers in what came to be called the "second serfdom." This repressed any tendency toward a more diversified farm economy, as was taking shape in parts of western Europe, locking in a grain-based economy founded on the labour of a semi-servile class of estate-bound labourers called the *instmen*. This development was unlikely to improve the dietary fare of the mass of the rural populace, and matters for them were to deteriorate even more during the nineteenth century, when desperate rural labourers from the east flooded in and the Prussian landlords eliminated what little material security rural folk had on the estates.[25]

In different regions of Europe, then, the advent of agrarian capitalism and the spread of market relationships marked a resurgent landed class bent on modernization, and the result was typically disastrous for the resident small-holder farmers. As their lives were impoverished and their families displaced, not surprisingly, their subsistence standard declined, often dramatically. An impact on diets was inevitable, though largely unstudied to date.

Much as people in our own era seek out cheaper foods when economic times turn hard, the displaced and impoverished agrarian folk of the early capitalist era were driven to rely more and more on cheaper grains exclusively. Among the Scottish people, for instance, oatmeal displaced a more varied diet incorporating animal proteins and, later, there was an increasing reliance on the potato when crop failures made traditional grains unafford-able and animal protein prohibitively expensive. This latter event was sig-nificant because the potato is a crop considered to have lesser nutritive value than grains and to be noticeably absent in proteins and essential B vitamins.

Alex Gibson and Christopher Smout provide one of the few studies that link changes in agrarian structure to diet.[26] They found that in the case of Scotland, the degradation of diets in the seventeenth and eighteenth centur-ies happened precisely with the expansion of markets for foodstuffs there, and with the expansion of the power of the landlord class. Possibly other fac-tors were at play, including a demographic increase by the early seventeenth century that would have put pressures on families to source lower-cost food-stuffs, but a more compelling explanation derives from the strong evidence of the increase in the power and influence of the landlord class in the seven-teenth and eighteenth centuries. This, of course, was likely aided by the com-petition for land among a more numerous peasantry. As Gibson and Smout argue, in Scotland, the independent peasantry had relatively little success compared with elsewhere in Europe in securing their free holdings and was largely reduced to tenant farming by the local lairds, if not forced out of farming entirely by 1750 or so. They also note that a diminishing of the clan warfare and return to relative peace may have played a role in this outcome. In this case, peace may have not led to prosperity but rather to further pres-sures on tenants from clan leaders who were no longer as dependent upon their loyalty and willingness to fight.[27]

SUGAR: FROM ELITE FOOD TO MASS CONSUMPTION

The rise of capitalism was to provoke world-encompassing economic and social changes, and some of the transformations it wrought occurred in what we refer to now as the global South. The rise of estate and plantation agriculture in the New World to supply European markets was the counterpart of the land clearances and rural disruption in England and parts of Europe in that it was fundamentally disrupting of long-established social and economic relationships, and bathed in blood and widespread hardship for the majority. It too had fundamental impacts on the shaping of food environments and the prevailing dietary regime. Of particular importance here is the development of a sugar economy.

There is likely no more powerful example of the disastrous effect on humanity that the commodification of foodstuffs can have than is provided by the rise of the cane sugar industry. Cane sugar came to be the most prominent of sweeteners in human diets over the last couple of hundred years, only very recently being eclipsed by corn-based sweeteners produced through genetic engineering. As these sweeteners entered into the commodity circuits via an industrial production process, each had dramatic effects on human diets.

The massive undertaking of European capitalists in the New World, oriented to expanding sugar production under the plantation system using slave labour, was a path-breaking development. Besides the catastrophic social destruction and dislocation this activity caused African populations, together with very considerable environmental damage in the New World that only increased over time as the system expanded,[28] the sugar plantation owners had a dramatic impact on the availability of sugar in Europe. This was particularly so once the Industrial Revolution transformed processing toward the mid-nineteenth century.[29]

Sugar was, of course, not the first of dietary sweeteners. Before cane sugar and other more recent sweeteners appeared in diets, sweet foods were commonly used. It may be useful to think of sweet foods as having a more "organic" relationship to diet than sweeteners. Sweet foods are typically consumed in a more natural form and can and have been consumed on their own. Sweeteners, on the other hand, are more commonly associated with the modern industrial era and are rarely consumed on their own but are an adjunct to an industrial process, typically to make foods more palatable. There are exceptions to this dichotomy, of course, as in the case of sugar's being used for its preservative function before the industrial era.

Among the first, if not the first, sweet foods and undoubtedly the most symbolically important is honey. Honey occupies a special place among sweet foods, and as the first sweetener. In her classic and comprehensive *A History of Food*, Maguelonne Toussaint-Samat begins her study with an examination of honey, which she describes as "a food both miraculous and natural," a "delicious nourishment ... that has an element of reward about it."[30] Its use by humans reaches back to Palaeolithic times, as rock paintings attest to, and it occupied an important place in the cuisines of the ancient Mediterranean civilizations.

The honey bee we know today, *Apis millifera*, is thought to have arrived from Asia originally. A species of honey-producing insect existed in the Americas as well and, from the early Mayan civilizations through to the Aboriginal cultures of North America, honey occupied a special place among foods. This exalted food was woven into the legends of the ancient Greeks, indeed into their very myths of creation of the world. As Toussaint-Samat notes, "The implication is that honey, the first food, dates from the creation of the world, and existed even before the bees brought it to mankind."[31] On the other side of the globe, the ancient Maya of Central America believed that "the bee was born of the Universal Hive at the centre of the earth. Golden to the sight, burning to the touch, like the sparks of the volcanoes, it was sent here to awaken man from apathy and ignorance."[32] Several ancient Mediterranean civilizations, including the Babylonians, Sumerians, and Cretans, buried the most revered members of their societies with honey to enjoy in the afterlife, because it denoted immortality.[33]

With the emergence of hierarchically organized societies, honey and the bee colonies that produced it came to be prized by the nobility and the powerful. As skills in beekeeping developed, so too did the exclusivity of its consumption. Toussaint-Samat notes that among the ancient Romans, only consuls were allowed to eat honey, while the pharaohs of Egypt and their priests kept the best honey and wax for themselves. In a later era, Charlemagne mandated that French peasant farmers produce honey and pay the emperor two-thirds of the honey produced as tax in kind.[34]

What, then, has the history of honey to do with current dietary dilemmas and nutritional decline? Perhaps it is only that in our distant past humans looked to honey, other sweet foods, and, later, other sweeteners such as cane sugar, as a break from the grinding monotony of prevailing diets for the majority, and as energy-dense foods that our evolution in a food-scarce environment gave us a natural predilection for. This alone would have given these foods an exalted place among foods. That honey became wrapped up in the tapestry of mythology of various civilizations enhanced its status and desirability. In an important sense, this history set the stage for what was to occur in the age of industrialized food as sweeteners and sweet foods that were for the great majority of human history very minor dietary components in the life of most people came to occupy centre stage in the emerging industrial diet of the twentieth century.

But by the time this happened, there was already a history of cane sugar and its rise to importance in European diets. Sugar arrived in Europe along with spices such as cardamom, nutmeg, and pepper from the East after 1100 AD as a relatively rare and expensive trade good. Its consumption had clear class dimensions for a very long time, and it was consumed regularly if perhaps sparingly by the wealthy from the mid-thirteenth century onward. As Sidney Mintz notes in his *Sweetness and Power*, sugar was not a significant part of the English diet, except for the wealthiest, until the seventeenth century.[35] At that time, he continues, it had several uses – as a spice or condiment, as a medicinal agent, as a decorative material, as a sweetener, and as a preservative. The custom of using sugar in these various ways came from older cultures – from the Far East and the Arab world of the Mediterranean region, among others. Sugar does not enter into the English diet in a major way until the late eighteenth century, Mintz maintains, when it could be said to have truly become a food: "By that time sugar had moved beyond its traditional uses, and – in Britain at least – was actually altering the ancient core-fringe, complex-carbohydrate–flavouring pattern of the human majority, in a revolutionary fashion."[36]

Through his consideration of the cuisine and cookbooks oriented to the various strata of the English upper classes, Mintz makes the case that for a long period of the history of that society, sugar was a symbol of power, a key ingredient in myriad dishes that graced the tables of the wealthy.[37] This fact in itself undoubtedly gave sugar a certain cachet among the emergent middle and working classes in a later era, when "it was transformed from a luxury of kings into a kingly luxury of commoners."[38]

This transformation began well before the nineteenth century. Estimates of English sugar consumption per capita in 1700 were a relatively insignificant 4 pounds, but by the beginning of the next century, that had increased more than four times to about 18 pounds. Other imported foods and beverages, including tea, coffee, and spices, were also being consumed in substantially greater quantities, even if their increase was not so dramatic as that of sugar.

FIGURE 3.1

Consumption of refined sugar in the United Kingdom, 1700-1959

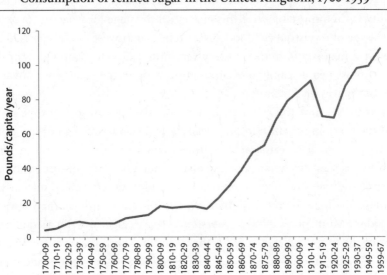

SOURCE: Adapted from G.N. Johnstone, "The Growth of the Sugar Trade and Refining Industry," in *The Making of the Modern British Diet*, ed. D. Oddy and D. Miller (London: Croom Helm, 1976), 60.

As the nineteenth century dawned, "the English population was already accustomed to sugar – if only in small amounts – and [was] eager for more."[39] By the latter half of that century, the technological revolution that transformed sugar production and processing in the colonies and drastically cheapened the cost of transport helped sharply reduce sugar prices for the English as well as other Europeans. By then the British were consuming an astounding 90 pounds per head. The British Parliament's repeal of legislation protecting colonial sugar producers with the advent of a free trade policy again cheapened sugar, as sugar from Cuba's slave economy began to pour into English markets (see Figure 3.1).[40] A similar pattern of sucrose consumption has been noted for the Netherlands, Sweden, Norway, Denmark, and the United States.[41] In the latter, the dawn of the nineteenth century saw Americans consuming a modest 8.4 pounds of sugar, but over the course of the century, the American diet was sweetened immensely. In 1905, some 70.6 pounds per person were being consumed.[42]

Sugar entered the English mass diet in several ways, ways that typically had roots in upper-class consumption patterns of an earlier era. This pattern for the dispersion of sugar may have been found, with local variations, in the mass diets of other European societies of the time as well. One conduit was what were, up to the eighteenth and nineteenth centuries, luxury beverages: tea, coffee, and chocolate, to which sugar was added as a sweetener. The English peculiarity, of course, was the development of what Mintz terms the "tea complex," which came to permeate the entire English class structure over time. One of the social customs that developed with this complex was the serving of sugar-laden confectionaries to accompany the beverage, these sugary treats becoming a second conduit. Another conduit was preservatives in the form of fruits preserved in a sugar syrup and myriad jams and marmalades, which became readily accessible once sugar prices fell by the mid-nineteenth century and the industrial canning industry began to displace cottage production. Preserving fruit in a sugar syrup had been another elite custom in earlier times. In addition to its use as a beverage sweetener and preservative, sugar in the form of treacle, or molasses, was used to sweeten porridges and puddings, and was later refined into a golden syrup similar in appearance to honey.[43]

The sum total of these dietary changes led to sugar's taking a remarkable place in the diet of people in several European countries and in the United States. As noted, by the latter part of the nineteenth century, the British were consuming an extraordinary ninety pounds per head, with consumption per capita in other European countries and the United States equally as high.[44]

SUGAR AND NUTRITIONAL DECLINE

The contemporary association of sugar-laden edible products and the degradation of diet was foreshadowed by an earlier period of nutritional decline, and the root causes of the earlier phenomenon bear remarkable general similarities to more recent causes as well. The historical study of sugar illuminates the past to help us understand the present.

The rapid expansion of industrial manufacturing in Britain in the eighteenth and nineteenth centuries absorbed more and more of the displaced agrarian population but dictated an employment regime that made impossible the domestic routines of an agrarian life. In particular, the rising employment of poor women outside the home led to a decline in traditional culinary practices in the home that had provided for a relative dietary diversity. In its place, new hot beverages, especially tea, sweetened with by then much-cheapened sugar, came to form more and more of the dietary regimen in the households of poor industrial workers, including children.[45]

Various authors have noted that the diets of working-class operatives in the newly industrializing areas of England and Scotland after 1850 showed marked nutritional deficiencies, especially in protein, and animal proteins in particular. The new industrial workers were forsaking, for the most part, the healthier rural diet, with its mainstay of cooked oatmeal porridge and milk, for a new diet that was ever more dominated by white bread and butter – with the latter being progressively replaced by jam later in the nineteenth century (when sugar duties were abolished) – supplemented with the staple hot beverage, tea. As one historian of the English diet has observed,

> White bread and tea passed, in the course of a hundred years, from the luxuries of the rich to become the hall-marks of a poverty line diet ... Whereas they were mere adjuncts to the tables of the wealthy, they became all too often the total diet of the poor, the irreducible minimum beyond which lay only starvation ... And in the circumstances of early industrialization this type of diet had an additional advantage that it could always be produced close at hand and required little or no preparation.[46]

We usually consider the impact of time pressures on diet as a problem very much characteristic of the late twentieth and early twenty-first centuries, with two-earner households and multiple job holdings putting food preparation time at a premium, if it is available at all. A more historical view, however, demonstrates that it is not so contemporary a problem at all. In fact, as the rural populations of Europe were being dispossessed of their lands in the eighteenth and nineteenth centuries and yoked to industrial machines by the emergent forces of capitalism, lack of time coincided with dietary decline, even when incomes were rising. Economic pressures forced many wives into the industrial workforce, with consequences for the family meal that are all too recognizable today. As another historian has argued about industrialization in the lowlands of Scotland, citing an investigation from those earlier days,

> The organization of the jute industry provided opportunities for female labour, so that many housewives went out to work in Dundee. Nutritional standards declined further and sharply when the wife

went out to work. "When the mother is at work there is not time to prepare porridge or broth in the 'diet hour' ... usually breakfast and dinner become bread and butter meals. As the school interval for dinner is not the same as the mill 'diet hour' the children have to unlock the house and get 'pieces' for themselves."[47]

In a further comment that resonates with contemporary dilemmas, the author notes,

> Pressure on the housewife's time was in itself a sufficient explanation of the choice of an inferior diet. The need to save time rather than the need to economize or to maintain nutritional standards determined the choice. Most noticeable was the increased consumption of bread ... The cooking of vegetable broth was neglected in the cities. So long as vegetable broth was used extensively the Scottish custom of eating few vegetables in any other form was unimportant. Where the housewife had to go out to work, the preparation of broth was practically impossible.[48]

It needs to be emphasized here, of course, that these women were being forced essentially by dire economic necessity to seek wage work outside the home.

Summarizing available evidence on these matters, Mintz argues that several points can be made regarding diets in the United Kingdom in the nineteenth century. First, food choices were very often a product of available time and not solely one of relative costs. Second, fuel was an important cost, and thus food not requiring fuel for cooking was especially attractive. And third, a wife's leaving the house to work for wages had a restrictive effect on family diet, favouring the purchase of the convenience foods of that time, store-bought bread, sweetened preserves, and tea. The latter when served as a hot beverage helped replace, at least symbolically if not nutritionally, the lost foods that had been a staple of the poorer households – the broths, cooked porridges, butter, milk, and homemade beer.[49]

Direct evidence of the health impacts of the rise in sugar consumption, at least in Europe, were clear after 1700, Moore notes.[50] The study of human skeletal remains in Britain provides an interesting example. Over a two-thousand-year period beginning in the pre-Roman Iron Age, wear and diseases of the teeth on that island suggest a high degree of dietary stability, at least of starches, right up until the seventeenth century. A coarse black bread made from stone-ground rye or barley flour was thought to be a carbohydrate staple for this extensive period, and sugars and refined carbohydrates generally were uncommon in the diet of the majority. The powerful sugar interests were to change this, however. As Moore notes, "During the seventeenth century the pattern of dental caries began to depart from its ancient form [and] by the end of the nineteenth century, in fact, the pattern of dental caries both in its prevalence and in its distribution had become virtually identical with that of today."[51] The only good news in this change was that, with the transition away from relatively unrefined carbohydrates, wear and tear on teeth was considerably reduced.

One of the insights we can gain from this brief historical overview of sweeteners is that the contemporary adulteration of diets with sweeteners has been conditioned by prior historical developments. First, the long history of sweeteners in the European diet, and one that privileged them as food for the rich, gave them status they might have otherwise lacked. Second, early industrial capitalism had brought onto the historical stage two complementary processes: the transformation of sugar production in the New World, which had the effect of radically cheapening it, and the transformation of the working lives of many of those affected by the industrialization in the Old World, in such a manner that horrendous time pressures of work created a demand for the convenience of (by then relatively cheap) sugar. And this was all long before pre-sweetened breakfast cereals and other sugar-laden edible commodities had ever been dreamed of. The contemporary business of adulterating food for profit had only to build on earlier dietary transformations while taking advantage of a new range of pressures introduced by the evolving political economy of capitalism.

If the deterioration of dental health owed much to the success of the sugar interests in expanding the market for their product in Europe, it was likely related also to the rapid increase in the consumption of other refined carbohydrates, particularly flour.[52]

THE BEGINNINGS OF THE INDUSTRIAL DIET, 1870-1940

If you're going to America, bring your own food.

— Fran Lebowitz, "Fran Lebowitz's
Travel Hints"[1]

THE FACTORY SYSTEM OF PRODUCTION of modern capitalism undermined artisanal small-scale production in numerous economic sectors before it began transforming the production of food. By the late nineteenth century, however, factory methods of modern industry had begun to be applied to food. The emergence of industrial foods and the constitution of the first industrial dietary regime occurred in North America after 1870 or so. What made this dietary regime unique was not only the rapid industrialization of food production with the early consolidation of food manufacturing corporations but also the advent of mass marketing. Mass marketing greatly facilitated the "normalization" of a diet increasingly composed of highly processed edible commodities. It also played an essential role in making the industrial diet a mass diet.

The pioneering role played by the flour-milling industry in producing a widely used semi-durable industrial food makes it a good candidate for having inaugurated the industrial diet. Moreover, it was millers in the United States that led the transformation in this sector to industrial methods in the years after 1870, and American food entrepreneurs were to take the initiative in the industrialization of other foodstuffs in the following decades. Even today, American transnational food and beverage corporations largely dominate the push to establish the industrial diet on a truly global basis. For this reason, the industrial diet might also be referred to as the "American diet."

Industrial milling methods produced a shelf-stable flour that lent itself to being marketed and distributed on a nationwide basis as early as the closing decades of the nineteenth century. The industrialization of other major sectors of the food economy, from fruit and vegetable preserving to meat-packing to ready-to-eat breakfast cereal processors, was soon to follow and would rapidly come to be dominated by giant, horizontally integrated factory establishments producing large volumes of standardized product at low prices. As businesses in these other sectors adopted and innovated mass-marketing strategies, and with the added impetus given this enterprise by the advent of commercial radio, industrial foodstuffs gained increasing penetration. This was even true during the calamity of the Great Depression when, despite initial declines, per capita consumption of processed edible products remained fairly stable and even saw substantial increases in the case of certain products, including soft drinks.

The state's role in this first dietary regime is limited by the ideological commitment of governments to the principles of classical liberalism and the very restricted role that was given to government in the minds of political elites at the time, elites who generally embraced this ideology until the calamity of the Depression forced its reappraisal. Nevertheless, unfettered profit making had, by the latter part of the nineteenth century, some obvious drawbacks, and these were nowhere more apparent than in the food business. In response to egregious practices in the food business, typically involving the dangerous adulteration of food and drink and/or grossly unsanitary conditions, a number of rapidly industrializing countries adopted some form of legislation to curb the worst excesses of business in this sphere. Nevertheless, a hallmark of this first industrial food regime was, for the most part, minimalist state involvement in terms of regulation and very little in terms of the price supports and subsidies to farmers and agribusinesses that came to define the decades after the Second World War.

CHAPTER FOUR

FROM PATENT FLOUR
TO WHEATIES

From start to finish the new [roller milling] method was radically
different from stone milling.

— Richard Perren, *Economic History Review*[1]

White flour, so much prized by housewives as superior, was instead
a distinctly inferior product.

— Elizabeth Etheridge, *The Butterfly Caste*[2]

T HE MOMENTOUS DIETARY CHANGE that characterizes the latter half of
the twentieth century could not have occurred without firm foundations for this transformation having being laid in earlier times. These foundations of the first industrial dietary regime were largely a product of the
latter part of the nineteenth century and the early decades of the twentieth.
Even though industrial capitalism predates the nineteenth century, the dynamic technological changes that are one hallmark of this economic system
began to have a more pronounced effect on the structure of capitalist business enterprise only after the 1850s. By the late 1800s, rapid technological
change both within and outside the food industry (e.g., railroads) had opened
up opportunities for leading capitalists in such areas as flour milling and
meat-packing to reorganize their enterprises so they could firmly dominate

what was becoming an integrated national market. Understanding the market power that they achieved in this period is crucial to understanding the ability of these companies to pioneer the mass marketing of new processed foods later on.

In organizational terms, oligopolistic control of markets, achieved typically by swallowing up competitors producing similar products in an orgy of horizontal integration that is characteristic of late-nineteenth-century capitalism, proved to be a decisive enabling condition for the transformation of the food environment that was to follow. The leading role of a few American food and beverage firms in shaping the era of mass marketing was integrally linked to the processed-product innovation of the early twentieth century. This innovation marked not only a groundbreaking shift away from a dependence on the production of undifferentiated commodities, like flour, by the leading firms but also an historically significant change from homemade foods to processed foods on an unprecedented scale.

TECHNOLOGICAL CHANGE, CONSOLIDATION, AND DIETARY IMPACT

Pioneering developments undertaken by American food-processing enterprises beginning in the years after 1850 would soon place them at the forefront of this sector of industry and put them in a position to dominate markets in the most developed countries throughout much of the twentieth century. It was at this time that a dialectical relationship between technology and the social form of food enterprises becomes particularly important. The spread of market relations meant competition among entrepreneurs in the emergent food-processing economy, and this in turn gave impetus to innovate technologically to reduce costs and increase profits. As we shall see, technology is not necessarily neutral in its effects, and it can significantly influence future developments in terms of the scale and form of enterprise. Changes in scale and form of enterprise, in turn, have implications down the line for the adoption of technology later on, and so on.

Ultimately, the dialectic between technology and the social organization of the food business within the overarching context of a maturing industrial capitalism could not but have profound effects on diets and nutrition. Just as the spread of market relations within largely preindustrial Europe had deleterious consequences for the diets of many, the ascendance of industrial capital in the food economy had decidedly negative outcomes from a nutritional perspective. The interesting phenomenon of the industrialization of cereal-processing activities is largely neglected yet illustrates well what happened.

The Industrialization of Flour Milling and Dietary Decline

We have seen that the expansion of markets and the accumulation of capital in the agrarian sphere have historically had very deleterious effects socially, and from a nutritional perspective as well. Similar outcomes, at least in the nutritional sphere, attended the early industrialization of food processing. Flour making is a particularly interesting case to examine, in a number of respects. For most foods, the shift away from domestic production in the home to industrial processing is a relatively recent event, dating from after the mid-1800s or even a good deal later. This is true for preserved meats, milk and cheese, bread, jam, and other foodstuffs. The same is not true for flour, however: grinding of grain in private enterprises specifically devoted to this task occurred much earlier. Given its early mechanization and the centrality of grains in the diets of Europeans and their descendants living in North America, it is not surprising that flour and grist milling was the leading industry by the value of product in the United States of the 1870s, and some 50 percent larger than textiles.[3]

Typically, the grinding process for grains was powered by water or wind, and used millstones to do the actual grinding. In the nineteenth century in England, a few of the leading millers had adopted steam power, freeing the owners from a dependence on nature, but even by 1870 it was estimated that two-thirds of grain milling in England was still powered by water.[4]

Traditionally and still up until that time, mills used mostly locally produced grains, which for the most part were also locally consumed. There were reasons for this. Stone milling was accomplished by pulverizing the wheat grains, or berries, in an operation that produced a wheat meal coarse by today's standards. The nutritional advantage of this was that the wheat meal contained all parts of the grain mixed together (germ, bran, gluten, and endosperm),[5] preserving the maximum nutrition that could be gained from the food. Although a relatively small portion of this wheat meal would undergo a further sifting process to achieve a whiter flour for those who could afford it (but containing, ironically, fewer nutrients), most flour was of this coarser type. Grain so processed retained elements that were susceptible to spoilage, in particular oils in the germ, which also contained important nutrients.[6]

Longer-term storage of flour and shipment to distant markets were not favoured by such a process, in other words. This kept markets local, and indeed it has been argued that in England at this time, trade in flour probably went no more than thirty miles, and only for the largest mills.[7]

The limitations of this type of situation, dictated as it was by the physical characteristics of the product, and no doubt by limitations in transport, would not have been a problem for millers until the logic of the new economic system made itself felt. The opening up of vast new grain-growing territories in North America, Argentina, and Australia; the developing international trade in grains and flour; a period of momentous technical change; and, later, the pressures of consolidation and trust formation among the most powerful enterprises forced major changes to the industry. These changes had in their turn serious impacts on the nutritional contribution of grain to the diet of millions.

A key development underlying structural changes to grain processing was the historically unprecedented territorial expansion and state-sponsored settlement schemes in the United States. After the years of the Civil War, the victorious Union Army was sent west to bring "order" to territories granted by treaty to various Aboriginal nations, but by then being invaded by thousands of prospectors and other fortune seekers. One of the first of these mass invasions of Aboriginal territory occurred with the discovery of gold in the Black Hills of what became South Dakota, an area sacred to the people of the Sioux Nation. Other white invasions followed, and with them the violent, drawn-out tragedy that had as its outcome the complete subjugation of the Plains Indian nations and the parcelling up of their lands for distribution among the waves of incoming white settlers.[8]

Some years later, the Canadian government, threatened by the territorial spread of its neighbour to the south and its expansionist doctrine of manifest destiny, launched a state-sponsored settlement program of its own in the vast territories west of Lake Superior. Spurred by such stimuli as the prospect of 160-acre land grants on the Prairies, settlers from eastern Canada, the United States, the British Isles, and to a lesser extent the European continent flooded into what were to become the provinces of Manitoba, Saskatchewan, and Alberta in the years after 1901.[9] Many travelled west to try their hand at wheat farming, my grandparents among them, despite the fact that they often lacked the skills or aptitude for it. Some were to survive as farmers and establish the Canadian Prairies as one of the greatest wheat-growing regions of the world.

One of the key outcomes of this unprecedented extension of the agricultural frontier was to bring into the increasingly global market immense quantities of hard wheat varieties that were better suited to the prairie ecology. These hard wheats were not processed particularly well by the existing stone-milling technology, which was better suited to soft wheats predominating in the eastern United States and in Britain. The hard spring wheats that began to flood in from the west after 1870 were better handled, however, by the new technologies that had already been developed by Hungarian inventors to improve the efficiency of milling the hard wheats that predominated in that region of Europe. Richard Perren describes the process involved in the new "roller-milling revolution":

> From start to finish the new method was radically different from stone milling ... By using rollers, the process became one of gradually reducing and separating the different portions of the wheat in various stages. The first set, called the break rollers, split open the husk, and the floury part, known as middlings, was sifted out from the bran. It then passed through further pairs of fluted rollers, after each of which the stock was again sifted and any remaining coarse material removed. The chief advantages of the system were that it was mechanically more efficient, requiring less power to grind the same amount of [grain], and produced a larger proportion of fine white "patent" flour, whereas millstones produced more coarse "household" grades.[10]

In the United States, flour milling was dominated by water power and the use of millstones up until the 1870s, but by that time certain milling capitalists had already begun to expand their influence by dramatically expanding their mills. The emergence of early capital concentration in this business was particularly evident in the city of Minneapolis, where the Mississippi River provided abundant water power at the St. Anthony waterfalls. This power was initially used by the logging industry, but it was not long before mills to grind wheat were also established to service the local market.[11] The location of this city between the developing prairie wheat economy to the west and the burgeoning urban markets of the east proved strategic for flour millers as the agricultural frontier, and hard wheat production, advanced.

Two Minneapolis businessmen, Cadwallader Washburn and Charles Pillsbury, became prominent after their success in building what were for the time very large water-powered mills, and for their willingness to risk techno-logical innovations. These industrial millers sought advantage over the com-petition by marketing a whiter flour, and the firm Washburn Crosby and Company was successful in employing a new sifting and regrinding process that eastern millers had experimented with. This process removed more of the bran from the hard spring wheat, which made for a stronger flour with superior baking qualities, yielding more bread than flour from the winter wheat varieties.[12] This purifying system, called the "new process," produced a cleaner-looking, whiter flour. It also produced handsome profits for these innovators for a few years until the wider industry also began using the pro-cess. This whiter flour was advertised as made by a patented process; after-ward, the term "patent" came to describe the new type of flour.[13]

Ever keen to achieve a competitive advantage, in the late 1870s Washburn sent an engineer by the name of William de la Barre to Hungary to secretly investigate the new roller-milling technology developed there. Posing as a worker, de la Barre gained access to milling operations in Hungary, making sketches of the machinery that enabled Washburn, with certain adaptions, to fabricate the technology in Minneapolis. His firm became the first flour mill to introduce the roller-milling process in the United States,[14] and between 1880 and 1890 others were to emulate him in order to achieve the efficiencies this technology brought with it, in particular, savings on labour costs.[15]

The influx of hard spring wheats from the prairie lands to the west that were the varieties farmers found most suited to the prairie ecology posed a problem for the old milling technology, as mentioned.[16] This was because millstones tended to pulverize a portion of the hard, friable husks of the grain, making a darker, less desirable, and lower-priced flour than that of the soft wheats that had previously predominated. As the prairie hard wheat pro-duction in the United States dramatically expanded, it was not long before all the millers in Minneapolis, and the leading mills elsewhere in the country, found good reason to adopt the new system.[17]

It was therefore a combination of pressures from the rapidly changing market for wheat (which was itself a product of complex geopolitical, eco-nomic, and sociological factors), the shift from soft to hard wheat varieties, and the systemic logic of capital accumulation in a competitive market en-vironment that produced an important nutritional change in the dietary environment. The transition from stone grinding to the roller technology helped further the process of refinement already begun by some millers when stone milling predominated. As the milling companies concentrated, they required much larger markets to service their expanded capacity and operate efficiently,[18] which in turn expanded distance and time to final consumption.

By further refining the flour and thereby eliminating the more perishable parts of the grain, and the wheat germ, in particular, milling companies ensured that flour would have enhanced storage qualities, making it possible to service a larger market area. The removal of the germ and bran in the refinement process then coming into existence meant loss of many of the essential nutrients found in the grain, and notably the loss of the B vitamins, calcium, iron, phosphorous, and magnesium.[19] The significance of this was driven home only decades later, however, when the relationship between vitamin deficiency and disease was better understood.

NUTRITIONAL IMPACT OF THE NEW MILLING PROCESSES

Even before the nutritional deficiencies of flour became an issue, questions were raised about the millers' practice of bleaching flour to achieve the whitest product possible. Although questions about the nutritional effects of bleaching were apparently raised by the nascent breakfast cereal companies, it was a preoccupation of researchers at North Dakota's agricultural experimental station, and later the US Public Health Service, as was the overall nutritional quality of flour.[20] The latter raised the issues of the lessened digestibility of bleached flour and the small amounts of nitrites being produced by the flour-bleaching process.

The milling industry, for its part, proved to be thoroughly committed to protecting the white patent flours that leading firms had based their reputations on. In addition to these reputations, which were backed up by some years of considerable advertising dollars expended to create public demand for the whitest flours, they had also invested heavily in milling technology to produce white flour from hard spring wheat, and bleaching technology as well. Moreover, artificial bleaching eliminated a long and expensive aging process that millers would otherwise have to incur.[21]

When the US government seized flour shipments in 1910 and a judge ruled that the presence of harmful substances in the flour (nitrates) was sufficient reason to bar the product from interstate commerce, the millers' national association appealed the case to the Supreme Court. In 1914, the millers won their case, with the court being unconvinced by the prosecution's argument

FIGURE 4.1

Percentage of nutrients available in refined versus whole wheat flour

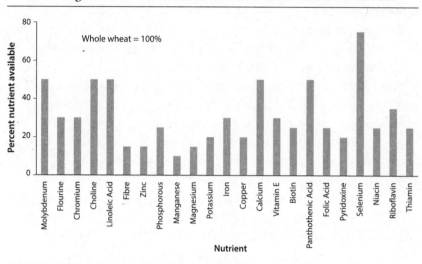

SOURCE: Adapted from Glen L. Weaver, "A Miller's Perspective on the Impact of Health Claims," *Nutrition Today* 36, 3 (May/June 2001): 115.

that bleached flour was potentially injurious to health.[22] The milling industry was able to continue its artificial bleaching practice largely unfettered by government controls thereafter.

Flour milling was one of the first industrial endeavours to eliminate a time-consuming chore for the household that had existed since the earliest domestication of plants thousands of years ago. Nevertheless, it was only by the late nineteenth century that major changes in the nature of the processing technology would have a serious effect on nutrition. As Figure 4.1 indicates, the separating out of the various components of the grain that was the nutritional hallmark of the new processes after 1870 had a nutritional impact that was nothing less than dramatic.

It has been known for many decades that refined white flour is nutritionally deficient and that it is the process of enrichment at the mill that attempts to compensate for this. Indeed, the absence of the bran from the final product means that approximately 25 percent of the selenium, 70 to 80 percent of the fibre, and a substantial amount of the zinc have been removed, and the amount of several other minerals, including iron, significantly reduced.[23] Other significant reductions occur in the essential B vitamins and vitamin E (see Figure 4.1). Given that at the time grains were an important part of the daily sustenance of people, and especially the poorest elements of the population, it was hardly surprising that the replacement of an important foodstuff by one that was substantially degraded in nutritional terms would have health consequences.

It is not well understood that this nutritional deficit lasted as long as it did. Indeed, well-known histories of nutrition covering this period largely gloss over it.[24] If we consider that the roller-milling transformation of the flour industry was largely a phenomenon of the late 1870s and 1880s, at least in the United States, and that the widespread enrichment of flour products did not take hold until the 1940s in the United States and Canada,[25] it is apparent that for a period of roughly sixty years, there existed a serious artificial nutritional deficiency in a major foodstuff for millions in North America. The same could be said for much of Europe, although there the milling industry's widespread adoption of roller milling took longer in some places. In Britain, for instance, a low growth in demand for flour and especially the prevalence of soft wheats amenable to stone-milling technology forestalled the change for some years until the increasing influx of hard American wheats and other factors favoured conversion to roller mills there as well.[26]

The nutritional deficiency of flours refined by modern industrial processes is not something that was discovered in relatively recent times, as I have noted. The efforts of industrial millers to compete via ever greater product refinement was not confined to producers of wheat flour; it was evident also with millers of corn and rice. The health consequences of excessive refinement began to be better understood after 1900. The link between polished white rice and the incidence of beriberi was beginning to be understood, thanks to the work of Edward Vedder of the US Army Medical Corps, who had done research in the Philippines on tropical diseases. Vedder had become concerned with dietary deficiencies he believed were caused by the production of polished white rice whereby processing eliminated the bran portion of the grain. Table 4.1 shows the extent of the deficiencies resulting from this process. His experiments had shown that patients suffering the later stages of beriberi could be cured of the disease with a dietary regimen that included an extract of the rice polishings contemporary milling had eliminated from milled rice.[27] It took others outside the United States to link his work with the disease pellagra.

Pellagra was known in Europe, and particularly Italy, and in the United States it was particularly prevalent in the South by the turn of the century. The symptoms were rough, scaly skin, typically taking the form of symmetrical lesions on the hands and arms, top of the feet, or back of the neck, or in a

TABLE 4.1

Vitamin B content of brown and white rice

	Thiamin (mcg/g)	Riboflavin (mcg/g)	Niacin (mcg/g)
Brown rice	3.69	0.50	53.8
White rice	0.60	0.25	18.1

SOURCE: Adapted from F.C. Blank, *A Handbook of Food and Nutrition* (Jodhpur: Agrobios, 2007), 52.

butterfly-shaped design across the nose. This was accompanied by severe disturbances of the digestive tract and nervous system. In acute cases it was usually fatal. It was gradually recognized that pellagra was most common among the poor and in institutional settings in which diet was very limited, and was much more frequent among women than men. Its high incidence in the South made it a health problem of the first order in the United States.[28]

The linking of pellagra to poor diet and attendant poverty was to prove an arduous task in the United States, however, as the medical profession there was imbued with the relatively new germ theory of disease, and this was much in favour as an explanation of pellagra. Others argued that the most likely cause was the toxins associated with rotten corn. The Englishman F.M. Sandwith built on the 1906 work of fellow countryman Frederick Gowland Hopkins examining the negative health impacts for mice fed a diet lacking in the amino acid tryptophan and advanced the idea in 1914 that pellagra might be due to a nutritional deficiency. Another scientist working in England at that time, Casimir Funk, argued that modern milling methods may be stripping grain of its nutritive value and leading to a nutritive deficiency, causing pellagra. In the United States, as Etheridge has argued, it was Joseph Goldberger who made the most progress uncovering the roots of this disease.

Goldberger, a medical researcher with the federal Public Health Service, had been studying the incidence of pellagra in the southeastern United States and conducting careful empirical investigations of his own. He began to link the disease with extreme poverty and the very limited diet associated with it, while systematically refuting other popular theories about its principal cause. Poor Southerners, and particularly the rural proletariat associated with the textile towns, who were forced to live on extremely low wages compared with their counterparts elsewhere in the country,[29] consumed a diet that was predominantly wheat bread, flour, molasses, pork, and lard. Added to the findings of Goldberger around 1915 were those of others who saw the nutrition-disease link in their research. One Southern medical researcher published an article in 1916 in *Scientific American* indicating that he had found no cases of pellagra in North Carolina villages that were unserved by the railroad and thus where water-ground or whole-grain cornmeal was still exclusively used. He argued that modern milling destroyed the nutritive protection against pellagra found in the whole grain.[30] At the same time, Public Health Service researchers published an article in the service's bulletin *Public Health Reports*, highlighting the nutritional loss in bread products produced by modern milling. As Etheridge notes, their article pointed out that

> white flour, so much prized by housewives as superior, was instead a distinctly inferior product. Made entirely of but one part of the grain – the starchy endosperm – it did not contain the same nutritive value it had when it included the germ and the bran as well. The modern roller mill, introduced into the United States in 1878, had definitely changed the food value of this staple of the diet. Highly milled flour and cornmeal kept better than whole-grain type but contained less protein, ash and fat than old fashioned products. More importantly, highly milled products contained fewer vitamins, or "certain essential accessory food substances" which were located in the outer layers of the grain and perhaps in the germ.[31]

Later, nutritional science more fully confirmed the essential nutritional contributions made by the various constituents of the wheat berry that were being refined out by the industrial grain-milling enterprise.

The milling industry quickly moved to counter the possible damage to its interests that such a published report could cause. The editor of the organ of the milling interests, the *Northwestern Miller*, telegraphed the Surgeon General the day after the Public Health Service article was published, protesting against the "vicious, untrue and wholly unjust attack upon the milling industry," and later that year sought a hearing before the secretary of the treasury to defend their interests. The Public Health Service was forced to agree to consult the industry before commenting in future on the "technical" aspects of milling.[32]

The reaction of the milling industry at this time to criticism of the nutritional integrity of its products was not to be the last occasion for millers to defend their right to continue to produce a product that had long had much of its nutritional value refined away. An episode some decades later serves to illustrate once again that the industry would use whatever argument it could muster to attempt to defeat threats to its perceived interests. The context was the period of food shortages in Europe that immediately followed the Second World War. Under pressure to appear to be taking action to help alleviate the critical shortage of flour, the federal government advocated measures to bolster the American flour supply by increasing the extraction rate in the milling process. Millers had argued that this could damage the "quality" of the standard bleached white patent flours. Through their leading trade journal, they argued that enlightened consumers demanded white flour and bread. The editorial in the *Northwestern Miller* proclaimed that

> the preference of the people of this country for fine, white flour and its delicious baked products is conclusively established by the fact that, after a half century or more of attacks by phony nutritionists, less than 3 percent of the nation's flour consumption is coarsely ground or so milled as to contain any fibrous parts of the wheat berry. The simple fact is that white flour and bread ... are made that way solely because in this enlightened land the consumer does not like wheat husks anymore than he likes potato peelings, pea pods or the shells of nuts.[33]

The journal's editorial on this matter continued in this vein, arguing that "white bread continues to be the preference, without exception, of those peoples whom we regard as the most enlightened in their ideals as well as in their standards and manner of living."[34] Absent from their arguments, as in earlier days, was any effort to take responsibility for the industry's concerted effort to shape consumer "preferences." Instead, the tack taken by the industry was to argue vehemently for the "natural" character of such "preferences."

FLOUR MILLERS LEAD FOOD INDUSTRY CONSOLIDATION

In the final decade of the nineteenth century and the beginnings of the next, powerful economic forces took hold of those industries that had grown up around the cereal bounty of the vast North American prairie farm economy. In both the milling industry and the baking industries, the large industrial plants that had been given particular impetus by the momentous technical changes of the time were being brought together in new forms of business organization, variously labelled "combinations," "trusts," and "holding companies," and under the control of fewer but much more powerful owners. These changes were to create the most appropriate conditions for the successful consolidation of more elaborated, industrially produced, processed cereal products in the early twentieth century on a scale never seen before in history. The market power that derives from a high degree of industrial consolidation is critical to the large-scale mass marketing campaigns that have the potential to change dietary patterns over time. The details of the economic and organizational formation from this part of the food business provide a window into the formation of today's food industry as a whole.

Early Factors in the Formation of the Processed Cereal Giants

A combination of factors led to a high degree of concentration of the milling industry in the United States even by 1890, with the Minneapolis milling capitalists leading the way. The latter had reaped the surplus profits that came the way of early innovators of successful technologies, using this capital to dramatically expand their mills and buy out competitors. They were geographically well situated to control much of the hard spring wheat supplies coming in from the west, and it was this kind of wheat, combined with the new milling methods, that yielded the fine patent flour that came to be preferred by bread makers in US markets and abroad. Millers in other locations found it difficult, if not impossible, to obtain a homogenous supply of the hard wheat and so were at a competitive disadvantage.[35] The larger mills found it prudent to source supply from a much bigger area than the small mills to ensure that they always had the quantity of wheat at the quality they wanted and that they would not be disturbed by calamities that might adversely affect farmers in one particular locality. Smaller mills were more dependent upon local supply, however, and much more vulnerable to supply disruptions.

Other advantages also accrued to larger millers that over time helped ensure their dominance. Through a process of backward integration, they expanded into the grain elevator business, which gave them certain advantages over mills that could not. In the area of transportation, they had the advantage in leveraging better freight rates from the railways; indeed, Charles Kuhlmann argues that this was perhaps the most important advantage.[36] If preferential treatment by the railroads gave them advantage over smaller millers in the shipment of flour, it was not uncommon for the same preference to be shown them on the grain-elevator side of the business. In this case, it was often the efforts of farmers to set up cooperative elevator operations that were prejudiced by the special treatment accorded the privately owned grain elevator companies by the railroad interests.[37]

The development of the export market, in western Europe especially, gave the largest millers another key advantage over the mass of smaller milling firms. As Kuhlmann writes,

> When the market broadened to include most of western Europe, and single orders for ten thousand to fifteen thousand barrels became fairly common, the advantage clearly moved to the side of the large mills. To secure such orders it was necessary to control large manufacturing capacity to be able to fill orders promptly and to make sure that the flour would be of uniform quality.[38]

By the late 1880s, Minneapolis had become the most important flour-milling centre in the world, and ownership of the mills had become highly concentrated. This was made even more so by the depressed market of that decade, and the entrance of English capital that consolidated two of the largest firms.[39] By 1890, almost 90 percent of the city's milling capacity was in the hands of four large corporations.[40]

The centralization of the milling industry was given further impetus by the process of merger in the baking industry sector. Bakeries too had been transformed by the Industrial Revolution, into factory-type assembly-line establishments that used machinery to sift flour, mix and knead dough, and form loaves that could be mechanically loaded into and out of large ovens.[41] As with milling, the concentration of capital within large bakery enterprises was soon to be followed by the bringing together of independent firms under a few large corporate organizations. Kuhlmann notes several examples, such as General Baking Company, which was formed in 1911 to acquire the holdings of twenty-six bakeries in fifteen large cities. Another was the Continental Baking Corporation, which constituted a combination of 103 bakeries in eighty-one US cities from coast to coast. Also in 1911, but across the border, a few leading bakery owners from Toronto and Winnipeg joined forces with a Toronto financier by the name of Cawthra Mulock to form the Canada Bread Company, an organization that would eventually control half of Ontario's bread market.[42]

In addition to this threatening development, the rapid expansion of the new retail chain store phenomenon and the concentrated buying power these stores represented posed a further threat to the milling companies.[43]

Although we may view the replacement of the independent grocer by super-market chain stores as a phenomenon of the latter decades of the twentieth century, and indeed as a contemporary phenomenon in Asia and Latin America, in fact, large corporate forms of food retail emerged much earlier. These initially did not use the more familiar supermarket format but instead cobbled together under the control of one company food vendors in specific sectors, whether they be meat stores, bakeries, or processed dry good vendors. In this way, the chain store type of corporate organization was born. It was only later, and especially after the Second World War, that the supermarket format emerged as a predominant format, and increasingly one controlled by fewer and fewer chain companies.[44] As in so many areas, US firms pioneered the way, and by 1914 the A&P Company already had some 650 stores in its operation, and by 1924 it had over 11,000.[45] The emergence of such powerful buyers could not have but caused considerable concern among the milling interests.

The horizontal integration that was to consolidate the flour-milling indus-try within just a few powerful players really took root in the late 1920s, how-ever. In the United States, James Ford Bell was head of one of the two main Minneapolis flour millers, the Washburn Crosby Company. He was looking for a way to survive declining per capita consumption of flour in the 1920s and the attendant reduced profits. As other industrialists in other spheres of business had demonstrated, reducing cutthroat competition through a strat-egy of consolidation was one proven strategy to guarantee continued sol-vency. In 1928, Bell aggressively embarked upon this path and in the process managed to form the largest milling company in the world, which became known as General Mills Inc.[46]

Industrial consolidation was very much underway in Canada as well by the early twentieth century, and as Charles Davies notes, between 1909 and 1912, 275 companies were merged to form 58 larger corporations.[47] The mill-ing industry was evidentially no exception to this trend. A special investiga-tive report by a federal commissioner under the auspices of the Combines Investigation Act several decades later starkly noted that, as in the Canadian bread-making industry, in the early decades of the twentieth century, flour milling had become concentrated in a very few large corporations and then represented by the Canadian National Millers Association (CNMA):

> Since at least 1936 there have been continuing efforts on the part of
> the principal milling companies to secure and maintain agreements
> amongst themselves and with others which would fix common

prices for the sale of flour, rolled oats, mill feeds and coarse grains which they sold ... Unquestionably the design of the members of the C.N.M.A. was to establish common prices for all of their products and thus to completely eliminate price competition amongst themselves.[48]

This report also drew attention to another key feature of the Canadian cereal grain economy at that time. This was the strategy of the larger milling companies to secure financial control of the larger bakeries. In a process of forward integration, these milling companies sought to secure the flour business of the bakeries they had acquired. The Maple Leaf Milling Company, for example, had secured a controlling interest in the Canada Bread Company by 1922, and later in the same decade it came to control Eastern Bakeries and Canadian Bakeries Limited as well. By the end of the 1920s, it controlled baking companies in almost every province and had thereby secured buyers for one-seventh of the flour used by all bakeries in the country.[49] In the same period, the Lake of the Woods Milling Company secured control over baking companies serving the Toronto market and those in several western cities, while the Ogilvie Milling Company secured control over bakery companies with a major presence in Montreal and several Ontario cities.[50]

The transformation of the means of production in this manner was itself dependent upon prior technological developments and vast infrastructural projects on the transportation front. But this transformation also called forth new ways of sourcing materials, and new means of warehousing and distribution. Above all, it necessitated new and vastly scaled-up approaches to selling product. The massive factory establishments being built even before 1900 by food manufacturers in areas such as flour milling were often built upon the expectation of an ever-expanding demand, a demand that could not be left up to chance and fortuitous circumstance. Fortunately for the food capitalists of that era, the instruments for stimulating demand were becoming available through the incessant drive for technological change that had been a central leitmotif of industrial capitalism since its inception. The early years of advertising, of pushing product for profit on a mass scale and employing the new mass media as the central instrument to do so, are important if we are to understand the tremendous power that transnational food businesses have to reshape diets today.

CHAPTER FIVE

Pushing Product for Profit

Early Branding

The entrepreneurs of the breakfast food industry ... almost singlehandedly destroyed the traditional American breakfast.

—Harvey Levenstein[1]

Twice as Much, for a Nickel Too

—1930s Pepsi ad inaugurating the era of
supersizing

In science you need to understand the world; in business you need others to misunderstand it.

—Nassim Nicholas Taleb, *The Bed of
Procrustes*[2]

W HAT WAS UNIQUE ABOUT the last years of the nineteenth century and the first decade of the century to follow, and how did it affect the food economy and, ultimately, shape diets? The answers to these questions will help us understand how the consumption of highly processed novel edible commodities became in a sense "normalized" in the United

States. This process of "normalization" of processed edible commodities lies at the heart of the constitution of the industrialized dietary regime.

Certainly, it was an era of far-reaching technological change. It also encompassed seismic shifts in the scale of enterprise and new complex organizational forms creating private firms with multiple operations spanning a nation. Very notably, it was a time that saw the emergence of marketing machinery of unprecedented scale and penetration, what came to be called mass marketing. These factors mark this era as one of fundamental transformation in so many realms, but no less so in the realm of food. Indeed, it was an era when the most powerful food-processing companies, as food historian Harvey Levenstein has argued, "aspired not only to respond to consumer demands but to shape them."[3] In a few decades, the long century and a half of competitive capitalism drew to a close, to be replaced by what economists Paul Baran and Paul Sweezy termed "monopoly capitalism."[4]

The early origins of the industrial diet in the nascent branding practices emerged in the last decades of the nineteenth century, only to expand tremendously in scope and sophistication by the 1920s. A few leading exemplars of this phenomenon, including Kellogg's and Coca-Cola, illustrate how certain foods were being redefined from the simple commodity form, which they had largely become as markets grew to global scales, to something more with the branding enterprise of early mass advertising. But what was the context that set the stage for this process to occur, and what was the role of advertising and branding more generally in terms of its political-economic significance?

Throughout most of the nineteenth century, even while commodities such as sugar, coffee, tea, and wheat were being sourced from around the world and transported to the leading centres of industrial capitalism, finished products coming out of this system had for the most part fragmented and localized markets. Manufacturers generally sold their products through brokers and jobbers and did not control the final distribution of their goods. Wooden clippers had shrunk oceanic distances considerably, and iron-hulled steamships did so even more by the 1850s and after. Nevertheless, internal trade before the spread of railroads was a much slower and expensive process.

Unquestionably, the massive canal building projects early in the century helped develop the beginnings of national markets. In the United States, the first Erie canal was finished in 1825; it was 547 kilometres long and had eighty-two locks providing a lift of 210 metres. For several decades, this canal served as the chief traffic artery for both passengers and freight travelling between the northeast and what was then the west, and it became the main artery for grain shipments from the west to New York City.[5] The canal linked trade up the Hudson River in eastern New York State with developing population centres across upper New York State all the way to Buffalo, which then developed into a major centre for industrial enterprise, including flour milling, and trade for points west on Lake Erie and beyond.

To the north in what was to become Canada, the first Welland Canal was finished in 1829. Almost fifty kilometres long, it had twenty-five locks, which linked the western end of Lake Ontario to Lake Erie and provided Canadian towns and emerging cities on the north shore of Lake Ontario with relatively inexpensive and quick access to American and Canadian markets much farther west. By linking the two lakes with this canal, comparatively low-cost inland water-borne shipping could be accomplished for an impressive distance of approximately 740 kilometres, from Kingston on eastern Lake Ontario to the Detroit-Windsor region of western Lake Erie.

Nevertheless, despite these advances, the size of the Great Lakes posed real dangers to the schooner sailing vessels that then dominated commerce. Certain hazards to shipping, principally powerful storms late in the season and geographical obstacles such as Long Point in Lake Erie, that became the graveyard for many dozens of ships over the nineteenth century, made commerce a less than predictable enterprise. So too did the often-fickle summer winds on the lakes, though even more significant were the freeze-ups, which hindered commerce greatly, in terms of critical water transport, during several of the coldest months of the year.

The construction of a network of railroads in North America was a necessary condition for overcoming fragmented markets. It not only represented a quantum leap in terms of the speed by which goods could be shipped but also made it possible to overcome much of the obstacle that climate posed to the internal shipment of goods during winter months. Combined with another technological marvel of the time, the telegraph, it allowed the far-sighted to contemplate the marketing of their products in an entirely new way. At the same time, with the aid of technological advances in other areas, there occurred the expansion of the tools of advertising to new levels of sophistication and power.

THE MATERIAL BASIS OF MASS ADVERTISING: THE OLIGOPOLY PHASE OF CAPITALISM

Mass advertising today is all too often accepted uncritically as a natural component of the capitalist world, yet such a view is historically inaccurate and mystifies the real role and tremendous costs to society represented by what has been termed the "sales effort." More on this later, but for the moment suffice to say that much of the contemporary food industry is utterly dependent upon mass advertising, whereas historically it was the site of many of advertising's most important and innovative manifestations. It is also worthwhile to note that as a significant economic phenomenon, mass advertising and the branding process it came to entail was a child of powerful tendencies that remade capitalist economies in the latter nineteenth century.

Central to this remaking was the concentration of capital. With food processing, as in most other sectors, this entailed the aggrandizement of individual firms as profits were reinvested into the firm to expand production and purchase new, often labour-saving, technologies. But also integral to this process was the centralization of capital, a different process that typically involved one leading company's buying up other independent firms in the same line of business. This process of horizontal integration entailed consolidating these formerly independent entities under the control of one individual corporate entity. Once centralized sufficiently to control business affairs in a particular sector, these economic organizations earned the name of "trusts" or "combines" and also "holding companies" by their critics of the time. They had thus become organizations endowed with tremendous market power that allowed them to set prices, to the detriment of their suppliers.

Indeed, broad sectors of society, and especially the numerous family farm populations in rural North America in the early twentieth century, were spurred to organize themselves economically in the form of cooperatives, and politically in populist agrarian parties such as the Progressive Party in the United States and the National Progressive Party in Canada, precisely to combat the tremendous economic and political power of the various trusts in the farm-implement sector, the grain-elevator and -milling sectors, in the railroad business, and in the meat-packing industry.

As several subsectors of the food industry – flour milling, meat-packing, vegetable processing – came to be characterized by the oligopoly structure of just a few sellers dominating their markets, the political-economic conditions changed sufficiently to qualitatively reshape the way the competitive process worked. In an influential book published over forty years ago, at a time when a critical social science was just emerging in the United States out of the academic deep-freeze represented by the 1950s, Baran and Sweezy succinctly summed up the significance of the change from competitive to oligopoly trust-ridden capitalism:

Under conditions of atomistic competition, when an industry comprises a multitude of sellers[,] each supplying only a small fraction of a homogeneous output, there is little room for advertising by the individual firm. It can sell at the going market price whatever it produces; if it expands its output, a small reduction of price will enable it to sell the increment, and even a small increase of price would put it out of business by inducing buyers to turn to its competitors who continue to offer the identical product at an unchanged price ...

The situation is quite different when the number of sellers is small and each accounts for a large proportion of an industry's output and sales. Such relatively large firms are in a position to exercise a powerful influence upon the market for their output by *establishing and maintaining a pronounced difference between their products and those of their competitors* (emphasis added).[6]

Baran and Sweezy then go on to articulate what I believe is at the core of mass advertising as it has developed in modern times. It was relevant for the first breakfast foods marketed, and it is uncannily accurate today for understanding the success of iconic firms of the digital economy such as Apple:

This *differentiation* is sought chiefly by means of advertising, trademarks, brand names, distinctive packaging, and product variation; if successful, it leads to a condition in which the differentiated product ceases, in the view of consumers, to serve as close substitutes for each other. The more telling the effort at product differentiation, the closer is the seller of the differentiated product to the position of monopolist. And the stronger the attachment of the public to his particular brand, the less elastic becomes the demand with which he has to reckon and the more able he is to raise his price without suffering a commensurable loss of revenue. (emphasis added)[7]

The Role of the Pure Food Law

The history of branding might have taken a different course if it had not been for the implementation of the Pure Food and Drugs Act of 1906. Although brought in mainly to deal with widespread adulteration of food and beverages and unsanitary processing facilities (see Chapter 8), this law had the perhaps unintended consequence of bolstering the conditions that would make it worthwhile for food processors to invest substantial sums in developing their brands, and in reinforcing them over time. Previously, it was not uncommon to pirate brands of another company and thereby benefit from the investment in that brand without having to pay for it. This was the case with the flour-milling industry in its early years, for example, where branding of flours had become established well before the turn of the nineteenth century. By stepping in with a pure food law, the state was laying essential groundwork for branding to really become established. As the organ of the flour industry noted in 1915, "There are certain requirements of the [federal pure food] law, such as prohibition of any deceptive statement on the label and demand for truthfulness of statement of name of manufacturer and place of manufacture, which operate strongly in the interest of legitimate branding and, to the same degree, discourage the brand thief."[8]

As manufacturers concentrated and centralized their operations, the relatively modest efforts at advertising their products conducted by the retail trade were more and more taken over by the manufacturers themselves. In the United States by the 1890s, advertising expenditures had already risen to $360 million, seven times what they were in 1867. By 1929, only some thirty years later, the revenues spent on advertising had increased approximately 1,000 percent over those of the 1890s, reaching $3.4 billion.[9] Truly a new era had dawned in terms of how products were being marketed.

By the early twentieth century, the leading food manufacturers had built very large production facilities and had bought up other manufacturing firms in their branch of production in a process of horizontal integration. The mass-production capabilities that resulted were on a scale that was historically unprecedented. As Richard Tedlow succinctly notes of business organization at this time, "Mass production demanded mass advertising."[10]

The organizational centralization of millers and other cereal processors, in addition to protecting them from the increasingly centralized power of the "buyers" (e.g., chain food-store companies), provided the financial wherewithal to push the relatively undeveloped enterprise of "pushing product" through advertising to a truly national level. Cereal-based product manufacturers had a pioneering role in this development, first via the new medium of radio and later with the advent of television and, by century's end, Internet-based communication. This prominence was to continue despite the rise of a host of other powerful consumer-oriented manufacturing and service-based industries later in the century.

Tedlow describes what he terms "Phase II" of the history of marketing development:

This was the era of the national mass market, in which a small number of firms realized scale economies to an unprecedented degree by expanding their distribution from coast to coast ... In Phase II the national product market was dominated by an aggressive leading company or a small number of such companies. Through advertising and publicity, through forward integration into company-owned wholesaling, through franchise agreements with retailers, through creation of sales programs and their implementation, and through the systematic analysis of carefully collected data, the large firm came to exercise an impact on the consumer market far greater than anything contemplated in Adam Smith's day.[11]

FROM THE SMALL-SCALE TO THE NATIONAL MARKET: MASS ADVERTISING CHANGES THE WORLD

The new era was a period when foods and beverages would be commoditized to a degree yet unknown in human history. To be sure, technological innovations laid the groundwork for this historically unprecedented extension of the commoditization of food. Steam engines had shrunk distances on sea and land, the telegraph and the telephone facilitated greatly the organization of far-flung productive enterprise, and new processing innovations allowed for a dramatic increase in output with much less labour. This was true in the canning industry, for example, where new machine crimping processes replaced labour-intensive soldering of cans, so that by 1910 the American canning industry was turning out 3 billion cans of food annually.[12]

Yet the new era was the era of nascent brands, rather than commodities per se. In one sense, the branded product was a commodity to be bought and sold, just like any other commodity. However, it was not like any other commodity in important respects. It was a product that was successfully differentiated in the minds of consumers as superior to other similar products available in the marketplace. Originally, this differentiation may have been assisted by a processing innovation of some kind that rendered the finished product somewhat different from the myriad others available. For example, as Levenstein has noted, the Van Camp company was able to distinguish its pork-and-beans product from the many available as what was then a staple food by adding tomato sauce to its recipe. But even firms that had made a significant change in the nature of their output had to make their innovation widely known to survive the harsh competition that was to come. This could be done only via the new techniques of mass advertising, which required unprecedented expenditures as well. Not all who embarked upon such expensive publicity campaigns for their products were successful, but few who did *not* would survive long into the new era of American capitalism.

Some spectacularly successful companies innovated primarily in the area of advertising and promotion. This was largely true of the vegetable processor H.J. Heinz: "Heinz arranged demonstrations of his product at grocery stores, offered a money-back guarantee, opened his factories to public tours, gave away millions of samples, and invested heavily in the most expensive form of advertising of the time, the electrically illuminated sign."[13] A few other would-be food entrepreneurs were to employ the powerful new techniques of mass advertising even more successfully than Mr. Heinz, however. One of these was to found a fortune via the production and marketing of a breakfast cereal; the other was to do so with a soda fountain product. In neither case were the products particularly novel, as there were many similar competing products available. Through marketing prowess and organizational innovation, the promoters of products in these categories created powerful processing empires that were to play leading roles in transforming diet over the next century.

BREAKFAST CEREALS:
ICONIC PRODUCTS IN THE AMERICAN DIET

What has come to be known as the breakfast cereal industry emerged in part as a separate entity to the flour-milling industry and, in part, it was an organic evolution of the latter. One would think that flour-milling firms were in a favoured position to launch an industry that essentially entailed the further processing of the product they had long been producing. It was notably entrepreneurs outside the milling industry, however, who were important to the development of what was to be a spectacular financial success of the processed-food industry, namely ready-to-eat cereal-based breakfast foods. Marketed as a healthy cereal-based alternative to existing foods, "ready to eat" breakfast cereals came to form the cornerstone of the American-style breakfast in the decades after the turn of the century. In the process, inevitably, they were to have nutritional consequences of considerable significance, particularly later on in the twentieth century when a new generation of heavily sugared products were introduced on a massive scale.

Cereal-based breakfast products appeared shortly after the mid-nineteenth century in the United States and were typically meant to be cooked at home and served hot. Although a meal of cereal-based porridge or gruel had long been the custom of people in various parts of the globe, a few entrepreneurs now believed money could be made by packaging a ground or rolled cereal meal and making it available to the growing urban middle class in particular. By the 1890s, the North Dakota Milling Company was advertising its Cream of Wheat as "the new breakfast food" in the *Ladies Home Journal*, and was one of the first attempting to attract customers with offers of free sample packages and cookbooks to those who mailed in a request.[14]

Gregory Price has argued that the processing innovations of granulation, flaking, and shredding led to the first successful national marketing of a "ready to eat" cereal product, one that could be eaten cold. A pioneer in this regard was Henry Perky of Niagara Falls, New York, in 1894. It is unclear how successful he himself was at achieving a wide acceptance for his product, but what he called "Shredded Wheat" became firmly established as a breakfast food of North Americans once it was sold to the much larger National Biscuit Company, later Nabisco, in 1928.[15] Also in the 1890s, C.W. Post's Postum Cereal Company was advertising its product Grape-Nuts in the *Ladies Home Journal* as a product that was "fully cooked and pre-digested."[16] He also produced a cornflake product called Toasties and was the first, according to Price, to advertise his ready-to-eat products nationally.[17] In this endeavour Post was in fierce competition with several other entrepreneurs located in Battle Creek, Michigan, which was to become, under the eventual dominance of the Kellogg's company, a geographical centre for the transformation of breakfast menus in North America and, much later, in other parts of the globe. As Levenstein notes,

> The entrepreneurs of the breakfast food industry ... almost single-handedly destroyed the traditional American breakfast. Historically, industrial and economic development has been accompanied by the substitution of meat for grain in the diet. Yet while that was indeed the trend overall from 1870 on in America, the breakfast food manufacturers managed to promote the opposite process at breakfast: the replacement of the traditional slabs of meat with various forms of highly processed grain.[18]

THE EARLY BREAKFAST CEREAL INDUSTRY AND DIETARY HEALTH

The early breakfast cereal entrepreneurs, beginning with those who promoted some form of cooked cereal product, were typically keen to link their products to a presumed health benefit, or to convenience, or both. Without accurate information on what people were eating on a regular basis, particularly for breakfast meals, it is difficult to come to firm conclusions about the impact of the packaged breakfast-food industry on North American diets at that time. Some authors have argued that late-nineteenth-century breakfast meals were dominated by large quantities of meat. Studies of the meat industry note the leading role of pork in the diet of Americans in the early decades of the nineteenth century, and the increasing consumption of beef as settlement extended onto former Aboriginal lands of the Great Plains and very large areas of grasslands became available for agriculture. By 1900, per capita consumption of beef in the United States had almost reached that of per capita pork consumption, at sixty-seven pounds, compared with about seventy-two pounds annually for pork.[19] Pork consumption declined after 1900, as did that of beef, until about 1950, when an era of cheap feeds made beef relatively inexpensive once again.[20]

The transition to cereal-based breakfast foods that gained momentum at this time may have reduced the relative importance of animal-based proteins in the morning meal, as corn- and wheat-based packaged products grew in prominence. To the extent that people were embracing cereal products made from the nutritionally deficient flours that had become standard products of the milling industry, the intake of certain minerals and vitamins would likely have been affected, as the era of artificially "enriched" flours was not to occur for another forty years. Nevertheless, a stronger case for the negative dietary impact of this industry can be made for the period after the Second World War. By that era, a mature breakfast cereal industry had become highly economically concentrated and had turned to the aggressive promotion of a spectrum of sweetened cereal products, and to directing this promotion at the youngest segments of the population.

The breakfast cereal industry at this time is notable for more than the inauguration of a shift in the dietary patterns at the morning meal: it should be recognized for the leading role it took in the history of branding of foods. Given the centrality of branding as a force in shaping diet in later years, it is worthwhile giving some attention to the early manifestations of this phenomenon.

BREAKFAST CEREAL ENTREPRENEURS PIONEER BRANDING

The two leading Minneapolis milling companies had for many years pioneered the process of creating branded product in the flour business by widely advertising their patented flours. Together with the Pillsbury Flour Mills Company, Washburn Crosby and Company had been the first to establish branded flour products on a national scale in North America with its "Gold Medal" flour. It is curious that the entrance of the milling companies into the ready-to-eat breakfast cereal business lagged behind pioneers such as C.W. Post and the Kellogg brothers. Nevertheless, in the early twentieth century, the General Mills company – an amalgam of five milling companies, including Washburn Crosby and Company – did become a major ready-to-eat cereal manufacturer and proved an innovator in the way it used its financial resources to incorporate the new medium of radio into its advertising campaigns. This new medium was exploited to promote its first ready-to-eat product, Whole Wheat Flakes (later renamed Wheaties), introduced in 1924.[21] In what the company claims was the first radio singing advertisement, the producers of Wheaties had a quartet promote the product on radio in the Minneapolis area in 1926. The positive effect of advertising on sales in this medium was eventually recognized, and the company took its singing advertising campaign to the emerging national radio audiences in 1929.

General Mills also began sponsoring radio broadcasts of local baseball games in the 1920s. By the early 1930s, this had led to much broader-based ad campaigns incorporating sports celebrity endorsements to bolster its ready-to-eat brand, beginning with Lou Gehrig as the first sports figure to be featured on its cereal boxes. The company followed this in later years with endorsements from sports icons such as Babe Ruth, Jackie Robinson, Ted Williams, and Mickey Mantle. These featured celebrity endorsements were to continue for future decades, and to be complemented with more complex campaigns regarding sports and health. During the Cold War years, General Mills linked its Wheaties product to the Eisenhower administration's quest to raise the fitness of American youth to European levels. It signed on an American Olympic champion as director of its Wheaties Sports Federation, and used the federation to link the brand to support for fitness and sports programs.[22]

KELLOGG'S CORN FLAKES AND BREAKFAST CEREAL OLIGOPOLY

If General Mills was the most prominent food manufacturer to link its new processed products to sports, physical fitness, and health more generally in the early years of the twentieth century, it was not the only one, nor even the first. The link between food and health was increasingly on the minds of the growing middle class in North America by the end of the nineteenth century, for a number of reasons. The germ theory of disease had become popularized by that time, for one thing, and concern with cleanliness was one result. Muckraking journalists highlighted the manifest excesses of unregulated capitalism in a variety of spheres, including the food sector. Upton Sinclair's exposé of the meat-packing industry in his book *The Jungle*, which presented a disturbing picture of sanitary and labour conditions in the packing houses, was an enduring example of this. Powerful interests in the food industry proved keen to exploit this concern with health when it was to their advantage, and it was in several instances.

The elder of the two Kellogg brothers, John Harvey, was by the end of the nineteenth century a well-known American surgeon and director of a famous sanitarium in Battle Creek, Michigan, affiliated with the Seventh-Day Adventists. Dr. Kellogg's younger brother, Will, was the unofficial manager of the sanitarium and took an important role in developing, producing, and marketing health foods for patients, which were sold through their newly created Sanitas Food Company. An early innovation was to let cooked wheat stand for several hours before running it through rollers and baking the resulting flakes. This palatable product was marketed as Toasted Wheat Flakes. The brothers had a ready if limited market without the need to do much in the way of advertising, as they were able to sell product to other Seventh-Day Adventist sanitariums in the United States and abroad. This generated enough capital to expand production and encourage work on new products.[23]

The evident demand for new breakfast-meal innovations spurred imitators to quickly copy any product that looked successful. The profits of pioneer innovators were difficult to protect in what then approached much more of a free market than anything that prevails today. Employees of successful innovators were often hired away by upstart competitors and then encouraged to reveal trade secrets about recipes of their former employers. Battle Creek became a centre for entrepreneurs intent upon cashing in on the new public interest in ready-to-eat breakfast foods. By 1902, local competitors had copied products marketed by the Sanitas Food Company and had largely eroded the modest profits it had generated.[24]

It was soon to be evident that the most successful entrepreneurs were those who figured out a way to circumvent the cutthroat competition that relatively free competitive markets inevitably entail. Among the first of these in the food business was C.W. Post. Post is a man of particular interest because he was an innovator in the exploitation of the new tools of mass advertising and the branding of processed products. A one-time patient of the senior

Kellogg at his sanitarium, Post was a salesman who apparently used his business acumen to develop a product that was very much like a cereal coffee substitute developed by the Kelloggs and served to patients at the sanitarium. But his tremendous success with the product came only when he decided to concentrate heavily on advertising. Capitalizing on the fascination with health food innovations at this time, Post advertised his Postum Cereal as a "builder of nerves, red blood, and all-round health."[25] He gave the same advertising attention to another item that resembled the granola product that the Kelloggs had been producing for the sanitarium for over twenty years. Marketed by the brand name Grape-Nuts, it too had commercial success that outshone rivals many times over.

The younger Kellogg, Will, ended his difficult relationship with his more famous, but domineering, brother in 1906, and with the assistance of a St. Louis insurance man by the name of Charles Bolin he incorporated the Battle Creek Toasted Corn Flake Company in that year. With the example of C.W. Post in the new realm of mass advertising close at hand and his own long-time product-development experience, along with the fortuitous relationship he had struck up with a pioneer publisher of business magazines and books, Arch Shaw, the younger Kellogg was now in a position to carry through on ideas in ways that had not been possible while working with his elder brother at the sanitarium. In particular, he would be able to weld together his ready-to-eat breakfast product with equally innovative advertising strategies that eventually gave him the critical advantage over the host of breakfast cereal competitors of his day. Had Kellogg been content to market the new corn-based product he invented in the manner typical of that time, it is highly likely that it would have been quickly copied and his future in the food business would have been much less spectacular. The breakthroughs his company made on the mass advertising front served him well, though, and helped end the era of competitive markets in this sector of American capitalism.

With the lessons learned from the experience of having had breakfast products he created duplicated by others who then seriously undermined his sales, the younger Kellogg became convinced that distinguishing his product from others in the mind of the public was the route to success. According to sources cited by his biographer, Horace Powell, Kellogg decided at the outset to advertise extensively and intensively. He used strategies such as blanket house-to-house sample drop-offs in targeted cities and in 1906 gambled on an expensive full-page ad in a leading magazine of that time, the *Ladies Home Journal*, that tempted housewives with a year's supply of his cornflake product if they could persuade their local grocer to order a case of it for their customers. By year end, Kellogg had spent on advertising a sum that was almost three times the company's initial working capital.[26]

A fire that destroyed the company's main factory in Battle Creek at this time of great advertising outlay would have spelled disaster for a typical breakfast food processor. Nevertheless, in a statement that sums up the power that the machinery of advertising was beginning to confer to those who knew how to manipulate it, Kellogg's business partner is reported to have written that "the fire is of no consequence. You can't burn down what we have registered in the minds of the American women."[27] The success in the next few years of this company in dominating the national market in the United States was to demonstrate that this statement was hardly empty rhetoric.

In the following years, Kellogg pushed hard to maintain his cornflake product's image in the public mind, coming up with audacious advertising ploys and a variety of gimmicks and creative advertising copy that managed to consistently create what today we call "buzz." Whether it was sponsoring the largest electric advertising sign ever seen in a Times Square, New York, promotion of his product or offering large prizes for the best ears of corn at county and state fairs across the country, the company spent heavily on advertising that emphasized repetition and continuity. As sales expanded, so too did the advertising budget, so that by 1940 the company had spent an astounding amount of money on advertising for that era, some $1 billion over the thirty-four years of its existence.[28]

In the early days of Kellogg's fledgling company, more than a hundred cornflake products had been marketed in the United States. Technology had existed for some time to produce this type of food product on a large scale, and concentrated forms of organizational enterprise had proven effective for the most powerful players in other sectors of American business in the last decades of the nineteenth century. Nevertheless, the breakfast food industry was characterized by numerous small competing enterprises until a few capitalized on the machinery of advertising that was then being perfected. The benefits to those who grasped the power of advertising via the new mass communication technologies were to be very considerable, and not long in coming. It is remarkable that this fragmented sector of the economy was, in less than three decades, to become one of the most highly concentrated sectors of the food industry. By 1935, the breakfast cereal industry was dominated by four firms – Kellogg's, Post, Nabisco, and General Mills – which together controlled almost 70 percent of the market.

COCA-COLA:
MARKETING SO SUCCESSFUL IT BECOMES CULTURE

Branding as a phenomenally successful tool for transforming diet is no-where better illustrated than with the rise of soft drinks in America and the ascendance of what became its premier representative, the Coca-Cola Company. In the United States, the earliest uses of carbonated soda water in the early nineteenth century mimicked its European usage as primarily for medicinal purposes. Nevertheless, entrepreneurs fairly quickly saw a market for carbonated flavoured refreshments without soda added. According to a standard historical source on the industry, these innovations to the trad-itional carbonated soda water are the key reasons this effervescent refresh-ment has been considered predominantly American in origin.[29]

Coca-Cola was created in an era when fortunes were to be made by mar-keting unregulated patent medicines, and indeed patent medicine entrepre-neurs were probably the most significant initiators of what has become modern advertising.[30] Atlanta resident Dr. John Pemberton's concoction bore the earmarks of that time – part medicine and part beverage. It also contained, among its various ingredients, extracts of coca leaves and kola nuts, which provided its stimulant qualities.[31] The use of coca leaves in bev-erages was not unheard of; in fact, a coca-laced wine called Vin Mariani became extremely successful in Europe and later the United States just be-fore Pemberton began pushing his product.[32] Pemberton's advertisements reflected the product's origins, touting its medicinal qualities as well as its value as a refreshing and rejuvenating beverage.

Pemberton was noted for spending about 90 percent of the receipts of his first production of cola syrup on advertising, mainly oil-cloth signs pinned to drugstore awnings.[33] The next year he advertised on Atlanta's horse cars and was selling forty times as much syrup as the previous year. But as Mark Pendergast makes clear in his authoritative, and unofficial, history of the company,[34] Pemberton's genius in concocting pleasing beverages was not matched by his business acumen or disciplined approach to expanding sales. It took another man, Asa Candler, and Pemberton's former partner, Frank Robinson, to bring the business smarts and advertising brilliance together behind the product and push it to the forefront of the pack, once they had successfully gained control of the rights to the product in 1887.

Throughout much of the nineteenth century, soft drink refreshments re-tained their attachment to drug stores and elaborate marble soda fountain facilities; absent was the contemporary focus on bottles and cans as the means of product delivery. This had much to do with the difficulties of transporting bulk goods such as bottled soft drinks any distance, and even more so the cost of bottles, which were individually mouth-blown for much of the century and lacked satisfactory closure devices. By 1903, the bottle problem was largely solved by Toledo-based Michael Owens and his automated bottle-manufacturing technology. Toward the end of the nineteenth century, various successful bottle enclosures were invented, with the most successful being that of William Painter, who invented the metallic bottle cap known as "the Crown." This device, with its early cork liner, was to become the standard closure mechanism before long.[35]

THE ASCENDANCE OF COCA-COLA:
BRAND FOCUS AND INTENSE ADVERTISING

With major technological issues largely resolved by around 1900, the stage was set for major competitive battles to emerge among various carbonated beverage manufacturers. Just in the cola segment there were many emergent brands, some of which were still existent by mid-century, including Chero-Cola, Cleo Cola, Dixi-Cola, Gay-Ola, Key Kola, Koca-Nola, Lime Cola, Lotta Cola, Marbert Cola, Mingo Kola, Nichol Kola, Pepsi-Cola, Pop Kola, Roxa-Kola, Royal Crown Cola, and Triple Cola – to name only a few from the incredible array of carbonated brands that populated the America market.[36] Ginger ale was the most popular of the carbonated beverages, with a company called Clicquot Club emerging as a dominant player, especially in the New England states. It is credited as being among the first of the beverage companies to use national advertising, in around 1907, to push its products from a regional to a national level of awareness.[37]

How did one of these early beverage companies – Coca-Cola – come to so dominate not only the cola market but – along with what became its main rival, Pepsi-Cola – the non-alcoholic beverage market generally, and not just in the United States but on a global level? More than one factor accounts for this, of course, but marketing strategy was key and came to define successful marketing for years to come. Another strategy was litigation, to deal with imitators that were undercutting Coca-Cola's market at every turn, but this came later, once its product had already attracted national attention and was deemed worth imitating.

Possibly the first of Candler's successful business decisions was to tie up loose ends concerning copyright for Coca-Cola and buy out the one outstanding holder of the rights to the product, depositing the documents verifying this transaction with the US patent office. Beyond this, an early key to Candler and Coke's success was to put aside the other products he was then also pushing, including patent medicines, and marshal company resources behind his one cola product that had a proven record of consumer acceptance. In addition to narrowing the focus of his business, Candler decided to invest heavily in advertising. Throughout the 1890s, hefty increments in product sales year over year, despite recessionary times in the wider economy, proved the wisdom of this strategy, and by 1895 the company was selling about four times as many gallons of its principal product as it had started the decade selling.

As Pendergast notes, "The key was advertising." In the early years, Candler was spending over half the total amount he spent in raw ingredients on advertising, much of it in new territories where there was no history of the product. Candler's partner, Frank Robinson, has been credited with having the brains behind the decision to remake Coca-Cola into a more socially acceptable beverage by de-emphasizing its medicinal qualities and radically simplifying the often wordy advertisements that were then typical. Ads that once proclaimed Coca-Cola as "Harmless, Wonderful, Efficient ... Relieves Headaches ... Gives Prompt Rest" and "The Ideal Brain Tonic and Sovereign Remedy for Headache and Nervousness ... It Makes the Sad Glad and the Weak Strong" were fairly drastically refashioned to emphasize a much simpler, and ultimately more powerful and effective, message. Coca-Cola was "Delicious and Refreshing," period. It was an important move, as it turns out, for the twentieth century was to be an era less tolerant of the laissez-faire ways of patent medicine capitalism that characterized nineteenth-century America.[38] In particular, the tolerance of narcotic drugs in beverages was coming to an end and, by the early years of the new century, Candler was finally forced to change his winning formula and remove the small quantities of coca leaf–derived cocaine that were part of the original formula.[39]

Beyond simplifying the message, the product's appeal was enhanced and the potential market broadened with the use of artistically rendered graphic images that depicted up-and-coming respectable middle-class men and, even more typically, women as well. The typical "Coke boy," as one company publication on the history of its advertising images notes, "is a young man on his way up, an aspiring student or rising junior executive. He works hard, he relaxes in the most fashionable way possible ... a combination sportsman, professional and all-around 'nice guy' ... Similarly, the Coca-Cola girl the company depicted, in its magazine ads and calendars in these early days has 'sex appeal, but a man can take her home to Mother.'" Depicting women drinking the product was central to the advertising strategy almost from the beginning, it would seem, and in fact the company's first effort with the new tactic of celebrity endorsement involved the opera star Lillian Nordica, in a time when every town and city of reasonable size boasted an opera house.[40]

Candler is credited with being the first to use national advertising to push his beverage product, and his 1901 budget for advertising reached $100,000,[41] an almost unheard of amount of money to be directed to advertising in an era when many sectors of manufacturing spent little if any revenues promoting product. Slightly over ten years later, the ad budget had escalated to over $1 million.[42] He cleverly used a combination of push and pull advertising techniques to firmly establish Coca-Cola with consumers. Timothy Muris and colleagues describe the strategy as follows:

> To push the product through the drugstore distribution channel, a sales force was recruited and druggists were offered heavy discounts on their first orders of syrup. Consumer demand pull was generated by distributing free coupons redeemable for a first glass of Coke, and by blanketing drugstores, train stations, town squares, and consumers with signs, calendars, clocks, and other premiums to build brand awareness and brand image.[43]

Coca-Cola's advertisements were to be found virtually everywhere even by the turn of the twentieth century. When asked some years later by the Internal Revenue Service during a court trial what kinds of vehicles his company advertised on, Candler is reported to have replied that he did not know of any types of vehicles that the company did *not* advertise on.[44] By 1913, the company was placing its advertising on an estimated 100 million items, from Japanese fans to baseball cards and everything in between. It was clearly a pioneer in what later came to be called saturation advertising.

Distributors and soda fountain owners were left with a strong incentive to expand sales. Company finances from the period show that Candler's total expenses (ingredients, labour, advertisements, and so on) came to about $1 per gallon of syrup that was sold retail for $6.40 by the soda fountain operator. Candler sold the syrup to distributors for $1.29, leaving a handsome profit to be made by distributors and fountain operators and thus a strong incentive to stimulate sales.[45] This built-in incentive program apparently worked, as annual sales continued to show strong year-over-year increases.

COCA-COLA: A PIONEER IN PRODUCT PLACEMENT

As Candler and his partner understood, handsome profits could be made from a product that sold for just a few pennies if consumers basically liked its taste, if the product was aggressively advertised, and if the product was widely available so that the advertising came to good effect. Meeting this last condition is where the beverage company played a true pioneering role.

A central factor in making Coca-Cola a ubiquitous product in early-twentieth-century America was the almost accidental adoption of a new strategy to allow the product to be bottled on a national scale. Candler had been suspicious of bottled product, which because of technical limitations had in the past often been an inferior product. Nevertheless, in 1899, Candler signed a contract with two aspiring bottling entrepreneurs that, uncharacteristically for Candler, gave away the rights to bottle the product in exchange for a fixed guaranteed price for syrup. In return, he appeared to receive little other than guarantees that the quality and "purity" of the product would be maintained, and assurances that bottling the product was the surest way to spread its consumption across the land. Candler seemingly had little to lose, however, since he was not required to advance any of his own capital for the venture, and if things worked out he would benefit from even greater increases in syrup sales.[46]

The evolution of this bottling venture is a story in its own right, but the point here is that it helped tremendously in opening up possibilities for product placement that could never have occurred with the old soda fountain system as the principal venue for product distribution. Once the bottling franchise model was set up, the capital of others was used to set up local bottling operations across the country. Having the product in bottles allowed it to be placed in a vast variety of sites where soda fountains were unpractical. It also led to an extension of the target market well beyond the upwardly mobile white middle class.

In the end, the bottling franchise venture proved to be a dramatic success, so that five years after Candler signed the fateful contract, 120 bottling plants had been set up, covering almost every state. As one successful Southern bottling entrepreneur summed it up, bottling of Coca-Cola had put it into the hands of "thousands of merchants in the suburbs and outlying districts of every city, in the stores of every country town and village, and in the homes of thousands of people where it had not been possible to put Coca-Cola before."[47] The product was well on its way to becoming the best-known brand of American capitalism, and a mainstay of the American diet as well.

It is worth reminding ourselves that branding is and was a strategy that profit-seeking business organizations use for one ultimate reason, to push more product out the door. In these terms, the American soft drink industry, with Coca-Cola leading the pack from the early years of the twentieth century, has been supremely successful. This success is not a phenomenon of just the last few decades. It was quite the contrary, in fact.

The figures on cases of soft drinks sold in the early twentieth century show that soft drink companies have been playing a significant role in shaping the American diet for the past hundred years. Already by 1910, these companies had managed to boost consumption to 65 million cases, and this was to be just the beginning. By 1920, annual production had reached approximately 175 million cases, and fewer than ten years after that it had grown spectacularly to over 272 million cases, which amounted to a per capita annual consumption of fifty-three bottles per American. It is remarkable that by the end of the 1930s, and despite the impact on incomes of the Great Depression, the industry had been able to increase consumption of its product by another

FIGURE 5.1

Annual US per capita soft drink consumption in the early twentieth century

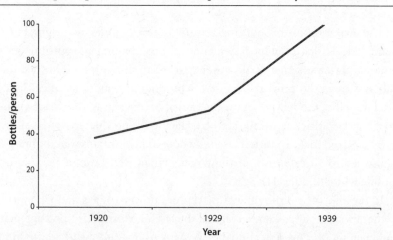

SOURCE: John J. Riley, *A History of the American Soft Drink Industry* (New York: Arno Press, 1972), 137, 142, 148.

dramatic increment, with annual production approaching 500 million cases, which signified a per capita consumption of almost a hundred bottles per person annually (see Figure 5.1).[48]

The dietary impact of this is not gauged only by the number of bottles consumed per person, however. Competitive pressures within the industry, heightened by the straitened circumstances of the Depression years, were bringing about innovation in container size. Supersizing is not a recent invention: the struggling Pepsi-Cola Company, begun in 1903 and reincarnated since then, had expanded its bottle size 100 percent in 1933 in a desperate attempt to boost its flagging sales fortunes. It promoted what in today's terms seems a modest twelve-ounce size to compete with Coca-Cola and other companies that used what had been a standard six-ounce size.[49] Once it had tied this change to a successful ad slogan – "Twice as Much, for a Nickel Too!" – a few years later, sales increased dramatically. This was essentially the dawn of supersizing.

Mass Marketing and the Normalization of the Industrial Diet

At one level, mass marketing was a development that allowed the companies that used it most successfully to come to dominate the markets in which they did business. It was an innovative corporate strategy that proved to be essential to survival and growth in the era of competitive capitalism. But as we look back in time, mass marketing must be appreciated for something else as well, something far more important in societal terms. It was a key ingredient in the efforts of a number of food manufacturing firms to have their *processed* food products supplant what people were eating, and drinking. It began to make highly processed foods – industrial foods – acceptable at a time when most people's diets were dominated by what we call today "whole foods," or at least foods that underwent fairly minimal processing before consumption.

The commoditization of foods essentially entered new territory as mass marketing proved to be a powerful tool in gaining acceptance for products that were increasingly reconstituted foods, shaped by ever more complex industrial processes. The door was being opened for the chemical revolution that would occur in later years when food manufacturers would be able to market a wide spectrum of processed edible products using a phenomenal arsenal of chemical additives. I would argue that the way was also being prepared for a general willingness to accept the genetically modified foods that appear later in the twentieth century. Indeed, it could be argued that the efforts of food manufacturers in North America over the previous century to inculcate a widespread acceptance of highly processed foods was likely a central factor in the uncritical acceptance of these genetically engineered foods in recent times.

PART 3

THE INTENSIFICATION OF THE INDUSTRIAL DIET, 1945-80

T HE INDUSTRIAL DIET DEMANDS our attention first and foremost because it involves the degradation of whole foods, and, in the case of a growing array of edible products, it has spawned a plethora of nutrient-poor processed edible products. It would take many years before the health-debilitating nature of these products came to be fully appreciated. Today, some medical authorities have been willing to go so far as to argue for their being labelled as "edible pathogens."[1] This view, however, isn't widely accepted. And it certainly wasn't in the period covered by the second industrial dietary regime.

Three basic processes have been responsible for degrading food. These processes, which essentially affect the production and processing of food, are the simplification of whole foods, the speed-up of the turnover time of capital employed in the food sector, and the growing use of macro-adulterants in producing edible commodities.

Although each of these processes is inherent in the first industrial dietary regime, they are deepened and extended in the second. Another sign that a qualitative change in the industrial dietary regime has occurred is the intensification of the industrial diet that took place in the post–Second World War years. Intensification, it will be remembered, was seen as a central motif of the second food regime by its advocates as well.

I see two institutional forces as critical to this intensification process: the supermarket chain store and the fast-food retail chain. Each of these institutional spheres experienced extraordinary consolidation of the business enterprises in their respective spheres, so that by the latter part of the twentieth century a few very powerful corporate players had established dominant positions. These players came to exercise exceptional market power that allowed them tremendous leverage, leverage applied in different ways to shape food environments and ultimately mass diets, in the process engrossing their bottom lines enormously.

The supermarket chain store and the fast-food chain each played considerable roles in determining how people ate in the postwar years. In this regard, and as a critical dimension of the intensification of the industrial diet, I refer to a complex of business strategies and practices that I attempt to capture with the concept of spatial colonization. This concept is meant to comprehend the strategies and practices food corporations developed to secure the visibility and availability of their products in the food environments of society.

I am particularly concerned with the spatial colonization of nutrient-poor edible commodities, or "pseudo foods." I first used this term in an article published some years ago to refer to a wide spectrum of nutrient-poor edible commodities that are typically high in sugar, fat, and salt – as well as in the often prodigious calories they provide – and low in key nutrients such as proteins, minerals, and vitamins.[2] The term was meant to include what are traditionally thought of as junk foods, but it was meant as a more inclusive category that would incorporate a wide gamut of products not usually considered as junk foods but which are nutrient-poor nonetheless. Examples in the breakfast cereal and fruit juice product categories abound, as they do in other edible product categories. Supermarket chain stores have become the primary site for the spatial colonization of these products. It is not the only one, however. In recent decades, the phenomenon of the convenience chain store has become an even more intensive site for this process and an ever more ubiquitous feature of food environments worldwide. And then there is the restaurant chain-store phenomenon.

Fast-food chain stores emerge during the first industrial dietary regime, in fact, but they morph into the ubiquitous phenomenon we recognize today only in the postwar era. Needless to say, they have become a central venue for the diffusion of nutrient-poor foods and beverages, but not the only one worthy of mention. Another form of restaurant operation, often referred to as the "full service" or "sit down" restaurant, has also taken on the consolidated chain-store corporate form, and, as recent research demonstrates, has become a potent vector for getting high-sugar, -fat and -salt foods and beverages into the contemporary mass diet. The concept of spatial colonization can be applied to both these forms of corporate restaurant operations as well, but in this case it has more to do with the colonization of suburban and urban real estate than with store shelf space, and these types of restaurant establishments' extraordinary success at dominating away-from-home eating options. Taken together, the astonishing success of these institutional forces has signalled a dramatic shift in eating from the domestic sphere to outside it, which in itself is a distinctive characteristic of postwar dietary regimes.

In different ways, the rise of these two institutional forces signals a dramatic loss of control over what we eat and of knowledge of culinary tasks – a veritable deskilling of kitchen work, as some have argued.[3] Of course, such a loss of control and knowledge begins in much earlier times, indeed, at the dawn of industrial capitalism when the rural folk of England were being moved off the land and into the cities to search for wage work in the then new factories. No longer able to produce what they ate, this swelling urban proletariat also found less time to prepare food. Both the inability to produce food and time pressures on culinary tasks are still with us. As a showcase for processed edible commodities par excellence, the modern supermarket of the postwar era played handmaiden to a food industry making products bought by a consuming public that was ever more willing to give up knowledge and control over the culinary realm in return for the perceived benefits of convenience. Lubricating this transition, of course, were billions of dollars in advertising expenditures.

On the other hand, the fast-food chain corporation streamlined and cheapened the eating-out experience. More than this, it nurtured a lifelong market by skilfully targeting children and youth empowered by new-found liberties and considerable disposable income. As meal getting moved out of the domestic realm into non-domestic food environments, the control over what was in our food and how it was prepared, both of which impinge on the health benefits food provides, was progressively diminished.

It remains to comment on the extent to which the state played a different role in the postwar dietary regime. The second food regime is argued by its proponents to be characterized by a notable state interventionism. This interventionism came in different forms. Prominent among them in the US case were public policies such as the PL 480 program, which helped deal with problematic grain surpluses by taking wheat off a glutted market and distributing it as food aid to the Third World, where "cheap American grain led to the displacement rather than the commodification of traditional foods."[4]

The full impact of this policy on diets in these recipient countries is an important issue that remains to be adequately researched and about which I can say little here.

The American state was also seen to be active in promoting the transformation of livestock production from handicraft methods practised along fairly extensive and low-intensity lines to intensive scientifically managed continuous production systems. This included policies encouraging the feedstock industry that was central to the developing meat complex, which had international dimensions.[5] This meat complex, which more and more subordinated nominally independent farm operators to highly concentrated processor-integrators,[6] had clear dietary impacts to the extent that it provided low-cost meat in high volumes to a burgeoning fast-food industry, and later a full-service restaurant industry, to which it became integrated in significant ways.

CHAPTER SIX

SPEEDING UP
THE MAKING OF FOOD

Those who can move faster through the various phases of capital circulation accrue higher profits than their competitors. Speed up nearly always pays off in higher profits.

—David Harvey, *The Enigma of Capital*[1]

Chicken breast cholesterol concentration was similar ... to those in feedlot bison and feedlot steers.

—D.C. Rule, K.S. Broughton, S.M. Shellito, and G. Maiorano, "Comparison of Muscle Fatty Acid Profiles and Cholesterol Concentrations of Bison, Beef Cattle, Elk and Chicken"[2]

I didn't claw my way up the food chain to end up eating vegetables.

—T-shirt slogan

IN APRIL OF 2010, I FOUND MYSELF on a tour of a large meat-packing plant that processes beef cattle. Having visited this plant some years before, I noted that it had been considerably modernized by its new owner, a global food-processing and trading giant. But these changes were not what stayed with me after the visit. What was hard to forget was the overwhelming and penetrating smell, noise, and dampness that goes with such a facility and the disturbing feeling I had being in close proximity to a mechanized process that was reducing large numbers of warm-blooded vibrant beings of another species to a series of edible components. And there was one other observation that stayed with me from this visit: the startling amount of whitish-yellow fat that covered the freshly skinned carcasses as they proceeded along the *dis*assembly line. The necks and most of the backs of the slaughtered cattle were thick with layers of fat, as were the loins and even the sides of their legs. I asked myself whether such fat-laden animals were typical of beef cattle in earlier times. I was to find out that a better understanding of why beef cattle are so heavy with fat provides important insights into the wider process of the degradation of the food we eat.

TURNOVER TIME AND OUR FOOD

No process bears the imprint of the current political economy of food more clearly than that which I call the speed-up in turnover time. In a thoroughly commoditized economy, the quicker that capital invested in one end of the productive process can be realized in a profitable sale at the other end, the more profitable will be the investment, all other things being equal.[3] As an example, an investment in broiler hen production by company A that can produce chickens ready for market in twelve weeks instead of the twenty-four weeks needed by company B will yield twice the level of profit over a given period, all other factors being equal. This is because company A can achieve twice the output over the twenty-four-week period, even if it makes exactly the same level of profit as company B on each chicken that is sold.[4] From the perspective of the producer and the food-processing entrepreneur, reducing the turnover time of capital invested, even by a small amount, seems like a very good idea. But is it a similar bargain from the perspective of the rest of us who are interested in a nutritional meal?

We have already examined how a cereal grain such as wheat was substantially altered by a technological process rooted in political-economic, rather than nutritional, considerations, and what this meant for the nutritional quality of the main product produced thereafter. We can consider other key components of the industrial diet, such as red meat, and ask, What makes red meat a nutritionally problematic food today? No doubt, most would respond that it is the high fat content, and they would be largely correct.[5] But it is less well

scientists and animal welfare advocates have made considerable progress in exposing the consequences of this system of agriculture for farmers, for rural communities and their environments, and for food safety as it affects the general public, as well as the deleterious effect it has had on the animals we eat.[23] What has received much less attention are the nutritional consequences of this form of intensive industrial agriculture favoured by agribusiness. This is where my own attention to CAFOs focuses, and in particular on the effects of this system on the quality of the fats we ingest when we eat meat produced by it. A few words on the science of fats may be useful beforehand.

In popular nutrition discussions, much focus has been given in recent years to the subject of fat. The overarching message has often been misconstrued as meaning that all fat is "bad" and should be avoided, period. Nutritionists have known for a very long time, of course, that the human organism requires this macronutrient for its survival. However, eating enough fat to be healthy is today just not an issue that most of us need to worry about, though eating enough of the "good" fats maybe is.

The important question these days is not whether we need fat to survive, but rather which fats are dangerous and which ones have beneficial effects. In other words, rather than being concerned only about the total amount of fat in our diet, we need to consider more carefully the relative amounts of the different dietary fats we consume.[24]

It is saturated fats and trans fatty acids, or trans fats, that have received the lion's share of concern recently. (I consider the negative impacts on health of these two kinds of food fats in more depth in Chapter 2.) Trans fats, at least the kinds that are dangerous for our health, are a product of the hydrogenation of vegetable oils. Saturated fats, which are fats that are solid at room temperature, are ingested by us principally when we consume animal products. Saturated fats are a problem for two reasons.

First, like other fats, saturated fats contain slightly more than twice the calories per gram than does protein or carbohydrates and, thus, when consumed excessively, are a potent contributor to overweight and obesity. In fact, in North America, fat consumption increased dramatically over the twentieth century. And although people have heeded warnings about the dangers of consuming too much red meat and have shifted to lower-fat meats, the substantial increase in the consumption of cheese and other high-fat dairy products undoubtedly has blunted the positive health benefits of this.

Second, they are linked to heart disease and certain types of cancer. The potent effects of diet are suggested by the fact that by the end of the twentieth century, Americans still had six times the level of coronary heart disease than the Japanese.[25] This was despite a decline in the disease in the United States in recent years.

CAFOs have an impact on the amount of saturated fats in the meat we eat. Studies that have compared steers raised in this system with steers and wild ruminants that are range-fed – that is, raised on the grasses they have evolved to eat – provide rather dramatic evidence of this. Total calories from fat in the muscular meat in these studies was about *twice* as high in feedlot steers as it was in range steers and wild ruminants.[26] If we consider the total fat found on the bodies of confinement-fed beef cattle, the comparison is even more dramatic. Indeed, wild ruminants have been estimated to have about *one-seventh* the fat of confinement-fed cattle.[27] The amounts of fat I observed on the carcasses of beef cattle in the processing plant I visited are, therefore, far from what we might expect with animals raised on their natural diet of grass.

Raising the meat we eat within the CAFO system affects another dimension of the fat profile of meat that we should be aware of. I refer to the polyunsaturated fatty acids found in meat. Polyunsaturated fatty acids, or PUFA, are generally divided into two groups, the n-6 PUFA and the n-3 PUFA (also known as omega-6 and omega-3 polyunsaturated fats respectively). A considerable amount of research around the world has indicated that a lower dietary ratio of n-6 to n-3 PUFA is associated with a lower incidence of cardiovascular disorders and with other positive health outcomes. Indeed, Palaeolithic diets were thought to have a ratio of 1:1 in this regard. The ratio in Western diets today is thought to be more like 15:1.[28]

Studies from the early 1980s found that when the muscle meat of cattle that had spent their lives moving around range lands consuming what they have evolved to eat was compared with a sample from feedlot-raised cattle, the former were found to have less of all kinds of fats except for omega-3 fatty acids. The higher presence of the nutritionally desirable omega-3 fats was credited to the high levels of these fatty acids in the forage that range cattle consumed.[29]

When cattle were compared with such wild ruminants as antelope, deer, and elk, it was found that the wild ruminant meat had higher levels of polyunsaturated fatty acids than either range or feedlot steers. Nevertheless, in its lipids profile, the range steers had more in common with wild ruminants and their relatively higher levels of polyunsaturated fats than they did with corn-fed steers confined to the feedlot system.

Recent studies have been able to carry out a more sophisticated analysis of fatty acids in range-fed and feedlot-fed animals, and overall the results have tended to support the earlier research. Indeed, the differences in dietary regimes can have substantial impact on the ratio of n-6 to n-3 polyunsaturates, with one study of beef cattle showing a ratio of 1.3:8.6 for cattle raised on grass compared with cattle raised on conventional feed grains. The former ratio is much more in alignment with the ratio of polyunsaturated fats that we humans are thought to have had in our diets for most of our existence.[30]

Whether comparing the ratio of polyunsaturated fats to saturated fats or the ratio of the beneficial omega-3 polyunsaturated fats to other polyunsaturated fats, the evidence has pointed to the health benefits of consuming range-fed animals, whether they be bison, beef cattle, or elk, compared with those animals fed a corn-based diet via the feedlot system.[31]

BEYOND BEEF

The decline in red meat consumption has been made up, for the most part, by increases in the consumption of other kinds of meat. Americans eat almost two hundred pounds in total of red meat, poultry, and fish per capita annually,[32] most of it produced within the CAFO system. So the CAFO system is not confined to beef production; indeed, other kinds of animals we eat for meat are more fully integrated into a pure CAFO system than are beef cattle. Poultry is a case in point – and a significant issue given the swing away from red meats to white meat, and to chicken in particular.

Many people have shifted their meat consumption to the so-called white meats, including chicken, to avoid the negative health consequences of the higher levels of saturated fats that characterize red meats like beef, yet the feeding regime of industrial poultry producers has rarely come under scrutiny. Poultry raised in the industrial CAFO system – which accounts for just about all such meat consumed in developed countries and many developing countries as well – also carry large fat deposits by the time of slaughter. Anyone who has cooked a factory-farmed chicken, turkey, or duck in the oven cannot but be aware of the large quantities of liquid fat produced by the time the bird is cooked. When cooled, this fat will solidify, indicating that it consists largely of saturated fats. Depending upon how such poultry is cooked, it is possible for considerable amounts of these saturated fats to be consumed while eating this purportedly healthier meat.

However, even taking care to remove from poultry meat the skin and copious amounts of yellowish-white fat underneath it before cooking, we are not getting the nutritional benefits from the meat that we should be. Why is this so? It may surprise many to learn that the lipids profile of skinless breast meat of chicken raised in the feedlot confinement system with corn-based feeds compares unfavourably to that of grass-fed ruminant "red meat" animals such as bison and beef cattle in terms of its effects on our cardiovascular system. The authors of one study note that

> at the levels of fatty acids observed, results of the P/S [polyunsaturate versus saturate] and the n-6/n-3 comparisons suggest that the fatty acids ... of range bison, range cows and elk would have the most beneficial profile compared to either feedlot bison, feedlot steers, or chicken breast as it relates to cardioprotectiveness ... [Moreover], chicken breast cholesterol concentration was similar ... to those in feedlot bison and feedlot steers.[33]

In other words, poultry meat reflects some of the same nutritional dilemmas as red meat because it too is a product of the industrial feed complex and the CAFOs that produce it.

The effect of a grass-fed regime versus a confinement regime on fat profiles of meat is apparently also reflected in the lipid profiles of eggs produced by chickens raised under each of these regimes, perhaps not surprisingly. In a 2002 study comparing lipid profiles, free-range hens with access to grass produced eggs with three times the omega-3 fatty acids than hens raised on conventional feeds in a confinement system.[34]

The impact of using the confinement system for raising the food we eat goes beyond the fat profiles of the end products, and so it makes sense to examine how confinement agriculture is affecting other areas of nutrition as well.

CONFINEMENT AGRICULTURE
AND THE DECLINE OF VITAMINS AND MINERALS

Animals such as beef cattle and pigs raised for meat were not, of course, always subject to a confinement regime. It is only in the last few decades that this system has become well established, and for animals such as swine, a complete confinement regime has become the norm. As this occurs, animals are blocked from access to forage and soil, which were traditional sources of nutrients for pigs, for instance.[35] As might be expected, after swine have spent some time under the confinement regime, nutrient deficiencies were noticed, particularly deficiencies of vitamin E and selenium, which have been shown to be rectified when animals were raised on pasture.[36] Confinement-raised animals require supplements in their feed to address the nutritional deficiencies created by the confinement system itself.

The shift to confinement systems of egg production is also fairly recent. For example, still by the mid-1950s, almost half of the chickens raised for egg production on farms in England and Wales were raised on a free-range basis. However, less than twenty years later, 95 percent were raised within a confinement system, and principally the battery system, where birds are confined to cages.[37] Early studies examining the nutritional differences of eggs produced under various management systems indicated relatively few variances, with the important exceptions of some vitamins, notably B12 and folate, which were significantly higher in the eggs of free-range birds. Differences in some of the other vitamins were not evident likely because feeds of confinement-raised hens were being enriched with vitamins.[38] More recent studies have noted that free-range hens allowed access to grass produced eggs with higher levels of vitamin E as well. In fact, their eggs had three times the levels of this vitamin compared with those of hens raised on conventional feed in confinement.[39]

MILK AND THE DOWNSIDE OF THE MORE-IS-BETTER APPROACH

There are other mechanisms, in addition to those considered above, whereby modern industrial stock-raising shortchanges eaters while enhancing the bottom line for producers and processors. Proponents of conventional modes of farming have recourse to numerous examples to make their case, and one of the most often used comes from the dairy industry. In the northern hemisphere, dairy breed diversity has given way to the dominance of one breed of cow, the Holstein-Friesian. As butter-fat content of milk became less desirable, and as a breed's capacity to output milk grew in importance, the Holstein-Friesian breed proved to be better able to meet market needs than other cattle bred for milk production, such as the Guernsey and Jersey Channel Islands breeds. Careful breeding over many years, along with new feed management regimes, has resulted in animals able to produce astounding quantities of milk – up to fourteen thousand pounds of milk per year per animal.

As it turns out, nature does not allow us to achieve these kinds of productivity gains without a cost. It has become apparent that the amount of vitamin E and the antioxidant beta carotene excreted by cows in their milk is independent of the amount of milk they produce. What this suggests is that as selective breeding, special feeds, and bovine growth hormone injections (allowed in the United States but banned in Canada and the European Union) boost the quantity of milk from each animal, the amount of this vitamin and antioxidant decline relatively per unit of output. The significance of this for human consumers is not well studied, but it is thought to be a significant factor for the health of the cow's immune system, and to reduce the ability of milk products to resist oxidation.[40] Cows with healthier immune systems have less incidence of problems such as mastitis or inflammation of the udder, and therefore less need for antibiotics, a benefit for the animal, the farmer, and, presumably, the human consumers of milk.

FOOD "BY THE POUND" VERSUS ITS NUTRITIVE VALUE

For long-standing historical reasons, humans the world over adopted and continue to employ food procurement practices that use weight and quantity as the main criteria for determining value. Cosmetic appearance as well has always had, and still has, a role in determining the value of food, perishable as much of it is. In the end, the industrial dietary regime has fully embraced valuations based on weight, volume, and cosmetic appearance, and we are all the poorer for it.

The CAFO system, together with genetic research oriented to creating animals designed for the system, represents the most profitable way to produce a pound of meat for the entities that control it. These entities are not, incidentally, usually the primary producers, but rather the corporate integrators that manage much of the on-farm decision making, and process and market the meat produced.[41] By speeding up the turnover time of capital employed in the production process, the CAFO system delivers a pound of meat at a price that cannot be matched. But this is only because the costs of this system are rarely accounted for. Several, but not all, of these costs have been well documented. Given that Americans alone are estimated to raise and kill almost 10 billion animals a year to eat their meat,[42] the issues concerning this segment of the food economy are fairly enormous.

Among the well-documented costs are those to the environment, which result from having far too many animals on a limited land base, without the possibilities for rational nutrient (manure) to recycle back into the soil, and therefore the very real dangers of contaminating local and regional water resources. For example, in South Carolina, where the hog industry has concentrated a large number of CAFOs, the extraordinary flooding that periodically occurs has caused the overflow of the massive manure reservoirs associated with the CAFOs, leading to very widespread contamination of rivers, lakes, and streams.[43]

Another consequence of the system is the violence it regularly does to the animals involved. Although the degree of violence varies from one operation to another, the system inherently reduces animals to nothing more than another production input in a large mechanized organization.[44] To expect animals to be respected and humanely cared for under this type of regime is unrealistic.

A further cost of the CAFO system that is becoming better understood is contamination by pathogenic bacteria. By favouring rapid growth with feeds that are not part of the natural diet of animals raised for meat, CAFOs have increased the risk of serious contamination by pathogenic bacteria such as E. coli. Raising cattle on feeds they were not designed to digest increases the presence of an acid-resistant strain of E. coli in their manure. This acid resistance is thought to allow the pathogenic bacteria to better survive in the acidic environment of the human gut, with devastating consequences for the human host.[45]

Beyond the dangers of pathogenic bacteria are serious hazards such as mad cow disease, or bovine spongiform encephalopathy (BSE), which is believed to have been spread by another inappropriate feeding practice driven by market pressures to reduce feed costs. In this case, inexpensive proteins derived from BSE-infected parts of dead cattle were mixed into cattle feed, unwittingly introducing a potent mechanism for spreading the deadly prion that is responsible for this fatal brain-wasting disease. In the country where this practice was carried out most widely – Britain – the spreading of BSE to other cattle and eventually to humans resulted in the virtual collapse of its beef cattle and dairy industries, the destruction of hundreds of thousands of animals, over one hundred human deaths, and an agrarian economy devastated for years. Since this disaster, authorities in Britain and other jurisdictions claim to have curbed such feeding practices.

Together with a highly concentrated slaughtering industry, the industrial CAFO system has created the conditions for widespread food safety crises that not only are tremendously costly when they occur but also inevitably have the potential to affect large numbers of human consumers.[46]

Finally, alongside these better-documented costs is the cost to human health that comes from the nutritionally degraded meat produced by this industrial food regime. For generations we have overvalued quantity and appearance, and dramatically undervalued – indeed largely overlooked – the real nutritive value of what we buy. As long as the lowest price per pound remains at the top of our value criteria for food, meat laden with harmful fats delivered by the CAFO system will be the order of the day.

Evidence shows that this is slowly beginning to change, at least for a small proportion of consumers who are willing to pay for meat from animals raised on grass, as nature designed them to be, and within smaller-scale operations that are less damaging to the environment and more humane to the animals involved. Animal protein produced in this manner is typically much more costly, however, than the CAFO-derived product, and inevitably so, one might argue, as long as the real costs of the CAFO system remain unaccounted for. Healthy, responsibly raised meat is certainly possible, then, but not likely ever at a price that makes it feasible to consume in the quantities presently eaten by many in developed countries. Rather, for most of us, its future may be more as a special adjunct to a diet in which vegetable proteins remain the day-to-day staple.

CHAPTER SEVEN

THE SIMPLIFICATION
OF WHOLE FOOD

AMONG THE FUNDAMENTAL processes degrading food once an industrial dietary regime becomes established is one I term "simplification." It is a process that takes various forms, some more visible than others. A visit to the supermarket will easily illustrate its more visible forms. Apples, potatoes, onions – produce many people buy every week – come in just a few predictable varieties, when the number of known varieties may extend into the hundreds or even thousands, as is the case with apples. However, this drastic varietal simplification is often essentially invisible, as with industrial agriculture's radical reduction of seed varieties of our major grain crops to a very few. This radical reduction in biodiversity has been flagged by numerous experts as a dangerous trend that is making humankind vulnerable to possible catastrophic events down the road. This is one dimension of the process of simplification, then – the dramatic reduction of the varietal bounty that nature presents us in the form of numerous varieties of edible vegetables, fruits, and grains.

There is another dimension to the simplification of our diets, and like the varietal decline in seed grains, this dimension is also largely invisible to most of us. It entails the reduction of more complex whole foods into simpler components of the original food, with dramatic loss of nutrients the frequent outcome.

I admit that it may be hard for many to buy my argument that our contemporary industrial dietary regime has entailed a dramatic simplification of the foods potentially available to us. Are not the offerings of any typical supermarket proof enough of the tremendous diversity in the modern food economy, compared with earlier times? To this challenge, I would reply that, as is so often the case, things are not always what they appear to be, and this is nowhere more true than in our food system.

FOOD PROCESSING: SIMPLIFICATION MADE INVISIBLE

My argument about simplification may seem implausible because of the invisibility of much of it, and because the details of what once existed have been lost with the passage of time. Regarding the invisibility of this process of simplification, we might profitably turn again to the story of wheat flour. The complexity of the wheat berry from a nutritional standpoint was no doubt modified to some degree by earlier processing technology, but not too much, in fact. In any case, without some kind of processing, the rock-hard wheat berry is unavailable to us as a food source. Stone grinding of wheat, leaving as it did the bran and germ of the seed in the resultant flour, retained much of the nutritional richness wheat had to offer. Technological change within the profit-driven context of nineteenth-century capitalism, however, with novel sifting and roller-milling technologies, brought consumers of flour – in Western countries, the broad mass of the population – a nutritionally deficient food. What had been real whole-wheat flour had been reduced and simplified for reasons having nothing to do with nutrition, and this whiter and seemingly cleaner end product was successfully marketed to a public wary of long-standing adulteration and happy to embrace a more long-lasting product. Other widely consumed edible commodities that might qualify as examples of this kind of nutritional simplification abound: white polished rice that has its nutrient-rich bran removed, processed apple juice made without the benefit of the nutrient-rich skin, heat-treated vegetable and fruit juices in general that have had nutrients destroyed by the pasteurization process used to kill bacteria and prolong storage life, and so on.

Defenders of present arrangements would likely reply that any initial deficiencies found in processed foods can and have been rectified, and perhaps point to flour as a case in point. Food companies *have* compensated for the nutritional deficiencies produced by modern milling technology, they might argue, through the enrichment of flour with synthetic vitamins, while still providing the convenience consumers desire.

Does this counter-argument to my simplification thesis hold up? Only partially, for the following reasons. This artificial "enrichment" by the milling industry does not actually resuscitate the original nutritional value of the whole grain. For one thing, it still has left the final product bereft of the fibre necessary for a healthy diet. True, whole-fibre breads are becoming more available, but only after many decades of bread being produced by wholly fibre-deficient flours. And still a great variety of baked goods consumed still are made from refined white flour.

On the other hand, more recent discoveries of micronutrients called phytochemicals have allowed for an even better appreciation of how modern flour-milling methods have degraded the nutritional value of grains. Phytochemicals have been found in a number of studies to be responsible for reduced risk of cardiovascular disease. In addition to this, recent studies in the lab have indicated they may have an important protective role in preventing the proliferation of cancer via a variety of physiologic mechanisms, including the mediating of hormones, the enhancement of the immune system, antioxidant activity, and facilitating substance transit through the digestive tract.[1] As has been the case with industrialized milling since the late nineteenth century, the removal of the bran and germ from the white starch-rich endosperm has also, it turns out, removed the great majority of the valuable phytochemicals from the grain and thereby greatly diminished its antioxidative potential as a human food. It is also believed that some of the phytochemicals that are particularly plentiful in grain are not as available in fruit and vegetables.[2]

The relatively impoverished phytochemical content of the endosperm of the wheat that is used to make standard white flour, compared with the bran and the germ, is illustrated by Figure 7.1.

Simplification of the kind illustrated in Figure 7.1 is a simplification of the plentiful nutrients in whole foods due to processing technology that has been shaped by market-driven incentives. Historically, this has been done to facilitate durability and reduce spoilage, thereby reducing costs to processors and distributors. But there is another kind of simplification that is integral to industrial dietary regimes: varietal simplification. This is the radical reduction in the biological diversity of foods available to us more generally, to a relatively few varieties whose genetic traits are favoured by those who control the industrial food system. Paradoxically, this process of simplification

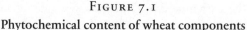

FIGURE 7.1
Phytochemical content of wheat components

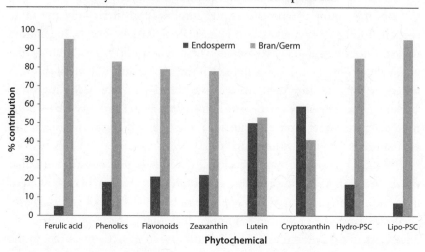

SOURCE: Adapted from Kafui Kwami Adom, Mark Sorrells, and Rui Hai Liu, "Phytochemicals and Antioxidant Activity of Milled Fractions of Different Wheat Varieties," *Journal of Agricultural Food Chemistry* 53, 6 (2005): 2302.

has been made possible by ever more complex techniques and technologies. We are starting to learn more about the downside of this other dimension of the process of simplification as it has affected vegetables and fruits. Let's take a closer look at how the loss of genetic diversity first occurred in agriculture.

AGRICULTURE AND VARIETAL SIMPLIFICATION

Some of the same criteria dictating simplification in the cereal industry, such as the need for increased durability so that produce could withstand prolonged shipping and storage times, have been at work in dictating fruit and vegetable variety selection. However, different criteria also came to bear. For example, the mechanization of tomato harvesting played a role in eliminating tomato varieties that could not withstand the demands of machine harvesters. Far from being some inevitable development with the progress of industrialization, the move to machine harvesting has its roots in forces that are eminently social and political.

William Friedland, Amy Barton, and Robert Thomas demonstrated in their classic study of California agriculture almost three decades ago that the mechanization of crops such as tomatoes and lettuce was impelled by certain developments, including growing political opposition to the Bracero Program that brought cheap Mexican labour into the state. Other significant factors were the growers' resistance to unionization of the agricultural labour force, and legislation that attempted to curb some of the most exploitive labour practices in agriculture. Added to this was the growers' very slim manoeuvrability over price because of the oligopoly control over processing and canning exercised by a few firms.

In the case of tomatoes that were grown for processing in California, production went from hand harvesting to almost completely mechanical harvesting during the 1960s. A key to the success of this transition for the growers was the development of a new tomato variety that could withstand the rigours of mechanical harvesting. In this regard, we see the state, in the form of the Davis campus of the University of California, playing a pivotal role in conducting the research necessary to develop the new plant variety, and also the experiments necessary to perfect harvesting machinery.[3] The state, therefore, has at times been a crucial handmaiden in the simplification processes that have transformed food environments to enhance the profitability of corporate food production and processing. And the dictates of mechanical harvesting, which typically has its roots in the political-economic realities of agricultural labour markets, play a role in determining the narrowing of plant varieties with other key fruit and vegetable species as well.

There are few fruits and vegetables that have seen a reduction in their diversity in our food system as radical as the potato (*Solanum tuberosum*). A food that was widely cultivated by the Andean highland peoples of South America had tremendous variation in its place of origin because of the widely varying ecology of numerous intermontane valleys. In fact, it has been argued that the potato has the greatest amount of biodiversity of any major food crop,[4] and thousands of varieties are believed to exist.

This genetic richness is today largely denied to most people. A major factor underlying this reality has been the rise of the fast-food industry and its embracing of the frozen french fry. An Idaho food-processing entrepreneur named J.R. Simplot has been given credit for pioneering the development of the frozen french fry product. It was a product that could be baked but which really had taste appeal only when deep-fried. Indeed, I can recall my mother serving baked frozen french fries when I was a child, and although they were a bit of a novelty and a welcome break from the monotony of mashed potatoes, they simply were not that appetizing. Deep-frying them helped their taste but was a time-consuming and costly affair, and never really caught on in a big way in the family kitchen.

On the other hand, deep-frying was something that fast-food outlets could readily do. In fact, the early entrepreneurial impetus behind the McDonald's fast-food chain, Ray Kroc, clearly saw the frozen french fry as central to the appeal of his burgeoning restaurant chain.[5] Why was the deep-fried frozen potato so warmly embraced by the developing fast-food industry? Put simply, it was cheap to buy and immensely profitable to sell. In his investigation of the food industry, Eric Schlosser found that fast-food companies bought frozen french fries from processors for about thirty cents a pound and resold them after deep-frying for about six dollars a pound. For their part, farmers received a few cents a pound for the potatoes they shipped to the processors.[6]

From the point of view of genetic diversity, however, the fast-food industry has been a disaster. Only very few varieties, among them the Russet Burbank and the Netted Gem, are viewed as desirable by the few multinational food processors – principally McCain Foods and Simplot – that now dominate the industry in North America and increasingly globally. And as people have come to embrace fast food, they also embrace the frozen french fried potato, instead of the greater diversity of potato varieties available as fresh product. We need to ask what this drastic reduction in genetic diversity among potatoes presently consumed has meant from a nutritional perspective. Are there real nutritional benefits of having a cornucopia of varieties available for our dinner plates? To answer this question, I turn to another popular food, the domestic apple, and new research suggesting some surprising answers to these important questions.

Not Just Any Apple a Day Keeps the Doctor Away

Isn't one apple just as good as another in terms of the health benefits they confer? I do have sympathy for the nutritionists' argument that getting people to eat any fruits and vegetables at all instead of myriad unhealthy edible products presently being consumed is a major victory. This is particularly true for North American children and adolescents: recent surveys reveal that their fruit and vegetable consumption is wholly inadequate.[7] This fact was reinforced by my own experience with recent fieldwork examining high school food environments in my home province, Ontario. I was stunned to find that in several of the high school cafeterias I studied, each serving several hundred students a day, only three to five pieces of fruit *in total* each day were being purchased. When cookies, brownies, muffins, or cakes were options, fresh fruit was generally shunned as a snack option by just about everyone.[8] However, as efforts to turn this sad situation around gain momentum (see Chapter 13), we need to give more scrutiny to the fruits (and vegetables and grains) themselves that are seen as healthy alternatives.

It was research at a federal government agricultural lab linked to my university that strongly suggested that one apple is not, in fact, as good as another. And if that is so for apples, might it not be true for many other fruits and vegetables that have been genetically "improved" by those who organize our food system? The problem, as we have seen, is that the "improvers" had a number of goals in mind in selecting varieties for the marketplace, but the nutritional value of the variety selected was almost certainly not one of them.

A few years ago, I came across a newspaper article mentioning research about nutrient differences in commonly available varieties of the everyday apple, *Malus domestica*. Upon rediscovering the article in my files, I noted that the lead researcher was stationed practically next door. I resolved to pay him a visit. As it happens, the evidence of considerable variance in the nutritional benefit from one apple variety to another came to light by fortuitous means.

Comparing the nutritional content of fruits coming from divergent geographical areas with differing soils, climates, and agricultural practices is problematic: What differences are produced by the environment rather than being a result of the varietal characteristics alone? Dr. Rong Tsao, who works for Agriculture Canada in a laboratory in Guelph, Ontario, was able to get around the problem through a bit of luck. He had a student whose family owned an orchard that happened to grow most of the varieties that have typically been found in our supermarkets, eight in all. Indeed, this number of varieties is greater than what has been available in most North American supermarkets over much of the last fifty years.

To keep the research manageable, he focused on a certain type of nutrient present in apples, but one that is thought to be significant for health: antioxidative phytochemicals. Antioxidants other than vitamins had been shown in laboratory research some twenty years ago to be linked to the prevention and reduction of cancer and cardiovascular diseases and to the stimulation of the immune system. Indeed, numerous studies have indicated that these particular antioxidants have a stronger ability than the antioxidant vitamins C and E and beta carotene to neutralize excess free radicals, which are linked to

FIGURE 7.2
Phytochemical differences of two apple varieties

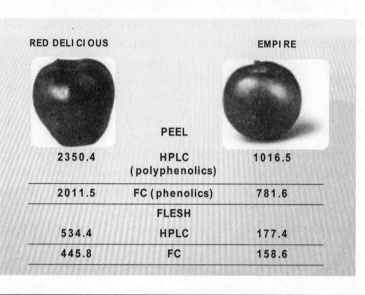

RED DELICIOUS		EMPIRE
	PEEL	
2350.4	HPLC (polyphenolics)	1016.5
2011.5	FC (phenolics)	781.6
	FLESH	
534.4	HPLC	177.4
445.8	FC	158.6

SOURCE: R. Tsao, "Polyphenolic Profiles in Eight Apple Cultivars Using High Performance Liquid Chromatography," *Journal of Agriculture and Food Chemistry* 51, 21 (2003): 6347-53.

major diseases such as cancer and to a series of degenerative diseases as well.[9] A second generation of research on phytochemicals is attempting to move from the lab to see what the benefits might actually be with living subjects. The hope is to eventually learn which of the thousands of such chemicals are beneficial and in what circumstances.[10]

Among the eight varieties included in Tsao's study, very significant differences in antioxidant levels were discovered (see Figure 7.2). At one end of the spectrum, the lowest levels of antioxidants are found in one of the most popular varieties planted in eastern Canada's apple orchards, the Empire. The most widely grown apple in Ontario, the McIntosh, did not fare much better. At the other end of the spectrum, an apple that is less popular today than some decades ago but still widely present in our food system, the Red Delicious, had the highest levels of antioxidants. The Red Delicious apple was discovered in 1875 as a chance seedling found growing on the farm of Jesse Hiatt in Peru, Iowa. It became favoured by retailers in the twentieth century for its renowned shelf life.[11] In Tsao's study, the Red Delicious variety was found to have levels of antioxidants in its skin (where most of these phytochemicals are found) that were almost 300 percent greater than those in the Empire variety. In declining production for many years, this variety is having somewhat of a renaissance as consumers turn increasingly to organically farmed fruits in North American markets.

Is this significant difference in nutritional value by variety a characteristic of the apple species alone? Logic would suggest that it is not, but this subject has yet to attract much research. Interestingly, there are a few indications of significant nutritional variation in other species, notably onions and raspberries. Research at Cornell University conducted by Dr. Rui Hai Liu and his associates along the same lines as the apple research noted above found that extracts from different varieties of onions had significantly dissimilar impacts on two types of cancer cell cultures. Those varieties with the highest phenolic and flavonoid content showed the highest antioxidant activity and were correlated with the highest levels of inhibition of cancer cell proliferation. Levels of antioxidants differed considerably among varieties, from 600 percent difference between the highest and lowest levels for phenolics to a remarkable 1,100 percent difference between the most potent and least potent varieties in the case of flavonoids, challenging the commonly held notion that one onion is much like another.[12] Generally, yellow and red varieties outperformed white varieties, and shallots scored very high as well.

Research on raspberries yielded results that echoed those on apples when it came to differences in certain tested phytochemicals and resultant antioxidative activity, with the darkest red varieties yielding the highest scores. In this case, however, the effects of extracts of each variety did not yield significantly different effects in terms of inhibiting proliferation of cancer cells in the lab; rather, all had a significant inhibitive effect. It was concluded that chemical components in the berry other than those tested likely were having the beneficial effects.[13]

The Cornell research also makes a strong case for the health benefits of phytochemicals found in whole food, principally fruit and vegetables, rather than ever more popular supplements. This research has indicated that there are thousands of phytochemicals in foods that vary in molecular size, polarity, and solubility. This, in turn, could affect how they are absorbed and distributed in different cells, tissues, and organs in the body. This balanced natural combination of phytochemicals is found only in whole fruits and vegetables, and the researchers note that this natural combination cannot simply be mimicked by dietary supplements.[14]

THE VARIETAL DEFICIT

Today, one is likely to find a few more varieties in supermarkets than was common a few decades ago, and organically grown produce as well, to supplement produce cultivated under the conventional pesticide regime. Nevertheless, it is remarkable how few varieties are present, whether it be of apples, potatoes, carrots, or tomatoes. The artful displays of produce abundance that is part of the supermarket's theatrical magic create the illusion of abundance of healthy food, but it is an abundance in quantitative terms mainly. Varietal abundance there is not.

Varietal differences have been all but eliminated by the supermarket chainstore system in the case of potatoes, and most other vegetables for that matter (e.g., carrots, celery, beets, onions) and, at most, a meagre *colour* diversity exists in a few cases. So instead of having a healthy choice of one of the thousands of known potato varieties, one is typically left to choose between red skinned, yellow flesh, and the standard white potato. With onions it is red, yellow, or white, for the most part. For tomatoes the choice does not extend much further, and any new choices are often more apparent than real, as with tomatoes with part of the vine left attached. Here standard tomato varieties, often grown hydroponically and having never had their roots in real soil, are left with part of the vine attached so as to give the impression of a more natural and different product.

What are key criteria dictating which varieties will qualify for approval in our food system? One overriding criterion for numerous vegetable crop varieties is their suitability for mechanical harvesting. In the case of tomatoes, California led the shift to mechanical tomato harvesting several decades ago, a shift that was made possible with the development of a few thick-skinned tomato varieties that would withstand mechanical harvesting.[15] Varietal diversity was the first casualty of this development. Since then, the same criterion has dictated the fate of other vegetable species, whether it be peas, where taller varieties fell out of fashion as shorter varieties suited to machine harvesters became the norm, or lima beans.

Given the highly globalized nature of the contemporary food system, one might expect much more diversity. The case of *Malus domestica*, the common apple, illustrates the reality, however. Instead of North American Granny Smith apples, many Granny Smith apples now come from Chile, South Africa, or New Zealand. Yet, though the provenance of the apple changes, typically by the season, the extremely limited varietal mix does not, at least not in any significant way. Globalization makes sense to merchants and retailers, as it provides relatively cheap fresh product from low-wage countries throughout the year, and it also helps keep prices they pay to local North American producers down. But although some food-industry pundits would have us believe otherwise, globalization has contributed very little, it would seem, to enriching the diversity of essential nutrients that we derive from fruits and vegetables. On that score, there is much more promise from the contemporary renewal of interest in locally produced food. For a basic truth of the food system is that an astounding varietal diversity of some of our commonly eaten fruits and vegetables was once ready at hand in local stores, country markets, and rural fall fairs.

The common apple is once again a case in point, at least for several regions in North America. Years ago, while undertaking fieldwork on farmer-food processor relationships in the Atlantic Canadian province of Nova Scotia, I came across historical documents enumerating more than 130 apple varieties grown in the relatively tiny geographic area of the Annapolis Valley by the early twentieth century. In 1916, the secretary of agriculture of the province published a report on fruit growing in Nova Scotia that provided a *partial* list of the varieties then grown there. I note these in Figure 7.3. The report notes that commercial growers would be advised to choose a relatively small subset of these varieties to plant, "so as to have the picking and marketing distributed over as wide a season as possible."[16] Here, we see already, early in the twentieth century, how strictly commercial criteria were beginning to dictate which varieties would be grown.

At the time of my research in this region (mid-1980s), one was lucky to find five varieties in Nova Scotia supermarkets. Elsewhere in Canada the situation was no different. In southern Ontario, a major Canadian fruit-growing area, some eighty-four varieties were reported to be cultivated by 1880.[17] Less than one-tenth of this number is available to us today. In fact, my own 2008 survey of six supermarkets selling in my home city of 120,000 people turned up an average of seven apple varieties. All stores had pretty much the same seven varieties as well. Those stores offering organic produce typically had a couple more varieties. I have visited supermarkets in numerous North American cities and have not found the situation to be much different. Better than it used to be, possibly, but far inferior to what was commonly available to rural populations at least a couple of generations ago. The remnants of this rural bounty in days past persist, of course, in many rural areas, along country roads, and on abandoned farmlands. Long-forgotten apple cultivars can still be found that provide an amazing spectrum of taste, colour, and perhaps unique nutritional benefits. Every fall I conduct a search for new varieties

FIGURE 7.3

Partial list of Nova Scotian apple varieties, ca. 1916

Alexander (Emperor)
Allington Pippin
Arabka
Arkansas Beauty
Baldwin
Baxter
Ben Davis
Bethel
Bietigheimer
Bismark
Bienheim Orange
  Pippin
Bottle Greening
Borkins
Bough Sweet
Bramley Seedling
Calkin Pippin
Canada Baldwin
Canada Red
Chenango Strawberry
Clayton
Clyde Beauty
Charles Ross
Colvert
Cooper Market
Cornish Aromatic
Cox Orange
Cranberry Pippin
Crimson Beauty
Duchess
Dudley
Danvers Sweet
Delicious
Early Harvest
Esopus Spitzenburg
Fall Pippin
Fallawater
Fameuse (Snow)
Gano
Gilliflower
Gideon

Gloria Mundi
Golden Pippin
Golden Russet
  (American)
Golden Russet (English)
Golden Sweet
Gravenstein
Grimes Golden
Haas (Fall Queen)
Honey Sweet (Winter
  Sweet Paradise)
Hubbardston
Hublon
Hunt Russet
Hurlbut
Ingram
Jacob Sweet
Jenneting
Jersey Sweet
Jewett Red
Jonathan
Jones
Kent Pippin
Keswick Codlin
Kitchener
King
Lady Finger
Lady Sweet
Late Strawberry
Longfield
Longworth
Louise (Princess Louise)
McIntosh
McMahon
Maiden Blush
Mann
Mother
Newton Pippin
  (N.Y. Pippin)
Nonpareil (Roxbury
  Russet)

Northern Spy
North West Greening
Ohio Pippin
Ontario
Orange (of New Jersey)
Patten Greening
Pewaukee
Peck Pleasant
Pine Apple
Porter Pippin
Pound Sweet
Pumpkin Sweet
Red Streak
Red Sweet Pippin
Red Russett
Ribston Pippin
Rolfe
Rome Beauty
Rose Red
Salome
Scarlet Pippin
Scott Winter
Seek-No-Further
  (Westfield)
Shackleford
Shiawasse
Smokehouse
Stark
Sutton Beauty
Swaar
Swazie
Sweet Greening
Tolman Sweet
Thompson
Twenty Ounce (Cayuga
  Red Streak)
Twenty Ounce Pippin
Vandevere (Newton
  Spitzenburg)
Victoria
Wagener

▶

◄ FIGURE 7.3

Wealthy	Winesap	Winter Pippin
Wellington	William's Favorite	Wolf River
Western Beauty	Wilson's Red (Red June)	Yellow Bellflower
White Apple	Winter Banana	(Bishop Pippin)
White Graft	Winter Bough	York Imperial

Source: Commissioner Public Works and Mines, "Fruit Growing in Nova Scotia," reprinted from *The Annual Report of the Secretary for Agriculture, Province of Nova Scotia for the Year 1916* (Halifax: Commissioner Public Works and Mines, 1917), 162-63.

that are now growing unattended along roadsides and on abandoned farms in my own part of southern Canada. I am amazed each year by the new discoveries that are to be had. Unfortunately, very few people in urban North America seem to be aware of this still existing diversity.

The real variation in *Malus domestica* is actually far more astounding than I had imagined. The 1916 report on fruit growing in Nova Scotia mentioned above suggests there were perhaps two thousand apple varieties known at that time. Frank Browning's highly informative book titled simply *Apples* quotes a Cornell University apple researcher who contends there are over six thousand apple varieties on record.[18] Other authorities use figures that are considerably higher. The comprehensive Brogdale website (www.brogdale. com) in the United Kingdom illustrates in its alphabetized listing more than eighty apple varieties whose names begin with the letter "A" alone. Whatever the true number, there is no doubt that the great majority of us are exposed to only an extremely small sample of known varieties of one of the most popular fruits in the world. One report notes that four varieties account for almost 70 percent of the continental market, while in Canada two-thirds of total apple production comprises three varieties – McIntosh, Red Delicious, and Spartan – and one-half of all apples grown in Canada in recent times were the McIntosh variety.[19]

This drastic varietal decline, and the lack of general knowledge about it, has several causes, one of which has to do with changes in popular culture that have come with urbanization. Browning, for example, argues that the apple was intimately woven into the history of European peoples going back several thousands of years and that this traditional relationship was transported to the New World, where it was revitalized and reshaped. He notes that in the United States, the public would experience the diversity of this species at regular apple tastings that were a mainstay of fall fairs that evolved out of an earlier agrarian economy and were driven by the priorities of that economy. In more recent times, fall fairs are driven by other priorities and now occur earlier, before most apples ripen. Our relationship with a foodstuff that was a rich part of the dietary tapestry is now largely broken. The highly urbanized population today is lured by ultimately much more powerfully marketed entertainment options than fall fairs, in any case.

Other forces have also transformed our relationship with the common apple, forces that have reduced this fruit to a bland, standardized commodity devoid of the nuanced flavours that marked the myriad varieties existing widely in North America even a few decades ago. Apple diversity, and we may conclude the diversity of fruits and vegetables commonly eaten in general, has been a victim of a globalized commodity system that prizes a few traits above all else. A report quoted by Browning suggests a few powerful factors influencing this result: "The emergence of a global trade in apples ... has skewed the search for new varieties to a few very limited criteria: hard, pretty fruit that both do well in storage and have enough shelf life to hold their crispness for a full week at normal room temperature."[20]

The global trade in fresh apples is itself dependent upon and a product of changes in food retailing over the course of the twentieth century. In that century, chain store forms of corporate organization took over much of the food retailing business, to be followed by the integration of the supermarket format, especially after the Second World War. As the retail sector became ever more concentrated and centralized, it proved efficient to swallow up the middle man function of the wholesaling distributors, a move that gave retailers more clout vis-à-vis the largest processors. These processors were themselves undergoing powerful bouts of corporate concentration.

Centralized distribution systems owned and operated by national retail chain-store companies favoured a bias toward uniform, standardized fruit and vegetables that could meet narrow cosmetic criteria and taste standards. Only the largest growers could consistently provide this, and they could offer retailers the added benefit of reduced administration costs because the latter could now deal with relatively fewer sellers of fruit and vegetables. The diverse small-farm community, settled as it was in myriad ecological niches across the northern United States and southern Canadian landscapes, was increasingly passed by in favour of what were in reality a relatively few corporate grower-packers in just a few geographical areas.

In North America, Washington State has come to be the favoured location above all others, and within it a few mega-grower-packers are especially dominant. Stemilt Growers is a prominent example of where the orchard industry is going. Once relatively modest apple growers in Wenatchee, Washington, the Mathison family that founded the firm decided in the 1960s that better gains were to be made by incorporating a packing operation into their orchard business. Over the years, their business expanded many times over, to the point at which it now incorporates a massive state-of-the-art packing plant that can customize the 12 million boxes of apples it ships to major corporate retail clients with exacting specifications regarding varieties, grades, and sizes. To feed its immense packing operations, the firm incorporates 350 other "associate growers" to ensure the supplies it needs.[21] In recent years, the company sought out investment opportunities abroad with the establishment of a Chilean subsidiary that exports apples and cherries from Chile. Estimated annual sales in 2010 of apples and other fruit are in the $200 million range.[22]

THE LOSS OF NUTRITIONAL TREASURES

The issue for those wishing to promote better nutritional outcomes, then, is somewhat complicated. The almost infinite variety of tastes and textures offered by *Malus domestica* has been dramatically reduced by the insertion of the apple into global commodity chains. The mundane supermarket offerings of this fruit in no way do justice to its rich potential as an attractive snack food in terms of taste and makes it all that more difficult to "sell" it to children and teens in particular. At the same time, new research into phytochemicals would suggest that the forces of simplification have left us with a much-reduced palette of micronutrients in our diet, not just in the case of apples but also with other commonly eaten fruits and vegetables. Future research may well indicate just how widespread this nutritional deficit truly is.

It is worthwhile bringing this issue back into our earlier discussion that attempted to situate our contemporary diets within the ample time frame of human evolution and the diets the human species evolved to eat. Prevailing diets in the long history of our species as hunting and gathering animals were without a doubt limited to the offerings of the particular ecological niches that scattered human populations found themselves in at any particular time. Nevertheless, we can imagine that, even so, the diversity of varieties within species eaten, not to mention the diversity of foodstuffs among species of plants and animals, was several orders of magnitude greater than the diets of even the most economically advantaged humans today. With this diversity came notable and potent nutritional benefits, including an impressive array of those very numerous phytochemicals that seem to play, in their yet-little-understood combinations and interactions, a rather pivotal role in protecting us from the cardiovascular disease and cancers that devastate human populations in the developed world at present.

The simplification of food environments, albeit within the overarching context of complex globally orchestrated networks of highly centralized transnational firms, is one critical dimension of what I have termed the "phenomenon of nutritional degradation." There is an even more basic level of the degradation of diets, of course. It is one that encompasses the glaring social reality that today, for substantial segments of the population, the varietal impoverishment of fruits and vegetable varieties is dwarfed by the fact that they are eating few fruits and vegetables of *any* kind, and those they do eat are often processed in ways that are particularly detrimental to health. In his investigation of the plight of the common apple, Browning quotes agricultural marketing specialist Desmond O'Rourke, who sums up the present-day situation rather well. He notes that apple consumption has basically stagnated, and that in contemporary food environments,

> potato chips ... [are] one of the key competitors to apples ... The real competition will not be so much between different kinds of fruits or different states but between the world supply of snack foods and the world supply of fruit ... The people we're really up against are Frito Lay, Coke, and Pepsi, the mega marketers of snacks.[23]

O'Rourke could have added a few other global snack food corporations to his list and also recognized that Frito Lay and Pepsi are one and the same corporation, making them an even stronger adversary than he imagines.

CHAPTER EIGHT

ADULTERATION AND THE RISE
OF PSEUDO FOODS

Used tea leaves were boiled with copperas (ferrous sulphate) and sheep's dung, then coloured with prussian blue (ferric ferrocyanide), verdigris (basic copper acetate), logwood, tannin or carbon black, before being resold.

> —Noel Coley, "The Fight against Food
> Adulteration"[1]

[With] countless new foods ... sugar, fat and salt are either loaded onto a core ingredient (such as meat, vegetable, potato, or bread), layered on top of it, or both.

> —David Kessler, *The End of Overeating*[2]

I N MANY OF THE FOOD ENVIRONMENTS we encounter on a day-to-day basis, it is becoming difficult to find whole foods in anything like their natural form. Healthy nuts are rendered unhealthy by prodigious amounts of added salt and sweet "honey" glazes. Yoghurt is laced with copious amounts of sugar or high-fructose corn syrup sweetener, typically the equivalent of seven teaspoons of sugar in a small serving size. Even plain oatmeal, a basic food that nourished generations of Scots and Irish in the hard times of centuries past, is now often packaged with surprising amounts of sugar and salt. What is happening, and how do we account for it?

The evolving story of the degradation of our food environments in industrial dietary regimes would be incomplete without examining one other "master process." In addition to the simplification of food environments and the speed-up in the complex mechanisms for producing food, we must add a further process that has become the *sine qua non* of the manufactured edible products that constitute the industrial diet. I refer to this as the process of macro-adulteration and examine how this process is different from the age-old practices of adulteration. As with the processes of speed-up and simplification, macro-adulteration is one that very much reflects the fundamental pressures of a market-driven, rather than nutrition-driven, food economy.

The edible products made possible by macro-adulterants have benefits to retailers, processors, and consumers. But they also have very significant costs, costs that are principally borne by the consuming public. The cost is chiefly to health. Three key macro-adulterants underlie the American diet: sweeteners, fats (primarily trans fats), and salt. In Chapter 2, I considered the health impacts of excess amounts of these in our diet. Now let's consider the adulteration of food in a historical context and explore what makes the current practices of adulteration qualitatively different from adulteration in times past – and whether the nutrient-poor edible commodities that saturate the American diet should be designated as pseudo foods. We'll also explore the importance of neurological factors in explaining the extensive use of macro-adulterants by the food manufacturers.

FOOD ADULTERATION IN HISTORY

The first thing to understand about the use of the term "adulteration" is that, as a social construct, its meaning has changed as society has changed. The history of adulteration of foods and beverages reaches back into antiquity. Derived from the Latin word *adulterare,* meaning to pollute or corrupt, the act of adulterating food was usually undertaken so as to cheapen the cost of producing a finished product, or to enhance its appearance, especially if the ingredients were inferior or spoiled in some way. Romans worried about the adulteration of wines, as did the Greeks, whereas the early Britons faced adulterations in their allotments of bread. Early references to food adulteration are found in the English Assize of Bread, dating back to about the year 1200, during the reign of King John. This statute was initially concerned with the quantity of bread that bakers were obliged to offer for sale.[3] Later legislation on adulteration in England also had an economic orientation in that it sought to prevent the seller from defrauding the government of taxes by scrimping on the quantities of flour in bread, and so on. Only later in the nineteenth century did health concerns become paramount and legislation come forward to begin to rectify the situation.

The early-nineteenth-century work of a German chemist by the name of Frederick Accum, who had migrated to England, and later in the century the efforts of a physician named Arthur Hill Hassall did much to change a situation in which the adulteration of foods and beverages was the rule rather than the exception. The meticulous research of Hassall in particular and its publication in the medical weekly *The Lancet,* edited by his colleague, surgeon Thomas Wakley, served to establish the wide prevalence of poisonous adulterants in the food of Londoners in the mid-nineteenth century. In fact, in a few short years after 1850, Hassall examined some three thousand samples of food and found that 65 percent of them were adulterated. His work also exposed manufacturers and merchants responsible for the sale of the adulterated foodstuffs, putting particular blame on the food manufacturers because special manufacturing methods and machinery were often necessary to successfully carry out the adulteration that Hassall's work exposed. As the historian Noel Coley notes,

> Hassall analysed the samples first with a microscope, and then with chemical tests as necessary. Before Hassall's time the microscope had been ignored as an analytical tool, but it proved invaluable for identifying foreign vegetable matter, living or dead insects, minute traces of adulterants, and crystals of foreign organic matter for which no chemical tests were available ...
>
> The microscope allowed him to estimate the amounts of adulterants present by counting the particles of foreign bodies, even when there were only traces. In one sample of mustard, for example, he estimated that there was one part of turmeric powder in 547 parts of mustard. He used chemical analysis to identify alum in bread, and iron, lead and mercury compounds in cayenne pepper, copper salts in bottled fruits and pickles, or Venetian red (iron oxide Fe_2O_3) in sauces, potted meats and fish.[4]

Then, as today, adulteration was typically a method manufacturers used to market inferior commodities to an unsuspecting public. The case of tea is instructive:

> By this time tea and coffee drinking had become popular in England but, being imported, both were expensive and as the fashion spread cheaper varieties were needed for sale to the masses. Many of these were not genuine tea and coffee but were made to look like the real thing by chemical treatment. Spent tea leaves and coffee grounds could be bought for a few pence per pound from London hotels and coffee shops. The used tea leaves were boiled with copperas (ferrous sulphate) and sheep's dung, then coloured with prussian blue (ferric ferrocyanide), verdigris (basic copper acetate), logwood, tannin or carbon black, before being resold. Some varieties of cheap teas contained or were made entirely from the dried leaves of other plants.[5]

Hassall used a threefold categorization to classify the kinds of adulterants in food then existing. The first category of adulterant was substances generally thought to be harmless that were added to food to reduce its cost and increase profitability for the vendor. This included chicory and baked horse liver, which were added to (relatively expensive) coffee, and flour, which was added to mustard powder, ground pepper, and ginger, for example. A second category of adulterant was substances that were largely indigestible but which were not considered to be acutely toxic. This included sawdust, brick dust, and bone ash. The third category was adulterants believed to be toxic for humans, including lead, arsenic, sulphuric acid, and mercury.[6]

Hassall's research helped push forward some of the first legislation in England, in 1860, to curb the most egregious cases of food adulteration, with later improvements to this legislation spurred by his work in the 1870s and afterward. The ebb and flow of politics, and the lobbying of commercial interests, affected the nature of legislation over time, and the latter's influence was seen in the revision of the Sale of Food and Drugs Act of 1875, by which the term "adulteration" was expunged from the legislation altogether.[7]

In Canada, the Inland Revenue Act of 1875 became the authoritative legislation dealing with the adulteration of food, beverages, and drugs, and it interpreted adulteration to mean "all articles of food with which was included any deleterious ingredients or any material of less value than is understood by the name."[8]

American concerns about adulteration through much of the nineteenth century reflected a preoccupation with the then rampant use of adulterants in various medicinal products. Food adulteration became a cause of public concern from time to time, as with the scandal over distillery "swill milk" in New York City. Distilleries there kept dairy herds in confined quarters and fed them the waste from the grain fermentation process. In the 1830s, a social reformer by the name of Robert Hartley campaigned against the "impure and unhealthy" nature of this milk produced by diseased animals eating an artificial diet, milk that was largely consumed by the poor of the city. The New York Academy of Medicine took up the cause as well, blaming the swill milk for the high infant mortality in the city, but failed to seriously address the issue, though a crusading journalist helped raise the ire of the public. In the end, corruption at the municipal level blocked changes until reformers successfully lobbied the state legislature to pass laws to deter the distillery practices and other standard efforts to adulterate milk for personal profit.[9]

Public agitation by women's organizations and consumer groups had been building in the closing years of the nineteenth century. They were responding to the growing evidence of widespread adulteration and other abuses by the increasingly monopolistic purveyors of foods and drugs. Despite this pressure, the vested interests benefiting from the existing situation could count on sympathetic politicians to block reform legislation time and again. Toward century's end, there emerged a catalyst for change, in the form of Harvey Washington Wiley. He was a physician and chemist working in the federal Department of Agriculture who was able to bring together the various forces in society agitating for "pure food" legislation into an effective pressure group on government. Nevertheless, it took a remarkable event, the 1906 publication of Upton Sinclair's *The Jungle,* a disturbing indictment of the Chicago meat-packing industry, to finally tip the balance in favour of reform legislation. In the words of James Harvey Young, in his chronicle of the passing of the landmark pure food legislation of that era, "[Sinclair's] few pages describing the filthy conditions in which the nation's meat supply was prepared turned the public's stomach, cut sales in half, angered President Theodore Roosevelt, and pushed through the Congress both a meat-inspection bill and the food and drug law."[10] The Pure Food and Drugs Act of 1906 gave a much more rigorous definition of adulteration than had ever existed in the United States. Food, the act stated, could be found to be adulterated in six basic ways. Young summed these up as the addition of any substance that reduced or injuriously affected the food's quality or strength; the substitution in whole or in part of any "valuable constituent"; and the concealment of damage or inferiority through mixing, coloring, powdering, coating, or staining. Further, in one of its most important and contested provisions, the law declared a food adulterated "if it contain any added poisonous or other added deleterious ingredient which may render such article injurious to health."

Also defined as adulterated food were food substances that consisted "in whole or in part of a filthy, decomposed, or putrid animal or vegetable substance, or any portion of an animal unfit for food, whether manufactured or not, or if it ... [was] the product of a diseased animal, or one that has died otherwise than by slaughter."[11]

It is the legislation's statement that food could be considered adulterated "if it contain any ... added deleterious ingredient which may render such article injurious to health" that is closest to the concept of macro-adulteration, the process that best describes adulteration in the modern food system.

ADULTERATION TODAY:
CONTEMPORARY WAYS TO DEGRADE DIETS

The issue of adulteration of whole foods was a serious issue in earlier times. Present governments regularly proclaim that our food system produces safe and healthy foods, but is that truly the case? Is adulteration a thing of our unregulated past? Much of the old-style adulteration has been dealt with by regulatory measures, including penalties to those who transgress, brought in by governments over the last one hundred years. Old-style adulteration still exists, of course. It may take the relatively innocuous form of the retailer selling water-logged ground beef, or chicken meat injected with a saline solution, in order to gain extra profits from a commodity sold by the pound. With the globalization of markets in the neo-liberal era we now live in, however, it may take on more sinister forms. A notable example came to light by 2008 and involved the widespread adulteration practices by Chinese food processors who were lacing dairy products and pet foods with the chemical melamine. In the case of dairy products, this was done to boost the apparent protein content of watered-down milk products. The adulteration of infant formula in this way led to the hospitalization of some fifty thousand infants in China and several deaths, while the melamine in pet foods led to an epidemic of illness and deaths of dogs and cats in the United States. Because of the globalization of our food system, this adulteration had effects far beyond China, contaminating food environments in Southeast Asia, the United States, and elsewhere.[12]

There is another form of adulteration, however, that I believe is of more concern to the majority of people, particularly in the more economically developed countries. Manufacturers *do* carry out a form of adulteration of foods and beverages, although rarely with acutely toxic poisons as they once did. It is done at a massive scale and affects very large sectors of the population, to the point that few of us are unaffected. This adulteration has serious and widespread health consequences and deserves much more attention than it receives. The adulterants, which I call macro-adulterants, for the most part are constituted by a few seemingly innocuous ingredients, principally sweeteners, fats, and salt. But in the quantities in which they are found in a broad array of processed edible commodities, these macro-adulterants add up in our diet, and their impact is hardly innocuous.

Adulteration is a matter that is inherently politically sensitive, not only because of the possibility of injury for the consumer but also because of the vested interests affected by attempts to curtail it. Coley notes that the chemist Accum, who pioneered work on food adulteration in England in the early nineteenth century, made powerful enemies when he chose to publish the names of merchants convicted by the courts of adulterating foods. Those enemies may have been involved in the authorities' bringing charges against him for allegedly damaging library books, and ending his career as an unofficial food policeman of the early nineteenth century.[13] I noted earlier how the cereal-milling interests in the United States had attacked those who questioned the nutritional quality of their products, including its adulteration with chemical bleaches. They were willing to pursue such matters all the way to the Supreme Court when they felt it necessary to protect their interests. The practices of macro-adulteration today are very likely to be as politically charged as was adulteration in times past.

WHY ARE THERE MACRO-ADULTERANTS?

Whole foods are regularly adulterated with sugar, fat, and salt in the process of manufacturing edible products for fairly basic reasons. They make food more durable, palatable, and easier to handle and therefore help boost sales and reduce costs to processors and retailers. There are other reasons, but these three explain a fair bit. The benefits, real and perceived, are not just for processors and retailers either, although they are the principal beneficiaries. Consumers also perceive benefits as well, and to suggest they do not would be unfair.

Consumers may perceive they get a deal by giving food more durability – rendering it more shelf-stable, in other words. Such products may be perceived to have added convenience in that they will last on the shelf for a considerable period without spoiling. Some macro-adulterants help create more palatable and easier-to-handle products, such as the hydrogenated oils used in peanut butter to produce a homogenized product that resists separation of the oil and solid matter, which would otherwise occur. One can argue that they make cheap edible commodities possible and thereby reduce cost-of-living expenses for many who choose to buy such products, whether they be processed soup, breakfast cereals, cookies and crackers, or fast-food fare.

Macro-adulterants reduce the costs to processors and retailers that would come with spoiled food and have made possible a plethora of edible commodities that have been sufficiently profitable to make some food-processing companies global giants in this sphere of the economy. The use of salt and sugar for their preservative qualities is nothing new, but in the era of industrial convenience foods, powerful economies of scale were to be had in concentrating production in large, highly automated factories. This, however, necessitated the transporting of product over long distances and the warehousing of product for periods that were not always easy to predict. The need for shelf-stable product that would not spoil for considerable periods was paramount in this system, in other words.

Another essential role of the macro-adulterants sugar, fat, and salt in the highly competitive profit-driven food industry is to enhance the desirability, or palatability, of the product. That food processors want to make their products appetizing to the broadest range of consumers is something that anyone can understand. However, with population-wide weight gains across societies happening so rapidly, serious questions are finally being asked about diets, and in particular, just what is in our (processed) food? We might also ask why it is that the foods the processing industry transforms needs so much of these macro-adulterants to make them palatable in the first place.

The snack food industry, for example, is known for its product claims along the lines of "You won't be able to eat just one!" In a culture of overblown advertising claims, it is almost remarkable that this kind would seem to have a good deal of truth to it. Few among us have not heard someone remark that is it hard not to keep eating snack product X or Y once the bag or box is open. Many of us might have made this remark ourselves. We are beginning to understand what food technologists and scientists must have understood for some time now: many edible products can be designed to have qualities that produce what quickly becomes an addictive eating be-haviour among those who consume them. I use the word "designed" here on purpose because what happens at the processing plant goes far beyond what nature provides us in what some are calling "whole foods." And it is not just snack products in a bag or box that have these qualities but a wide variety of processed edible commodities found in the supermarket, and also products served by restaurant chains of various kinds as well.

PSEUDO FOODS AND THE SUPERMARKET

My use of the term "adulteration" differs somewhat from its use by food and health authorities. For me, the process of macro-adulteration is intimately linked up with the appearance and rapid expansion of edible products that I have argued elsewhere can be usefully labelled as "pseudo foods."[14] This is a broad category of edible products that have sugar, fat, and salt as their main ingredients and which are generally considered by nutritional scientists to be nutrient-poor.

For some time, nutritionists and public health authorities had been warn-ing of the disturbing trend toward increased fast-food consumption and the popularity of what they, and indeed most of us, call "junk foods." Spurred by the growing evidence of population-wide weight gain in a host of developed countries over a relatively recent span of time, and the relative inability of medical and nutritional science to adequately account for it, some years ago I began explorations of a few key food environments in the first years of the new millennia. Given their salience in the lives of most people today, I chose to examine the supermarket chain store and school food environments.

Taking a new critical eye to the content of supermarkets, and the forms of marketing that have evolved there, I was impressed with both the prominence of what most of us understand as junk foods in the supermarket food en-vironment and the sheer volume of physical space they typically occupy there. Soft drinks and related beverages generally took up one entire aisle in the typical supermarket; in many cases, junk-food salty snacks (potato and corn chips, pretzels, and so on) and chocolate bars and related snacks also occu-pied an entire aisle of their own. Moreover, these junk foods were displayed prominently at a number of other places in the store (more on this in Chapters 10 and 11). The more time I spent examining supermarket products, the clearer it became to me that many products not conventionally thought of as junk foods were, from any reasonable nutritional standpoint, little better than those edible products we all recognize as junk foods. It seemed essential to capture this extra dimension of what was happening in the supermarket and elsewhere. To this end, I have argued that using the concept of pseudo foods is a useful way to appreciate the significance of this broad range of nutrient-poor edible products that saturates contemporary food environments.[15]

Why Pseudo Foods?

As Marion Nestle has masterfully illustrated in her 2002 book *Food Politics*, food is an especially politicized dimension of our contemporary world, even though many do not realize it is. Labelling foods, therefore, is to engage in a political act. When mainstream nutritional science argues that there are no inherently good or bad foods (presumably because even so-called junk foods provide energy to the body, if nothing else), it is taking a position that is arguably more political than scientific. I believe this position ultimately leads to much confusion over nutrition for most people and impedes progress to healthier eating. It may help to get back to basics.

The word "food" as a noun has its origins in the Old English word "fōda," which is of Germanic origin. My *Oxford Dictionary of English*, which is as good a source on the English language as any, defines food as "any nutritious substance that people or animals eat or drink or that plants absorb in order to maintain life and growth." Another popular source, this one digital, defines food as "anything eaten to satisfy appetite and to meet physiological needs for growth, to maintain all body processes, and to supply energy to maintain body temperature and activity."[16] The issue is, what do we call the growing mass of edible products that do little to "maintain life and growth" or "meet physiological needs for growth" and maintenance of "all body processes," but in reality, and in the quantities they are being consumed, do exactly the opposite? I refer to a growing proportion of edible products in contemporary food environments that are deleterious to the life-sustaining qualities of real food in that they degrade the health of the human organism, and presumably any other organism that consumes them in sufficient quantities, from dogs and cats to rats.[17]

It was in order to call attention to these nutrient-poor edible products, which are becoming ubiquitous in contemporary food environments, that I have argued for designating them as pseudo foods. Pseudo foods are generally processed edible commodities high in sweeteners and refined carbohydrates, fat, and salt and, other than the overabundance of calories they usually provide, are notably low in fibre and nutrients such as proteins, minerals and vitamins, and micronutrients (trace minerals and phytochemicals) that are essential for health. Pseudo foods are typically an important component in what has been termed in Britain the "high-fat, -salt, and -sugar (HFSS) foods," which are the subject of recent legislation that restricts advertising of them to children and youth.[18]

Edible products that qualify for the label "pseudo foods" would include many of the juice beverages sold today because of their high sweetener content and absence of the nutrients associated with products made from pure juices. Most of these products are made with less, often much less, than 25 percent pure juice. In its 2010 *Report of the Dietary Guidelines Advisory Committee on the Dietary Guidelines for Americans*, the US Department of Agriculture noted that per person "in 2008, almost two times more fruit drinks, cocktails, and ades (12.9 gallons per person) were available than fruit juice (6.9 gallons)" in the America food system.[19]

These compromised juice products constituted the *majority* of products in the juice category in all the Canadian supermarkets I studied.[20] I more recently surveyed numerous large supermarkets in cities in central Mexico and found that they typically do not have a single juice product that is 100 percent natural fruit juice. All were adulterated with added sweeteners.

Many of the frozen dairy products that are proliferating in supermarkets in recent years would be considered pseudo foods because of their high fat and sugar content and low levels of essential nutrients. Ice cream, the dominant frozen dairy product in supermarkets and one that now occupies much more shelf space than fluid milk, usually has about 50 percent of its calories coming from fat, although some varieties reach 70 percent.[21]

Pseudo foods include high-profile supermarket products such as presweetened breakfast cereals, which typically have four to five teaspoons of sugar per single serving size added to the nutrient-poor refined flours they are made from. When these products are added to the copious quantities of soft drink products, confectionaries, high-sugar and trans fat–laden baked goods, and salty snack products (mostly potato- and corn-chip products), which average 50 percent calories from fat,[22] we are dealing with a very substantial part of the modern supermarket food environment.

If these products were available only in the supermarket, it would be enough cause for concern, but, of course, this is not the case. In fact, they colonize other food environments, from video stores and gas station kiosks to hospitals, schools, and airports – and to a remarkably high degree. The process of what I term the "spatial colonization" of pseudo foods by large edible products manufacturers is a matter I deal with in Chapters 10 and 11.

In the schools, adulteration is present in various ways, but one in particular was driven home to me recently when I was asked to comment for a television program on a regional school board's proposal to ban chocolate milk. I thought I should get better informed about the product, and one of the things I discovered when I checked the sugar content of a popular chocolate milk product I knew to be in the schools in question was that it almost equalled the quantity of sugar in the same serving size of Coca-Cola. It was another example of a pseudo food.

I also knew from a survey I had done in these schools a few years earlier that students who drank milk invariably drank the chocolate milk product, and much less frequently plain white milk. The adulteration of milk, in this case, was almost certainly having a significant nutritional impact among many students, in the form of excessive calories.

The Rise of Addictive Foods?

Have edible products of various kinds been doctored to make them superpalatable and thereby encourage overeating? With new data showing an astounding 75 percent of adult Americans overweight, and Canadian, Australians, Britons, and others nationalities in rich countries not that far behind, and with evidence of weight gain and obesity becoming a global phenomenon, this is not a question that can be dismissed out of hand anymore. In the course of research on the emerging obesity epidemic embarked on just after the turn of the new millennium, I began exploring literature that examined how certain food additives affected our neurological system. Thanks in part to the valuable help of my research assistant, I was gaining insights into how food technologists and the companies that employ them use additives to enhance the taste and appetite appeal of foods. It was a fascinating – and disturbing – area to explore, but various constraints, including my own lack of training in certain scientific fields, limited progress, and the project was left aside. Fortunately, others have made significant contributions more recently to help us understand some widespread food industry practices.

Among the best-known recent efforts to expose the extensive use of what I would call "adulterants" is that of Eric Schlosser in his well-received book *Fast Food Nation: The Dark Side of the All-American Meal*. Notably, Schlosser alerts us to the fact that, in addition to the macro-adulterants I have mentioned, fast-food companies in particular rely on another group of food adulterants, chemical food additives, to make cheaply produced edible products palatable.

It was Schlosser who introduced the general public to the international flavour industry, companies such as International Flavors and Fragrances, Givaudan, Haarmann and Reimer, Takasago, Flavor Dynamics, Frutarom, and Elan Chemical, companies that "make processed food palatable."[23] As he eloquently argues, the chemical flavouring industry is quite capable of making, and typically is already marketing, chemical products that will faithfully imitate practically any flavour one is likely to find in whole foods, as well as imparting flavours such as smoke that in the past came from time-consuming cooking and curing methods.

The point of this industry, according to Schlosser, is to impart tastes to cheaply produced processed edible products so that they may successfully mimic more expensive whole foods. All consumers would like to imagine fresh strawberries being blended into the strawberry milkshakes they order, but fresh or even frozen strawberries are an expensive commodity. The taste they would impart can be had with infinitely less expensive but complex chemical additives, produced by the chemical flavouring industry. In Schlosser's words,

> A typical strawberry flavor, like the kind found in a Burger King strawberry milk shake, contains the following ingredients: amyl acetate, amyl butyrate, amyl valerate, anetol, anisyl formate, benzyl acetate, benzyl isobutyrate, butyric acid, cinnamyl isobutyrate, cinamyl valerate, cognac essential oil, diacetyl, dipropyl ketone, ethyl acetate, ethyl amylketone, ethyl butyrate, ethyl cinnamate, ethyl heptanoate, ethyl heptylate, ethyl lactate, ethyl methylphenylglycidate, ethyl nitrate, ethyl propionate, ethyl valerate, heliotropin, hydroxyphrenyl-2-butanone (10 percent solution in alcohol), α-ionone, isobutyl anthranilate, isobutyl butyrate, lemon essential oil, malton, 4-methylacetophenone, methuyl anthranilate, methyl benzoate, methyl cinamate, methyl heptinecaronate, methyl aphthyl ketone, methyl salicuylate, mint essential oil, neroli essential oil,

nerolin, neryl isobutyrate, orris butter, phenethyl alcohol, rose, rum ether, γ-undecalactone, vanillin, and solvent.[24]

These insights into the chemical-flavouring industry help us understand two things: why the fast-food industry is so very profitable (by keeping costs of raw materials down) and, importantly, how inexpensive processed commod-. ities can be made palatable to the human consumer. But there is more to this issue of palatability.

One of the most direct and credible responses to the question posed at the beginning of this section – just what is in our food? – has been given by David Kessler in his 2009 book, *The End of Overeating*.[25] In this remarkable work, Kessler does a masterful job of synthesizing a wide spectrum of relevant science that shows how what I argue are the main macro-adulterants – sugar, fat, and salt – plus the chemical-flavouring industry examined by Schlosser, play a key role in promoting excess eating of high-calorie processed foods. Here I am able to only summarize some of the key findings he presents; nevertheless, his arguments complement and extend very nicely my overall analysis.

The literature dealing with the factors that make certain foods highly palatable, or brings about, as one article frames it, the "craveability" or intense liking of certain foods, is not well developed.[26] Despite attempts to quantify the phenomenon, insights into the matter are few and scattered, and largely the preserve of industry insiders. Kessler's broad-ranging synthesis of insights from these very industry insiders and scientists concerned with biochemical and neurological processes governing food and behaviour helps fill this gap.

Kessler notes that animal experiments demonstrate the power of sugar and fat to stimulate appetite and motivate behaviour, and that there appears to be an optimal level, or "bliss point" for each macro-adulterant, at which these effects are most enhanced. Combining macro-adulterants, moreover, enhances the effect over and above what each might have alone. Rats fed their normal diet ate to a certain point and then curtailed their consumption, but when presented with food engineered with extra sugar and fat together, the animals began eating without restraint and become obese. Other experiments involved feeding rats with a "supermarket diet" of salami, chocolate chip cookies, sweetened condensed milk, bananas, milk chocolate, and peanut butter. Whereas rats retain their normal weight on their regular bland chow, on this "supermarket diet" they became obese. As Kessler observes, this research suggests that "the biological system that's designed to maintain energy balance can go awry when animals have easy access to a variety of foods that are high in sugar and fat."[27]

Foods that have the right combination of sugar, fat, and salt, Kessler points out, have a high hedonic value, giving us pleasure. He provides examples of edible processed products available in restaurants in North America, and increasingly globally, to illustrate:

> [With] countless new foods ... sugar, fat, and salt are either loaded onto a core ingredient (such as meat, vegetable, potato, or bread), layered on top of it, or both ... Potato skins [are] fried, which provides a substantial surface area for ... "fat pickup." Then some combination of bacon bits, sour cream, and cheese is added. The result is fat on fat on fat on fat, much of it loaded with salt.
>
> Buffalo wings start with the fatty parts of a chicken, which get deep-fried. Then they're served with creamy or sweet dipping sauce that's heavily salted. Usually they're par-fried at a production plant, then fried again at the restaurant, which essentially doubles the fat. That gives us sugar on salt on fat on fat on fat.[28]

Sugar and fat together have been found in experiments to be reinforcing in that they act to stimulate test animals to eat more than they would without these substances in their food. Animals in experiments were found to work much harder to access foods that have sugar and fat added. Scientists doing research on animals and eating note that rats will work almost as hard for sugar and fat-laden food as they would to access cocaine.[29]

According to Kessler, this experimental research points to the importance of cues, quantity, concentration, and variety. Cues are the locations and events associated with past consumption of palatable foods. The brain chemical believed to be involved in making these cues so potent in stimulating the desire for certain foods is dopamine. Distinct from the pleasure we receive from eating certain foods, dopamine is what motivates our behaviour and steers us toward food: "Cues associated with the pleasure response demand out attention, motivate our behaviour, and stimulate the urge we call 'wanting' ... With experience, the association between cues and food becomes even stronger ... we pursue the food more frequently, and the resulting pleasure leads us to repeat the behaviour. *A continuous cycle of cue-urge-reward is set in motion and eventually becomes a habit*" (emphasis added).[30]

Quantity becomes an issue with food that has a high hedonic value: evidence from animal studies, for example, indicates that animals are less likely to reach a point of satiety with such foods. The more there is available, the more that is eaten. As for concentration, laboratory animals have been found to consistently favour foods with higher levels of sugar and fat than those with lower levels, at least up to a certain point of concentration – the "bliss point."[31] The variety of sensory stimuli influences our desire to eat as well and plays a role in short-circuiting our body's balance mechanisms. In experiments, test animals fed only one kind of palatable food, such as chocolate, reached a point at which they seemed to become satiated with a taste and stopped eating the food. However, when also offered another food with high hedonic value, such as bananas, providing different taste stimuli, they continued to eat, ingesting even more food.

In the long hunting and gathering era of our Palaeolithic past, during which our genetic makeup was formed, diet was shaped by natural cycles: certain foods came available only at certain times of the year. With the advent of agriculture, diets became even less varied, or so experts on these matters have argued, at least for the vast majority of people. Up until very recent times, it was only the elite who benefited from a varied and abundant diet, and it was typically only they who became obese. Contrast this with the huge variety of energy-dense processed products available in today's supermarkets, together with their relative cheapness compared with actual necessities of life, at least in North America.

As Kessler observes, food processors have learned to use sensory variety to encourage greater consumption of a wide selection of edible products. Products are now frequently designed to have a variety of flavours and textures to achieve a highly palatable dynamic contrast. An example here might be a touch of cayenne pepper in sweetened chocolate, a highly palatable combination I was recently offered at a neighbour's party. And as Kessler argues, "The more potent and multi-sensory foods become, the greater the rewards they may offer and the more we learn to work for them."[32] I know I certainly went after my host for more of *those* chocolates, when I wouldn't have bothered with regular chocolate. The variety of sensory stimuli available in our food today, along with the extraordinary quantities of it that many can afford, is a phenomenon that is entirely novel in the history of human evolution and one that we are ill-equipped to cope with.

Sugar, fat, and salt act on our brain by "amping up," to use Kessler's phraseology, the neurons that are the basic cells of the brain. As he notes, it is the sense of taste above all that promotes the strongest emotional response in the brain. The neurons that are stimulated by taste are part of the opioid circuitry: "The 'opioids,' also known as endorphins, are chemicals produced in the brain that have rewarding effects similar to those of drugs such as morphine and heroin. Stimulating the opioid circuitry with food drives us to eat."[33] In addition to the pleasurable effects they provide, opioids are known to relieve pain and to calm us down and relieve stress. This is what we expect from our favourite "comfort foods," of course, and these comfort foods are typically products that are formulated with significant amounts of sugar, fat, and salt.

There is now evidence, argues Kessler, that the high levels of sugar, fat, and salt in the contemporary American diet act to essentially rewire the biological circuitry of our brains and thereby circumvent our natural ability to achieve energy balance, or homeostasis. New research supports the thesis of addictive foods and increases our understanding of the mechanisms by which they affect us.[34] The potential for an epidemic of overeating with food environments becoming saturated with products with high hedonic values is certainly there. For population-wide effects to become evident, however, other factors such as mass marketing also need to be taken into account, as well as the spatial colonization of food environments by companies producing such edible products.

CHAPTER NINE

THE SPATIAL COLONIZATION
OF THE INDUSTRIAL DIET

THE SUPERMARKET

If it's not in the face of customers, it can't sell well.

— retail food analyst[1]

To build pervasiveness of our products, we're putting ice-cold Coca-Cola classic and our other brands within reach, wherever you look: at the supermarket, the video store, the soccer field, the gas station – everywhere.

— Coca-Cola Company executive[2]

N UTRIENT-POOR PSEUDO FOODS have become ubiquitous in the present industrial dietary regime, and nutritional distortion has resulted. What were the enabling conditions established in an earlier era that allowed companies manufacturing nutrient-poor edible commodities to dramatically expand in the latter half of the twentieth century and, in the process, consolidate the industrial diet? A high degree of corporate concentration in certain sectors of the food business certainly undergirds the extraordinary power these firms have to colonize food environments with myriad pseudo foods notable for high levels of sugar, fat, and salt. The spatial colonization of food environments – and particularly the key institutional food environment of supermarket chain stores – by transnational snack food corporations has reached a point at which it inevitably endangers health by making what were once occasional treats into everyday eating and drinking experiences. We have yet to understand the full implications of this significant transformation of our food environment, much less figured out what to do about reversing the adverse effects this transformation has wrought on societies across the globe.

SPATIAL COLONIZATION

Spatial colonization is a concept designed to help us understand how certain realities of the contemporary food economy – differential profits, mass advertising, and corporate concentration and the market power it provides – come to affect the geography of food environments and the prominent role of nutrient-poor edible products within them. Ultimately, in the food business, if profits are to be realized, product must be sold. Intensive, incessant advertising has become a necessary investment for corporations marketing nutrient-poor edible products to maintain and expand their markets, but it is not sufficient alone. To translate manufactured demand into sales, it is necessary to secure the physical visibility and availability of the product within a particular food environment. The process of spatial colonization essentially refers to the power of food processors to place product in the most visible and effective selling spaces in a food environment. An industry spokesperson summed this process up concisely when commenting on the marketing of confectionery in supermarkets: "Confectionery sells confectionery – you must have a variety of products and you must have a variety of locations in your store. You should use a combination of feature and display for maximum impact ... If it's not in the face of customers, it can't sell well."[3]

Ensuring a product's physical visibility and availability can take different forms, depending upon the specific position of a food corporation within the wider food economy. In the case of fast-food corporations, for example, spatial colonization is more about securing desirable real estate in high-traffic urban and suburban locations, whether that is on city streets, in shopping malls, or in airports. In most recent times, these firms have seen opportunities open up that allow them to expand their reach into public sector–controlled spaces such as schools – from the primary level to the post-secondary level – and hospitals.[4]

For food and beverage manufacturers, on the other hand, product visibility has to be secured first and foremost in the supermarket food environment, although other marketing channels, including convenience store chains and vending machine sales in institutional settings are very important as well. In the telling words of a Coca-Cola Company executive, "To build pervasiveness of our products, we're putting ice-cold Coca-Cola classic and our other brands within reach, wherever you look: at the supermarket, the video store, the soccer field, the gas station – everywhere."[5]

In an earlier chapter I examined how the Coca-Cola Company really pioneered spatial colonization by following up on its early and hugely successful efforts at saturation advertising with a novel distribution system that decentralized production to independent entrepreneurs who were springing up to take advantage of advances in bottling technology. Availing itself of the capital and local knowledge of these entrepreneurs across the United States, Asa Candler's Coca-Cola Company was able to rapidly colonize early-twentieth-century food environments with its product in a way no one had yet managed.[6]

Before the process of spatial colonization could take its present-day effectiveness, however, it was necessary for certain structural conditions to evolve. These conditions are nothing less than a reflection, in the sphere of food, of the wider evolution of market processes in the late capitalist era within the most economically powerful countries.

THE STRUCTURAL BASIS OF SPATIAL COLONIZATION: CAPITAL CONCENTRATION AND CENTRALIZATION

The most fundamental of structural processes within the capitalist economic system that has enabled the generalization of the industrial diet was identified by classical political economists long ago, and remarked on by more recent authorities carrying on this tradition. This is the tendency for capital to become more concentrated and centralized over time. This tendency was given attention by the legendary Scottish economist Adam Smith, but it was most systematically argued later on by Karl Marx to be a basic law of capitalist economy. It is a process that entails successful firms' growing larger and larger via the process of capital accumulation. Beyond this, however, particular market advantages are to be had by swallowing up competitors and/or driving them out of business and thereby gaining the upper hand by controlling more and more of the market. This later process describes the centralization of capital.[7] The history of capitalism since Marx has proven the wisdom of his predictions on this score.

This process was impelled by the competitive struggle and aided considerably by the advent of the joint stock company, and by credit. It is a central irony of this economic system that although its ideologues espouse free enterprise and competition at every opportunity, the reality of business practice is that firms have historically jumped at the chance to restrict competition whenever possible and thereby gain the advantage.

This core tendency of the system had reached such proportions by the end of the nineteenth century, in the era of the great trusts and the "robber barons," that it provoked extraordinary reaction from disadvantaged sectors of society, especially the then numerous agrarian class. Ultimately, political elites, at least in the United States, realized that saving the system that benefited them most of all would require the passing of legislation to break up some of the most egregious examples of corporate monopoly and provide disincentive for it to reoccur.[8]

The food industry was not immune to this powerful concentration process, as we have seen with the example of flour milling. Milling entrepreneurs that had already accumulated considerable capital were later able to take advantage of new technological breakthroughs in the form of the roller-milling process that aided them in producing a more shelf-stable and consistent product. This in turn opened up opportunities for a few firms to transform their regional dominance into what became a commanding position at the national level. This was the case with the Pillsbury Flour Mills Company and Washburn Crosby and Company (later General Mills) of Minneapolis, for example. In the Canadian case, I noted a royal commission report documenting how a few milling firms had used mergers and buyouts of baking companies to centralize control over grain processing and maximize profits at the expense of consumers and smaller milling operations in the early decades of the twentieth century.

It can be economic crisis that proves to be the handmaiden for rapid centralization as well. In an earlier work I described this in the Canadian meat-packing industry, where in the Great Depression years of the 1930s J.S. McLean orchestrated the establishment of the meat-packing giant Canada Packers with the buyout and consolidation of several smaller distressed meat-packing firms.[9] This new firm came to dominate the meat-processing sector in Canada for decades thereafter.

TABLE 9.1
Major food and beverage market shares

Product	Company	Approximate % share US market
Ready-to-eat cereals	General Mills, Kellogg	60
Soup (wet)	Campbell	69
Salty snacks	Frito Lay (PepsiCo)	56
Carbonated beverages	Coca-Cola, PepsiCo	75
Cookies (packaged)	Nabisco (Kraft), Kellogg	50
Crackers (packaged)	Nabisco (Kraft), Kellogg	50
Candy	Mars, Hershey	75
Non-carbonated beverages	Coca-Cola, PepsiCo	75

SOURCE: James E. Tillotson, "The Mega-Brands That Rule Our Diet, Part 1," *Nutrition Today* 40, 6 (November/December 2005): 256.

Already by the turn of the twentieth century, some powerful joint stock companies in the North American food sector were looking toward consolidating their hold on regional markets and toward national market domination. Other upstart companies in relatively new product areas – carbonated soft drinks, ready-to-eat breakfast cereals, for example – were soon to achieve success in pushing aside competitive firms and surging toward market dominance. The extraordinary degree of market concentration in the US food industry can be seen from the data in Table 9.1.

BRANDING AND THE MASS MARKET

In the consolidation of the food industry, advertising has typically played a central role. The amassing of wealth by certain food companies, their takeover of rivals, and their centralization in a few hands of market control within various sectors of the food economy went hand in hand with the dramatic increase in the role of advertising. Creative and judicious use of advertising made rapid growth possible for Coca-Cola and Kellogg's, for example, and rapid growth allowed them to plough ever greater financial resources into advertising. The development of the mass print media, followed by radio, offered the possibility of consolidating a presence in much larger markets,

markets of a national dimension. This was the era of the emergence of the phenomenon of branding, then.

As we have seen with the pioneering example of the breakfast cereal industry, some manufacturers were learning that the way to dominate markets was through the development of brands, and the way to make a brand a powerful selling tool was to find creative ways to use the emerging forms of mass communication. This Kellogg did with his cornflake product, which at the time was just one of many cornflake products being peddled around the United States on a small scale by myriad food entrepreneurs. Marketing innovation was particularly important for the success of entrepreneurs who lacked access to considerable amounts of capital to push product through traditional retail channels. By offering consumers a free supply of his product for a year if they could get a local retailer to stock it, Kellogg used consumers as a force, rather than the power of an already consolidated and capital-rich company, to expand his production. Brand development plus marketing via mass communication, in some cases fuelled by infusions of capital from already highly concentrated and centralized corporate organizations, saw the early emergence and dominance of American food-processing giants in the first decades of the twentieth century.

Today, we live in a world of megabrands, and this includes the food economy. Developing a powerful brand is advantageous to food processors in many ways, of course. One of the most important is that it gives them clout in dealing with supermarket chain stores, which have become themselves very large and concentrated. From the perspective of nutrition and health, however, the result is much less salutary. The nutritional profile of many products with the biggest brand images often run counter to the basic nutritional guidelines advocated by health authorities. When it comes to the relative influence of megafood brands versus the influence of dietary guidelines promoted by governments, there is essentially no contest: the brands win hands down, as the authors of these very guidelines readily admit.[10] One observer of megafood brands has noted:

> Mega-brands, beyond their organoleptic attractions and functional benefits, also offer compelling associations, emotional and psychological product inducements, marketed by well-funded, highly professional organizations. The US Dietary Guidelines are long on lecturing what to eat, but short on telling how and limiting in their motivation.[11]

Had it not been for the calamitous event of the Great Depression, there is little doubt that a number of the firms that had established national brands in the food industry would have begun to aggressively globalize their products by the 1930s. As it happened, this development was largely delayed until after the Second World War. By that time, as Stephen Hymer remarked some forty years ago, the internationalization of the dominant national firms was paralleled and aided by the emergence of an international capital market:

> The multinational corporation's need for short-term loans and investment arising from the continuous inflow and outflow of money from all nations, never quite in balance, has encouraged international banking ... [And] its long-term financial requirements and excellent credit rating have broadened the demand for international capital mobility ... The development of the international capital market, in turn, gives multinational corporations increased access to the savings of many nations, enables larger undertakings to be formed, and fosters mergers and consolidations.[12]

DIFFERENTIAL PROFITS UNDERLIE MARKET POWER AND SPATIAL COLONIZATION

In the end, we must somehow explain why pseudo foods, or nutrient-poor edible commodities, have become so ubiquitous in contemporary food environments. How is it that products that have such negative nutritional characteristics now confront us at every turn? I believe that at the core of an explanation lies the fact that these commodities can be very lucrative, if the manufacturer is able to assert a monopoly or virtual monopoly on its production. The profitability of these kinds of edible products *is* a widely recognized and publicized fact, or so the trade journals of the food industry would strongly suggest. Manufacturers of these products, and retailers selling them, are able to receive better-than-average returns on them, something that alerts us to the existence of differential profits in this sector of the economy.

Differential profit is a concept that attempts to account for the fact that where foodstuffs are very highly commoditized, some food and beverage products attract higher returns, or profits, for their sellers than others. In a capitalist economy, profit and the rate at which it can be accumulated is the prime mover, the master compass that orients the flow of investment, whether it be in the food business or in any other sector. The rate of profit, or return on investment, plays a fundamental role in shaping the ways in which food environments are organized, in other words.

Generally, more highly processed foodstuffs – goods with more "value added" – have more attractive rates of return for retailers and processors. Foodstuffs that have undergone little or no transformation – for example, table potatoes, fluid milk, eggs, flour, and tomato paste, referred to in the food business as "commodity" products – typically have rather thin profit margins, and indeed some, like fluid milk, are often sold below cost by supermarkets as loss leaders primarily to attract customers to the store. On the other hand, products that have been created out of inexpensive, and often subsidized, raw commodities such as sugar, potatoes, wheat, and corn, with some processing and the addition of inexpensive chemical additives to create "value added," can be processed into very profitable branded commodities. Their success in the market will depend heavily on expensive advertising, however, and market control.

Reports in the trade journals of the food retail industry give an idea of the profitability of pseudo food–type products. *Canadian Grocer*, for example, reported that confectionery has grown to be one of the food retailer's largest categories in Canada, at $2 billion in sales annually. Sales have been growing at 5 percent a year. It is also a category that has consistently had among the highest gross margins, averaging 35 percent. This same trade journal quotes an executive of one retail chain store as saying about confectionery, "Healthy markups, good profits, reliable sales – there aren't many other grocery categories that can make the same claim."[13] Another high-profit category is constituted by potato- and corn-chip products and the like, which the industry refers to as "salty snacks." The main trade journal of the American grocery industry, *Progressive Grocer*, has reported that food retailers have indicated that salty snacks are the second most profitable product category for them, outpaced only by bakery products.[14] Powerful industry players have corroborated the profitability of these pseudo foods. For example, a representative of one of the world's largest salty snack manufacturers – PepsiCo's Frito Lay – claimed that although his company's products represented only about 1 percent of US supermarket sales in 1998, they accounted for about 11 percent of operating profits and 40 percent of profit growth for the average supermarket.[15]

Further evidence of the profitability of nutrient-poor edible commodities comes from industry data from chain store companies that control convenience stores in the United States, reported in *Canadian Grocer*. Gross margins for all merchandise averaged 33 percent, but the gross margins for pseudo foods were reported to be notably higher, ranging from 35 percent for cookies to 37 percent for salty snacks, 39 percent for ice cream, 43 percent for candy and gum, and up to 59 percent for soft drinks served in-store.[16] Finally, it is noteworthy that in Canada the snack food industry has been growing much faster than has the food industry as a whole. In fact, its growth from 1999 to 2009, measured in constant 1992 dollars, was 83 percent as compared with the overall growth of only 6 percent for the entire food and beverage industry.[17] The high returns on these pseudo foods allow for intense and incessant mass advertising, which helps explain how nutrient-poor products became central in food environments. But how does market dominance translate into lucrative profits? Some of our best evidence comes from the ready-to-eat breakfast cereal industry.

Oligopoly Equals Bigger Profits

Sugar- and salt-laden breakfast cereals are produced by a sector of the food industry that has been heavily concentrated for decades. Even by 1970, only four firms – Kellogg's, General Mills, General Foods, and Quaker Oats – controlled 91 percent of the sales.[18] A key benefit of this oligopoly situation, at least to these companies, is in the area of pricing. Frederic Scherer's well-known study of the breakfast cereal industry illustrates how oligopoly pricing works, and exemplifies the gap between the idealized world of competitive pricing in free markets as touted by orthodox economists and the real world of business today.

Scherer noted that a study of the breakfast cereal industry shows us that the Kellogg's company, the most powerful player for many decades, appears to have been successful in imposing a high degree of price discipline on its few competitors. Essentially, Kellogg's typically set the pattern of price changes, and almost always in an upward direction, and the other firms followed:

> Out of 15 unambiguous price increase rounds between 1965 and 1970 ... Kellogg's led 12. Kellogg's price increase was followed nine times by General Mills and ten times by General Foods. On only one occasion did neither follow ... *Leadership was sufficiently robust to permit price increases in times of both booming and stagnant demand.*[19] (emphasis added)

Through the mechanism of a price leader in a heavily concentrated sector, then, these firms were able to avoid much of the price competition that is supposedly at the core of a free market economy. It is notable that of the 1,122 price changes in the industry between 1950 and 1972, only 1.5 percent were list price reductions, with about half of these occurring in a single incident.[20]

One would expect this situation to be beneficial to the companies involved, and indeed it was. After-tax returns for the top five cereal manufacturers was an impressive 19.8 percent for the period 1958-70, at a time when returns for manufacturing as a whole was only 8.9 percent.[21] In addition, the US Federal Trade Commission stated that overcharging consumers by the few firms controlling this one sector of the food and beverage industry was costing consumers $100 million a year by the late 1970s.[22]

We can extrapolate the experience of the breakfast cereal industry to other product categories in which pseudo foods prevail, such as soft drinks, salty snacks, and chocolate bars and confectionaries. These categories tend to be even more tightly controlled by a few corporate players than has been the case in the breakfast cereals industry. The snack food industry in Canada, for example, is controlled by a very few multinational food manufacturers. The federal government reported that, by 2009, only four firms controlled 82 percent of the value of all shipments of snack foods.[23] Moreover, it is not often recognized that the corporate players that largely control the production and marketing of pseudo foods are among the largest of all companies in the food and beverage sector. PepsiCo, for example, with worldwide sales of $35 billion in 2006, makes more in profits each year than the total sales of most smaller food companies.

MASS ADVERTISING AND THE "NORMALIZATION" OF THE INDUSTRIAL DIET

For the industrial diet to become a ubiquitous, taken-for-granted part of everyday life, particularly when it constituted in many (but not all) respects a fairly radical departure from prevailing diets, some very powerful force or forces must have been at play. As we have seen, mass marketing was one of these forces. From the early twentieth century and the early efforts of such people as the breakfast cereal entrepreneur C.W. Post, the advertising industry and the food- and beverage-processing industry have carried on a close and mutually profitable relationship.

Mass advertising is the process whereby one particular firm's product becomes differentiated in the market place. This product differentiation has been the mechanism in the food system, and in the wider economy, that has allowed some companies to develop branded products, which in turn have allowed them to dominate their competition in the markets they sell in.[24] In the post–Second World War era, those food processors that were successful in establishing branded products via massive advertising expenditures achieved a favoured position in the food economy relative to other processors and also relative to food retailers that were themselves becoming more concentrated and powerful.[25]

Mass advertising and corporate concentration in the food business go hand in hand, then – they are mutually reinforcing processes. The high cost of mass advertising on media outlets such as network television means that only the largest companies have the deep pockets needed to gain access in the first place. The benefits that come from such advertising can be immense, however, and its ability to create and strengthen a brand has made these same corporations even more powerful over time. Furthermore, there are economies of scale that come to companies that do the most advertising, enabling them to buy advertising time from media corporations at cheaper rates than their competitors and thus gain market advantage. This process had progressed so sufficiently over the course of the twentieth century that, by the early 1980s, of the 1,100 food companies that were using major media sources to advertise their products, only 12 firms accounted for 45 percent of all advertising expenditures.[26]

Intensive advertising effort is a key means by which pseudo food companies have boosted their products into the prominent position they have in our lives. Food companies have always been among the most advertising intensive of industries. For decades, expenditures by food processors had exceeded those of any other broad manufacturing category.[27] Of the total advertising expenditure by food companies, spending on nutrient-poor pseudo foods takes priority. As Jennifer Taylor and colleagues note, research shows that advertising promotes more frequent consumption of foods that are less healthy, such as higher-fat, energy-dense snacks and much less frequently such healthy choices as fruits and vegetables.[28] Marion Nestle was one of the first to point out the link between mass advertising by food processors and the promotion of nutrient-poor edible commodities. She estimated that of the astounding $33 billion spent by food companies on all their promotional campaigns by 2000, almost 70 percent was spent on convenience foods, candy and snacks, alcoholic beverages, soft drinks, and desserts, whereas just 2.2 percent was for fruits, vegetables, grains, and beans.[29]

Despite pseudo foods' being unnecessary, and arguably quite harmful, from a nutritional point of view, a small number of corporations that market well-known branded pseudo foods spend an astounding amount of money each year to keep these products front and centre in the minds of consumers. By 2006, just the nine most powerful companies marketing pseudo foods spent a total of $9.187 billion on advertising their brands in the United States, which was approximately 544 times greater than the entire advertising budget for the US government's Department of Health and Human Services for that year.[30] Table 9.2 provides a breakdown for this group of sales and ad expenditure by company for the United States and for their global operations, in 2004 and 2006.

THE CASE OF SUPERMARKETS

I believe it is in the supermarket context that the phenomenon of spatial colonization – the effort to ensure the physical visibility and availability of product – is most clearly illustrated. In any case, this is where I began my empirical research some years ago in an effort to understand how manufacturers were colonizing shelf space. Subsequently, I have come to believe that the concept is useful beyond this particular type of institution, that indeed it can be used to understand the colonization of space in much broader terms, such as urban and suburban environments. Stretching the concept in this way is particularly useful in understanding the growing impact of fast-food outlets and convenience store chains, or "c-stores" in the parlance of the industry, in transforming food environments.

So how does the spatial colonization of fast foods and pseudo foods work within important institutional spheres such as supermarkets, and what is the spatial colonization of high-traffic urban and suburban space in North America and, increasingly, the global South?

Pseudo Foods in the Supermarket

In the developed capitalist countries, supermarket chain stores play a defining role in shaping food environments. This is not surprising, as they have come to control a tremendous proportion of the consumer dollar spent on food. Table 9.3 indicates the sales revenues of the ten largest American supermarket chains, which James Tillotson notes control about 80 percent of all groceries sold in US supermarkets.

As the most important food environment in terms of sales, supermarkets and their shelves are much-sought-after locations for pseudo food processors.

Table 9.2

Nine largest pseudo food manufacturers: US and world sales, and expenditures on advertising, 2004 and 2006

Company	US sales (millions $)[1]			World sales (millions $)			US ad expenditures, (thousands $)		
	2004	2006	% change	2004	2006	% change	2004	2006	% change
Burger King	7,700	8,392	9.00	n/a	2,048	n/a	542,143	379,459	-30.00
Coca-Cola	6,643	6,662	0.30	21,962	24,088	9.70	540,551	740,824	37.00
General Mills	9,441	9,803	3.80	11,070	11,640	5.10	912,455	920,466	0.90
Kellogg	5,968	7,349	33.20	9,614	10,907	13.40	647,097	765,089	18.20
McDonald's	6,525	7,464	14.40	19,065	21,586	13.20	1,388,862	1,748,345	25.90
Nestlé[2]	22,444	24,889	10.90	70,114	78,327	11.70	1,028,295	1,314,975	27.90
PepsiCo	18,329	22,178	21.00	29,261	35,137	20.10	1,262,160	1,322,721	4.80
Wendy's (Tim Hortons)	2,475	2,197	11.20	3,635	2,349	-32.90	435,776	435,209	-0.10
Yum! Brands[3]	5,763	5,603	2.80	9,011	9,561	6.10	779,396	902,047	15.70

1 All figures are in US dollars. Mars Inc. is a major manufacturer of pseudo foods, but data on sales were not available. Expenditures on advertising in the United States amounted to more than $658 million in 2006.

2 Sales are for the Americas, North and South. Ad expenditures are for the United States.

3 Yum! Brands owned KFC, Taco Bell, Pizza Hut, and A&W restaurants at the time.

SOURCE: *Advertising Age, Special Report, Profiles Supplement,* 2005, 2007.

TABLE 9.3
Leading US supermarket chains

Company	Sales in billions US$
Wal-Mart	138.0
Kroger	53.6
Costco	41.7
Albertsons	40.8
Safeway	33.6
Ahold USA	26.9
Supervalu	20.3
Publix	16.7
Loblaw	16.2
Delhaize	15.4
Total sales	403.2

SOURCE: James E. Tillotson, "The Mega-Brands That Rule Our Diet, Part I," *Nutrition Today* 40, 6 (November/December 2005): 260.

Supermarket chain-store companies, on the other hand, function as shelf-space landlords, renting out space in their stores to those companies that can afford to pay. The supermarket retail sector has seen dramatic concentration in a number of countries, most notably in Canada, Britain, and Australia. By 2010, an estimated two-thirds of the grocery market was controlled by three companies in Canada, for example.[31] This degree of concentration gives the few retailers that dominate this sector a good deal of power over processors and what they can demand to display their products.[32]

The special deals, discounts, rebates, and allowances that processors pay to "rent" the shelf space from the supermarket chains have, according to one analyst, allowed US food retailers to make up to one-third of their profits solely from these kinds of trade payments from processors to facilitate marketing of their products.[33] In Canada, a report in the late 1980s by an industry analyst writing in the *Globe and Mail* estimated that these payments amounted to $2 billion of the $32 billion in annual food sales at that time.[34] Given the secretive nature of these payments, current data on them are hard to come by, but it can be assumed that they have grown as overall food sales have grown.

There is, then, a high cost to being prominently displayed in the supermarket food environment. Fewer and fewer food processors are able to pay and, as a result, in most product categories the products of smaller firms have all but disappeared.[35] Hastening this trend since the early 1980s has been the push by most supermarket chain-store companies to develop and market their own store brands (for example, Wal-Mart's Sam's American Choice and Kroger's Kroger Value products in the United States; Loblaw's President's Choice brand in Canada) in the supermarkets they control. In this context, few companies can compete with the market power of the large concentrated corporations that dominate the production of pseudo foods.

The relationship between processor and the supermarket chain is not simply a landlord-tenant-type relationship; it is more complex than that. The success of transnational processing giants in transforming the supermarket food environment would also appear to have much to do with their active promotion of the mutual benefits to be had with pseudo food sales to the retail chain stores. The largest companies, Nestlé and Coca-Cola among them, communicate regularly to retailers via prominent advertising of preferred retail strategies to maximize sales in key trade journals such as *Progressive Grocer*. For their part, retailers seem eager to steal lucrative pseudo food sales away from other non-food chain stores, including drug store chains, when it comes to selling confectionery products, for example.

How is spatial colonization manifested in the geography of the supermarket? To begin, supermarket layout – the overall positioning of product categories – is noteworthy. Low-profit commodity items that most shoppers will purchase no matter what else they buy (milk, butter or margarine, eggs, and often bread) are placed at the back of the store, as far as possible from the entrance, so that customers will have to pass by less essential but more profitable products to get to them. Favoured locations in the supermarket include eye-level shelves (as opposed to the much-less-favoured bottom shelf) and unique product positioning, called special displays, that set product apart from competing brands and heighten visibility. Another "high rent" location is near store areas that must be passed by the customer, with the checkout counter being the most significant. In today's supermarket, particularly in the superstore-type format, spatial colonization often takes the form of massive "island" displays of a single product that are very difficult for the consumer to ignore.

But does the spatial manipulation of product have any real effect on sales? Market research would suggest that it indeed does. Research indicates the powerful effect of shelf position on sales, for example, and studies have suggested that the use of special end-of-aisle displays in supermarkets can boost unit sales by several hundred percent, even when no price reduction occurs.[36]

Can Someone Measure That?

It is one thing to argue that pseudo foods are colonizing our food environments; it is another to back it up with some real evidence. Certainly, we can demonstrate how significant the annual sales figures are for these nutrient-poor commodities, and this does give us a fairly good idea of how significant they have become in our lives. Nevertheless, it is not the same as having actual numbers to illustrate the process of spatial colonization in the supermarket. Unfortunately, these numbers have not been publicly available, and apparently no one had thought the issue important enough to study in a systematic way. In 2001, I decided to try to rectify this situation.

In 2001 and 2002, I conducted a study, with the help of a couple of very able research assistants, that involved visits to a number of supermarkets in the cities of Kitchener, Waterloo, Cambridge, and Guelph, all in an urban region in Ontario about an hour's drive west of metropolitan Toronto. Twelve of a total of twenty-four supermarkets existing in the region at that time were studied.

This study aimed to provide the first publicly available data on the spatial colonization of pseudo foods in the supermarket food environment. The stores surveyed included stores owned by all of the three main supermarket chain-store companies operating in Ontario. The study included the smaller, more traditional, supermarket format stores, as well as the largest superstore-type format that includes in-store pharmacy, florist and electronic shops, furniture, and so on. It also included store formats that are marketed as lower-price "no frills" stores. Because the industry in Canada is dominated by so few players, and because they tend to use fairly standard formats in organizing their stores, I believe that the stores included in the study are reasonably representative of what is happening in the industry.

Measures were taken of the linear shelf space devoted to all food items in each of the main product categories (e.g., breakfast cereals; juices; bottled beverages; salty snack products; bakery; dairy; meats; and fresh, frozen, and canned fruits and vegetables) and, as well, the linear shelf space devoted to pseudo foods in each category. In the end, for each store, there were data on the total linear shelf space devoted to food and beverages (non-food and non-beverage items were not measured) and on the total linear shelf space devoted to pseudo foods. Data were also available by major product categories on the relative proportion of foods and pseudo foods stocked in the store. In some product categories – bottled beverages, for instance – most of the shelf space was devoted to nutrient-poor soft drinks. In others, such as breakfast cereals, a smaller but still very significant portion of shelf space was devoted to nutrient-poor products, in this case pre-sweetened breakfast cereals. In each store, the number and content of all special displays were also recorded, but the linear footage of these was not. Since most of these displays market pseudo foods, the overall measure of the linear feet of shelf space pseudo foods occupy was inevitably a conservative one.

Our Findings

The average linear footage devoted to pseudo foods ranged from 26 to 37 percent of the total of linear footage devoted to edible goods in the stores we surveyed. For the twelve stores sampled in our study, the average proportion of pseudo foods of all foods measured was 31 percent. Pseudo foods are more likely to be found on the shelves that constitute the central area of each store, where they range from 35 to 44 percent of all edible products. This, of course, is the part of most supermarket food environments where entire aisles are devoted to bulk candies and chocolates, to cookie displays, and to soft drinks and high-fat and high-sodium potato- and corn-chip products.

It has come to be received wisdom among nutrition experts that the perimeter of the store is the healthiest area to shop, as that's where the freshest and least processed foods are to be found, and to some extent this may be true. However, the study pointed clearly to the fact that this is changing with the rapid growth of extensive high-fat and high-sugar ice cream snack displays, and the extensive use of special displays to promote pseudo foods, both of which tended to be located outside the central aisles in our sample.

Interestingly, there were no clear differences in the marketing practices regarding pseudo foods from one company to another. All the chain store companies appeared to be employing basically the same marketing strategies in promoting pseudo foods. There was evidence that the newest stores in the study employed more prominent mechanisms to promote pseudo foods, however. This typically entailed the use of massive special displays to market nutrient-poor products, rather than having a higher proportion of them on the regular store shelves. Retailers have got the message, then, that "smart" retailing means pushing pseudo foods in ever new and creative ways, above all else, and the easiest way to do this is to incorporate these strategies into newly constructed (and more spacious) stores.

One thing we noted was that in the supermarkets under study, an entire shelf – in the larger stores, the equivalent of two entire shelves – extending the full length of the central retail space is typically devoted to candies and chocolate bars, and these items were prominently displayed in many other locations in the store as well. Another observation was that in most stores, a dairy case occupying an entire aisle was devoted to high-fat and high-sugar ice creams and other such dairy products. Industry sources suggest that this is nothing more than the efforts by manufacturers and retailers to extend the consumption of these frozen snacks – high in sugar and fat – from the traditional summer months to the entire year.[37] In our study we noted that the more modern the supermarket, generally the more extensive was the ice cream case, indicating that pushing these types of obesogenic snack products is seen by food retailers as very good business as they rejuvenate their store formats.

Examining the breakdown within some major product categories illustrates the patterns we observed. I have already noted that in the newest and largest supermarket stores, an extraordinary amount of space was devoted to high-fat and high-sugar ice cream products. It was also typical to have over 90 percent of the linear footage devoted to frozen juice drinks occupied by high-sugar beverages that contained 25 percent or less – often much less – real fruit juice. The situation with canned and Tetra Pak juices was basically the same.

Another very lucrative category for the retailer is that of the ready-to-eat breakfast cereal products, and here from 55 to 80 percent of total shelf space was devoted to pre-sweetened cereals in the stores we studied. These products represent a potent vehicle for getting sugar into children's diets.[38] We can understand the readiness of retailers to market pre-sweetened cereals aggressively when it is understood that they are the fastest-growing segment of the fastest-growing product category of 569 product categories tracked by the information and measurement company Nielsen.[39]

With consumer research indicating that as much as two-thirds of brand selection decisions are made in the store,[40] and impulse purchases being a significant part of overall profits for retailers, it is not surprising that stores, in conjunction with leading processors, have had recourse to the use of special displays. Modern marketing makes maximum use of impulse purchasing behaviour, and not surprisingly, supermarkets place high-profit impulse items at the checkout. In the stores we studied, candies, chocolate products, and salty snacks were present at 80 percent or more of the checkout. The reality is that impulse sales are driven throughout the modern supermarket. Special display stands, hooks ("profit hooks," in industry parlance), and strips are now commonly positioned in the most visible locations of the store.

Although special display devices can be used, hypothetically, to market any manner of goods normally found in supermarkets, in practice we found they were overwhelmingly dominated by nutrient-poor edible commodities. The number of special displays of these pseudo foods in the sampled stores ranged from eight to a high of twenty-six, and on average there were nineteen of them per store. Since this research was undertaken, others have also demonstrated that the great majority of in-store supermarket promotion is for unhealthy edible commodities.[41] Figure 9.1 gives an idea of the extensive use of special displays in one of the supermarkets sampled, which was fairly typical of the other stores studied.

The supermarket food environment today carries a range of foods from all parts of the globe that is unprecedented in human history. For those concerned with the lack of healthy nutritional offerings available to the poor and marginal populations in even the richest societies, the presence of a supermarket is often seen as a positive element for inner-city core populations and for poor rural communities in which little other than fast-food outlets and convenience stores are to be seen.[42] Yet, despite this relative diversity of foods and beverages, we have seen that certain types of products receive privileged treatment in the supermarket food environment in terms of visibility and promotional effort. These products are too often nutrient-poor goods high in sugar, fat, and salt. Their presence in the supermarket is out of all proportion to their nutritional contribution to our lives, and their spatial colonization of the supermarket is a testament to the extraordinary influence of their manufacturers, and also to the willingness of supermarket chain-store companies to cash in on the monetary bonanza they represent.

C-STORES AND THE HYPER-COLONIZATION OF PSEUDO FOODS

If pseudo foods are so lucrative, why do not retailers in a profit-oriented economy specialize in just these edible products? The answer to this question is, of course, that to a large extent they have. They are called convenience stores, or c-stores, and they have become a global phenomenon. Convenience stores appear to be a peculiarly American innovation, emerging in the 1950s in the southern United States in particular, and as the supermarket phenomenon expanded, they played a role in displacing the mom-and-pop independent

FIGURE 9.1

Typical supermarket layout with special displays

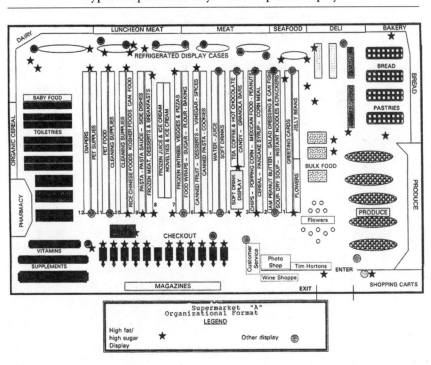

SOURCE: Anthony Winson, "Spatial Colonization of Food Environments by Pseudo Food Companies: Precursors of a Health Crisis," in *Critical Perspectives in Food Studies*, ed. M. Koc, J. Sumner, and A. Winson (Toronto: Oxford University Press, 2012).

small grocery store. By 1959, there were 2,500 convenience stores in the United States; by 1964, 5,000; and by 1967, 12,500.[43] Today, c-stores are big business, as Table 9.4 illustrates. Transnational oil companies are major players in the c-store business. The largest c-store corporations have thousands of outlets, and the top ten c-store chains alone have over thirty thousand outlets in the United States.[44]

North American companies generally favour franchising the majority of their c-store outlets. A major exception to this is the Quebec-based company Alimentation Couche-Tard, which still owns directly the majority of its outlets. One early 1970s analysis of the phenomenon of convenience store expansion noted that they typically carried a wide variety of goods that compared favourably with the supermarkets.[45] This is clearly no longer the case. C-store chains now offer shelf space that is saturated with pseudo foods.

TABLE 9.4

Top ten c-store chains

Company	# Stores	Sales (millions US$)	Country of ownership	Stores
7-Eleven Inc.	5,806	12,313	United States	7-Eleven
BP North America	5,166	12,845	United States	ampm, Mini Market, Amoco, Arco, BP, BP Express, B Connect
Shell Oil Products US	4,907	10,667	United States	Shell
Exxon Mobil Corp.	4,870	10,373	United States	Exxon, Mobil, Mobil Mart, On the Run, Tigermarket Express, Houston Tiger, Snack Shop
ChevronTexaco Corp.	4,024	8,999	United States	Chevron, Texaco
Alimentation Couche-Tard	2,838	6,318	Canada	Bigfoot, Circle K, Dairy Mart, Handy Andy, Mac's
Speedway SuperAmerica LLC	2,690	8,343	United States	Speedway, SuperAmerica
Sunoco Inc.	1,794	4,609	United States	APlus, Coastal, Optima, Sunoco
ConocoPhillips Inc.	1,756	3,982	United States	76, Conoco, Phillips 66
The Pantry Inc.	1,491	4,551	United States	Big K, Cowboys, Etna, Fast Lane, Golden Gallon, Handy Way, Interstate, Kangaroo, Lil' Champ, Minimart, On the Way, The Pantry, Quick Stop, SmokExpress, Sprint, TruBuy, Zip Mart

SOURCE: Convenience Store News, "The Top 100 Convenience Store Companies," 28 August 2006, http://www.csnews.com/.

Indeed, the spatial colonization of pseudo foods in this form of retail outlet far exceeds levels of the typical supermarket. Often there is little in the way of traditional foodstuffs in the store, especially in the chain-type operations. The exception might be milk and bread and perhaps eggs. During our research into the spatial colonization of pseudo foods in supermarket retail outlets, we also surveyed a small sample of convenience stores in the region. On average, we found that 70 percent or more of shelf space devoted to edible products was taken up by nutrient-poor pseudo foods, particularly salty snacks, chocolate bars, cookies, and soft drinks.[46] This is likely not a surprise to anyone who has had the occasion to search for something nutritious to eat in such retail outlets.

C-Stores Are Now a Global Phenomenon

The c-store phenomenon is a largely under-researched area, I should add, and my remarks refer to c-stores in North America. However, during fieldwork examining food retail operations across central Mexico in 2006, I was struck by the high degree of penetration of convenience chain stores in the urban areas of that country. The following year I encountered these types of chain stores in Argentina as well, including in the fairly out-of-the-way region of Argentine Patagonia. In both cases, the convenience stores I found in these countries had pseudo foods occupying considerably *more* than 70 percent of the shelf space devoted to edible products.

Convenience stores represent an important dimension of the contemporary food environment because of their extensive hours, often running 24/7, which is not often the case for food retail outlets offering healthier offerings. As well, c-stores are ubiquitous. Where not a supermarket, let alone a green grocer or farmers' market, is to be found for miles around, one is surely to come across a convenience store. More economically disadvantaged sectors of society have been found to be the most vulnerable in this respect. A Canadian study of the city of Quebec, for instance, found that its poorer neighbourhoods were ten times more likely to have pseudo food-laden convenience stores than were better-off neighbourhoods.[47] The lack of alternatives to c-stores poses a serious barrier to nutritional health.

Not only are food environments in poorer neighbourhoods less likely to have food outlets offering nutritious food but they are more likely to be the locus of fast-food operations. The proliferation of fast-food chains is the other key dimension of the reproduction of nutritionally compromised food environments and warrants attention.

CHAPTER TEN

MEALS AWAY FROM HOME

THE HEALTH BURDEN OF RESTAURANT CHAINS

[In the United States in 2006,] it would not be unreasonable to estimate that approximately $300 billion was spent on fast food of various kinds ... The reality of living in the United States today is that most Americans eat fast food of various types almost daily.

—James Tillotson, writing in *Nutrition Today*[1]

The energy density of the entire menu at fast food outlets is typically [about] 1100kJ/100g. This is 65 percent higher than the average British diet ... and more than twice the energy density of recommended healthy diets.

—S. Stender, J. Dyerberg, and A. Astrup,
writing in *International Journal of Obesity*[2]

Strong and consistent evidence indicates that children and adults who eat fast food are at increased risk of weight gain, overweight, and obesity.

—US Department of Agriculture, 2010[3]

CONVENIENCE IS A TERM that seems to find its way into every marketer's advertising strategy. Making things easy – convenience by another term – has long been popular with the consuming public in North America. And it seems the rest of the world is buying into the idea. In the realm of food, convenience is spelled "eating out," and it is a way of meal getting that has helped transform the way we eat. Aiding and abetting this transformation is the modern phenomenon of takeout foods, foods prepared by some (typically) for-profit enterprise for the purposes of eating in some other place, often at home.

The significance of the latter form of meal getting was impressed upon me two years ago when I was trying to purchase a new, and reliable, stove for my home. The salesperson, a man of some experience in the appliance business, asked me if my family cooked very much. When I said that we liked to prepare our own food as much as possible, he frankly informed me that the models I was considering were no longer really built for the rigours of regular cooking. Seeing my perplexed expression, he explained that the major lines of stoves are essentially designed to be used mostly for reheating food, food prepared elsewhere. I would have to consider a more expensive model if I wanted to use it to *cook* regularly – a telling sign if there ever was one that fewer and fewer people now cook for themselves, at least not on a regular basis.[4]

The evidence for letting someone else do the cooking is fairly dramatic, particularly for the United States (see Figure 10.1). Expenditures on food eaten away from home increased from about one-third of total food expenditures in 1970 to almost one-half of total expenditures by 2003.[5] In 2001, Canadians, for their part, were spending 30 percent of their food dollars eating out, and this figure has very likely increased over the last ten years or so.[6] Americans' and Canadians' annual spending on fast food alone is more than three times what the Germans and the Japanese are spending on a per capita basis.[7]

The reasons that help explain this shift in meal getting are varied and range from dramatic increases in time pressures on families with two-earner households to loss of culinary skills or, more commonly, the failure to acquire culinary skills. Each of these factors is rooted in political-economic, sociological, and cultural changes. Some might argue that increased disposable income is a factor as well, although the reality is that incomes for the majority of families have shown little improvement for much of the last twenty years, whereas eating food prepared elsewhere is a trend that has been only increasing.

Eating food prepared elsewhere is not, in itself, a trend that is inherently unhealthy. Aside from the joy and community that can come from food preparation, nutritious food prepared by others is just that – nutritious food

FIGURE 10.1

US per capita annual expenditures on food away from home, 1960-2005

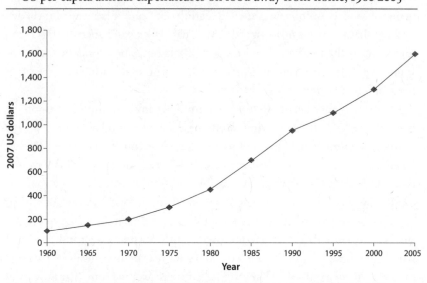

SOURCE: Urban Design Lab, Earth Institute, Columbia University, 2007, based on data from US Department of Agriculture Economic Research Service, "Food CPI, Prices and Expenditures Away from Home."

– and good for the body. Alas, in the real world, most people have to live in, to eat out or to buy takeout too often means eating industrial food, that is to say, it means adopting the industrial diet. More and more, meal getting represents a significant loss of control over how we prepare what we eat, and over what is in what we eat. Each is important. The loss of control in this area of our lives is one of the least examined but most significant dimensions of modern life, and it has major repercussions for health.

A very substantial proportion of the food eaten away from the home is captured by chain restaurant corporations. Chain restaurants have become the dominant form of restaurant operation in the United States and other developed countries, and will likely come to dominate those countries where they are as yet weakly established. These chains take on two predominant forms: the fast-food type of operation – McDonald's, KFC, Burger King, Wendy's, and the like – and the full-service chain operation. Among the most prominent of the latter are Olive Garden, Applebee's, IHOP, T.G.I. Friday's, Denny's, Outback Steakhouse, Chili's, and Red Lobster, to name only the largest, each having annual revenues in the billions of dollars. Remarkably similar to fast-food operations in terms of their typical corporate franchise structure, their space requirements make them more suited to the lower-cost real estate of suburban environments, whereas fast-food chains are seemingly able to infiltrate almost any environment in which human traffic makes it profitable, from hospitals, airports, banks, and schools to the old crumbling cores of ancient cities.

Together, the top four hundred restaurant chains reported $292 billion in aggregate global sales in 2007, from a total of 274,000 locations globally.[8] Yet, even though there are a multitude of chains, the ten largest among them control over 50 percent of global sales from chain restaurants. Within this top ten, two corporations stand out in particular, and they are both fast-food operations. The top two account for an astounding 30 percent of total global sales of the top four hundred restaurant chains.[9]

So what, exactly, is the contribution of chain restaurant corporations to the proliferation of the industrial diet? As we shall see, chain restaurants both contribute to the health burden on society and transform food environments outside the home.

Nutritional Impact of Chain Restaurant Food

Getting a handle on the nutritional impact of chain restaurant food is not an easy task because of the variety of chains and the seemingly wide spectrum of edible products they offer. Neither is it an impossible task, for there is a good deal of information provided on corporate websites of some, but not all, of the major chains.

Another factor that makes it easier to assess offerings is their standardized food: although fast-food chains vary somewhat in the products they promote, in the end they offer a remarkably standardized fare, something that has been argued contributes to their global success. This standardization is reflected in the leading chains' official documents, such as annual reports. One of the standard products served by most chain restaurants is french fries. Chicken and beef products, usually fried, typically constitute the mainstay of standard meals offered. Soft drinks are another component of the standard meal at an American fast-food chain, wherever one goes in the world.

To assess these restaurant chain products and ascertain nutritionally problematic areas of their offerings, it will be helpful to have an idea of what amounts established nutritional authorities are recommending for daily consumption of calories, salt, and fats, keeping in mind that these official recommendations reflect the interests of various stakeholders in our food system.

Dietary Recommendations: *Caveat Emptor*

Dietary recommendations are ultimately a product of a political process, the outcome of negotiations and compromises among various parties, or stakeholders, present in the forums in which they are established.[10] Nevertheless, they are widely available guidelines that bear the authority of government approval and presumably reflect, to some degree, prevailing scientific consensus on the benefits and dangers of different elements found in food. I say "to some degree" because the reality is that guidelines and policy on food are not shaped in a political vacuum but reflect the political economy of the food system. Guidelines for sugar intake is a case in point.

What is remarkable about sugar up until very recently is the lack of official dietary advice on it. Despite a growing body of evidence linking added sugars in processed foods and beverages to serious adverse health outcomes, including obesity and heart disease,[11] the official *Dietary Guidelines for Americans* for 2010 produced by the US Department of Health and Human Services, still does not recommend an upper limit for sugar consumption. The experience around the World Health Organization's 2003 Report *Diet, Nutrition and the Prevention of Chronic Diseases* that did recommend a specific upper limit of 10 percent of calories for daily sugar consumption, is instructive.[12] Upon the report's release, the US sugar industry, together with other lobby organizations of the America food industry, denounced the report and demanded from the US Secretary of Agriculture the American government's withdrawal of its substantial funding for the World Health Organization.

The aggressive lobbying in Washington to fight the recommendation provides a window into the process of dietary policy formation and the heavy role industry has in it. It is notable that by 2010, the American Heart Association was calling for recommendations of a limit on added sugars that were *one-half* those of the World Health Organization in 2003 (i.e., 5 percent of daily calories), and yet the "Key Recommendations" in the 2010 official dietary guidelines in the United States still did not have limits on sugars in the diet and advises consumers only to "reduce the intake" of dietary sugars.[13]

Recommendations for salt – or more correctly, sodium – consumption are the most clear-cut. For example, the American Institute of Medicine recommendations for daily intake for adults is 1.5 grams (1,500 milligrams) and slightly less for seniors. The *Dietary Guidelines* in 2010 advised consuming less than 2,300 milligrams of sodium a day. For children, the recommendation ranges between 1 and 1.2 grams (1,000 to 1,200 milligrams). However, for adults with hypertension, African Americans, and middle-aged and older adults, the federal authorities in the United States recommend an upper limit of 1,500 milligrams per day, or less than a teaspoon of salt, which is about 2,300 milligrams.[14]

As for fats, it is saturated fats and trans fats that are the leading problem. The US government's *Dietary Guidelines* advises a daily limit on saturated fats of twenty grams, for a person with an intake of 2,000 calories. Men would average somewhat above this daily calorie intake, and women somewhat below it, but 2,000 calories can be taken as a rough guideline for the daily need of an average adult with a sedentary lifestyle, which unfortunately includes the majority of adults in North America. The twenty grams of saturated fats, then, provides a useful benchmark upper limit for what authorities believe is a prudent guideline for healthy eating. This translates to less than 10 percent of daily calories from saturated fats.

Recommendations for trans fats have become much more restricted in recent years. The *Dietary Guidelines* recommend that 1 percent or less of fat intake be in the form of trans fats. Canada has taken a more relaxed approach to trans fats for some reason, asking food processors to limit these dangerous fats in foods to 5 percent or less and setting up a trans fat monitoring program. This program has surveyed restaurant, institutional, and retail food environments for the presence of trans fats and saturated fats in a wide variety of products over several years. Although the latest survey (2009) noted that some progress had been made to reduce trans fats in Canadian food products, the data indicate that dangerous levels still exist in some foods, particularly in many baked goods, such as pies, doughnuts, and Danish pastries, and that dangerous levels may exist in a number of other items, from french fries to processed chicken products. Many of these products are high in saturated fats as well.[15] The absence of point-of-purchase labelling requirements at the time of writing means that many consumers have no idea of the trans fats content, or the overall fat content, of any foods purchased outside of packaged food bought at a grocery store.

Fast Food's Nutritional Impact

How, then, do fast-food edible products fare? There is certainly support for the argument that they are obesogenic, or obesity promoting, because of their high energy density – their calorie content. For example, it has been estimated recently in a leading scientific journal dealing with obesity that fast-food menu items typically contain approximately 1,100 calories per 100 grams, whereas the average British diet is estimated to contain 670 calories per 100 grams. The caloric load of the fast-food meal, moreover, is noted to be *twice* the energy density of a healthy diet (which is considered to be 525 calories per 100 grams).[16] Another study, the first to examine the long-term (fifteen-year) impact of a fast-food diet, found that frequent fast-food consumption was positively associated with weight gain and the increased risk of insulin resistance and the development of type 2 diabetes.[17]

How does fast food shape up with respect to the dietary recommendations of government noted above? One approach that I think helps gauge its performance is looking at the combo meals because these are especially popular products promoted by most chains. Just one combo meal at McDonald's, KFC, or Subway exceeds the recommended 1,500 milligrams of sodium, for example (see Table 10.1). This is not that surprising when one realizes that, according to the nutrition information made available on the websites of these very restaurant chains, in a number of cases a *single* product item contains more than the 1,500-milligram limit recommended for hypertensive adults, Africa Americans, and middle-aged and older adults by the US government. For example, Burger King's Original Chicken Sandwich, Wendy's Baconator burger, A&W's Whistle Dog, KFC's Big Crunch Sandwich, Tim Hortons' Ham and Cheese sandwich, Subway's Meatball Marinara 6-inch sandwich, Pizza Pizza's Pepperoni 18-inch pizza slice, and its Bacon Double Cheeseburger 18-inch pizza slice each had 1,500 milligrams or more of salt. All of these chains, including McDonald's, had several other individual items containing close to 1,500 milligrams of salt.

The caloric impact of fast-food combo offerings is another area where these chain operations have a decidedly adverse impact. Figure 10.2 shows that for four of the most popular fast-food chains, the combo meal offering typically constituted about half of the recommended calorie intake for the entire day. In two of the cases, McDonald's and Subway, consumers of their combo meal would be ingesting between twelve and sixteen teaspoons of sugar in their meal package (five grams equals approximately one teaspoon).

One positive aspect of the examination of combo meals is that, in North America at least, the controversy over trans fats in recent years has spurred these fast-food chains to deal with the high amounts of it present in their products until recently. When we examine the practices of these chains more globally, however, the situation does not appear as positive. Notable here is a remarkable study that has compared the total fat and trans fat content in a meal of french fries and fried chicken bought at McDonald's and KFC outlets

FIGURE 10.2

Nutritional profiles of popular fast-food combo meals

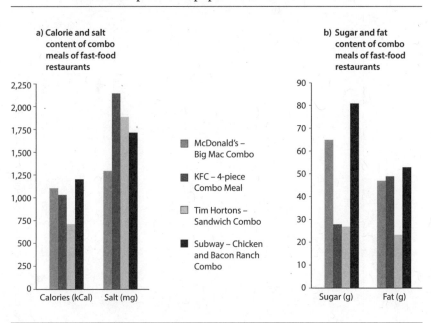

a) Calorie and salt content of combo meals of fast-food restaurants

b) Sugar and fat content of combo meals of fast-food restaurants

- McDonald's – Big Mac Combo
- KFC – 4-piece Combo Meal
- Tim Hortons – Sandwich Combo
- Subway – Chicken and Bacon Ranch Combo

SOURCE: Data from company websites, 2012.

in thirty-five countries. This study noted not only that these meals result in the ingestion of an extraordinary amount of total fat (from 41 to 65 grams at McDonald's and from 42 to 74 grams at KFC) but also that the harmful trans fats in these meals can vary by several orders of magnitude (from 0.3 to 10.2 and from 0.3 to 24.0 grams, respectively).[18] Moreover, these values can vary from one city to another within the same country. From a consumer's point of view, it is clear from this study that one can feel safe from trans fats only in jurisdictions where they have been more or less regulated out of the food supply, and to date Denmark is the only country where this is the case.

The combo meal findings do give us an idea of the likely nutritional outcome of eating fast food, but they do not do full justice to the potential harm that fast food represents. To illustrate this, it is necessary to look at the worst-case menu scenario that the fast-food giants offer. To this end, Table 10.1 presents a menu for four major fast-food operations that incorporates the highest-calorie product items under the four entree components: entree, side order, dessert, and beverage.

TABLE 10.1

Fast-food worst-case scenarios

Company	Product	Calories (kcal)	Saturated fat (g)	Sodium (mg)	Sugar (tsp)
McDonald's	Entree: Angus Burger	810	19	1,280	2
	Side dish: Large fries	560	3.5	430	–
	Dessert: Cinnamon Melts	460	8	400	5
	Beverage: Triple Thick Milkshake	560	9	420	19
	Total (% DV)*	2,390 (120)	39.5 (198)	2,530 (105)	26
Burger King	Entree: Triple Whopper	1,240	32	1,470	3
	Side dish: Poutine	740	13	2,500	1
	Dessert: Pie	300	12	210	6
	Beverage: Chocolate shake	950	8	590	39
	Total (% DV)	3,230 (162)	65 (325)	4,770 (199)	49
KFC	Entree: Boxmaster Sandwich	840	7	1,940	2
	Side dish: Poutine	860	12	2,450	1
	Dessert: Pecan tarts	350	6	140	5
	Beverage: Orange Crush (19 oz)	289	–	104	19
	Total (% DV)	2,339 (117)	25 (125)	4,634 (193)	27
Pizza Hut	Entree: Canadian P'Zone	1,960	22	2,820	1
	Side dish: Medium wings	320	5	1,180	–
	Dessert: Caramel Chocolate Cake	630	13	280	14
	Beverage: Orange Crush (19 oz)	289	–	104	19
	Total (% DV)	3,199 (160)	40 (200)	4,384 (183)	34

* Percentage daily value of appropriate nutrients as recommended by the US Food and Drug Administration for a 2,000-calorie diet. Includes adults and children four years of age and older. Figures are rounded to the nearest percent.

SOURCE: Company websites, March 2011.

The totals for calories, saturated fats, salt, and sugar of all the meal components in each restaurant chain menu is nothing less than deeply disturbing.
The restaurant meals represented here are not meant to represent a typical
meal choice, but they do represent a combination of products that these companies promote every day to millions of people around the globe. As such, it
is possible for consumers to avail themselves of some or all of them in the
course of eating there, and indeed, they would not be on the menus if they
were not being chosen by considerable numbers of their customers on a
regular basis.

FULL-SERVICE CHAIN RESTAURANTS:
NUTRITIONAL IMPACT OF A TYPICAL MEAL

How do the full-service restaurant chains fare? Although it would be mis-
leading to say there is a simple answer to this, it is possible to get an idea of a
diner's likely fate eating in one of these types of establishments. One way to
approach the matter is to compute from the various companies' own nutritional information (available on some, but not all, of their websites) to get
the nutritional profile of what we might call a "typical meal." I limit my focus
here to salt, fats, and calories.

I have chosen four of the largest American full-service restaurant chains –
Red Lobster, Olive Garden, Chili's, and Casey's – and attempted to estimate
what a typical meal would mean in terms of salt, calories, and saturated fat
intake. A typical meal for this purpose is constituted by a dinner entree, a side
dish, and a dessert. This typical meal is actually simply an average of the salt,
calories, and saturated fats in all the products offered among each of these
components – dinners, side dishes, and desserts – calculated from data available on company websites as of summer 2009. I do not include the contribution of a beverage, which would mainly affect the calorie intake, so the data
on calories eaten in a visit to such an establishment are quite conservative.

Salt

I have computed the average salt content of the standard meals offered by the
four leading American full-service restaurant chains – Red Lobster, Olive
Garden, Chili's, and Casey's. In all cases, this average was at or above 1,500
milligrams per meal, and with one it was very substantially above this figure.
Notably, Chili's meals on average contained about 3,700 milligrams of salt

FIGURE 10.3

Average salt and calorie content of a typical meal
at selected full-service chain restaurants

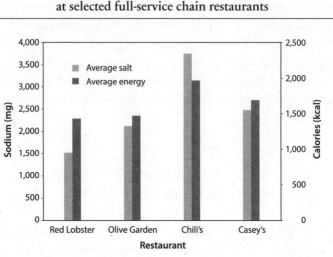

SOURCE: Data from company websites, 2009.

(see Figure 10.3). In other words, chances are that you will exceed your recommended daily salt intake with just one meal in any of these establishments.

Saturated Fats

How is one likely to fare with respect to saturated fats in popular restaurant chains, then? The typical meal of all restaurant chains exceeded the recommended saturated fat intake for the entire day. However, two chains, Chili's and Olive Garden, exceeded the recommended intake by *100 percent or more* (see Figure 10.4). In both cases, the typical dessert item alone exceeded the daily recommended saturated fat intake.

It is a basic nutritional fact that each gram of fat consumed contributes roughly twice the amount of calories as an equal amount of carbohydrates or protein (nine calories versus four calories). It is not surprising, then, given the high-fat nature of these typical meals, that the overall calorie content exceeded what is considered the daily energy needs for the average adult, and with just one meal. Presumably, consumers of these products will have other meals during the day, putting them well over a recommended calorie intake, and down the road a little bit farther to becoming obese adults, if they are not so already.

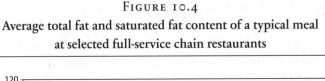

FIGURE 10.4

Average total fat and saturated fat content of a typical meal
at selected full-service chain restaurants

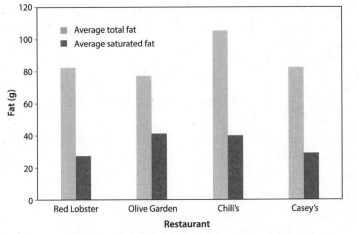

SOURCE: Data from company websites, 2012.

Healthy "Ethnic Food": The Myth

The explosion of restaurant offerings featuring cuisines adapted from other cultures has helped define the North American eating-out experience for quite some time now. The word that one need focus on here is "adapted." For although culinary exoticism has been popular for years and shows no sign of going away, the translation of foreign cuisines into North American eating contexts too often involves a reformulation of them to better mimic acquired tastes for sugar, fat, and salt. Cuisines that in their traditional forms do not promote the same kinds of chronic disease as the industrial diet, once transplanted, typically do.

This phenomenon would seem to hold whether one is referring to transplanted Mexican cuisine, Thai or Chinese cuisine, Indian cuisine, or Italian. Some of the major full-service restaurant chains noted above specialize in such offerings, and the nutritional analysis of their fare indicates that it is as problematic as any American fast-food chain's offerings. Moreover, a nutritional analysis by the *Toronto Star* of much more limited-scale restaurant operations offering some of these cuisines in the Toronto region suggests that avoiding big chain-type operations is not necessarily a way to avoid "ethnic food" with dangerous levels of sugar, fat, and salt. Popular menu items such as pad Thai and veggie thali were subjected to nutritional analysis as part of a series of articles evaluating popular "ethnic" meals. These dishes were found to be far from healthy, with levels of calories and sodium in a single meal, for example, that were approaching recommendations for a full day's consumption and fat content that actually exceeded daily maximum recommendations.[19]

TRANSFORMING MEAL GETTING

If there is a quintessential development that typifies the industrial diet for people around the globe, it surely is the fast-food chain phenomenon. Although the evolution of fast-food companies and their impact on transforming food environments warrants a complete study on its own, it is instructive to at least briefly chart their rise to prominence.

Fast food as a form of food preparation and consumption has been around since time immemorial, but it took on an institutional existence in the form of the chain restaurant only in the twentieth century, and it did so most vigorously in the United States. Historians of food have noted the pioneering role of the White Castle restaurant chain, and a few others, in breaking a trail for the fast-food giants that have come into global prominence. White Castle started in the early 1920s at a time in which the meat industry was still held in some disrepute as a result of widespread controversy around contamination and adulteration within the meat-packing industry, fuelled by Upton Sinclair's exposé in his 1906 book *The Jungle*. White Castle founder Billy Ingram sought to counter the skepticism by offering his beef hamburger meals in an establishment that strived to emphasize cleanliness, using gleaming white porcelain panels to help project an image of purity. As James Tillotson has argued, "[t]he historical importance of these first mover chains was that they favourably prepared Americans to such quick dining and their innovative approaches to food service created the consumer opportunity for out-of-city, quick-serve chains that would start to flourish in the 1940s and 1950s."[20]

These first chain fast-food operations were oriented to the central city environment, however, and not well placed to avail themselves of the new markets mushrooming after the Second World War in the surrounding suburbs. An exception to this was the chain of restaurants and hotels established by Howard Johnson in the late 1930s. According to Tillotson, Johnson was a pioneer in a couple of respects, and a bridge to the fast-food chain restaurant boom that occurred after the war. First, he located his establishments primarily outside the cities, on the rapidly expanding highway network. Second, he introduced the franchise management structure into the industry, something that had been invented earlier in the soft drink industry, and which had great success there. The owner of the franchise paid royalties to the originating company, which established clear rules for operating the franchise. It allowed the company to expand rapidly, using the capital of its franchisees.

McDonald's and Yum! Brands: The Fast-Food Juggernauts

I noted above that of the four hundred top restaurant chains, only two of them control 30 percent of global sales. These two are McDonald's Corporation and Yum! Brands Inc., a restaurant chain conglomerate that owns KFC, Taco Bell, and Pizza Hut restaurants, among others. These two fast-food juggernauts, along with a few smaller competitors such as Burger King, Wendy's, and Dairy Queen, are spreading their influence in dramatic fashion throughout eastern Europe, Latin America, Asia, and Africa, seemingly unhindered by critical analysis and commentary of their practices. They have become a potent force continuing the transformation of food environments around the world.

As Figure 10.5 demonstrates, the world's largest restaurant chain – the McDonald's Corporation – had languished as an essentially mom-and-pop operation for a number of years after its inception following the Second World War. Soon-to-be fast-food legend Ray Kroc reshaped the operation to take advantage of the explosion of suburban car culture in the 1950s, however, and had a hundred outlets by the late 1950s. Ten years later, the chain had ten times that number of restaurants operating and had begun its first foray abroad, with openings first in Canada and then Puerto Rico in 1967. By the early 1980s, the chain had over seven thousand restaurants, but even more significantly, it had operations in thirty-two countries. Along with Coca-Cola, which had preceded it abroad by several decades, McDonald's was becoming a pioneer in the globalization of the industrial diet. In fact, by 2008, the company could boast that it had a thousand restaurants in China alone, and over thirty thousand restaurants worldwide.[21]

With over $63 billion in global sales reported in 2007, McDonald's Corporation stands head and shoulders above all but one of even its closest restaurant chain competitors in terms of its ability to capture the away-from-home

FIGURE 10.5

Expanding McDonald's restaurant outlets, 1949-2009

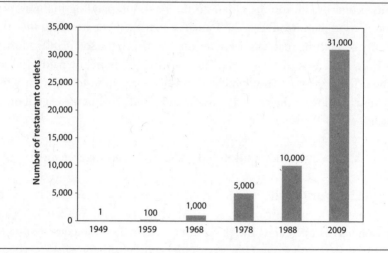

SOURCE: McDonald's Corporation, "History of Growth," http://www.aboutmcdonalds.com/.

eating dollar in the United States and in many countries abroad. Only the fairly recently cobbled-together Yum! Brands corporation, with its KFC, Pizza Hut, and Taco Bell divisions, can compare with McDonald's in these terms. Worldwide sales for this transnational were in the $30 billion range in 2007 (see Figure 10.6). This rival firm has itself a strong global presence, with restaurants in over a hundred countries by 2005. Indeed, it opened 780 restaurants in that year alone, boasting a total of an astounding 34,000 restaurants around the globe by 2005, outnumbering McDonald's in number of restaurant units and having 30 percent more restaurants than Wendy's and Burger King combined. Yum! Brands is especially strong in rapidly colonizing the world's fastest growing markets in the global South, with China being its priority target.

RESTAURANT CHAINS AND OBESOGENIC FOOD ENVIRONMENTS

The fast-food chain restaurant phenomenon, and its full-service chain restaurant counterpart, together with the forces that are impelling meal-getting outside the home, have truly changed not only the way we eat but also what we eat. It is not the only factor, as previous chapters illustrate, but it is certainly a major one. The restaurant chain juggernaut is predominantly led by

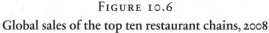

FIGURE 10.6

Global sales of the top ten restaurant chains, 2008

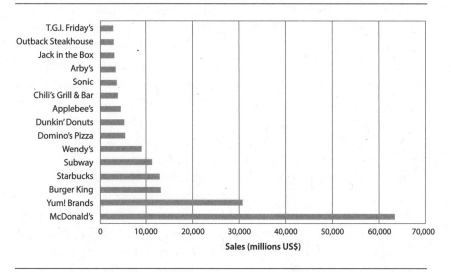

Source: "R&I Top 400 Segment Rankings," *Restaurants and Institutions*, 1 July 2008.

American corporations, another reason we might label this mass industrial diet the "American diet." Having colonized North America in the 1950s and 1960s, these US restaurant chains then launched aggressive expansion into western Europe. This region came to be the most important source of McDonald's revenues by 2008. Following the example of Coca-Cola decades before, these corporations also began to move into the global South, with Latin American countries being the preferred target markets initially. The remarkable economic growth of the two most populous countries, China and India, has led to a dramatic resurgence of American chain-restaurant overseas investments since the late 1990s, targeting these two markets. This investment dwarfs earlier forays into developing countries and will likely play a central role in reshaping a larger part of humanity's diet in years to come.

Taken together, these corporate food restaurant operations are potent forces in making people fat, or so I would argue. In other words, they are part of the process of transforming food environments into obesogenic, or fat-generating, environments. Some might argue that if the diet promoted by these companies were truly dangerous, governments would have intervened to protect the public from them. Others have argued that since no one is being forced to eat in these types of restaurants, it is a matter of individual choice and therefore should not be the concern of governments in any case.

These often-heard points of view deserve some attention, and I will comment on them briefly here before returning to them in the final chapter.

To the first argument I would point to the stunning lack of concern of governments in the West to intervene in markets no matter what dangers may be resulting from irresponsible corporate behaviour. The pro-market mentality and the anti-statist attitudes of politicians that have taken hold with the spread of neo-liberal ideology in recent times were patently evident in the unwillingness of governments to regulate in any substantial way the highly dangerous market in financial derivatives that burst asunder in 2008-09, which brought on global recession. If *this* kind of activity is left un-attended by governments, with all of its potential to damage society, it is no wonder there is so little interest in investigating and regulating the dubious nutritional practices of powerful food processors and retailers.

As to the second argument, which is perhaps the one most frequently voiced today with the libertarian ethos that pervades public discourse, especially in North America, two points bear repeating. First, the power of the mass advertising machine that energizes modern capitalism is a strikingly potent, if underappreciated, force for motivating human behaviour. When it is understood that much of the extraordinary expenses that go to powering this machine are deployed, in the food and beverage industry at least, to mo-tivate and direct consumer behaviour among children and youth, and to nor-malize a diet that is manifestly unhealthy, the arguments about freedom of choice are not quite so convincing. I note again that the advertising ex-penditures of just the top nine pseudo food manufacturers by 2007 were well over five hundred times larger than the total advertising budget of the US Department of Health and Human Services. It is hard to believe that this dramatic imbalance in the messages about what to eat has no consequence.

Second, I believe those who use the freedom of choice argument must somehow come to terms with the reality of the spatial colonization of these restaurant chains throughout our various food environments. Restaurant chains have become very big business indeed, and as such they have amassed the market power to push aside independent restaurants over time, and in so doing have eliminated alternative nutritional options. Moreover, as new com-mercial real estate is developed, these global corporations are typically the only restaurant venues that can sustain the rents demanded, so in the new food environments continually opening up, they are positioned to physically dominate as well.

Freedom of choice in meal getting presupposes the ready availability of viable options. Although exceptions do exist, in an inordinate proportion of food environments, real nutritional options are few, if they exist at all. The reality in more and more geographical settings – urban, suburban, and rural – is that there are a variety of unhealthy eating options, but few or no healthy eating options, and this is especially true for the majority of people of modest financial means.

GLOBALIZATION AND RESISTANCE IN THE NEO-LIBERAL ERA

T HE GLOBAL EXTENSION of the industrial diet in the 1980s and afterward has been dramatic. In the contemporary era, the global expansion of food transnationals has produced a qualitative shift in the prevailing dietary regime. Various factors underlie this globalization, but foremost among them has been the impact of neo-liberal policy frameworks. The Third World debt crisis was provoked by the monetarist policies of the Reagan government from 1982 onward and the extraordinarily high interest rates that were associated with them. The structural adjustment process initiated by the International Monetary Fund, the World Bank, and affiliated lending organizations, ostensibly to deal with this crisis, served to open up countries of the global South to various influences, including transnational agribusiness and food and beverage companies. Structural transformations in the societies of the global South were also very much part of the dietary changes that were to come. The chief vectors of the dietary transformation in the developing world have been, and still are, transnational supermarket and convenience chain stores, snack food transnationals and conglomerate food-processing firms with major snack food divisions, and American-based transnational fast-food corporations.

Further to the argument for a distinct dietary regime in the post-1980 period has been another qualitative shift in the role of the state with regard to food. This role has moved from that of intensive intervention via subsidies to producers, regulation of the food-processing sphere to ensure food safety, and promulgating policies to deal with agricultural surpluses and their export to the developing world, to one of much less intervention and relative withdrawal from the economic sphere and reorientation of the state's engagement with it. This change in government's role in the food economy has been countered by new forms of supranational regulation, however. Since 1995, these new forms have been concretized in the World Trade Organization and in the growth of private regulation in the form of private quality standards that are manifested especially through supermarket retail chains.[1] The growth of private standards is seen as a response to the dramatic growth in the international trade in food; the shift in trade and consumption of non-traditional and niche foods, in particular fresh fruits and vegetables; and the growth in demand for foods that are perceived to be craft-produced rather than massed-produced, to be of higher quality, and to have been produced in an environmentally sustainable way.[2]

In the realm of widespread dietary trends, these developments have been reflected in contradictory movements. At the global level, powerful forces have capitalized on momentous social and economic transformations in the global South and have aggressively promoted the penetration of the suite of nutrient-poor products associated with the industrial diet. In some of the developed countries, and in particular in North America, embracing the neo-liberal policy model has favoured what has been, effectively, the privatization of public sector food environments, from hospitals to primary schools to universities. Concretely, this has very often meant the colonization of these environments by fast-food chains and nutrient-poor pseudo foods.

On the other hand, it is undeniable that for a relatively privileged class of citizens, food options have become considerably more diverse and interesting. Gourmet and faux gourmet foods and foods representing a kaleidoscope of global cuisines populate many contemporary food environments, from supermarkets to shopping malls to upscale downtown restaurant districts. These dietary trends reflect complex changes in society, including substantial income gains for a section of the middle class over the last twenty years or so and powerful immigration trends in recent decades that have reshaped the ethnic mix of previously more homogeneous towns, cities, and regions.

Making sense of this apparent diversity of patterns is not particularly easy. However, too often, academic commentators lose sight, in their discovery of the new diversity of the food system, of the hard fact that for the majority of people confronted with neo-liberal realities in developed countries, good jobs are ever scarcer and incomes are trending sharply downward as inequality reaches levels not seen since the early twentieth century. Such realities make it hard, if not impossible, for the majority to participate in the diverse bounty to be found in contemporary food environments. Food and beverage companies have capitalized handsomely on the income squeeze faced by the majority with an ever wider array of processed products priced for this market. Unfortunately, the majority of these products are nutritionally compromised, and indeed many may be more correctly labelled "pathogens," as has recently been argued in a major Canadian medical journal.[3] I do believe, therefore, that the overall trend is for food environments to be continually degraded in this third food regime, despite clear-cut counter trends, and that this is true in developed countries and especially in the global South.

One further development in the realm of food and diet that cannot be overlooked is the one taking place in the so-called life sciences. With the application of new biological technologies by powerful corporate actors, "food is perceived almost like a drug," as Tim Lang and Michael Heasman have argued, "a solution to diseased conditions, part of a planned, controllable and systematic manipulation of the determinants of health and ill health."[4] What they term the "life sciences integrated paradigm" has already produced a whole variety of novel foods, or nutriceuticals, with purported health benefits that are widely proclaimed by the corporations that produce them. This response to the deficiencies of the industrial food industry is decidedly a corporate paradigm, and it will undoubtedly continue to influence the shape of diets in ways that we have yet to understand. This development does stand in opposition, however, to another notable trend that seeks more substantial and thoroughgoing changes to the current food system and the industrial diet that it supports.

In this regard, a constellation of factors has produced another defining characteristic of the most recent dietary regime – growing widespread resistance to the industrial foods of the industrial diet and the agricultural and processing system underlying it, and a growing determination among disparate groups and movements to reshape agriculture and food environments in alternative ways that are more sensible from an environmental and human health perspective, and which can reinforce, rather than erode, human communities. This complex and widespread resistance is difficult to capture, if only because of its diversity and relative neglect until very recently. I do believe it is a defining feature of contemporary times in the realm of food and diet and gives further credence to the notion that a distinct dietary regime has emerged in the last few decades.

CHAPTER ELEVEN

THE INDUSTRIAL DIET
GOES GLOBAL

India is clearly one of our priority markets ... It is time now to increase the depth of consumption.

— Steven Reinemund, CEO, PepsiCo, 2004[1]

Heart disease, cancer, chronic obstructive pulmonary disease and diabetes are no longer the lot of the wealthy. Chronic diseases have also become diseases of the poor.

— André Picard, *Globe and Mail*[2]

The idea that developing countries should feed themselves is an anachronism from a bygone era. They could better ensure their food security by relying on US agricultural products, which are available, in most cases at much lower cost.

— US Secretary of Agriculture, 1986[3]

T HE INTERRELATED COMPLEX of corporations that has come to dominate food processing, food retail, and away-from-home eating environments has at this point in North America and western Europe limited expansion opportunities. To put it bluntly, in this context the industrial diet is pretty well maxed out.[4] Fortunately for the largest of these companies, the world is indeed their oyster. As populous countries in the global South experience a spectrum of new economic opportunities, disposable incomes of emergent middle classes have been rising, and with them lucrative business opportunities for promotion of the industrial diet in virgin territories. The globalization of this diet to the developing world and the contemporary political-economic context that facilitates it are among the defining features of the third industrial dietary regime. Let's consider now what the corporate promoters of this diet have accomplished so far in the global South, along with evidence of the health impact of dietary transformations now underway in the region.

It is ironic that as the growing literature on the anthropology of food documents the tremendous diversity of dietary cultures around the globe, evidence of a growing homogenization of diets is also coming to the fore. To quote one of the foremost authorities on this subject, "Globally, our diet is becoming increasingly energy dense and sweeter [while] higher fibre foods are being replaced by processed versions."[5] In the last twenty years, there has been a phenomenal acceleration in the rate of globalization of the industrial diet to corners of the planet where it had only the weakest toehold previously. I am referring to India, China, and Southeast Asia, to South America, eastern Europe, and Africa. We can point to obvious changes that paved the way for this: the breakdown of Communism in eastern Europe and its transformation into capitalist dictatorship in China; the upsurge of neo-liberalism on the policy agenda in state after state, opening the doors to unrestricted foreign investments; and the expansion of middle classes in these societies with concomitant increases in disposable incomes. The spread of car culture in all of these regions has historically been associated with the rise of the industrial diet as well.

The global process of urbanization is another phenomenon that ultimately facilitates the acceptance of the industrial diet, with its emphasis on convenience and fast service. This urbanization is not, of course, some natural process but is itself in large part the product of the expropriation of masses of rural smallholders in country after country.[6] Neo-liberal agricultural policies and the open door it guarantees to low-cost subsidized agricultural commodities imported from such countries as the United States have played an important role in this rural exodus. All of this has been exacerbated in some regions by desertification and war. The long-standing unity of production and consumption characterizing peasant production in most parts of the world for millennia is being broken today on a phenomenal scale. As I argue in Chapter 1, once this unity is broken, the way is open for external forces, and especially profit-seeking enterprises, to take advantage of the newly created alimentary vulnerability and actively facilitate the transformation of diets in the pursuit of economic gain.

My intent here is not to explore these aforementioned themes at any length, for they have been well covered by others for the most part. What still needs attention, as far as the globalization of the industrial diet is concerned, is a focus on the direct agents in the spread of this diet, and in particular the corporate actors that are most directly responsible for dietary change. In this regard, it is worth reiterating that the industrial diet could just as easily be termed the "American diet" because of the prominent role of US food corporations in its evolution and contemporary globalization.

There are three main engines of change: transnational supermarket chain-store companies, transnational fast-food companies, and transnational companies directly marketing pseudo foods and junk foods. These actors play complementary and possibly mutually reinforcing roles in undermining more traditional dietary arrangements, arrangements that very often had beneficial nutritional characteristics, and replacing them with nutritionally compromised edible products. Before examining the agents of change, it is useful to consider some of the health outcomes related to dietary change that are presently reshaping the well-being of populations in the global South.

GLOBAL TRANSFORMATION IN DIET-RELATED HEALTH PROBLEMS

Obesity

Obesity, it need be remembered, is a major risk factor for the most widespread chronic diseases, and notably cardiovascular disease and type 2 diabetes. Approximately 85 percent of people with diabetes are type 2 according to the World Health Organization, and of these 90 percent are obese or overweight.[7] The emerging reality of overweight and obese populations in middle-income and low-income countries of the global South is the most visible aspect of diet-related health problems to come, and problems that have already arrived in some cases. For example, where data are available, we are also seeing rapid rises in obesity-linked health outcomes, including type 2 diabetes.

Annual increases in overweight and obesity are occurring at an astounding rate of more than 1 percent per year in many of these countries, including some with very large populations, such as China and Indonesia. These rates of increase are matched by only a couple of rich countries – the United Kingdom and Australia.[8] Nationally representative data on women aged twenty to forty-nine in thirty-six developing countries provided by Barry Popkin show a remarkable picture. The prevalence of overweight exceeds underweight among women in dozens of poorer societies today in both urban and rural areas. It is only in the very poorest of countries of the globe (e.g., India, Senegal, Central African Republic, Benin, Haiti, and Madagascar) that the prevalence of underweight still exceeds that of overweight, and this is generally only in the rural areas, not urban.[9]

Particularly disturbing are rapid increases in the incidence of obesity among children in these societies. Take only the most populous society, China. Data from the China Health and Nutrition Survey, which is a longitudinal study between 1989 and 1997, found especially high increases in obesity rates in urban areas. Among young children (two to six years), the prevalence of overweight increased from 14.6 to 28.9 percent, and that of obesity from 1.5 to 12.6 percent, during this period.[10] These data likely underrepresent the problem because the measures of overweight and obesity used were developed for Caucasian populations, and it is known that, at a given level of overweight, Asians are at higher risk for weight gain–related disease than are Caucasians. Different measures of weight gain among Asian populations, such as waist circumference or waist-to-hip ratios are thought to be more appropriate measures.[11]

The incidence of different types of chronic disease is closely linked to broad-based changes in diet and levels of urbanization, and to changes in lifestyle this urbanization brings with it, and there is considerable variation across countries in the global South. If we look at data on causes of death in Latin America, for instance, we see that communicable diseases in one of the least-developed countries, Guatemala, were still by the mid-1990s a leading cause of death, despite a slow rise in recent decades of chronic disease as a cause of mortality. At the other end of the spectrum, in relatively highly developed Uruguay, even by the 1970s, chronic diseases, in particular cardiovascular disease and cancer, were overwhelmingly ranked as the leading causes of death.[12]

Chronic Diseases

Getting a firm handle on chronic diseases in countries with less-than-adequate health monitoring institutions is a dodgy affair. It has been argued that in this context the rule of halves must be kept in mind, that is, the notion that approximately half of the commonest chronic disorders are undetected, half of those detected are not treated, and half of those treated are not controlled.[13] So, estimates of the incidence of chronic diseases related to diet and lifestyle are very likely to be underestimates.

What is remarkable over the last decade is the steady march of chronic disease in the developing world, where infectious diseases were until recently the overriding concern. By 2007, the World Health Organization was reporting that ischemic heart disease and stroke had become the leading cause of deaths worldwide, and together with chronic obstructive pulmonary diseases – all chronic diseases – were believed to be responsible for 27 percent of total deaths worldwide.[14]

Type 2 diabetes is a disease strongly associated with diet and lifestyle and therefore deemed to be largely preventable. A 2001 article in a major science magazine was already describing by that date the increases in numbers of people diagnosed with this disease worldwide as "explosive," with the disease "taking its place as one of the main threats to human health in the 21st century."[15] The incidence of diabetes (types 1 and 2) globally is expected to double between 2000 and 2030. Increases in the incidence of the disease are expected to be highest in the Middle East, sub-Saharan Africa, India, and Southeast Asia.[16]

Especially alarming is emerging evidence of the rapid rise in the incidence of type 2 diabetes in children and youth in a number of regions and countries. In Japan, the incidence of this form of diabetes has increased ten times between 1976 and 1995 for primary schoolchildren, and it has doubled for adolescents over the same period. In a disease clinic in Bangkok, Thailand, the proportion of new cases of type 2 diabetes rose from 5 percent in 1987 to almost 18 percent ten years later.[17]

With the spread of diabetes in developing countries, certain populations are known to be at particular risk because of genetic susceptibility to glucose intolerance and diabetes. Several Aboriginal populations have witnessed extraordinary increases in rates of obesity, for instance, and with it, rates of type 2 diabetes. The prevalence of diabetes among adults in Aboriginal populations has reached 40 percent for tribes of the central plains of the United States. Dramatic rural-urban differences have been reported across the globe, with urban Aboriginals at much greater risk than their rural counterparts. Interestingly, where Aboriginal populations still practise traditional agriculture and/or hunting and gathering lifestyles, the prevalence of type 2 diabetes tends to be much lower. Pima Indians who have had to give up traditional agriculture suffer diabetes at rates that are six times greater than those of Pima people who still practise traditional agricultural. A very low prevalence of diabetes is also characteristic of Aboriginals in Brazil who continue to follow traditional lifestyles and diets.[18]

Other populations are also thought to have a genetic predisposition to glucose intolerance and diabetes. More than twenty years ago, medical scientists were discovering that urban populations in South India had developed a similar (and relatively high) prevalence of diabetes compared with Indians living in urban agglomerations outside India, such as London.[19] Since then, India has become more urbanized and people more exposed to Western, largely American, dietary influences. A recent editorial in the *Journal of the Association of Physicians of India* has referred to India as the "diabetes capital of the world" because it now has the highest number of diagnosed diabetics of any country on earth. At the same time, this editorial warned about another related condition that was becoming very prevalent in that country as well: hypertension, a potent harbinger of cardiovascular disease. The prevalence of hypertension discovered by Indian researchers in recent studies is comparable to rates found in the United States.[20]

Data from African countries are more difficult to come by and often are not current. Nevertheless, studies published between 1999 and 2003 were reporting disturbingly high rates of hypertension in several nations. The prevalence of hypertension was approaching 40 percent among urban males in Tanzania, and ranged between 30 percent for all males (urban and rural) and 37 percent for all females studied in Morocco.[21] The prevalence of diabetes was high in Egypt and northern Sudan, where it approaches 10 percent of adults; as well, extraordinarily high rates of about 20 percent were reported for adults in Mauritius even by 1999 and of almost 30 percent among elderly "coloured" people living in Cape Town by 1997.[22]

How do we account for this devastating global explosion of chronic disease? Some would have it that these diseases are the inevitable result of unstoppable processes of modernization and urbanization, essentially "diseases of development" over which we have little control. Clearly, this is not the view taken here, nor by a growing number of voices emerging on these issues. Although we cannot point to only one or two factors to explain this disease phenomenon, I believe that the main determinants of diet and lifestyle that lie behind many of these trends are amenable to change, and, therefore, progress can be made through concerted efforts to turn around these trends. We have, after all, lessons learned from the fight against the tobacco transnationals to draw from, an experience that can shed light on what it takes to make significant population-wide advances for human health. Moreover, the experience with tobacco shows that state-sponsored programs of control and tax policies on these dangerous products have had substantial positive impacts in societies in which they have occurred. So, what are the prominent forces undermining dietary health in the global South? I believe it is possible to distinguish three main vectors responsible for the diffusion of the industrial diet in the global South: supermarket chain stores, transnational corporations marketing pseudo foods directly, and transnational fast-food corporations.

GLOBAL SUPERMARKET CHAINS AND THE INDUSTRIAL DIET

The emergence of the supermarket as a prominent organizational form of food retail in developing countries has been a recent and rapid development. Supermarkets had emerged by at least the late 1970s in a few countries, notably in Latin America, a trend that was picked up in the academic literature by the early 1980s.[23] Since the mid-1990s, however, there has been an explosion of change in food retail practices in the societies of the developing world. The great bulk of attention to this development has focused on the impact on the supply chain – specifically, the impact on small and medium agriculturalists seeking market outlets for their produce.[24] This is a significant concern, but it is dwarfed by the role of supermarket chain stores in providing a central impetus to population-wide dietary transformation, and the health consequences that will follow from this transformation.

I have made my case for the role of supermarkets in promoting the consumption of nutrient-poor pseudo foods in Chapter 10 and elsewhere.[25] My work in the Canadian context demonstrated that supermarket chain stores aggressively promoted nutrient-poor edible products high in sugar, fat, and salt, and in a variety of ways. It also demonstrated that these products dominated several product categories, including fruit juices and breakfast cereals, and that overall they constituted a sizable proportion – about one-third – of all supermarket shelf space devoted to edible commodities. This constitutes a process of spatial colonization of the food retail environment by pseudo foods. I have also argued that it is the realization of differential profits, that is, the extraordinary returns to be had on the sale of these pseudo foods, that best explains their prevalence in the food environments more generally. In addition, a related food retail phenomenon, convenience store chains, can be understood as representing a veritable hyper-colonization of food environments by pseudo foods because of the extremely high proportion of nutrient-poor products in the product mix of these types of stores. Where this convenience store chain phenomenon is becoming widespread, as it has in some Latin American countries, it can be seen as another potent contributor to the proliferation of pseudo foods in the global South.

Both supermarket and convenience store chains are transforming food environments of developing countries. In the supermarket realm, chain store retailers who have become truly global in their reach have been rapidly extending their corporate tentacles into countries that only a few years ago were thought to be too poor to attract such attention. At the national level in several developed countries, supermarket chains have for some time enjoyed oligopoly powers to the extent that just a very few firms controlled much of the market. This has been particularly true in the United Kingdom, France, Australia, and Canada, for example. In the latter, just two firms control over half of supermarket sales.[26] Their extraordinary market power has given these supermarket chains a high degree of control over the entire national food system.[27]

Supermarkets in Developing Countries

Recent research has documented the unprecedented pace by which the supermarket form of retail food selling is transforming Latin America, Asia, and Africa. A series of changes in the structures of economies in these regions have opened up new opportunities for the supermarket retail form. Among the most important of these changes are rapid urbanization; expansion of the middle class and with it a rise in disposable incomes for this segment of the population and the ability to purchase refrigerators; significant increases in female labour force participation; and the rapid growth of car culture and access to public transport. In the developed economies, indigenous supermarket chains have found their markets increasingly saturated and expansion blocked, especially in Europe, by restrictive zoning legislation.[28]

As supermarket chains spread in the developing world, they provide economically privileged strata of the population a broader array of fresh and relatively safe food, in a well-lit and clean shopping environment. They typically also provide such affluent customers with free parking, a not insignificant benefit in an increasingly car-oriented world. The adoption of neo-liberal economic policy in one country after another in the developing world in the 1980s and afterward opened up economies to foreign direct investment, and in particular, to the largest supermarket chain companies in the developed world: Wal-Mart, Carrefour, Tesco, Kroger, Ahold, Safeway, and Sainsbury's, to name only a few of the leaders.[29] Of the top thirty global grocery retailers, ten are headquartered in the United States, giving it a commanding lead, although French, German, and Japanese retailers are also strong.[30]

One of the foremost research teams documenting the spread of supermarkets in this context argues that this phenomenon has proceeded in four waves in the global South. The first wave began transforming major cities in Latin America, the second wave hit East and Southeast Asia, the third wave involved the smallest and/or poorest countries in the developing world, at which time secondary cities and towns affected by the first wave were being affected. The fourth and most recent wave, they argue, is affecting South Asia. As they note, "In a single decade Latin America had the same development of supermarkets that the United States experienced in five decades." However, even in this region there is considerable variation from one country to the next.[31] In other places such as China, for example, the control of supermarkets of retail food environments is at a much lower level, and while growing quickly, is likely to take many years to reach the levels seen in a number of Latin American countries.[32] Nevertheless, Wal-Mart, among other companies, is rapidly expanding its presence in that country and by 2009 reported 138 superstores in seventy-three cities, employing about ninety thousand people.[33] Figure 11.1 depicts the extent of supermarket control of food retail in a selection of Latin American nations.

The supermarket form of food retail was initially pioneered by local entrepreneurs in many cases. This was true of the mini-supermarkets that had emerged in San José, the capital city of Costa Rica, for example, by the time of my first sojourn there as a student in the late 1970s. They catered largely to a small upper middle class, whereas the great majority of the population, even in the capital city, frequented the large, and not particularly clean, municipal market and the many small food shops around the city.[34] Since that time, supermarkets chains have witnessed explosive growth in a number of countries. In Mexico, for example, their control of food retail grew from between 10 and 20 percent in 1990 to about 60 percent by 2005.[35]

Consolidation and multinationalization of the rapidly expanding supermarket sector in developing countries has also characterized recent times. Although indigenous supermarket chains emerged in some countries, it was

FIGURE 11.1

Supermarkets' control of retail food in selected Latin American countries

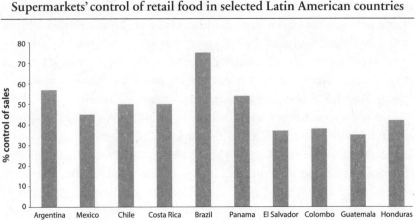

SOURCE: Thomas Reardon and Julio A. Berdegué, "The Rapid Rise of Supermarkets in Latin America: Challenges and Opportunities for Development," *Development Policy Review* 20, 4 (2002): 371-88.

not long before global supermarket chain companies established their presence, either through setting up their own operations or taking over local chains. These global chains controlled 70 to 80 percent of the top five supermarket chains in most countries in Latin America by 2003 in a process called multinationalization. Mexico was one of the few exceptions to this, and here, indigenous corporations retained firm control.[36] Some of these international retail giants were able to achieve profit rates as high as three times those obtained in home markets by investing in developing countries,[37] a factor that was no doubt very significant in the decisions of these giants to make rapid and substantial investments in years to come in the developed world. On the other hand, this sector of food retail has become highly consolidated very rapidly, with the top five chains controlling 65 percent of the supermarket sector as a whole in Latin America. The excerpt below from a Wal-Mart on-line publication illustrates the role of the global chains in transforming food environments in some countries:

> In 14 years, the company grew from a five-store company to become the third largest retailer in Brazil with sales close to R$17 billion. Two acquisitions propelled Wal-Mart Brazil through this transition: Bompreco's 118 stores in the Northern region of Brazil, and Sonae's

140 stores in the Southern region. With these acquisitions, Wal-Mart Brazil grew from a two to nine brand company with multiple store formats (retail, wholesale and soft discount). During the last two years, the company grew organically, building new stores for all brands across 18 states and the federal district.[38]

Observers of the tidal wave of supermarket chain expansion in the global South have also argued that, far from serving only a small well-to-do sector of developing societies, these chain stores have penetrated deeply into the food markets of the poor, spreading from big cities to even small towns, from China to Chile to Kenya.[39]

NUTRITIONAL IMPACT

Food analysts have argued that the most recent phase of capitalism has caused significant transformations in the food system, and supermarket operations there. Consumer demands and competitive pressure have brought about market differentiation, involving new kinds of processed foods; new attributes for "traditional" foods; and emphasis on quality, authenticity, and "goodness."[40] Certainly, this is where the cutting edge of food retailing is located, and it does characterize a part of the reality of modern supermarkets, especially in developed countries. Even there, however, one must be careful to distinguish the forest from the trees. Although a few provide a disproportionate share of supermarket profits by regularly consuming gourmet, exotic, fair trade, and organic products, the great majority of supermarket consumers are still consuming standard processed foods for the most part, with all the nutritional consequences this implies.

In developing countries, this point is even more relevant. The "exotic" foods now proliferating in developed country supermarkets are rare, if not totally absent. Supermarkets have another role here from a nutritional standpoint: introducing large numbers of people among the newly emergent middle classes to ready-to-eat breakfast cereals, processed cake mixes, reconstituted and artificially sweetened fruit juices, industrial baked goods, processed meats, and other goods of the industrial food system with which they may have only passing familiarity.

It must not be forgotten that, together with the role of supermarkets in the spatial colonization of pseudo foods, this process goes hand in hand with widespread and intensive mass advertising of these very same products. My own experience in Central America and Mexico suggests that the advertising push for these types of high-fat, -sugar, and -salt products generally precedes the proliferation of supermarkets. The manufacturers of modern pseudo foods, as quintessentially industrial edible products, typically builds on (and may mimic) traditional sweet and fatty foods made for special occasions by small-scale artisanal operations and the already existing taste for these foods that has developed over many generations.

FAST-FOOD TRANSNATIONALS

A second potent vector for the diffusion of the industrial diet throughout the developing world is fast-food chain restaurant corporations. This corporate form comes in indigenous variants and in the form of global transnationals, typically headquartered in the United States. The latter phenomenon is of primary importance not only because of these global transnationals' object-ive market power but also because, through their penetration of foreign mar-kets, they give impetus to the development of indigenous fast-food operations eager to emulate the products of the world-renowned fast-food brands.[41] Their copycat behaviour only adds impetus to dietary transformation.

Of the fast-food transnationals, none is as powerful and globally situated as McDonald's Corporation. This company has been highly successful in bringing the American way of eating to Europe over the past couple of dec-ades or so, to the point at which, after 2002, European outlets were returning to the company more revenues than did their US operations. By 2009, it was reported that the company operated a phenomenal 31,900 restaurants in one hundred countries.

McDonald's and its competitors grow by changing the way people eat. As I discuss in Chapter 10, an advertising model that aggressively targets children and youth has been central to their success. But as anthropologist James Watson and his co-authors note in *Golden Arches East*, the success of McDonald's in Asia is also due to the dynamic relationship of the corpora-tion with its host culture and not just the result of the advertising jugger-naut that it also represents. This dynamic relationship had to do with the way it incorporated into its local strategy children and youth, always a central motif for this company, but also with how it dealt with and adapted to other segments of the population, and how it took advantage of local customs. As Watson writes, what we are talking about here is a "localization strategy."[42]

What Watson and his co-authors essentially tell us is that corporations as successful as McDonald's do not owe their global impact to market power alone but also to an ingrained corporate culture that is sensitive to local conditions and strategies of market penetration that actively co-opt local managerial and cultural expertise in the quest to transform food environments and thereby engross their bottom line. Asian food environments in particular differed markedly from the kinds of edible products that McDonald's and other transnational purveyors of the industrial diet have on offer. In this context especially it would seem that targeting children and youth, those least ingrained with food habits and tastes foreign to the industrial diet, is the most likely route to success. And so it has been.

In China, as Yunxiang Yan eloquently demonstrates in his ethnographic study of the rise of McDonald's to success in the Beijing restaurant scene, the company was able to adroitly take advantage of local social and economic conditions, and in particular China's one-child policy that created millions of doting parents and grandparents focused on the welfare of a generation of "little emperors." By creating an environment that would reinforce the specialness of these single children and offering a reasonably affordable venue (for the emergent middle class at least) to celebrate the major events in the lives of these children, McDonald's became, during the 1990s, an institution that was more and more relevant to family life.[43]

The extent to which the company is willing to go to nurture relationships with children and thereby build a long-term customer base in China is suggested by the following passage:

> Aunt and Uncle McDonald [local variants of the company's Ronald McDonald character] do not confine their activities to the restaurant. After making friends with the youngest customers, the staff members who play Aunt or Uncle McDonald record the children's names, addresses, and birth dates on a special list called "Book of Little Honorary Guests." Later they visit the children's families and their kindergarten and primary schools. Congratulatory letters are sent to the children prior to their birthdays, with warm greetings from Uncle McDonald.[44]

Adapting to local exigencies has meant a departure from the rapid flowthrough of customers the chain encourages elsewhere, and, instead, building customer loyalty by offering restaurant space as a place to hang out for teenagers, and allowing adults, who tend to view McDonald's as much more of a formal dining event than do North Americans, to linger as well.

Other factors give North American fast-food chains cachet among the Chinese as well and facilitate the acceptance of this foreign fast-food cuisine. For one, eating at American fast-food restaurants can be seen by upwardly mobile parents as a valuable cultural experience for their children, one that may help them get on in their adult life.[45] In addition, the company's emphasis on cleanliness and hygiene, coupled with its advertising campaign highlighting the health aspects of its diet, impress a public disenchanted with the less-than-hygienic conditions associated with traditional food environments in China. And the set standardized menu that McDonald's provides is for some a welcome respite from the traditional arrangements of Chinese restaurants, where customers may often feel they are in competition with other patrons in providing the best (and typically most expensive) meals for their guests so as not to lose face. McDonald's, although not a cheap meal by local standards, provides a way to avoid this expensive reality of "competitive dining" that characterizes traditional Chinese restaurants.[46]

Finally, it has been noted that in China, as in many other places in the Third World, fast food is not something that is particularly new. Local food environments had been characterized by more traditional fast-food options long before McDonald's and its competitors arrived. What *is* new is more the industrialization of production with the American chains and, of course, the new types of edible products that it introduces. In the end, it is this last point that must be highlighted. Whatever credit these companies may be given for their business smarts in cleverly adapting to local culture and being sensitive to local peculiarities, it is the transformation of diets that they are promoting in their incessant pursuit of expanding their market and ultimately returns to shareholders that really matters, at least from a health perspective. As Yunxiang Yan writes of his interview with the general manager of a Beijing McDonald's, the goal "is to make McDonald's food part of the everyday diet of ordinary Beijing residents."[47] Any analysis that loses sight of this reality is less than inadequate, if not altogether irresponsible.

SPATIAL COLONIZATION OF FAST FOOD

Although innovative in their cultural sensitivity to the societies they operate in, McDonald's and its competitors are also concerned with the spatial colonization of their retail outlets in the markets they penetrate. Recently, McDonald's has undertaken a global repositioning as far as developing countries are concerned. While divesting itself of its Latin American holdings of some 1,570 restaurants in 2007, it refocused its expansion into the largest potential markets on the planet, China and India. The company planned to open 175 restaurants in 2009 alone in China and an even greater number of restaurants in India by 2015.[48]

Yum! Brands, second only to McDonald's in size and impact, has been even more aggressive in its penetration strategies for Asian markets. Even by 2004, this firm was spending $400 million annually to colonize China with KFC and Pizza Hut outlets and was boasting that it was well ahead of McDonald's in colonizing the critical Chinese market, with 1,792 outlets, compared with the latter's 735 outlets. Yum! Brands president noted in 2005 that there were over 300 million middle-class Chinese consumers who could afford the products the corporation sold, making China a larger market than the United States. Yum! Brands had built up its own food distribution system in China over ten years, and by 2005 had positioned its outlets in 360 cities. Substantiating my argument that a key strategy of global fast-food transnationals is spatial colonization of urban real estate, the annual report from 2005 notes that Yum! Brands has "one of the largest real estate development teams of any retailer in the world."[49]

Supporting the argument that it is in developing countries that fast-food transnationals see their major future growth, Yum! Brands reported 22 percent annual growth in its China business in 2005, along with franchise business sales growing 10 percent in the Caribbean and Latin America, 17 percent in the Middle East and North Africa, and 20 percent in South Africa.[50]

Another global fast-food player is Burger King Corporation. In addition to its penetration of Europe, where it is especially strong in Germany and the United Kingdom, it also has a strong position in Latin America, where it had by 2007 over nine hundred restaurants in twenty-five countries. Burger King boasts that it is a market leader in the fast-food sector in sixteen of these twenty-five countries, with total sales exceeding $800 million by 2007. The corporation is rapidly developing its presence in the Asia Pacific region as well, with over six hundred restaurants there in 2007, though about three hundred of these are in Australia. There, as elsewhere, "special products developed to satisfy local tastes and respond to competitive conditions" are part of the restaurant's fare, but always as a complement to the standard Burger King menu items, principally hamburgers, french fries, and soft drinks.[51]

ROLE OF PSEUDO FOOD TRANSNATIONALS

Global fast-food chains market their own edible products, but they also play an important role in marketing nutrient-poor edible products manufactured by some of the largest global players in the food and beverage industry world-wide. For their part, supermarket chains wield influence in promoting the industrial diet in great part due to the role they play in marketing these same products. Finally, the transnational purveyors of pseudo foods market their products in myriad other ways in their efforts to expand their profile and dominate these emerging markets.

Which are the key global corporations aggressively promoting pseudo foods and junk foods to countries of the developing world? It is, in fact, not always the usual list of suspects. With the concentration of capital in the food industry over the twentieth century, it became possible for the remaining suc-cessful food companies to diversify beyond their original product base into new and especially lucrative areas. Nutrient-poor edible products were one broad area that offered especially attractive returns, as I note in Chapter 10. Global food companies with incredible market power, such as Nestlé, Kraft, General Mills, and Kellogg's, not traditionally thought of as junk food pur-veyors, have become potent forces for the dissemination of nutrient-poor products in recent times. It may help to examine a few of these corporate giants to see what kinds of food environments they actually promote. To an important extent, it is directly at odds with the vision they have of themselves and wish to project to the world.

The Case of Nestlé

Nestlé is a true giant of the global food business. Formed in 1905 through the merger of a European condensed-milk company and a Swiss-based baby for-mula company, Nestlé began to market chocolates as well that same year. Junk foods, then, were actually built into its corporate DNA from the begin-ning. Headquartered in Switzerland but with a slight majority of sharehold-ers resident in the United States, this corporation had exceeded $100 billion in sales by 2007. Nestlé's global corporate slogan is "Good Food, Good Life." It has recently begun to position itself as a "Nutrition, Health and Wellness" company in its official documents.[52]

Nestlé has been, of course, the subject of considerable global nutritional controversy for several decades because of its global marketing of infant formula. Critics have charged that in the best case, infant formula does not confer the health advantages of breast milk, and in the worst case, as when it cannot be refrigerated or is mixed with contaminated water, conditions widely prevalent in the global South, it can kill infants.[53] Recent research has also indicated the link between formula-fed babies and higher incidence of obesity later in life.[54]

Another matter that has attracted much less controversy is the fact that at the same time the company markets its weight-management products through its recently acquired Jenny Craig division, it is also marketing globally a variety of high-calorie and nutrient-poor products through its confectionery and dairy divisions. By the 1980s, Nestlé had added to its confectionery arsenal with the purchase of chocolate bar maker Rowntree, and the Italian confectionery firm Buitoni-Perugina. In 2007, the company's sales of confectionery and ice cream worldwide approached $20 billion, constituting approximately 20 percent of total global product sales. Approximately $4.2 billion in sales of confectionery takes place in Latin America and the Caribbean, Asia, Oceania, and Africa.[55]

In recent years, Nestlé was seeing its most robust sales in the emerging markets of the global South – Brazil, China, the Philippines – and Russia. In fact, Asia, Africa, Latin America, and the Caribbean constituted about 30 percent of the company's $100 billion plus in global sales by 2007, indicative of the significance of investments by the world's largest food corporation in these regions to date. This company will inevitably play a leading role in transforming diets there.

The Case of Kraft

Kraft, for some time a division of the tobacco giant Altria Group Inc. (formerly Phillip Morris), was spun off as a separate corporate entity by 2007 and has become a processing giant with revenues exceeding $37 billion. Much like the conglomerate food giant Nestlé, Kraft has several large divisions within which it groups its products. And like Nestlé, Kraft seeks to position itself to take advantage of contradictory trends within the food industry, in particular, the growing interest of consumers for snack products on the one hand and for healthier products on the other. Kraft manufactures a range of nutrient-poor, high-glycemic products that constitute a very significant part of its overall business. Interestingly, it has recently appointed as its CEO an executive who was formerly the CEO of the salty snack division of PepsiCo, Frito Lay.[56]

FIGURE 11.2

Mondelēs International, revenue by product category, 2012

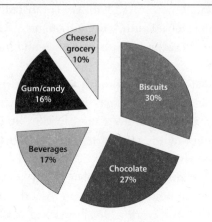

SOURCE: Mondelēs International Fact Sheet, http://www.mondelesinternational.com/
SiteCollectionDocuments/pdf/mondeles_int_fact_sheet.pdf.

Kraft's snacks division makes and sells primarily cookies, chocolate confectionery, salted snacks, and crackers, including leading products such as Oreo, Chips Ahoy!, Newtons, Peek Freans, Toblerone, Suchard, Marabou, Freia, Côte d'Or, SnackWell's, and many more. It also manufacturers presweetened cereals, including Honey Bunches of Oats, Pebbles, and Honeycomb. Collectively, these types of products amounted to 30 percent of Kraft's total net revenues worldwide in 2007,[57] growing to 38 percent with the more recent purchase of Groupe Danone's biscuit division. Figure 11.2 illustrates the corporation's overall product makeup. Although Kraft does not appear to be pursuing markets in the global South as aggressively as some other companies, it did have 123 of a total of 187 manufacturing plants in forty-four countries as of 2007, with forty-six of these being in Latin America, eastern Europe, the Middle East, Africa, and the Asia Pacific region.[58] Recently, it moved to enhance its exposure to the profits junk foods can provide through its expensive acquisition of the British candy giant Cadbury PLC. The explanation of Kraft CEO Irene Rosenfeld when asked what the takeover of Cadbury was all about is telling regarding where Kraft sees itself as a company: "It is very simply about growth, putting a larger proportion of our portfolio in growing categories like chocolate, gum and candy. It means a broader geographic footprint, especially in developing markets."[59] This controversial acquisition, it turns out, was only a preliminary move to be followed in 2012 with a major reorganization that saw Kraft spin off its North American grocery products division and rename the remaining corporate entity, with its powerful snack brands ($36 billion annual revenue), Mondelēs International. Now the world's largest snack purveyor, Mondelēs is committed to aggressively pushing its snack brands in developing markets (see the fact sheet on its website). It will likely become a major player in globalizing the industrial diet.

PepsiCo in India

The Pepsi-Cola company spent much of the twentieth century playing catch-up to Coca-Cola in the carbonated beverage business, but in more recent times this company has emerged as a major force in the food and beverage industry worldwide. With astute marketing in the 1980s and afterward, and the purchase of the salty snack processor Frito Lay, the fortunes of the company have changed dramatically. PepsiCo is now a major force to be reckoned with in the shaping of food environments around the globe, from Russia to India and everywhere in between. In its major national market, the United States, the company spent over $1.3 billion in advertising alone in 2006. By 2007, the company estimated the revenues from the sales of its products worldwide to be a staggering $98 billion.[60] Only Nestlé and Coca-Cola were of this size in the global food and beverage industry.

It is notable that in recent years, PepsiCo has chosen its chief executive officer from a developing country – Indra Nooyi, a management professional who received her early professional formation in India, one of the company's main target markets. PepsiCo has been very active, in fact, in using its marketing know-how about attracting new customers in the vast new markets offered by India and China. The company entered India in 1989 and, with forty-three bottling plants, claims to now be one of the largest multinational investors in the country, and its revenues show very strong growth, tripling every five years.[61] Although typically thought of as a manufacturer of soft drinks, PepsiCo's salty snacks division in India, as elsewhere, is the one that has seen the highest rates of growth. And whereas its initial strategy in India was apparently one of expanding its base of customers who were willing to switch some of their beverage consumption to soft drinks from more traditional drinks such as tea, more recently the company has switched its emphasis to one that attempts to "increase the depth of consumption."[62]

Much like global fast-food operations, PepsiCo shows evidence of considerable cultural intelligence as it seeks to penetrate local markets and, as in North America, it is appealing especially to the young. As the advertising text of its India website notes of one of its snack products, "From the land of 'tiffins' comes a new lip smacking flavour which embodies the spirit of the West. The new Kurkure Mumbai Chatpata flavour with a mix of mild spices, pepper, chillies and a dash of fennel. It will force your taste buds to say 'Majaama.'" PepsiCo India CEO Sanjeev Chadha has noted the company's strategy to "leverage local taste" preferences by developing extruded snack products that incorporate aspects of regional cuisine. He also notes that given the fact that half of Indians earn about a dollar a day or less, company success is linked to marketing product at a price point at which they can still be widely purchased. With this reality in mind, one of the company's salty snack products is marketed for the equivalent of one and a half cents a bag.[63]

With product innovation and advertising sensitive to local pop culture, PepsiCo has invested heavily to make its websites interactive and fun. Part of the attraction on its India website, for instance, is interactive video games one can easily play to pass the time. Its "What's Your Way" ad campaign posts various social dilemmas teens and young adults might find themselves in, and invites people to post their various solutions to these dilemmas online, with the possibility of getting their photo on a Pepsi-Cola can. Another feature of the website offers the possibility of uploading one's photo to be placed on a can of Pepsi-Cola, a photo of which is then posted on Facebook. A press release lays out the point of its Indian strategy: "It's all about connecting with Youth in their own space. Whether it is engaging with the 30 million youth on the internet, co-creating with the 6-odd million youngsters on social networking sites, or connecting with 250 million youth on their mobiles, the What's Your Way! campaign, is a conversation between the Youth and Pepsi in a fun environment."[64]

Coca-Cola and the China Market

No discussion of the globalization of the industrial diet would be complete without mention of the efforts of the Coca-Cola Company. Coca-Cola has been a pioneer in this regard, expanding the reach of its products before many of today's prominent transnational fast food and supermarket chains even existed. However, one cannot speak of a *recent* shift of operations to the global South in the context of this company. It has, in fact, penetrated numerous markets there for a very long time. What is new with Coke, then?

For one thing, markets have changed as the world has changed. New consuming populations are being created, both by the opening up of previously denied national spaces and by the surge in monetary incomes of tens of millions of citizens in the global South. With saturated markets in the developed world, and growing opposition to their role in promoting nutrient-poor diets from organizations in civil society and government, companies such as Coca-Cola have taken on a renewed interest of late in the global South, where nutritional consciousness is still at a very low level, and most especially in areas with dense populations where their presence was limited until now. India and China, with 2.5 billion people between them, are not surprisingly at the forefront of this new corporate expansion. Coca-Cola's recent activities in China serve as a potent example of what this company is trying to achieve in the near term in developing countries, where it expects 60 percent of its future growth to occur.[65]

The year 2009 witnessed an acceleration of Coca-Cola's interest in the vast potential that China offers for food and beverage transnationals. The company announced plans to invest $2 billion in just the following three years alone, along with its announcement to extend its reach by building bottling plants in the remoter central and western provinces of that country. This is on top of the thirty-eight bottling plants the company and its affiliated bottlers have already established in greater China. The size of the announced investment is in keeping with China having become the third largest market for Coca-Cola in the world. Moreover, in the context of a global economic decline, the company's growth in 2008 was still at an impressive annual rate of 19 percent.[66] This significant growth may have been partly because of the company's success in leveraging its brand in China through its aggressive marketing as a Beijing Olympics sponsor. Coca-Cola has a long history of involvement with the Olympic organization going back to the 1932 Games in Los Angeles. In Beijing, Coca-Cola took a page from marketing strategies pioneered by food industry giants such as General Mills long ago and prominently featured celebrity American basketball player LeBron James, along with Chinese basketball star Yao Ming, as part of the Coca-Cola Olympic Star Team.[67]

Coca-Cola is interested in China because, among other reasons, the market is potentially extremely large. Coca-Cola already controls more than one-half of China's soft drink market and 12 percent of its fruit and vegetable juice market, according to one mainstream business source.[68] And yet, from the point of view of consumption, this market has hardly been tapped when it is considered that with an annual per capita consumption of 28 Coca-Cola products per person, China is far below the level of consumption the company has achieved in Brazil, where the average is 199 company drink products per capita annually.[69]

The unhindered expansion of Coca-Cola in China, and other transnationals for that matter, is not a foregone conclusion. The recent blocking by the central government of the company's intended buyout of a large Chinese juice corporation demonstrates that even the largest food and beverage transnationals from time to time experience powerful local resistance, particularly when they misjudge local sentiments, or in this case, the investment guidelines of a powerful central government.[70]

THE GLOBALIZING DIET: WHERE WILL IT END?

The trends of the globalization of the industrial diet are sobering. Within a very short time, the diets of very large numbers of humans have been to some degree affected. I have tried to give an idea of what I believe to be the main vectors, or engines, behind this phenomenon. Have the diets of large sections of the population of developing countries been transformed, and do they now ingest ever greater quantities of nutrient-poor edible products on a daily and ever increasing basis because of the activities of the global supermarket and fast-food chains, and what I have called the pseudo and junk food transnationals? I do not believe anyone is yet in a position to answer this question definitively one way or the other. What can be said is that the emerging evidence on chronic disease strongly suggests that momentous changes in diets in these countries are underway, and that these changes are more advanced in certain regions and countries than others. Latin American countries were typically the first developing markets that American and European food and beverage corporations exploited. Not coincidentally, the most economically developed of these – the most attractive markets for foreign investment – are also the countries grappling with some of the highest rates of obesity and related chronic disease.

THE ENEMY WITHIN

A weakness of the foregoing analysis is that it suggests that dietary transformation is the responsibility of global food and beverage transnationals, and them alone. In my defence, I would plead that this analytical bias is in the end inevitable – it is simply an overwhelming task to consider seriously the local influences that also contribute to dietary transformation. Nevertheless, it is important to recognize the existence of forces at this level. In this regard, I would insist that, depending upon the context, it is also necessary to recognize that indigenous food and beverage manufacturers, and indigenous supermarket chain stores, have also made their mark fostering dietary transformation. It is essential to realize this, or else one can quickly fall into the error of seeking solutions to the impending health crises that these dietary changes portend solely by limiting transnational domination of local food systems. It cannot be forgotten that in lieu of the transnationals, their local imitators will be only too happy to flog a similar panoply of health-destroying edible commodities in their place. Indeed, they are presently doing so in many of the countries of the global South, and often so successfully that transnational firms are more than willing to buy them up to expand their market reach.

Solutions to the dilemmas indicated here are not ultimately rooted in a struggle to liberate societies from the damages of transnational edible products manufacturers and retailers, though their present power is inordinate and increasingly pervasive. In the end, the quest for meaningful solutions must entail a serious questioning of the economic system that subordinates nutritional quality and human health to the maximization of investor returns. To note but one example, an Indian or Chinese or South African or Brazilian corporation that manages to persuade its compliant local government that soft drinks in schools are both good for business and good for making up for cutbacks to educational budgets is no better than a foreign company that does so. In either case, diets are corrupted, and health is undermined. What must be addressed is the enabling context that allows these economic actors, whether national or foreign, to enrich themselves at the expense of human health.

CHAPTER TWELVE

Transformative Food Movements and the Struggle for Healthy Eating

Unhealthy weight is a problem of the body politic rather than a problem only of individual bodies.

> —Jane Dixon and Dorothy Broom, *The Seven Deadly Sins of Obesity*[1]

Can a society truly claim to be sustainable if it fails to invest in nutritious school food for young and vulnerable people?

> —Kevin Morgan and Roberta Sonnino, *The School Food Revolution*[2]

We are trying to create a different programmatic response to food vulnerability and it's called the community food centre.

> —Nick Saul, executive director, The Stop[3]

W E LIVE IN A TIME pregnant with contradictions. The industrial diet is being rapidly reproduced in developing countries while simultaneously being seriously challenged in the very societies in which it originated. These challenges constitute important evidence of a growing resistance to the powerful forces that bear responsibility for the degradation of diets over the last century or so. This resistance is the other side of the coin to those features of the third dietary regime discussed in the previous chapter. It would seem to be one of the defining characteristics of the contemporary dietary regime as well.

The industrial diet is progressively being resisted in developed countries through alternative ways of food provisioning that, to varying degrees, put a profit-oriented food system into question. Advocates of these alternatives to the dominant model see environmental, taste, social justice, local control, and animal welfare criteria as important, or even paramount. These challenges to the industrial diet and the production system that underlies it have been referred to by academics as "alternative food movements." As Wynne Wright and Gerad Middendorf have argued, these movements "signify a mounting reflexivity and new modes of action among producers, consumers, and activists in the production and consumption of food."[4] They include the slow food movement, the movement promoting organic foods, initiatives for fair trade foods, the growing interest in constructing sustainable food systems, the food sovereignty movement, and the tremendous recent upsurge of interest and activity around relocalizing food production. Although each of these movements has its own agenda, together, they include the revitalization of small and medium food producers, providing food for the poorest sectors of society, establishing producers' rights and equitable compensation for food production, environmental recovery and health, the rescuing of disappearing varieties and culinary traditions, and a revival in the appreciation of the crafts tradition in food production and preparation whereby food once found a central place in social activity and community affairs.

However laudable each of these initiatives is on its own, they do seem somewhat limited in terms of their social impact and more tuned to the concerns of specific (sometimes privileged) segments of society, with the exception of the push for a more sustainable agriculture – something presumably in the interest of all of us. The degradation of food environments around the globe that these struggles for healthy eating address, on the other hand, is a process that affects nearly all of us, though to considerably varying degrees. It is a process that educated and economically advantaged sectors of society have been better able to protect themselves from, of course. Even within these groups, however, the relatively high prevalence of overweight and obesity (in Canada, affluent adult males are the most overweight segment of the population) testifies to the pervasiveness of the factors that produce obesity and the now well-established negative health outcomes associated with this condition.[5]

The forces that are largely responsible for the degradation of food environments, then, are the objective basis against which a truly widespread movement is emerging to establish healthy food environments. The healthy eating "movement" is not yet particularly visible, and there have been few noisy demonstrations to proclaim its existence. It has yet to find a common theme and rallying cry. The struggle for healthy eating has not yet become a movement in the way that the suffragette movement for women's rights in the early twentieth century did, or the civil rights movement in the United States did in the 1960s. Yet, the degradation of our food environments that I have examined in the preceding chapters represents such a universal injustice that there is the possibility that the struggle for healthy eating will also, someday, become highly visible and truly transformative, the way the suffragette and civil rights movements were in their own time.

If this incipient movement has a central motif, it may well be that it is oriented to the struggle to ensure that maximizing health, rather than profit making, is the highest priority in the provisioning of food to the various sectors of society, and in particular the most vulnerable sectors, including children and youth, the old and infirm, and those who find themselves economically and socially marginalized. In fact, there is evidence that real progress in this direction is already being made.

TOWARD A HEALTH-BASED FOOD SYSTEM

The broader context of the struggle for healthy eating is the escalating phenomenon of population-wide weight gain and obesity, and the impact on societies around the globe of neo-liberal economic, social, and political policies. By taking hold of mindsets and subsequently reshaping the policy landscape, the forces behind the neo-liberal economic and political agenda have played their part in transforming food environments.[6] Neo-liberal approaches to food prioritize market-based solutions and profit taking over the nutritional health of children and youth. In more specific terms, they have expanded the reach of the corporate food sector and served to open up public sector food environments (e.g., schools, hospitals) to corporate control where before it was limited, particularly in developed countries such as Canada, with its relatively broad public sector involvement in education and health.

In the end, one can argue that the struggle for healthy eating is almost inevitably drawn into combat with the powerful forces degrading diets globally and undermining the well-being of billions on planet Earth. This prospective movement can also be seen to have parallel and overlapping agendas with some of the other alternative food movements presently receiving attention.

I see the struggle around healthy eating as a prospective alternative social movement of importance and one that goes to the heart of the contradictions that are produced by the capitalist control of food. This struggle is nothing less than a response to the very serious imbalances that characterize food economies today. Of course, like most if not all of the struggles that have proceeded it, this one can be expected to have to deal with internal differences and orientations. It is unlikely, for instance, that there will ever be complete agreement over which foods are healthy. Hopefully, however, there will emerge a general consensus on some of the fundamental and long-standing processes of the food industry that have degraded whole foods and transformed diets in manifestly unhealthy ways, as well as a growing resolve to counter these processes and practices. Indeed, it is my contention here that this has been happening for some time. I would also contend that confronting these processes and practices has the potential to lay bare the contradictions of producing healthy food within a profit-based political economy and better illuminate the need for alternative means of food provisioning in many areas where for-profit enterprise has manifestly failed to deliver a healthy diet.

THE FORMS OF STRUGGLE FOR HEALTHY EATING

The struggle for healthy eating takes many forms in North America, as it does in other societies in the developed world. It is useful to reflect a moment on what these different forms look like, before we think through what they may have in common, what prevents the various types of struggles from having greater effect, and what role academics and intellectuals in general have played and can play in future.

Within the state apparatus itself, and within the legislative chambers of government and the state health care bureaucracy, there has continued to be ongoing skirmishes between the forces that (broadly speaking) act in the public interest on food, nutrition, and related health matters and those pursuing more narrow corporate or sectoral interests. These skirmishes have amounted to considerable battles at times, when the stakes for the stakeholders are big enough, as Marion Nestle has demonstrated for the United States, for example, in her influential study titled *Food Politics*.[7]

In Canada, the highly charged debate several years ago over whether to allow the use of Monsanto's bovine growth hormone (BGH) in the nation's milk supply pitted "David" in the form of scientists working at the Health Protection Branch of Health Canada (the equivalent of the US Food and Drug Administration) against a formidable "Goliath" in the form of an alliance of the Health Protection Branch management and the corporate giant Monsanto itself. This battle included allegations of corporate bribes to federally employed scientists; the intervention of the Toronto Food Policy Council and the public broadcaster – the Canadian Broadcasting Corporation – which was willing to give the whistle-blowing scientists a platform for talking about their report that was critical of Health Canada's approval process on BGH technology;[8] and the not insignificant role of a popular former minister of agriculture and then senator, Eugene Whelen, who publicly declared that farmers had no need for Monsanto's technology.[9] Given the centrality of dairy products in the Canadian diet, it was not altogether surprising that once the scientific controversy was made public, significant wider debate would ensue. In any case, BGH was not approved in Canada, and a recent major film documentary and book on Monsanto notes that these Canadian developments played a role in the subsequent European ban on BGH there.[10]

The controversy over BGH in Canada illustrates the complex nature that the struggle for healthy eating is likely to take. It illustrates, for example, the tensions within the state over such issues, and it shows us that to treat the state as a monolithic entity is a mistake when searching for effective avenues to advance a healthy-eating agenda.

This affair, as it turns out, has been one of the few, but notable, Canadian victories in recent times for the public good rather than the transnational corporation. It has had implications further afield, as well. In the United States, concern about BGH has been growing, with a few prominent scientists raising concerns over BGH milk since the early 1990s, and more recently in France.[11] In the United States, by 2007, a major American food retailer – Kroger – had announced that it would complete the transition of the milk it processes and sells in all of its stores to a certified BGH-free supply by February 2008.[12] This incident illustrates the potential of having wider forces drawn into struggles that are organized to protect the public's right to a healthy food supply.

In Canada, as in the United States, government action on healthy eating has taken other less dramatic but nonetheless significant forms – new labelling legislation, for example, and also some limited initiatives around trans fats. On the issue of the dangers of trans fats to human health, it is worth noting that nutritional scientists had warned government authorities about them three decades ago, but to no avail.[13] Nevertheless, in these contexts, the struggle has been largely contained within the state itself. Those wishing to constrain more forthright and thoroughgoing reforms to food regulations have been more successful at limiting the damage to their interests.

Advocates from civil society and lower-level state actors in the form of public health authorities had, in conjunction with allies within Health Canada, some success in bringing forth new legislation requiring labelling of food and beverage products with (but not all) nutrient values, as well as trans fat contents, where such labels were not required and typically absent before. This is also a victory for the public good, though a limited one. Loopholes in the labelling legislation allow food processors to essentially hide unhealthy amounts of certain ingredients such as sugar and salt in unrealistic "suggested serving size" amounts, while dangerous trans fats in food are labelled but not banned, as they could be and have been in Denmark. Significant here is a recent report that found that many of the foods examined in Canada still contained dangerous amounts of trans fats,[14] despite controversy over them in the media. Indeed, a potent indicator of the ongoing problem trans fats constitute is provided by Canadian studies of breast milk, indicating that these fats still exist in disturbingly high levels in mother's milk.[15] The trans fat issue can be seen as one that illustrates the limited gains to be made by waiting for voluntary corporate action on even the most egregious forms of dietary pollution, and the imperative of having state regulatory mechanisms in place to achieve real positive change for healthy eating.

SCHOOLS AS A SITE FOR HEALTHY EATING ACTIVISM

Arguably, a more dramatic representation of the actual struggle for healthy eating has been taking place in the institutional contexts of the schools. As Kevin Morgan and Roberta Sonnino argue in their pioneering book *The School Food Revolution*, "Whatever the national context or cultural setting, the reform of school food raises some of the most compelling ethical, political and economic questions that a society can ask itself in the 21st century."[16] School food environments matter because they constitute a major site for meeting the nutritional needs of children and youth.[17] As Michele Simon has argued, school food environments are an important institutional site that presents advantages for those wishing to advance the cause of healthy eating that do not exist in other institutional contexts.[18]

School food environments have indeed become contested terrain where civil society advocates, the state, and corporate private interests have engaged in a series of clashes, the most visible being in the United States and Britain. As major institutions that occupy a sizable portion of government budgets in the developed world, schools have borne much of the brunt of cutbacks associated with neo-liberal economic policies. In the United States, school food-service programs were regular line items in local school district budgets but must now be completely self-supported, and federal reimbursements for lunch programs fell between 1995 and 2000. Selling nutrient-poor products – essentially fast food, junk foods, and pseudo foods – have been one of the few ways to relieve this fiscal constraint.[19] Chronic funding shortfalls have been only one aspect of the story, of course, but it has been crucial in opening up the schools, from the primary level to the post-secondary level, to elements of the corporate food sector.

As Janet Poppendieck has noted, with federal funding cuts in the United States, local school boards were forced to act like for-profit enterprises and reduce the cost of food and labour while expanding their customer base.[20] This has had unfortunate nutritional consequences. Labour costs were lowered by reducing, often drastically, the foods produced from scratch, replacing these with semi-processed edible products that could simply be reheated. This was a phenomenon I noted in my research on school food environments in Ontario, and it was part of the degrading of school food environments in Britain as well.[21] In some US jurisdictions, the prepackaged food manufacturers even provided the freezers for their reheat meals. In Canada and the United States, kitchens that could once prepare large numbers of meals from scratch have been transformed into giant reheat operations that provide semi-processed edible products to students.[22] These are the same nutrient-poor types of products that earned the label "cheap processed muck" in the British context.[23]

The advantage for school boards in reorienting kitchens to reheat operations is that they could employ kitchen staff for reduced hours, and thereby pay them as casual labour rather than as full-time workers with benefits. It also meant that lower-skilled and therefore cheaper labour could be hired.[24] These changes were part of a broader neo-liberal approach to education brought in by conservative governments in one country after another in the 1980s and 1990s, an approach that seriously degraded school food in the interest of saving a few dollars or pounds in the education budget. With a shortsightedness that is nothing less than astounding, the actual health costs down the line were not accounted for.

Multinational beverage and snack food manufacturers (often one and the same, as with PepsiCo and Nestlé) have been especially willing to provide money to schools in exchange for the opportunity to gain further beachheads in the public domain and to cash in on the lucrative youth market, which they view as pivotal to their profitability.[25] In Manitoba, about a third of schools reported having sponsorships from a food and beverage company in 2001, with the overwhelming majority of agreements made with a multinational corporation, typically PepsiCo or Coca-Cola.[26] Provincial surveys of school food environments in several jurisdictions found that they were heavily saturated with nutrient-poor products.[27] Recent literature has also documented the influence of multinational soft drink corporations in the school food environment in the form of "pouring rights" in American schools.[28] A notable survey of principals in Minnesota, for example, found that 77 percent of high schools in the state had signed a contract with a soft drink corporation.[29] Another study of a nationally representative sample of schools in the United States found that 72 percent of senior high schools had a contract that gave a company the right to sell its products in the school.[30]

Concerned parents and professionals (particularly in the field of public health), but also teachers and sometimes school administrators, have led the fight to take back school food environments from corporate beverage companies and fast-food vendors that have infiltrated schools made vulnerable in years past by chronic underfunding by state authorities. They have been assisted, directly or indirectly, by the efforts of researchers, especially in the medical and nutritional sciences, who have carefully documented the growing phenomenon of weight gain and obesity among children and youth, and established a growing body of science indicating the links between the dramatic population-wide weight gains in recent decades and serious negative health outcomes.

This struggle over school food environments has taken on different forms in each national context, according to different conditions, actors, and legislative arrangements, but in every case it has been a response to the deplorable state of school food and the growing threat (including the threat to state and provincial budgets) of the obesity epidemic among children and youth. So where are we now with broad-based efforts to rescue school food environments?

Britain has taken a lead in this regard (and in related matters, such as legislation limiting advertising by the junk food and fast-food transnationals). Reacting to public embarrassment over the quality of the state-funded school food program, a situation orchestrated in part by celebrity chef Jamie Oliver in his popular television series *Jamie's School Dinners*, but also influenced by Scottish social policy innovations and the long-standing efforts of civil society organizations such as the Soil Association, the Blair government was cajoled into action to address the situation once it had become defined as a national problem of some urgency.[31] The political crisis over school food led to the setting up of the School Food Trust in 2005, with £15 million in government funding to promote the health of schoolchildren and improve the quality of food supplied to schools and consumed there. Its chief goals are to:

- ensure all schools meet the food based and nutrient based standards for lunch and non-lunch food
- increase the uptake of school meals
- reduce diet-related inequalities in childhood through food education and school based initiatives
- improve food skills through food education, and school and community initiatives.[32]

Efforts to improve the nutritional disaster that characterized British school food are ongoing and have experienced problems, but there is evidence that real progress has been made.[33] The British case points out the possibilities for a renewal of progressive state intervention at the national level on the issues of food, nutrition, and health, matters that have traditionally been the domain of the federal state in many societies.

It is useful to consider the factors that made possible state action to address food nutritional quality in Britain. Four stand out. First, the contemporary phenomenon of the celebrity chef allowed an individual – chef Jamie Oliver – to emerge as a catalyst for change. Important here is the fact that he was among the first of the relatively few celebrity chefs who "get it" when it comes to healthy eating. Second, there existed in Britain well-developed civil society organizations working on food and agricultural issues, the Soil Association being one of the most prominent. Third, there existed growing awareness within the state, but the general public as well, of the rapidity with which population-wide weight gains have occurred and the potential health time bomb this implies. Fourth, Britain has been one of the few developed societies in recent years to have had a national government with a moderately progressive orientation – this cannot be insignificant.[34]

In the United States by the end of the 1990s, if not before, the signs of organized public resistance to the penetration of the school food environment by fast-food and beverage corporations were evident.[35] Since that time, the

Surgeon General and professional groups have begun to call for change,[36] activists and some celebrity chefs have decried the existing state of affairs, public consciousness has been raised by civil society organizations such as the Centre for Science in the Public Interest and such cinematic triumphs as Morgan Spurlock's brilliant *Super Size Me*, and local healthy eating initiatives have begun to proliferate. Slowly, some governments have begun to take action. State governments in the United States, rather than federal authorities, have been the sites of policy initiatives, which is not particularly surprising given the lock that corporate America had over the Bush White House.[37] Mary Story and her co-authors reported that twenty-three states have adopted legislation limiting the times and/or types of "competitive foods" (typically fast food) available in schools, while a few major city school districts, including Los Angeles, New York, and Chicago, have moved to ban soft drinks and high-fat snack foods in school vending machines.[38]

In Canada, where provincial governments have authority over education, the response has been limited in terms of concrete legislation, but, increasingly, provincial governments have moved beyond the information-gathering stage and have been galvanized into action. The motivations behind such action are not clear but are likely a combination of warnings from professional dietitians about the poor quality of school food environments,[39] evidence on the proliferation of poor nutrition products from their own surveys of provincial schools, mounting evidence of high rates of childhood obesity, and in at least one case, the prospect of dire financial costs to government associated with the latter.[40] In any case, since 2006, several provinces have moved to dramatically revamp nutritional guidelines for schools so as to reduce or eliminate nutrient-poor food and beverage products. It remains to be seen whether these will receive strong enforcement, but it is a very hopeful development.

FARM-TO-SCHOOL PROGRAMS

Alongside these formal government actions have been a host of more informal, localized initiatives to promote healthy eating in schools. Of particular note is the proliferation of farm-to-school programs, which typically have improvement of the school food environment as one of their objectives but may also be seen to contribute to community health more generally.[41] These programs exist throughout the United States, Canada, and Britain and have been spurred by factors such as concern over the rise of obesity, desire to improve the situation of agricultural producers, rising health care costs, a desire to improve environmental practices, and the quality of school meals.[42]

As Amanda Marshall argues in reference to the federally funded National School Lunch Program in the United States, "The United States has long recognized its responsibility to feed schoolchildren; farm to school is one of the ways to ensure that schoolchildren are not just being fed, but *being fed well*" (emphasis in original). She noted in 2006 that in just over ten years, approximately nine hundred farm-to-school projects and programs have sprung up in some thirty states, the National Farm to School Network has been formed, and legislation supporting local procurement or farm-to-school initiatives has been passed in at least thirteen states.[43] Among the most original is the Marin Organic project in Marin County, California, which collects organic produce and dairy products from growers around the county and from a local processor and makes deliveries of these whole organic foods to public and private high schools.[44] (More on this in the next chapter.)

In Britain, considerable interest in securing healthier foods for schools and other public sector institutions from local provisioners, including directly from farm operations, has developed. There, obstacles posed by treaties related to the European Union have made local provisioning difficult, but creative ways are being worked out to manoeuvre around regulations.[45]

Marshall has advanced several points that she considers most relevant in transforming farm-to-school initiatives from individual projects to the whole school level, whereby these limited initiatives can take on a more systemic character. Key considerations include the pre-existence of a fertile school culture that is open to initiatives on nutrition and the environment; the existence of a champion or champions at the local level with the vision to make the initiative broader and deeper; the need to meld bottom-up with top-down initiatives; recognizing that longer-term sustainability requires buy-in at the level of government at some point; acknowledging that inspirational stories can be essential to motivating change; bringing in partners to broaden the healthy-eating initiative and secure needed expertise; responding to previously identified needs within the school and community; and building on positive experiences and small successes.[46] These, then, are some of the most prominent manifestations of initiatives that take on the agenda of transforming contemporary food environments so that nutritional health, rather than profit making, can become the central motif of food provisioning. One might point to other initiatives, both within and outside institutional domains, that share this agenda in one form or another, and indeed there is much potential for synergistic linkages with activists involved in food security organizations; those interested in promoting green forms of provisioning, in particular the local food movement; and even slow food advocates.

It is a testament to the success of healthy eating initiatives and activism so far that some of the world's most powerful food and beverage transnationals have been forced into a strategy of effective retrenchment. This is illustrated, for example, in PepsiCo's public commitment not to market its highest sugar offerings in US schools.[47] Clearly, such voluntary actions can be seen as an attempt to forestall possible legislation such as has been implemented in Britain, which could seriously impair the company's ability to reach the highly profitable children and youth markets.

THE PROGRESSIVE POTENTIAL OF TODAY'S HEALTHY-EATING STRUGGLES

The struggle for healthy eating, perhaps not surprisingly, has taken forms that have within them the seeds of a more radical critique of the food system. The logic of challenging contemporary conditions in schools typically forces challengers to confront the legacy of neo-liberalism, at least at a basic level, and consider the substantial disadvantages that citizenry face with a disempowered state sector. Quite unlike a number of other alternative food movements, this struggle has the potential to challenge the hegemony of neo-liberal discourse more generally by pointing to the manifest contradictions in policies that systematically privilege corporate purveyors of edible product over children's health, the health of other vulnerable populations, and the public in general. An important illustration of this has been the neo-liberal restructuring of educational institutions and the serious cutbacks these have entailed. These cutbacks have produced unexpected negative consequences for vulnerable sectors of society as they open a very wide door to powerful corporate actors that produce nutrient-poor commodities, a reality that has been documented by several important studies in the United States.

In the United Kingdom, where the balance of forces at the federal level has been markedly different from that in the United States, the federal state was essentially goaded into action in ways unprecedented in contemporary times, legislating an "ad ban" on corporations wishing to push junk food and fast food in television programming oriented to children and youth.[48] The once unchallenged prerogatives of the market have taken a direct hit with this legislation, and with the precedent it sets for reformers elsewhere to try to achieve the same and, indeed, to push the legislation further.

Is a renewal of state-initiated progressive legislative reform of food environments along the lines of that undertaken in Britain, and indeed the extension and deepening of what has been achieved there, a realistic possibility elsewhere? Is it worthwhile pursuing, or should efforts be concentrated on grassroots initiatives? My view is that a strategy that embraces *both* is one to be favoured, but that at different times and places an emphasis on one or the other may be the most effective. I take a realistic look at the prospects in the concluding chapter. Before doing so, I take a more in-depth look at case studies of what I consider to be catalytic organizations and exemplars among the widespread initiatives aimed at resisting the degradation of food environments and promoting healthy eating.

CHAPTER THIRTEEN

CASE STUDIES OF
A TRANSFORMATIVE FOOD
MOVEMENT

FOR NUMEROUS YEARS NOW there has evolved a broad spectrum of sites in which the struggle for healthy eating is taking place. In the process, food environments, at least in some of the developed countries, are beginning to be reformed, if not transformed. Of those organizations involved in this broad struggle, some have played particularly significant roles. I see these roles as being essentially inspirational and catalytic, in the sense that these organizations have been exceptionally innovative and have demonstrated what is achievable in transforming food environments. They have shown the potential to precipitate real change in that they have been uniquely successful in forging a link between the food economy, on the one hand, and significant food environments – schools – on the other, a link that has advanced healthy eating outcomes.

The case studies considered here, of two of these kinds of organizations, in no way exhaust the variety of developments occurring, even in North America. They do provide inspirational experiences in the sense that they have each achieved significant progress in making local food environments healthier, and have done so in a way that also engages and strengthens local food production. One is more rural based, and one urban based, one American and one Canadian. Their stories can be added to the emergent literature examining efforts to transform food environments in a key institutional sphere in modern societies: schools.

MARIN ORGANIC

My introduction to the California organization known as Marin Organic was through a discussion I had with a colleague and inspirational figure in my local food and agriculture scene, Jennifer Sumner. Jennifer had encouraged me to visit the organization, and I first managed to arrange for this on the way back from a trip to visit family in Australia. And so, in the spring of 2006, I found myself amid the stunning rolling green hills and small lakes that typifies parts of Marin County, just north of San Francisco. The county had emerged as a hothouse for environmental organizations engaged in various kinds of educational efforts, and several of the county's agricultural producers had become interested in organic agriculture years earlier. Marin Organic developed as an expression of the desire to preserve county land in agriculture and enrich marketing opportunities for local producers. It has since expanded its reach.

I had become interested in Marin Organic when I heard that it was trying to spark the creation of durable relationships between the numerous organic farms in the area and county schools. School food environments had been seriously degraded in much of the United States and Canada over the previous decade or more, and the idea of infusing them with fresh organic produce definitely caught my attention. Farm-to-school programs were spreading throughout different parts of the United States, but Marin Organic's focus on organic produce seemed to be unique. However, organic produce is generally more labour-intensive to produce than non-organic and therefore more expensive. How could schools that in most jurisdictions have been dealing with funding cutbacks realistically embrace organic food? I learned that it had not been easy to engage schools at first. Organic produce was more expensive in Marin County, as elsewhere. But this is where the organization became creative, as I discovered during a long discussion with then executive director, Helge Hellberg, outside its offices over the Cow Café in the heart of Marin County.

Helge talked about how the organization had managed to make fresh organic produce and dairy products affordable for county schools. A key to this was the fact that something like 20 percent of produce was regularly left in the field because it did not meet the exacting cosmetic specifications of buyers. This was perfectly good produce that was left to rot and yielded no other benefit than the compost it provided for the next crop. What if an effort could be mounted to recover this food?

Historically, peasants in Europe and elsewhere had been granted the right to glean the landlords' lands after the harvest, gathering any leftover grain for their own subsistence. Jean-François Millet's 1857 painting *The Gleaners*, depicting three poor peasant women gleaning grain in the French countryside is perhaps the best-known portrayal of this age-old phenomenon. Resurrecting the practice of gleaning in Marin County to lower the cost to schools of organic produce seemed to me like a brilliant solution.

At the time of my first visit, Marin Organic was receiving a list of "gleanable" foods from local farmers by the end of each week. At that point, the organization would have to arrange labour to glean the fields if farmers were not able to do it themselves. As I was to later discover, this gleaning activity also included organic dairy products from a local processor when perfectly edible product could not be sold to buyers for one reason or another, which happened from time to time. As Helge told me, although the price of organic produce was generally higher than conventionally grown produce, when supplemented with the free food recovered by gleaning, the cost of the organic food Marin Organic could supply was competitive with the food the schools were previously buying. Increasingly, he noted, the schools the organization deals with value the quality of the food they receive.

In 2006, when the program was just getting underway, Marin Organic was enriching some five thousand school meals per week; local producers were getting back about $40,000 from the program annually, and about sixty thousand pounds of free food were being gleaned annually. This gleaned food was not undercutting the market price that farmers received for their produce because without it they would not have had schools buying their produce at all. Gleaned produce helped grease the wheels of the process, in other words, a process that was providing a significant revenue stream to farmers.

Although there had been initial resistance in school kitchens to the prospect of integrating organic produce into their meals, this was being resolved. This process had been helped along by organizing visits by kitchen staff to organic farms in the county so they could better appreciate the value of the produce they were receiving from Marin Organic. At the time of my first visit, about twelve schools had begun to buy food through Marin Organic, though a few of these were passing on some of the food to other schools as well. In total, about twenty schools and community centres were regularly receiving food via Marin Organic, and by the time of my second visit in 2007, some forty institutions were being serviced. The organization reports it was reaching ten thousand students with its organic food by 2010.[1]

Creative ways had to be found to meet the various costs in mounting this farm-to-school program, including delivery costs and staff expenses. One way the organization was meeting its expenses was through the relationship it had established with a private company that was emerging as a giant in the global IT industry – Google Inc. This company is located in California's Silicon Valley, not too far from county producers. Led by forward-thinking management, Google was open to enriching its employee cafeteria with Marin County organic produce. With some five thousand employees, Google constituted a significant revenue stream. In addition, Google supplied, free of charge, 150 gallons a week of used cooking oil, which Marin Organic has processed into biodiesel for the truck it uses to deliver produce to schools, thereby saving on fuel expenses.

A year after my first visit, I was able to return to Marin County. This time it was to prove to be more of a hands-on visit – getting in the truck, visiting farms, talking to farmers, picking up produce, and distributing very early the following day all of the produce we had collected to county schools. Orchestrating these tasks was Scott Davidson, who proved to be deeply knowledgeable about both the farm operations we were visiting and the schools receiving the organic bounty.

The Farms

Each week, Marin Organic is in touch with farmers to see what produce is available. With that information, Scott makes a consolidated list which he then emails to the schools every Thursday morning. Schools, in turn, email, fax, or phone in their food orders by Friday afternoon. That evening, Scott will call farm operators with the school orders, so that they will have a couple of days to harvest. In this farm-to-school process, then, Marin Organic is the catalyst that makes the idea of a farm and school food environment relationship actually happen. It has forged the crucial connections and gets done the critical administrative tasks and financial transactions that make this relationship function for both farmers and schools.

What kinds of farms get involved with this type of program? It surely is not the industrial-scale corporatized farm producing thousands of acres of soybean, corn, wheat, or the like that typifies much of North American agriculture. Nor is it the extensive integrated vegetable and fruit operation exporting to the entire continent that typifies central Californian agriculture. Rather, they are typically much smaller-scale operations, unique in their diversity as they attempt to take advantage of the varied ecological niches provided by Marin County's striking geography. Of the roughly thirty-five farms in the county, Marin Organic was dealing with eight to ten of them as regular suppliers. During my tour with Scott, we picked up produce at a cross-section of these. They were varied operations that gave one an appreciation for the agricultural diversity of the county. One of the first farms we visited, nestled in a small valley, was growing olives, lemons, lettuce, and specialty herbs. Its olive groves extended beyond the rolling hills surrounding the farm buildings. It featured an elegant boutique, where it sold directly to locals and tourists some of its products. Another much smaller operation grew herbs, garlic, and lettuce; raised organic beef; and produced organic soup. An even smaller operation grew herbs and salad greens primarily. A larger farm had extensive fields of organically grown lettuce, some of which it had just harvested and boxed as we arrived.

The farms we visited all helped to contribute to the agrarian economy of the county, which still constitutes an amazingly beautiful pastoral environment relatively close to an urban agglomeration and all the development pressures associated with it. Indeed, there was considerable evidence of suburban expansion in the eastern part of the county. The county's ecological niches provided a unique environment to produce some of the healthiest produce available by organic methods. But it was easy to see agriculture being displaced from this bucolic setting if it was not carefully nurtured. Marin Organic's programs, and especially its farm-to-school project, took on added significance for me in this context – as having a potentially growing role in ensuring the sustainability of what remains of this distinctive agrarian setting.

The Schools

The next phase of my second visit involved distribution to the schools. It proved to be no less interesting than the farm visits for someone with as strong a sociological bent as I have. I was impressed by the diversity of the schools, for one thing, both in terms of their physical infrastructure and size, and in terms of the student populations from one school to the next, even within a county that appeared to have a largely affluent population in keeping with its relatively expensive real estate.

One of the first schools we visited was a large suburban public high school where visible minorities constituted most of the student body. The kitchen was massive and decidedly industrial in design, and had been converted to function mostly as a reheat operation. This conversion has happened across the United States and Canada as underfunding resulted in staff cuts that no longer made from-scratch food preparation feasible. Instead, semi-processed edible products that could be reheated in giant ovens came to dominate meal times. Typically, these products were less than ideal from a nutritional perspective. Clearly, the fresh organic vegetables Marin Organic was providing were an improvement on the rather bleak menu options I saw available. It was also fairly clear that much more would have to be done to make this food environment a healthy one, and that a farm-to-school project could only be a part of any realistic effort to promote healthy eating there.

We also visited another large public high school in a decidedly more affluent neighbourhood. Here, the kitchen was also large, but it was not principally a quick-serve reheat operation like that of the previous institution we had visited. Although some of the menu options were clearly high in fat and sugar and anything but nutritious, others were definitely healthier. More of the meals were being prepared from scratch, and there seemed to be more openings for the type of produce and products Marin Organic could provide. It was here that we dropped off a large order of gleaned organic yoghurt, which that day the school received free of charge, in addition to the vegetable produce it purchased from Marin Organic.

Some of the schools we made deliveries to were private, and they too exhibited diversity, though it was more in terms of their physical structures than among their student populations, which appeared to be predominantly white and upper middle class. One of the schools, in an old converted church property, had a quirky, casual atmosphere that seemed to personify the relaxed and creative educational setting that one expected to find in California. It was a far cry from massive teenage "warehouses" that typify many secondary educational institutions in the United States and Canada, and which were closer to my own high school experience. It was hard not to be envious of those lucky students.

Another private high school was set among the rolling hills and valleys. Its Corinthian pillars at the entrance, together with the luxury vehicles in the parking lot, suggested its exclusivity and select clientele. Indeed, the parents of these fortunate students could be expected to hand over more than $20,000 per child annually for the privilege of having them attend, I was told. As I chatted with the kitchen staff during the preparation of the noon meal, I could see evidence of a high degree of acceptance of organic foodstuffs. Not only did the school buy from Marin Organic but it was using considerable quantities of organic produce grown in neighbouring Yolo County. In line with the overall ethic of choice that schools everywhere in North America seem to embrace, the sumptuous cafeteria, with its gorgeous valley views, featured a range of menu options, including pizza and hamburgers, but also very healthy entrees. Fruits and vegetables were in abundance at the excellent salad bar. Basically, the difference between it and the large public high school we had first visited was like night and day.

A Few Contentious Issues

Viewing the efforts of Marin Organic first-hand was inspirational in that it represented a multi-faceted approach that had the promise to reinvigorate local agriculture and at the same time revitalize degraded food environments. My visits to the various school partners of its farm-to-school program also brought to the fore the serious realities that will confront any effort to resist the degradation of food and encourage healthy eating. In particular, the realities of social class, race, and stark economic inequalities pose formidable obstacles to making the struggle for healthy eating more than the struggle of the privileged few. I left the county inspired by Marin Organic's effort to link farm to school, but also with nagging doubts. Is it possible to incorporate those segments of society that would most benefit from healthier food options into the struggle for healthy eating? Or will the structural barriers that typify capitalist society more generally determine that the promise of healthy food – what some have cynically termed "yuppie chow" – is relegated to the relatively affluent and educated? To confront these critical issues are strategies developed by another type of catalytic social organization at the forefront of the healthy eating movement.

FOODSHARE: COMMUNITY FOOD SECURITY AS A TRANSFORMATIVE TOOL

Almost a continent away and nestled in a spacious Toronto high school rendered "surplus" by declining inner-city enrolments, an organization named FoodShare orchestrates dynamic food and community-development programs. The organization was created in 1985 by Reverend Stuart Cole, who was motivated to do something about hunger in inner-city Toronto. It started as a coordinating body for food banks, which were just beginning to expand in the city, and had a budget of $20,000 and a half-time staff member. Today its budget is $5.5 million, with over fifty full-time staff. Nevertheless, its early orientation toward hunger and food insecurity helps to explain why FoodShare looks at the food system through the lens of social justice for low-income people. Its programs strive to put into practice the concept of community food security, which has been described as a situation in which all community residents obtain a safe, culturally acceptable, nutritionally adequate diet via a sustainable food system that maximizes community self-reliance and social justice.[2]

For many years now, FoodShare's executive director has been Debbie Field, a woman who has had the opportunity to think long and hard about food, health, and community in our contemporary society, and figure out how to change what is wrong with present arrangements. As we walked around FoodShare's impressive food warehouse facilities one day, Debbie offered the following analysis:

> Capitalism creates food that's killing people, and what's killing people is not whether it's organic or conventional, [but rather] because it's packaged with too much salt and too much sugar. This is where the whole student nutrition movement has to be situated – in this crisis. We have problems and they manifest themselves in different ways, but they're all about the commodification of food. Our [goal] as progressive people is to de-commodify at least basic foods and convince policy makers that basic foods need to be subsidized.[3]

Debbie explained that what is unique about FoodShare is not only its size, relative to anything else like it in Canada, but that, as an organization engaged in transforming food environments, it has a decidedly multi-faceted approach. Although there may be larger organizations in the United States coordinating student nutrition programs or inner-city community gardening initiatives, or promoting farmers' markets, FoodShare is unique in that it brings all these initiatives together under one roof.

If there is a central motif to what FoodShare is all about, it can be boiled down to the promotion of food environments that are healthy, affordable, culturally appropriate, and when possible, locally sourced. From its pioneering role in creating the Good Food Box – now replicated in many other communities – to its present-day multi-dimensional orientation toward food, the organization has put itself in the lead in progressive food circles and in the struggle to change food environments in Toronto and beyond. It is worth considering just how it has gone about this.

FoodShare prides itself in taking a holistic, or as staff put it – "from field to table" – approach to the food system. In other words, its operations range from growing, processing, and distribution right through to purchasing, cooking, and consumption.[4] The organization has positioned itself as a multi-faceted modelling of solutions to change the food system, in conjunction with the involvement of community partners. As Debbie told me, what FoodShare is really intrigued by is solutions that will help low-income people and farmers, but also help deal with the massive crisis of obesity and diabetes by in some way subsidizing basic whole foods. She pointed out that leading writers on food, from Michael Pollan and Alice Waters in the United States to the slow food movement's Carlo Petrini in Italy and renowned Indian food activist Vandana Shiva, have decried the emergence of a two-tiered food system whereby the rich increasingly access good whole foods while the less well-off have to make do with industrialized packaged edible commodities and fast food. Indeed, she has argued in the organization's newsletter that we need food justice, along with local food and sustainable food production.[5]

FoodShare sees itself as a pioneer, demonstrating what is possible and then going on to play a mentoring role for others, helping them adapt solutions to their own circumstances. As the organization's Strategic Plan notes, "Each of our embryonic models (our programs) provides a snapshot of what a good, healthy food system might look like."[6] Going back some twenty years or so, FoodShare was instrumental in facilitating a number of the city's first community gardens and kitchens in low-income neighbourhoods. Since then it has played a significant part in creating a model of what a universal student nutrition program could look like. It also takes seriously the need to advocate for changes in public policies on student nutrition.

The wide gamut of programs FoodShare has established in the short twenty years or so of its existence is nothing short of inspiring. It is worth listing them, by the title FoodShare has given for each: Field to Table Schools; Focus on Food youth internships; Good Food Box; Good Food Markets; Fresh Produce for Schools and Community Groups; Baby and Toddler Nutrition; Community Kitchens; Field to Table Catering; Power Soups; Community Gardening; Composting; Beekeeping and Urban Agriculture; and FoodLink Hotline.

School Food

FoodShare is the community-development component in a larger coalition of organizations that are spearheading the struggle for healthy eating in

Toronto schools. Among the other participants are the Toronto Partners for Student Nutrition – an organization that includes school boards and foundations aligned with school boards – the Student Nutrition Advisory Council, and Toronto Public Health. As is typical elsewhere in the province, decisions about school nutrition programs involve group decision making.

To understand the situation of school food in Toronto, as elsewhere in Canada, it is useful to know that Canada is the only developed country without a federally funded national school nutrition program.[7] Education is largely a provincial responsibility, and school food environments are dealt with at this level. Until quite recently, school food environments have been largely neglected at this level as well. Fortunately, this has begun to change.

One thing that makes the understanding of how school food environments are organized in the province rather difficult, at least at the secondary school level, is the fact that, typically, food provided in cafeterias is a separate affair from foods provided via school nutrition programs, where these exist. In many, if not most, of Ontario's school districts, the cafeteria food is provided by private caterers.[8] For the most part, we are speaking of large corporate food-service companies focused on the bottom line, not student nutrition and health. Student nutrition programs, on the other hand, are community programs housed in schools.

FoodShare's Lori Nikkel, who was heading up her organization's efforts on the student nutrition front when I visited, explained to me that changes at the level of the provincial government have been very important factors in their ability to ramp up programs to provide nutritious foods to the city's schools.[9] Ontario, as with other provinces, had effectively pursued a policy of not-so-benign neglect when it came to school food. Largely as a result of this, school food environments had degenerated to a state that was often nothing short of deplorable, a reality I discovered when doing onsite research into high school food environments in a nearby large school district in 2004-06.[10] School food environments in other provinces were in similar shape.[11]

The significance of student nutrition programs becomes clearer when one realizes that, according to an insightful recent taskforce report on nutrition by the Toronto District School Board, 41 percent of the students in the board's secondary schools are not eating breakfast before arriving at school, and 21 percent are not eating lunch. The figures from schools in the poorest districts, typically those with large visible minority populations, are even more startling. There, 68 percent of students report not eating breakfast, 54 percent report not eating lunch, and 6 percent report not eating dinner.[12]

Given these stark statistics, it can be appreciated how important the new provincial funding initiatives for a breakfast meal program actually are. However, funding is only for breakfast programs and is capped at 15 percent of total program costs. The rest must be raised locally from parents and through fundraising, a very difficult task for the poorest schools. In Toronto, the public school board received the equivalent of twenty-four cents per meal for primary schools and forty-eight cents per meal for high schools.[13] School lunches still receive little support.

With provincial revenues for each program capped at 15 percent of its total costs, the need is overwhelming for local organizations to fill the gap. FoodShare does its part by supporting the creation of some two hundred morning-meal programs in low-income neighbourhoods in the city.

One of the most concrete means by which FoodShare supports school nutrition is its delivery of fresh fruit and vegetables to 180 of the city's schools each week. When child care centres and community agencies are added, FoodShare's fresh fruit and vegetable boxes are reaching some 250 sites a week. This is orchestrated out of the voluminous space the organization's food warehouse now occupies in what were the high school's workshops, where industrial trades were once taught.

FoodShare understands that schools need fresh healthy whole foods, and that simply dropping off such foods to the schools is not going to ensure success in reinventing school food environments. To this end, it has taken a lead in establishing a culinary skills program whereby students visit the facilities, which include a teaching kitchen. In addition, the Field to Table Schools program has eighty-four workshops so far that reinforce existing educational curriculum and strive to make food literacy a part of students' lives.

Beyond this, FoodShare has also begun to support the expansion of school gardens by delivering crucial educational materials and providing staff support to promote gardens and devise ways to have schools gardens maintained throughout the summer. The lack of correspondence between the Canadian growing season and the school term is a thorny issue to resolve, but FoodShare is exploring ingenious ways to overcome it. These include involving daycares that exist in some schools to take initiative in summer garden maintenance, fundraising to pay for a summer gardener, and a program whereby a family adopts the school garden for a week during the June-July period, when school is out. FoodShare has even worked out a novel arrangement with local public health authorities to provide training to public health nurses, who, as part of their rounds in Toronto schools, can keep an eye on the health of the school garden. This latter initiative struck me as especially ingenious in that it seeks to make constructive use of personnel in a publicly funded service, personnel who would be going to the schools in any case as part of their regular duties.

FoodShare's role in sparking the transformation of school food environments is matched outside the school ground. Without this organization, many neighbourhood farmers' markets would not exist, simply because producers do not see it as economic to supply the smaller markets, given the low volume of sales. FoodShare can agglomerate the demand from several markets and offer to buy enough produce to make it viable for local farmers to drive into the city with their products. In this way, a number of the poorest neighbourhoods now have fresh produce that is also locally or regionally produced, whereas before such neighbourhoods may have been essentially food deserts. As Debbie Field remarked about these micro–food markets in poor neighbourhoods, "They [the market organizers] order from us, and they mark it up a little bit and we deliver it to them. It's community development. A lot of what we are doing is about community development as well as food."

THE WAY FORWARD

Transformative organizations such as Marin Organic and FoodShare are part of an incipient alternative food movement that today defines the struggle for healthy eating. In their different ways, each organization has been a critical element in bringing together disparate actors in the food system in such a way that healthy eating is enhanced, smaller farm operators receive support, and a community of interests is being advanced. They have each been a vital part of the upsurge in interest in alternative food systems, an interest that is mushrooming in many parts of the world in recent years.

In the complex and dynamic food scene that is Toronto, FoodShare has been joined by other innovative alternative food provisioning organizations, including The Stop, which strives to incorporate community building and poverty reduction into its proactive social justice–oriented food activities.[14] Each organization is led by an individual with a broad vision of what their organization needs to accomplish, but a vision tempered with a pragmatism that can translate inspiring ideas into workable solutions. A new research initiative I'm involved with that is probing alternative food networks across

Ontario has discovered the positive impact these two Toronto-based models have had elsewhere, and the diversity and vitality of the alternative food system that is establishing beachheads in community after community.[15]

The two organizations I have foregrounded here are noteworthy examples of the kinds of change afoot, but they in no way exhaust the spectrum of activities characterizing the healthy eating struggle presently underway. They do, however, offer innovative approaches to one particularly salient food environment: schools. The question arises, however, whether such efforts are enough to provoke real change.

Kevin Morgan and Roberta Sonnino have eloquently demonstrated in their cross-societal examination of school food that, even among the developed countries, the challenges facing school food advocates differ dramatically from one country to the next. In countries such as Britain, the United States, and Canada, where recent political culture favoured market-based solutions, provisioning school cafeterias has been viewed as just one other service to be put out to the private sector for tender, and where the lowest-cost bidder could expect success. This approach may work for provisioning pencils and notebooks, but it has proven to be a disaster when it comes to provisioning vulnerable youth with their nutritional needs. The evidence on the health and physical fitness of children and youth in Canada and the United States, for example, is cause for major concern and is a dark foreboding of a health disaster in the making.

The good news on this subject is that some governments have started to grapple with toxic school food environments. I have alluded to promising changes in Canada at the provincial levels, although there remains an astounding inattention to the issue at the federal level. In Britain, the scandal of school food provoked a revamping of cafeteria nutritional standards, and positive change. Fresher and healthier food is now being served, but, not surprisingly, the price of school meals has gone up significantly. Also not surprisingly, according to a 2007 survey, 75 percent of local authorities report that the number of school meals purchased has dropped, and many private caterers are having difficulty making ends meet.[16] There are lessons to be learned here, no doubt. My research on school food environments, together with the research of others, suggests that the following issues are especially important:

• Having fresh, whole food in schools is essential but not enough. Attention must be paid to how it is prepared, and this requires investing in staff with the culinary skills and time to prepare tasty food from scratch.

- Pricing of healthy food is critical, as students are price sensitive, and if it is undercut by cheaper processed foods either in the school or available near to schools, progress will be limited. Subsidizing healthy food is essential and will pay huge dividends down the line with healthier citizens in the future.
- The foregoing points suggest the importance of near-school food environments in affecting the efficacy of promoting healthy food in schools. Preliminary research suggests that fast-food and junk food vendors target schools in their location strategies,[17] and that the presence of their products has impacts on distorting school food environments. Legislation creating junk-food- and fast-food-free zones around schools would go a long way to solving this problem.
- Means must be found to avoid students from low-income families who receive food in school and at subsidized prices from being stigmatized, which at present heavily burdens the school lunch programs in the United States. There are various solutions to this problem, with Italy's perhaps being the simplest: every student gets the same wholesome standard meal at lunch, regardless of ability to pay.
- Allowing nutrient-poor food and beverages into the schools is essentially a matter of being "penny wise and pound foolish." The quick revenues gained by granting pouring rights to soft drink companies solve immediate problems at the expense of the health of children and youth. Governments have begun to take action to ban such products from the schools, but they also need to follow up and increase funding to schools to make up for lost revenues. In many jurisdictions, this is a matter of restoring funding for education that was taken away in an earlier period of neoliberal cutbacks to the public sector, cutbacks that have often had disastrous consequences, and nowhere more evident than with school food environments.
- Complementing reforms to school food environments must be reforms to policies on physical activity in schools. De-emphasizing elite school sports and building in regular physical activities for all students at all grade levels is essential.

Attempts to reform school food environments will likely run up against entrenched vested interests and hostile value orientations in the wider society. In the United Kingdom, and now in Canada, conservative media have given voice to elements in society who employ the freedom of choice argument to oppose government intervention regarding food and advocate the return of junk foods and other nutrient-poor products to school cafeterias because, they argue, "this is what kids want."[18] Putting aside the corporate entities that certainly stand to benefit from this backlash, it is interesting to note that these advocates of the status quo have typically not extended their arguments for freedom of choice to include the use of tobacco and alcohol in schools. The ethical standards of society for these products, which these advocates have been wont to challenge, have not yet been extended to health-damaging edible products – pseudo foods and junk foods – or at least not in the minds of many. My sense is that we are in a transitional period, and at some point the broader public may well consider it socially unacceptable to have these products widely available in schools. In the meantime, those in government and civil society who work to promote healthy eating in schools can expect a backlash, and their success or failure in dealing with this backlash may well determine the features of school food environments in days to come.

And what of efforts to combat degraded food environments outside the realm of schools? Are there signs of progress, and what are the prospects for positive change? There does seem to be a case to be made that progress is occurring primarily in areas in which identifiably vulnerable populations exist, with the schools being the most significant in this regard. Recently in Canada, hospital food environments have become a new site for food environment transformation. For some time, hospitals had been a locus of fast-food operations and junk food vendors, which provided underfunded hospital administrations with welcome rental income. Even here there are indications of unease – and resistance. In Toronto's Hospital for Sick Children, for example, a resident pediatrician recently started a Facebook group called "Burger King should NOT be allowed to operate at Sick Kids Hospital" in an attempt to influence the decisions of administrators who were about to award new slots in the food court of Canada's largest pediatric hospital. The fast-food corporation was forced to terminate its operation at the hospital, though a couple of other fast-food companies still remain.[19] Elsewhere, initiatives have been made to substantially increase the component of locally grown food on hospital menus and menus of other institutions, including daycares, primary and high schools, and universities.[20]

The prospects for reshaping food environments so that nutritional criteria come foremost is, nevertheless, still a most daunting task in practically any society one chooses to consider. The forces degrading diets are powerful, and growing more powerful each year, and their reach is ever more extensive. Meanwhile, there are structures in society that aid and abet their propagation. It is time to make a sober assessment of the prospects for more general positive change and to seriously consider what still needs to be done.

CHAPTER FOURTEEN

Toward a Sustainable and Ethical Health-Based Dietary Regime

We showed that we could get people to eat anything we marketed. Now all we have to do is build a food distribution system that favours real food, and market that.

> —Mark Bittman, "How to Save a Trillion Dollars"[1]

If price spikes don't change eating habits, perhaps the combination of deforestation, pollution, climate change, starvation, heart disease and animal cruelty will gradually encourage the simple daily act of eating more plants and fewer animals.

> —Mark Bittman, "Rethinking the Meat-Guzzler"[2]

A valuable debate [over the food system] has begun from an environmental health perspective; there now needs to be debate beginning from a human health perspective.

> —Tim Lang and Michael Heasman, *Food Wars*[3]

Growing evidence of the widespread and ever increasing damage that industrial diets have wrought on human health makes it critical that a transformation of food environments and the reshaping of mass diets be placed at the forefront of struggles for human progress wherever possible. But what principle, or principles, should orient efforts in this direction? The thrust of my arguments so far is that positive health outcomes must come to the forefront in reshaping our food system. But this may quickly be seen as problematic given that many of the people motivated to rebuild our food system would seem to have other priorities. This is an issue that must be given consideration.

Many who are interested and active in food movements now are motivated by one or more of a few basic concerns. The concern for the environment is probably the most widely shared one today. Issues including the carbon footprint of food production, the dependence on chemical pesticides and fossil fuel–based fertilizer, and the pollution burden of factory farming, to name only the most prominent, drive the fervent desire to put the food system on the path to sustainability. The good news is that there is a virtuous relationship between a more sustainable food system and a healthier diet. The concept of the double pyramid tells us why.

THE DOUBLE PYRAMID

Healthy food and sustainable food production are largely compatible goals, and this fortuitous fact allows us to foresee a future in which the proponents for each can come together in a united push for real change. The concept of the double pyramid illustrates how these twin goals reinforce each other (see Figure 14.1). Developed by the Barilla Center for Food and Nutrition and based on sound evidence, the double pyramid describes a possible virtuous transition in our food system that is good for people, good for other animal species, and good for the environment.

Many people are familiar with the food pyramid, promoted for many years by health authorities in the United States and the World Health Organization as a guide to a healthy diet. Essentially, healthy foods that should be eaten in greatest quantity are at the broad base of the pyramid, whereas less healthy foods, typically foods high in sugar, fat, and salt, occupy the narrow upper echelons of the pyramid. It is a device that is not without its problems, but it has not been without its utility as a general guide to

FIGURE 14.1

The double pyramid

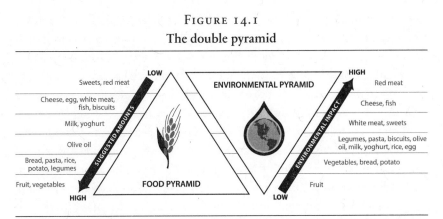

SOURCE: Barilla Center for Food and Nutrition, *Double Pyramid: Healthy Food for People, Sustainable Food for the Planet,* 2011, http://www.barillacfn.com/.../pp_doppia_piramide_alimentazione_eng.pdf.

healthier eating. What happens when we calculate the ecological footprint of producing the different foods highlighted in the food pyramid, as measured by their relative needs for resources such as fossil fuels and water to produce them?

The evidence indicates a strong inverse relationship between health impact and environmental impact. In other words, the healthiest foods have the least environmental impact, whereas the least healthy foods have a very heavy environmental impact. What does this mean in practical terms? Basically, by eating a diet largely based on fruits and vegetables, and secondarily legumes and complex carbohydrates, including potatoes and various whole grains, we are minimizing our environmental impact on the planet. In addition, by minimizing consumption of the foods that health authorities the world over advise us to consume little of, so too are we minimizing the high environmental costs entailed in their production. Foods that are responsible for the highest ecological footprint in terms of carbon emissions and water usage are red meats; close behind are white meats (chicken and pork), fish, and processed dairy products, notably cheese.

Does this mean that being environmentally responsible requires a largely vegetarian diet? If the existing system of animal protein production – that is, factory farming – continues to dominate, it is hard to get away from the conclusion that indeed it does. Although increasing numbers of people are choosing to go the vegetarian or vegan route, many will not for reasons of ingrained taste preferences, adherence to cultural traditions, or whatever. To this I would also point to the evidence of our Palaeolithic past that fairly clearly shows the significant role of animal protein in human diets for much of our existence. The rejoinder to this last argument might well be that, unlike our Palaeolithic past, humans number in the several billions today, as opposed to perhaps a few hundred thousand then, and the impact of animal protein production to feed this mass of humanity has exceedingly grave environmental consequences and in its present form is in no way sustainable.[4]

Added to the environmental impact are the ever more pressing ethical issues posed by factory farming of animal protein. As awareness of the conditions of animals in factory-farm operations becomes more widespread, the attractiveness of eating these animals diminishes, at least for many. To this we might also add the dangers from pathogenic bacteria encouraged by factory farming, together with the evidence that factory-farmed meat results in a source of protein exceptionally high in saturated fats and an imbalance in the omega fatty acids (see Chapter 6).

Is a diet with a substantial component of animal protein inherently ecologically damaging, unhealthy, inhumane, and fraught with danger from pathogenic bacteria? This is certainly grounds for fractious debate. I believe there is a strong case to be made that it *is* all these things within the present CAFO, or factory farming, system. But what if this system were rejected and animals were raised as they once were, perhaps with relatively benign technological aids to increase productivity? What might this look like?

It would mean raising cattle on lands that are natural grasslands for the most part, without the fattening process in feedlots and hormone implants as well. It would mean raising hogs on a much smaller and more humane scale, with ample room to raise their young and access to the outside and fresh air. It would mean letting chickens range more freely in an environment that resembles more closely a barnyard of old rather than the crowded death camp environment of a factory poultry farm, where feed is laced with non-therapeutic doses of antibiotics to suppress diseases among overcrowded birds and stimulate growth. It would mean jettisoning the devastating fish-killing technologies presently employed in global fisheries that are quickly destroying wild fish stocks worldwide, and employing technologies of times gone by that allowed fish stocks to reproduce year after year. It would also mean rejecting much of the present fish-farming methods in favour of methods that were demonstrably environmentally benign – if these can be designed, as some argue they can.

Changes of this nature are not novel suggestions, of course. But they would allow for a number of positive things to happen. These include the possibility of proper nutrient recycling on the farm and serious reductions in the environmental impact of raising livestock, poultry, and fish. They would also permit much more humane methods of animal rearing to take place, methods that would be more in agreement with the ethical beliefs of many.

Is there a cost to changes of this nature? Of course there is. Costs would be both monetary and non-monetary. In monetary terms, animal protein will very likely cost more, perhaps substantially more. Factory farming has made meat relatively cheap, no doubt about that. But that is only because the real costs to society, to the animals, and to nature have not been priced into it – polluted waterways, fouled air, decimated fish stocks worldwide, tragic outbreaks of pathogenic bacteria,[5] and as I have argued earlier, less-healthy meat bulked up with saturated fats and deficient in good fats. And then there is the ethical cost – hard to measure but there nevertheless – of abusing other sentient animal species for our personal use when alternatives to nourish us are clearly available.

A completely sustainable, healthy, and ethical diet is an ideal to strive for but one that may never be reached. Yet, we can envision a diet that moves a good distance in this direction, one that even includes animal protein, though not occupying the same place in our diet as it presently does. As hard as that may be for some to accept, this would be a good thing – for our health, for the environment, and for the animals involved.

If evidence supporting the double pyramid is taken into account, then there does appear to be support for the argument of a strong overlap between the interest in ensuring sustainability and the interest in securing nutrition and health. That is very good news, and the issue for the future is how to unite the energies of both camps in a push for real change. It also forces us to face a difficult question: To what extent is real change possible within existing political-economic arrangements?

REAL BARRIERS TO A HEALTH-BASED DIETARY REGIME

The previous chapters have presented a wide spectrum of evidence that, under the profit-based food system over a period of many decades, the dominant tendency has been to degrade whole foods for a variety of economic reasons and reproduce the resulting industrial dietary regime and the degraded foods it implies on an ever expanding global basis. Under the big tent of an overarching capitalist economy, where profit making takes precedence, is what I have termed the "third industrial dietary regime" capable of being fundamentally shifted to a point at which *healthy eating* takes precedence in the shaping of mass diets? To an important degree, this is an empirical question. Can a case be made that the dominant for-profit food system is moving toward self-correcting for the long history of degraded food it has provided? Or is it undermining concerted efforts to reform those food environments I discussed earlier?

In making the case for the defence (the defendant here being the dominant food system), one might point to evidence in almost any respectable supermarket in the developed world. Supermarket chain stores have come to be, of course, the primary channel for food procurement in the developed world and are rapidly becoming so in developing countries too.

Advocates of the present system can argue that there are plenty of healthy options in the average supermarket, and it is just up to the consumer to make healthy choices. The ethic of individual responsibility plays strong in this argument, and it strikes a chord with many as libertarian ideology becomes more prominent in society. In response to this argument, I would suggest that, although there is almost always room for the exercise of individual responsibility, it must be recognized that the realistic possibilities for doing so are very often much more limited than advocates for the status quo would argue.

First of all, the asymmetries that now exist in the marketing machinery devoted to food consumption are dramatic and *must* be part of the discussion. Simply put, extraordinarily powerful corporations spend an enormous amount of money pushing nutrient-poor edible commodities, essentially pathogenic pseudo foods that undermine health. The exceptional profitability of these edible commodities is what motivates their purveyors to advertise them heavily and spend prodigious sums to secure their visibility in food environments. Moreover, much of this advertising push is aimed at kids and teens, most of whom are in no position to really understand the consequences of what they eat.

On the other side of the equation, for various reasons, societal resources spent on healthy-eating messages are several orders of magnitude smaller. In fact, as mentioned earlier, in the United States over the last decade, the top nine companies selling fast food and nutrient-poor pseudo foods annually have spent up to five hundred times as much on advertising as the federal government's Department of Health and Human Services has spent on all manner of health-promotion messages. The latter cannot in any realistic way be expected to counter the corporate pseudo-food messaging that saturates our everyday world.

The end result of this deluge of intensive advertising has been the normalization of a degraded, industrial diet with disturbing health impacts. In recent decades, powerful new strategies and technologies have been rolled out, such as product tie-ins with characters in highly successful Hollywood movies, and food photography has made major advances in enhancing the visual appeal of products, especially in the fast-food industry.[6] In the end, the normalization of the industrial diet has meant that a suite of nutrient-poor edible products has been made socially acceptable – indeed, highly desirable.

A second but related point is that these same nutrient-poor products are secured by the influential corporations that own them in virtually every food environment possible, whether in the private or the public sphere. This process of spatial colonization also entails enormous costs: consider the billions spent by pseudo food purveyors in slotting fees to secure the best shelf space in supermarkets or by fast-food chains to secure the most prominent real estate in urban and suburban environments. This reality has long been true of developed economies, and it is a central investment goal of globe-spanning processors and retailers to make this reality of the developed countries also a reality in the global South. By the end of the first decade of the twenty-first century, we can say that they are well on their way to achieving this goal.

Food environments have been impoverished in ways not so apparent, of course. In the supermarket one will no doubt find that relatively healthy, nutritious food options do indeed exist. Indeed, one could argue that they always have, to some degree. I am speaking here of the array of fruits and vegetables any supermarket carries, including vegetable proteins of various kinds, some fresh, others frozen or canned. However, even here, as I document in the chapter dealing with the simplification of foods under the industrial dietary regime, the apparent abundance of fruits and vegetables in the typical supermarket belies a serious varietal deficiency, and with this drastic varietal simplification very likely comes a nutritional impoverishment as well.

In the case of animal protein, supermarkets and restaurant chains carry relatively inexpensive animal protein options, something that might be seen as further evidence of the robust nature of our contemporary food system. But here again, my discussion of the speed-up of the production process in the industrial dietary regime context indicates that this abundance of animal protein is ultimately much more costly than we might imagine. In addition to the other issues associated with factory-farmed animal protein, factory farming produces animal meat that is extraordinarily high in dangerous saturated fats. It is also characterized by an imbalance between the omega-6 and omega-3 fatty acids when compared with meat from animals that eat what they were designed by nature to eat. This imbalance is to the detriment of the health of humans who eat such meat. Finally on the matter of meat, the concentrated industrial meat processors' colonization of food environments with cured, processed meats of all kinds, products that play to retailers' desires for shelf-stable product and consumers' desire for convenience, has served to undermine health by increasing the danger from widespread foodborne pathogen outbreaks and by introducing dangerous adulterants (e.g., nitrites) into the diets of many people.

The impact of profit making on the production of our food goes considerably beyond this, however. Whole foods are regularly, and extensively, adulterated with sugar, salt, fat, and a wide variety of chemical additives in a system that is oriented to taking the cheapest food ingredients possible and making them durable, and palatable, and therefore more saleable and ultimately highly profitable.

Ironically, it is the most nutrient-poor categories of products in our food environments that have been the most lucrative. Much like what occurred with tobacco manufacturing, the high returns from pseudo foods have encouraged the centralized control of their production within the hands of a few corporate entities that have subsequently become extremely profitable and economically powerful. With this power has come inordinate influence in shifting dietary preferences. In fact, these corporations have come to be among the most powerful players in our food system. The implications of this reality have yet to be fully appreciated by those who wish to turn around degraded food environments.

The Hold of Neo-Liberalism

For those intent on constructing healthy and sustainable food systems, there are further real barriers that must be confronted as well. The most formidable of these is the wider political-economic model that orients our economies. Another is the reality of time compression affecting the lives of many citizens today. A third barrier is what I have referred to as the ethos of individual responsibility, an ethos that pervades societies in the West, and especially those in the Anglo-Saxon world.

There is no doubt that the profit motive within a market-based economic system has been a potent force for transforming the modern world. As an engine for wealth creation, such political-economic arrangements have proven to be unsurpassed. Indeed, one might argue that it is precisely this success that blinds many to the abject failure of a profit-oriented economy to serve up healthy and sustainable food. This blindness is not restricted to perceptions of the food system, of course; it extends to many areas of society.

The neo-liberal political-economic model that now holds sway in most countries provides a definite structural barrier to transforming dietary regimes, for a couple of reasons. In addition to the definable and concrete legislative barriers to renewed government regulation set down in many trade agreements designed to liberalize trade over the last twenty-five years or so, there is a less tangible but arguably more resilient barrier to change. This barrier manifests itself in the form of the pervasive buy-in to the ideology of neo-liberalism itself.

The ideology of neo-liberalism shows remarkable tenacity, despite its many colossal failures over the last decade or so – think of the economic collapse of the neo-liberal showcase republic of Argentina in 2001, the meltdown of Enron and WorldCom in the United States and their extensive economic and social repercussions, the exploding economic inequalities in one society after another since the onset of the neo-liberal era, and most recently, the global financial meltdown occasioned by blind faith in a deregulated private banking system as the best guardians of the nation's financial well-being. Despite these events, and many more one could enumerate, governments in most of the developed countries continue to evince a decidedly neo-liberal outlook, governments presumably elected by citizens who are similarly in tune with this ideology.

The foregoing, I believe, explains much of the reluctance of governments to really tackle the forces degrading diets, despite the rapidly escalating health calamity posed by accumulated evidence of rather dramatic rises in the incidence of weight gain and obesity among the general population, including especially disturbing increases among the youngest members of society. This, in spite of an escalating media concern and public awareness of the issue since the early years of the new millennium.

Nevertheless, the reluctance of governments to take positive action in cleaning up food environments cannot be ascribed solely to the power of multinational actors in the food system, nor to buy-in to neo-liberal thinking on the part of citizens. I see two further obstacles to change. Each resides in civil society. One factor that cannot be overlooked is related to the time compression that characterizes the lives of many. The last issue is what I will term the "ethos of individual responsibility and freedom of choice." Each of these factors needs to be considered by advocates of healthier eating environments.

Time Compression

The matter of time compression is a reality that has resurfaced in recent decades, thanks to factors such as the decline of the stay-at-home spouse and also the demise of well-paying middle-class employments in the neo-liberal era, often necessitating working at two jobs or working overtime hours on a regular basis to make ends meet.[7] Time compression was, it will be remembered from Chapter 3, an issue with working-class women in the early industrial era. Now, as then, nutrient-poor convenience foods have invaded the home food environment, and work environments as well, while fast-food operations proliferate outside the home. Although the gold standard for positive nutritional outcomes is a carefully prepared home-cooked meal, the objective realities of contemporary work lives make this difficult, if not impossible, for many to organize on a regular basis.

Not only is time at a premium for families as perhaps never before, but where once the educational system developed culinary skills among at least one crucial segment of the population – young females – for decades, such programs have fallen by the wayside, in part a reaction against a value system that viewed women alone as responsible for culinary tasks. What seemingly nobody foresaw was the fact that if *no one* knows how to cook, *everyone* will become dependent upon someone, or more usually a corporation, to do it instead. With this comes a loss of control over what is in meals and how they are prepared. This situation has provided the food industry with tremendous opportunities to market semi-processed or fully processed industrial foods of questionable nutritional benefit designed for quick reheating to fill in for the genuine home-cooked meal. The health outcomes of this situation are too often of a negative kind.

Ethos of Individual Responsibility and Freedom of Choice

The emphasis placed on individual responsibility in life outcomes varies from one culture to another, so the weight of this factor cannot be said to affect all societies in the same way. One might argue that in Western cultures it is perhaps the most prominent value orientation within what is sometimes referred to as the "Anglo-Saxon world" – notably the United Kingdom, the United States, Canada, Australia, and New Zealand, though other cultures also hold to it to varying degrees, of course. This value orientation encompasses the notion – still common in society – that if only individuals made better lifestyle decisions, then much of the contemporary problem with weight gain and obesity, and the negative health outcomes associated with these, could be avoided. Along with this view comes the notion that no one should have to pay for, or be inconvenienced by, unfortunate dietary decisions others have made.[8]

There is almost always room for the exercise of individual responsibility, yet this view utterly fails to explain why so many individuals began making bad dietary decisions over the last twenty years or so, the period during which obesity has come to be a first-order health issue. It fails to account, as well, for the host of disturbing developments in the food industry that I have examined in this book.

The value placed on the freedom to choose is also a thorny issue to confront. Freedom of choice is a value imbedded in market-dominated economies generally, and nowhere more trenchantly than in the United States. A thoroughgoing exploration of this value orientation is not possible here, though it might be noted that the strategy of using the issue of freedom of choice was one employed by the tobacco industry in an earlier time, when initial efforts to curb its dangerous products were being mounted. Indeed, an industry lobby organization called the Center for Consumer Freedom was initially funded by a large grant from America's biggest tobacco manufacturer; it has lobbied on behalf of restaurant chain corporations as well.[9]

With reference to children and youth, the notion of freedom of choice runs quickly up against the fact that these are immature human beings who still require substantial education and guidance and who are not in any position to adequately assess the nutritional choices available to them, let alone many of the other choices some would argue they should be able to make. We don't allow them the freedom to choose to bring guns to school, or drink alcohol in school hallways, or smoke in class, or a number of other matters, but supposedly we should allow them complete freedom to choose the basic eating options that determine their very physical, and to an important degree psychological, well-being.

Moreover, the market, dominated as it is in the food sector by so few powerful players, offers little in the way of real freedom of choice in the first place. The apparent diversity of product lines is undercut by the fact that in almost any product category, the majority of product lines are owned by a few food industry giants. Even more significant is that these products are shaped in nutritionally crucial ways by an economic logic that prioritizes a healthy return on investment above all other criteria, and certainly above the health of the consumer. Under this logic, as we have seen in earlier chapters, the nutritional degradation of whole foods is a predictable outcome.

Finally, the argument for freedom of choice is further undermined by the extraordinarily imbalanced reality of advertising in the food system. Nutrient-poor, degraded edible commodities are marketed by global food and beverage giants with extremely deep pockets. Their advertising budgets for these products are colossal in comparison to the ad budgets, should they exist at all, for basic, healthy whole foods such as unprocessed fruits, vegetables, and nuts, for example. The mass marketing of pseudo foods saturates our daily lives, whether it be while walking down the street or on the bus or subway, while watching television, or while surfing the Internet. Ad expenditures for these products are far, far larger than the advertising budgets for healthy-eating messages funded by any government health ministry one could possibly name. This reality, I believe, puts the lie to the argument that one could possibly have *real* freedom of choice in what to eat in many contemporary societies.

Advocates and activists in the struggle for healthy eating, whether it be in the schools or in the wider society, should realize that successfully confronting the forces degrading diets is about more than marshalling evidence for their cause. Much of this book, of course, has been precisely about marshalling evidence of the degradation of diet and the need for change. Yet, struggles in other realms have taught us that this is not enough. It will also be necessary to deal with the persistent value orientations that inhere in the dominant ideology if there is to be success.

Advocates and activists of healthy eating will have to learn to frame the inevitable debates in a different way because the ethos of individual responsibility and freedom of choice, for example, are deeply entrenched. Arguments grounded in this ethos have been, and will be, used by the food industry and its supporters to try to block any real change to the existing situation. Those hoping to transform food environments will have to take seriously the advice of people like George Lakoff, who has brilliantly argued that it is essential to reframe the debate in order to achieve social change. As he has noted,

> Frames are mental structures that shape the way we see the world. As a result, they shape the goals we seek, the plans we make, the way we act, and what counts as a good or bad outcome of our actions. Our frames shape our social policies and the institutions we form to carry out our policies ... Reframing *is* social change.[10]

Part of a successful strategy to transform food environments, then, is one that pays careful attention to dominant value orientations and the arguments that ultimately will be used to convince people that food environments that prioritize a return to health are superior to those that prioritize healthy returns to investors. Responding to the value orientation of freedom of choice, for example, can mean demanding that real freedom of choice in the realm of food means that healthy and affordable food be available to all, a situation that simply does not presently exist, as ever mounting demands on food banks make abundantly clear. Indeed, the current system has proven to be increasingly unable to offer affordable food that is also healthy food and has therefore proven to be a barrier to real freedom of choice.

NEVERTHELESS, "THE TIMES THEY ARE A-CHANGIN'"

It is hopeful that, despite all the obstacles to change presented above, there is reason to believe that the resistance to the degradation of food environments in civil society is gathering momentum. The emerging movement to promote healthy eating, together with other struggles around food, have put the dominant food system on trial. What I describe as catalytic organizations for change in the previous chapter, using the examples of California's Marin Organic and Canada's Toronto-based FoodShare, are becoming noted exemplars of how to bring this change about in their own spheres of influence. These examples are at the cutting edge of reshaping food environments and their agricultural support structure. They are inspiring some of the most engaged young activists today to pay attention to what is happening to food as a potential crucible in which different elements can interact and produce something altogether new and exciting. Moreover, there is evidence of a real widening of the seismic impact of this movement.

A physician who has become a hugely popular media celebrity – Dr. Oz – has for some time confronted America's problem of dramatic population-wide weight gain and obesity. Of late, this influential television and radio personality has moved into territory where no medical authority within mainstream media has dared to go before: advocating a shift to a mainly plant-based diet. In the course of advocating for this shift, he has become strongly critical of the role of dairy products in the industrial diet and noted that they are the leading vector for ingesting saturated fats. His advocacy of a plant-based diet is openly predicated on a shift away from the meats that have heretofore been a mainstay of the industrial diet as well. Not very long ago, it was unheard of for a major media personality to advocate such views and risk incurring the wrath of the powerful meat and dairy industries because any that did could expect to pay a high price for doing so.

Another contemporary example that springs to mind is the role of once staunchly conservative medical authorities on the food front. One of the world's leading medical journals, *The Lancet,* argued as early as 2002 that "more radical solutions should be considered: taxing soft drinks and fast foods; subsidizing nutritious foods, like fruits and vegetables; labelling of the content of fast foods; and prohibiting marketing and advertising to children."[11]

In Canada, the Canadian Medical Association has taken on increasingly strong views about the need for governments to deal with pseudo foods. Beginning in 2008, the association began calling for taxes on the junk foods that saturate food environments everywhere. In early 2011, its journal called for a much wider campaign of concrete government measures to confront the plague of toxic edible commodities aggressively promoted by major players in the food manufacturing industry and by food retailers of all kinds. Among the measures advocated were banning fast-food chains from school and health-facility food environments, placing graphic warnings on pseudo food packaging, and passing legislation that would dramatically reduce the health-damaging salt that is packed into many nutrient-poor edible commodities.[12]

More recently, a call came from this quarter to label many of the products of the industrial diet as "edible pathogens." The Canadian Medical Association has also warned against health organizations' entering into co-branding arrangements with food corporations. The association noted in an editorial that "through these partnerships, the food industry seeks to emphasize that inactivity – not the promotion and consumption of its calorie-rich products – is the prime cause of obesity."[13] These are surely hopeful signs of positive change even within the dominant institutions of society.

What If Governments Get Active Again?

One does not have to go too far back in history to discover times when governments played a more active role in the food economy. The second food regime discussed in Chapter 1 was such a time, and, in countries such as Australia and Canada, a state-regulated central selling agency was created to market grains and protect grain growers from the predations of grain speculators who had ruled markets up till then. Various forms of supply management came into existence in the dairy sector as well, in several countries, to protect both producers and consumers from certain practices of the dairy processors that had jeopardized the viability of farmers and the safety of the milk supply during the tumultuous years of the Great Depression.[14] In an even earlier era, governments intervened to promulgate legislation to protect the public from the rampant practices of food adulteration. In capitalist societies more generally, history shows that political conjunctures arise that allow for government action that may run counter to the short-term interests of the corporate sector. It is possible to imagine a much more activist state role with respect to food, one that goes beyond the as yet rather timid attempts to reform school food environments, for example. If governments can mandate higher fuel efficiency in the automobile sector despite trenchant resistance from the powerful auto companies, and far-reaching tobacco control policies despite multi-million-dollar lobbying campaigns from the corporate tobacco oligopoly, so too can they nurture healthier food environments through a combination of policies.

Among the earliest and most articulate advocates of more active policies to deal with obesogenic food environments have been Kelly Brownell and Katherine Battle Horgen in their important book, *Food Fight*.[15] They note key developments that will be necessary to empower a social health movement that could yet be the force that galvanizes governments to take decisive action to enable the transformation of our current dietary regime.[16] Among them are the existence of a crisis, a critical mass of scientific evidence, social attitude changes among the general public, and political leadership willing to stand up to intense industry pressure. To this list I would add the importance of reframing the issues, as argued above, to place the food industry's hobby horses of individual responsibility and freedom of choice in their proper place. Finally, I would also make a case for the necessary role that civil society actions play in bringing about needed state policies.

With respect to this last point, it is not at all clear that the diverse goals of what some have called alternative food and agricultural movements have been very effective in pressuring governments for substantial policy changes on the food and agriculture front. For this to happen, a minimal condition is that a good deal more convergence must take place among the main strands of civil society activities in this realm. This would mean that those who struggle for change around sustainable agriculture, around a healthy-eating agenda, and around support for small and medium producers and their communities, three key nodes on the alternative front, need to come together to promote a mutually beneficial agenda. Moreover, a major part of this agenda needs to recognize the importance of re-engaging the state apparatus, which has heretofore been largely immobilized though political elites' embrace of neo-liberal policies and their corporate backers.

It is hard to imagine scaling up the real advances that have been made at local levels without bringing the state back into the equation. One need only recall the progress made in the realm of social welfare during the twentieth century – social security, the minimum wage, the right to organize, the right to free medical care (in some countries) and unemployment insurance, to mention some of the most prominent advances – for one to appreciate the potential of governments to make better lives for their citizens. The contemporary tendency for activists to treat the state as irrelevant for progressive social change plays squarely into the hands of those blocking such change. The point is not to abandon a role for the state in struggling for change, but rather to demand a better deal from it and be prepared to devote energies to work for political change at this level.

What Might Healthy Food Environments Look Like?

Finally, and since this chapter advocates a turn to a sustainable and ethical health-based dietary regime, it is only appropriate to consider what healthy food environments might look like. It is possible to map out general ideas here, but it doesn't make sense to suggest anything too specific – the world is too diverse in terms of cultures, tastes, and economic possibilities, not to mention the range of geographical and ecological possibilities for growing food. To envision a health-based food regime I draw inspiration from the lessons provided by advocates of the Palaeolithic diet. There is a good case to be made that a modified version of this diet is a good starting point for envisioning what healthy eating in the future should look like. I would argue for a modified Palaeolithic diet for two reasons. First, the Palaeolithic diet's emphasis on animal proteins is problematic because of the resource strain this puts on the planet, and because for nutritional and ethical reasons cheap meat produced by factory farming is less than desirable. Because animal protein produced on a sustainable and ethical basis is inevitably going to be considerably more expensive, it is imperative that vegetable protein substitutes be the mainstay of the dietary regime of the future. This does not mean animal proteins cannot have a place; they just cannot be as central as they are presently. Rather, they should be much more of a special-occasion addition to the diet for people who still desire them.

What are the most basic features of such a dietary regime? I would suggest it must entail whole foods, minimally processed; relatively high amounts of protein, largely vegetable but sustainable and ethically produced animal protein when affordable for those who accept its consumption; more complex carbohydrates derived from fruits, vegetables, and legumes and a radical reduction in refined carbohydrates from grains, especially wheat; and greater recognition of the nutritional problems associated with diets loaded with the saturated fats associated with dairy products, leading to a shift to healthy substitutes that are already available to provide the minerals, vitamins, and protein associated with dairy. Finally, minimally processed foods and an emphasis on plant-based foods will provide a much healthier diet in terms of fat intake, reducing especially saturated fats, implicated in cardiovascular disease. Fats will be largely polyunsaturated or monounsaturated, with much higher consumption of the beneficial omega-3 fatty acids than is typical of the industrial diet.

This shift in diet will have further dramatic health benefits. In particular it will promote:

- radical reduction in the sodium levels in our diet, and the widespread hypertension associated with it, as well as increased potassium levels, in accordance with diets that prevailed for most of our existence as a species
- a much better pH balance in the body with a reduction in acid-producing foods, in turn leading to better bone health as it reduces the calcium leaching believed to be caused by a diet high in acid-producing foods
- much higher intake levels of phytochemicals, vitamins, minerals, and antioxidants than are associated with the industrial diet.[17]

This shift in diet will have fairly dramatic environmental benefits as well, including:

- a very significant reduction in the carbon footprint resulting from food production, in terms of fossil fuels expended and methane produced
- lower consumption of increasingly scarce water resources in comparison with a diet heavy on animal meat consumption, and especially beef consumption
- A dramatic freeing-up of agricultural land for the production of human food rather than animal feeds.

Any health-based dietary regime of the future that we might envision will have to strongly reflect the constraints that 7 billion plus humans place on the carrying capacities of our land and ocean environments. In other words, it must become truly sustainable and not merely pay lip service to the term. Finally, a health-based dietary regime provides many more possibilities for a humane food system that firmly rejects the egregious practices against the other animal species that are ingrained into the system of factory farming.

Constructing a healthy, ethical, and sustainable dietary regime is nothing short of a monumental task, to be sure. It necessarily entails confronting a number of entrenched vested interests because it really means transforming the entire food system. And yet, it is surely the only sensible course of action before us.

NOTES

Introduction

1 The slow food movement began as a protest in 1986 against the establishment of a McDonald's fast-food restaurant near the Spanish Steps in Rome. Carlo Petrini is a founding member and the most famous person associated with the movement. The movement's website notes that its philosophy is that "everyone has a fundamental right to the pleasure of good food and consequently the responsibility to protect the heritage of food, tradition and culture that make this pleasure possible," http://www.slowfood. com/. See Geoff Andrews, *The Slow Food Story: Politics and Pleasure* (Montreal and Kingston: McGill-Queen's University Press, 2008).

2 Useful contributions include Laura Raynolds, "Re-embedding Global Agriculture: The International Organic and Fair Trade Movement," *Agriculture and Human Values* 17, 3 (2000): 297-309; Julie Guthman, *Agrarian Dreams: The Paradox of Organic Farming in California* (Berkeley: University of California Press, 2004); Alan Hall and Veronika Mogyorody, "Organic Farming in Ontario: An Examination of the Convenionalization Argument," *Sociologia Ruralis* 41, 4 (2001): 399-422; Laura DeLind, "Transforming Organic Agriculture into Industrial Organic Products: Reconsidering National Organic Standards," *Human Organization* 59, 2 (2000): 198-208.

3 Important contributions in this area include Gavin Fridell, *Fair Trade Coffee: The Prospects and Pitfalls of Market-Driven Social Justice* (Toronto: University of Toronto Press, 2007); Gavin Fridell, "The Co-operative and the Corporation: Competing Visions of the Future of Fair Trade," *Journal of Business Ethics* 86, 1 (2009): 81-95; also see Raynolds, "Re-embedding Global Agriculture"; Daniel Jaffee, *Brewing Justice: Fair Trade Coffee, Sustainability, and Survival* (Berkeley: University of California Press, 2007).

4 The intense interest in local food has been scrutinized by Robert Feagan, "The Place of Food: Mapping Out the 'Local' in Local Food Systems," *Progress in Human Geography* 31,1 (2007): 23-42; Clare Hinrichs, "The Practice and Politics of Food System Localization,"

Journal of Rural Studies 19 (2003): 33-45; and Hilary Tovey, "'Local Food' as a Contested Concept: Networks, Knowledges and Power in Food-Based Strategies for Rural Development," *International Journal of Sociology, Agriculture and Food* 16, 2 (2009): 21-35.

5 Among the many important contributions, I would note Peter Singer, *Animal Liberation*, 2nd ed. (New York: New York Review of Books, 1990); Peter Singer, ed., *In Defense of Animals: The Second Wave* (Malden, MA: Blackwell Books, 2006); Jim Mason, *An Unnatural Order: Uncovering the Roots of Our Domination of Nature and Each Other* (New York: Simon and Schuster, 1993); Cass R. Sunstein and Martha Nussbaum, eds., *Animal Rights: Current Debates and New Directions* (New York: Oxford University Press, 2005); and Jeffrey Moussaieff Masson, *The Face on Your Plate* (New York: W.W. Norton, 2009).

6 Tim Lang and Michael Heasman, *Food Wars: The Global Battle for Mouths, Minds and Markets* (London: Earthscan, 2004), 300.

7 US Department of Agriculture, "Energy Balance and Weight Management," in *Report of the Dietary Guidelines Advisory Committee on the Dietary Guidelines for Americans, 2010* (Washington, DC: Centre for Nutrition Policy and Promotion, 2010), http://www.cnpp.usda.gov/.

8 I cite a number of studies that support these conclusions in Chapter 2.

9 The Body Mass Index is the ratio of body weight to squared height in metres (kg/m^2). Although BMI is highly correlated with adiposity, it is not considered a true measure of it (see K.R. Fontaine and D.B. Allison, "Obesity and Mortality Rates," in *Handbook of Obesity: Etiology and Pathophysiology*, 2nd ed., ed. G. Bray and C. Bouchard [New York: Marcel Dekker, 2004], 767-85). One's BMI can be influenced by age, gender, ethnic background, dietary habits, and physical activity. Despite some shortcomings, BMI is widely accepted today as an indicator, although evidence that waist circumference (central adiposity) is a better measure of risk of cardiovascular disease has led to an argument for adding it to BMI to improve the measure of health risks associated with any given weight. For discussion of this issue, see, for example, George A. Bray, "Don't Throw the Baby Out with the Bath Water," *American Journal of Clinical Nutrition* 79, 3 (2004): 347-49.

10 See Gyorgy Scrinis, "On the Ideology of Nutritionism," *Gastronomica: The Journal of Food and Culture* 8, 1 (2008): 39-48.

11 Ibid., 40-41.

12 Figures quoted in Mark Bittman, "How to Save a Trillion Dollars," *New York Times*, 12 April 2011.

13 The literature on these themes is extensive. Notable early examples of the Latin American context include Warren Dean, *Rio Claro: A Brazilian Plantation System: 1820-1920* (Stanford, CA: Stanford University Press, 1976); Edelberto Torres Rivas, *Interpretación del Desarrollo Social Centroamericano* (San José, Costa Rica: Editorial Universitaria Centroamericana, 1973); Jim Handy, *Gift of the Devil: A History of Guatemala* (Toronto: Between the Lines, 1984); Thomas H. Holloway, "The Coffee Colono of São Paulo, Brazil: Migration and Mobility, 1880-1930," in *Land and Labour in Latin America*, ed. Kenneth Duncan and Ian Rutledge (Cambridge: Cambridge University Press, 1977), 301-22; David J. McCreery, "Coffee and Class: The Structure of Development in Liberal Guatemala," *Hispanic American Historical Review* 56 (1976); Marco Palacios, *Coffee in Colombia, 1850-1970* (Cambridge: Cambridge University Press, 1980); Anthony Winson, "The Formation of Capitalist Agriculture in Latin America and Its Relationship to Political Power and the State," *Comparative Studies in Society and History* 25, 1 (1983); and Anthony Winson, *Coffee and Democracy in Modern Costa Rica* (London: Macmillan, 1989).

More recent contributions dealing with agrarian change in the global South include A.H. Akram-Lodhi and C. Kay, eds., *Peasants and Globalization: Political Economy, Rural Transformation and the Agrarian Question* (New York: Routledge, 2008); Henry Bernstein, "Land Reform: Taking a Long(er) View," *Journal of Agrarian Change* 2, 4 (2002): 433-63; Henry Bernstein, "Agrarian Questions from Transitions to Globalization," in Akram-Lodhi and Kay, *Peasants and Globalization*; Saturnino Borras, Cristóbal Kay, and A. Haroon Akram Lodhi, "Agrarian Reform and Rural Development: Historical Overview and Current Issues," in *Land, Poverty and Livelihoods in an Era of Globalization*, ed. A.H. Akram-Lodhi, S. Borras, and C. Kay (London: Routledge, 2007), 1-40; Annette Demarais, *La Via Campesina: Globalization and Power of Peasants* (Halifax: Fernwood Publishing; London: Pluto Books, 2007); and Gerardo Otero, *Farewell to the Peasantry: Political Formation in Rural Mexico* (Boulder, CO: Westview Press, 1999).

Chapter 1: Between Producers and Eaters

1 From the *Merriam-Webster Online Dictionary* (2007), http://www.merriam-webster. com/dictionary, and *the American Heritage Dictionary of the English Language*, 4th ed., respectively.

2 Harriet Friedmann and Philip McMichael, "Agriculture and the State System: The Rise and Decline of National Agricultures, 1870 to the Present," *Sociologia Ruralis* 29, 2 (1989): 93-117.

3 See Hugh Campbell and Jane Dixon, "Introduction to the Special Symposium: Reflecting on Twenty Years of the Food Regimes Approach in Agri-Food Studies," *Agriculture and Human Values* 26 (2009), 261-65.

4 See M. Aglietta, *A Theory of Capitalist Regulation* (London: New Left Books, 1979).

5 Campbell and Dixon, "Introduction to the Special Symposium," 263.

6 Alfred Crosby, *The Columbian Exchange* (Westport, CT: Greenwood Press, 1972).

7 Alan Davidson, "Columbian Exchange," in *The Oxford Companion to Food*, ed. Alan Davidson (Oxford: Oxford University Press, 1999), 207.

8 See Paul Mantoux, *The Industrial Revolution in the Eighteenth Century* (London: Jonathan Cape, 1961). Mantoux indicates he is following Marx's lead in his understanding of the timing of the development of the factory system (36).

9 The first argument is made by Eric Schlosser in the very popular documentary *Food, Inc.*, http://www.takepart.com/foodinc/film; the latter argument is made by Friedmann and McMichael, "Agriculture and the State System."

10 Friedmann and McMichael, "Agriculture and the State System," 95-103.

11 Ibid.; John McCallum, *Unequal Beginnings: Agriculture and Economic Development in Quebec and Ontario until 1870* (Toronto: University of Toronto Press, 1980).

12 See R.L. Jones, *History of Agriculture in Ontario, 1613-1880* (Toronto: University of Toronto Press, 1946), and Anthony Winson, "The Uneven Development of Canadian Agriculture: Farming in the Maritimes and Ontario," *Canadian Journal of Sociology* 10, 4 (Fall 1985): 411-38.

13 A point made by Friedmann and McMichael, "Agriculture and the State System."

14 This is argued by Eric Schlosser in the widely disseminated 2009 documentary on the contemporary food system titled *Food, Inc.*

15 Cited in James Harvey Young, *Pure Food: Securing the Federal Food and Drugs Act of 1906* (Princeton, NJ: Princeton University Press, 1989), 108.

16 Marx saw competition and the rise of credit as providing a particular impulse to the concentration and centralization of capital. See Karl Marx, *Capital*, vol. 1 (Moscow: Progress Publishers, 1977 (repr. of English edition, ed. Frederick Engels [London: S. Sonnenschein, Lowrey, 1887]), 586-87.

17 More details on the development of the early Canadian canning industry can be found in my *The Intimate Commodity: Food and the Agro-Industrial Complex in Canada* (Toronto: Garamond Press, 1993), chap. 5.

18 A pioneering case in this regard was the Dakota Milling Company's advertising its Cream of Wheat hot cereal in the *Ladies Home Journal* in the 1890s. C.W. Post also advertised his Grape-Nuts cereal in that journal during those years. See *Ladies Home Journal* 18, 8 (1901): 18. The rapid expansion of Kellogg's in the early twentieth century and the central role mass advertising played in its success over numerous competitors is documented in Horace B. Powell, *The Original Has This Signature: W.K. Kellogg* (Englewood Cliffs, NJ: Prentice-Hall, 1956).

19 Harvey Levenstein, *Revolution at the Table: The Transformation of the American Diet* (New York: Oxford University Press, 1988), 33.

20 On the effects of modern milling technology in degrading the nutritional quality of wheat, see Glen Weaver, "Percent Nutrition Reduction Whole Wheat Flour versus Flour," *Nutrition Today* 36, 3 (May/June 2001): 115. For evidence of the impact of processing technology in the ready-to-eat cereal industry in increasing the glycemic index of the processed grain, see Janette Brand, Philip Nicholson, Anne Thorburn, and A. Stewart Truswell, "Food Processing and the Glycemic Index," *American Journal of Clinical Nutrition* 42 (December 1985): 1192-96.

21 This occurs in the context of the obesity epidemic, of course, although the major emphasis, particularly in political circles, continues to be on activity levels rather than diet, and when on diet, the focus has been almost exclusively on advice to shy away from weight-promoting foods and rarely on the economic system that promotes an obesogenic diet. Alarm within the medical community is growing, however, and a recent article in the *Canadian Journal of Cardiology* argued for the labelling of junk foods in our diet as "pathogens." See Norm Campbell, Kim D. Raine, and Lindsay McLaren, "'Junk Foods,' 'Treats,' or 'Pathogenic Foods'? A Call for Changing Nomenclature to Fit the Risk of Today's Diets," *Canadian Journal of Cardiology* 28, 4 (2012): 403-4.

22 See Harvey Levenstein, *The Paradox of Plenty: A Social History of Eating in Modern America* (Berkeley: University of California Press, 2003), 31.

23 Ibid., 25. I document a similar pattern in the Canadian dairy industry at the time in Winson, *Intimate Commodity*, chap. 4.

24 Levenstein, *Paradox of Plenty*, 27.

25 Friedmann and McMichael, "Agriculture and the State System," 103.

26 Ibid., 104.

27 Ibid., 105; Winson, *Intimate Commodity*.

28 Friedmann and McMichael, "Agriculture and the State System," 106.

29 For data on US meat consumption over time, see Ian MacLachlan, *Kill and Chill: Restructuring Canada's Beef Commodity Chain* (Toronto: University of Toronto Press, 2000), 312. MacLachlan notes that beef consumption per capita declined from 110 to 66 pounds between 1975 and 2000.

30 Eric Schlosser, *Fast Food Nation: The Dark Side of the All-American Meal* (New York: Houghton Mifflin, 2001), 121.

31 See Susan Mann and James Dickinson, "Obstacles to the Development of a Capitalist Agriculture," *Journal of Peasant Studies* 5, 4 (1978): 466-81.

32 The point about the time pressures faced by many women by the 1970s is made forcefully in an interview with Wallace McCain of McCain Foods, one of the foremost purveyors of convenience foods in North America and abroad, who explicitly notes that his company's product line was oriented to cater to women who face such time pressures (see the documentary *Potatoes*, National Film Board, 1976).

33 See Winson, *Intimate Commodity*, 123, fig. 4.

34 The prominent role that potato chips and sugar-sweetened beverages play in weight gain was discovered in a large twenty-year study published in 2011. Red meat and processed meat were the next two most significant obesogenic foods. See D. Mozaffarian, Tao Hao, E. Rimm, W.C. Willett, and F.B. Hu, "Changes in Diet and Lifestyle and Long-Term Weight Gain in Women and Men," *New England Journal of Medicine* 364 (23 June 2011): 2392-404.

35 See Anthony Winson, "Bringing Political Economy into the Debate on the Obesity Epidemic," *Agriculture and Human Values* 21, 4 (Winter 2004): 299-312.

36 For my examination of the phenomenon of spatial colonization of nutrient-poor products, what I call "pseudo foods," in the supermarket context, see ibid.

37 The relevant literature here has grown to be far too large to cite in its entirety, but the reader can gain a better appreciation of the research linking weight gain to adverse health outcomes by consulting the following recent studies. For an extensive survey on the science examining the relationship between weight and early mortality, see K.R. Fontaine and D.B. Allison, "Obesity and Mortality Rates," in *Handbook of Obesity: Etiology and Pathophysiology,* 2nd ed., ed. G. Bray and C. Bouchard (New York: Marcel Dekker, 2004), 767-85; J.E. Manson, W. Willett, M. Stampfer, G. Colditz, D. Hunter, S. Hankinson, C. Hennekens, and F. Speizer, "Body Weight and Mortality among Women," *New England Journal of Medicine* 333, 11 (1995): 677-85; and I.M. Lee, J.A. Manson, and C. Hennekens, "Body Weight and Mortality: A 27-Year Follow-Up of Middle-Aged Men," *Journal of the American Medical Association* 270, 23 (1993): 2823-27. For recent surveys of literature examining the relationship between obesity and disease, see Manson et al., "Body Weight and Mortality among Women"; A. Must and R.S. Strauss, "Risks and Consequences of Childhood and Adolescent Obesity," *International Journal of Obesity* 23 (Suppl. 2) (1999): S2-S11; Tim Lobstein and Rachel Jackson-Leach, "Estimated Burden of Paediatric Obesity and Co-morbidities in Europe: Part 2; Numbers of Children with Indicators of Obesity-Related Disease," *International Journal of Pediatric Obesity* 1, 1 (March, 2006): 33-41; and Pamela Abrams and Lorraine E. Levitt Katz, "Metabolic Effects of Obesity Causing Disease in Childhood," *Current Opinion in Endocrinology, Diabetes and Obesity* 18, 1 (February 2011): 23-27.

38 Knowledge of this phenomenon has been considerably enhanced by the insightful research of Thomas Reardon and his co-researchers. See, for example, Thomas Reardon, Peter Timmer, Christopher Barrett, and Julio Berdegué, "The Rise of Supermarkets in Africa, Asia, and Latin America," *American Journal of Agricultural Economics* 85, 5 (2003): 1140-46.

39 "R&I Top 400 Rankings," *Restaurant and Institutions,* 1 July 2008.

40 Barry M. Popkin, "Global Nutrition Dynamics: The World Is Shifting Rapidly toward a Diet Linked with Non-Communicable Diseases," *American Journal of Clinical Nutrition* 2, 84 (2006): 289-98.

41 J. Luo and F.B. Hu, "Time Trends of Obesity in Pre-School Children in China from 1989 to 1997," *International Journal of Obesity* 26 (2002): 553-58.

42 See the World Health Organization, "Obesity and Overweight," *Global Strategy on Diet, Physical Activity and Health,* 2003, http://www.who.int/dietphysicalactivity/; Popkin, "Global Nutrition Dynamics"; Sarah Wild, Gojka Roglic, Anders Green, Richard Sicree, and Hilary King, "Global Prevalence of Diabetes," *Diabetes Care* 27, 5 (2004): 1047-53; and Orit Pinhas-Hamiel and Philip Zeilter, "The Global Spread of Type II Diabetes Mellitus in Children and Adolescents," *Journal of Pediatrics* 146 (2005): 693-700.

43 See the account in Lorine Swainston Goodwin, *The Pure Food, Drink and Drug Crusaders, 1879-1914* (Jefferson, NC: McFarland and Company, 1999), chap. 11.

44 Friedmann and McMichael, "Agriculture and the State System," 112.

45 See William Friedland et al., "'Chasms' in Agro Food Systems: Rethinking How We Can Contribute," *Agriculture and Human Values* 25, 2 (June 2008): 197-201.

46 For the British legislation, see Ofcom, *Television Advertising of Food and Drink Products to Children: Statement and Further Consultation*, 2006, http://www.ofcom.org.uk/. For Spain, see Lisa Abend, "In Spain, Taking Some Joy Out of the Happy Meal," *Time*, 1 December 2009, http://www.time.com/time/world/.

47 For evidence of fast-food and junk food vendors colonizing food environments adjacent to high schools, see S.B. Austin, S. Melly, B. Sanchez, A. Patel, S. Buka, and S. Gortmaker, "Clustering of Fast Food Restaurants around Schools: A Novel Application of Spatial Statistics to the Study of Food Environments," *American Journal of Public Health* 95, 9 (2005): 1575-81, and Anthony Winson, "School Food Environments and the Obesity Issue: Content, Structural Determinants, and Agency in Canadian High Schools," *Agriculture and Human Values* 25 (2008): 499-511.

48 I make this argument in Anthony Winson, "The Demand for Healthy Eating: Supporting a Transformative Food 'Movement,'" *Rural Sociology* 75, 4 (2010): 584-600. In parts of the global South, it is the food sovereignty movement that has gained some traction in the struggle to resist the globalization of the corporate food model, at least in some contexts, and which at present offers the greatest resonance with small farmers and potentially consumers there.

49 For "nutritionalization" of the food economy, see Jane Dixon, "From the Imperial to the Empty Calorie: How Nutrition Relations Underpin Food Regime Transitions," *Agriculture and Human Values* 26 (2009): 321-33.

50 For a discussion of industry lobbying and success in changing regulations around what health claims can be made for food products in the United States, see Marion Nestle, *Food Politics*, 2nd ed. (Berkeley: University of California Press, 2007), chap. 11.

Chapter 2: Discordant Diets, Unhealthy People

1 Nassim Nicholas Taleb, *The Bed of Procrustes* (New York: Random House, 2010), 5.

2 Loren Cordain, S. Boyd Eaton, Anthony Sebastian, Neil Mann, Saffan Lindeberg, Bruce A. Watkins, James H. O'Keefe, and Janette Brand-Miller, "Origins and Evolution of the Western Diet: Health Implications for the 21st Century," *American Journal of Clinical Nutrition* 81 (2005): 342.

3 These generational calculations are largely derived from S. Boyd Eaton, Marjorie Shostak, and Melvin Konner, *The Paleolithic Prescription* (New York: Harper and Row, 1988), 26.

4 Peter Unger, Frederick E. Grine, and Mark F. Teaford, "Diet in Early *Homo*: A Review of the Evidence and a New Model of Adaptive Versatility," *Annual Review of Anthropology*, 35 (2006): 211.

5 Ibid., 212.

6 Ibid., 214.

7 On the percentage of plants in previous diets, see A.L. Zihlman and N.M. Tanner, "Gathering and Hominid Adaption," in *Female Hierarchies*, ed. L. Tiger and H.T. Fowler (Chicago: Beresford Food Service, 1978), 163-94; on the more recent analysis, see L. Cordain, S.B. Eaton, J. Brand Miller, N. Mann, and K. Hill, "The Paradoxical Nature of Hunter-Gatherer Diets: Meat-Based, yet Non-Atherogenic," *European Journal of Clinical Nutrition*, supplement 1, 56 (2002): 42S-52S.

8 See Julia Lee-Thorp and Matt Sponheimer, "Contributions of Biogeochemistry to Understanding Hominin Dietary Ecology," *Yearbook of Physical Anthropology* 49 (2006): 131-48.

9 Unger, Grine, and Teaford, "Diet in Early *Homo*," 220.

10　This is the thrust of the article by Unger, Grine, and Teaford, ibid.
11　Unger, Grine, and Teaford, "Diet in Early *Homo.*"
12　This point and subsequent discussion is heavily influenced by the path-breaking article by Cordain et al., "Origins and Evolution," 341-54.
13　See R.J. Stubbs and S. Whybrow, "Energy Density, Diet Composition and Palatability: Influences on Overall Food Energy Intake in Humans," *Physiological Behavior* 81 (2004): 755-64.
14　Marion Nestle, *Food Politics*, 2nd ed. (Berkeley: University of California Press, 2007).
15　See Loren Cordain, *The Paleo Diet* (Hoboken, NJ: John Wiley and Sons, 2002), 4.
16　Ibid.
17　Cordain et al., "Origins and Evolution," 341.
18　Ibid., 350.
19　Ibid.
20　Ibid., 341.
21　Ibid., 342.
22　As a member of the Sodium Working Group, a Canadian federal task force, noted after the release of its report calling for a dramatic reduction of salt levels in processed food, "Every year that we delay there are tens of thousands of premature deaths and cardio-vascular events, [and] billions of dollars of health care costs, that could be avoided." See Carly Weeks, "The Spoonful a Day Challenge," *Globe and Mail*, 30 July 2010, 1.
23　Etienne Patin and Lluís Quintana-Murci, "Demeter's Legacy: Rapid Changes to Our Genome Imposed by Diet," *Trends in Ecology and Evolution* 23, 2 (2007): 56-59.
24　Ibid., 58.
25　There is an extensive recent literature on the prevalence of celiac disease. Some notable studies include Catherine Dubé et al., "The Prevalence of Celiac Disease in Average-Risk and At-Risk Western European Populations: A Systematic Review," *Gastroenterology* 128 (2005): S57-S67; C. Catassi, I.M. Ratsch, E. Fabiani, et al., "Coeliac Disease in the Year 2000: Exploring the Iceberg," *Lancet* 343 (1994): 200-3; and Alessio Fasano et al., "Prevalence of Celiac Disease in At-Risk and Not-at-Risk Groups in the United States," *Archives of Internal Medicine* 163 (2003): 286-92.
26　David Ludwig, Joseph Majzoub, Ahmad Al-Zahrani, Gerard Dallal, Isaac Blanco, and Susan B. Roberts, "High Glycemic Index Foods, Overeating, and Obesity," *Pediatrics* 103, 3 (1999): 1.
27　World Health Organization, "Obesity and Overweight," *Global Strategy on Diet, Physical Activity and Health*, 2003, http://www.who.int/dietphysicalactivity/.
28　W.H. Glinsmann, H. Irausquin, and Y.K. Park, "Evaluation of Health Aspects of Sugars Contained in Carbohydrate Sweeteners: Report of Sugars Task Force, 1986," *Journal of Nutrition* 116, 11 (1986): S154.
29　See Jack Challen, Burton Berkson, and Melissa Smith, *Syndrome X: The Complete Nutritional Program to Prevent and Reverse Insulin Resistance* (New York: John Wiley and Sons, 2000), 16.
30　Jim Mann and A. Stewart Truswell, eds., *Essentials of Human Nutrition* (Oxford: Oxford University Press, 2007), 328.
31　Mary T. Bassett, "Diabetes Is Epidemic," *American Journal of Public Health* 95, 9 (2005): 1496.
32　P. Hogan, T. Dall, and P. Nikolov, "American Diabetes Association: Economic Costs of Diabetes in the US in 2002," *Diabetes Care* 26 (2003): 917-32.
33　Ron Goeree, Morgan Lim, Rob Hopkins, Gord Blackhouse, Jean-Eric Tarride, Feng Xue, and Daria O'Reilly, "Prevalence, Total and Excess Costs of Diabetes and Related Complications in Ontario, Canada," *Canadian Journal of Diabetes* 33, 1 (2009): 35-45.
34　Mann and Truswell, *Essentials of Human Nutrition*, 329.

35 Ibid., 329.
36 Eaton, Shostak, and Konner, *The Paleolithic Prescription*, 88-93.
37 Chellam, Berkson, and Smith, *Syndrome X*, 19-20.
38 See D.J. Jenkins, T.M. Wolever, R.H. Taylor, et al., "Glycemic Index of Foods: A Physiological Basis for Carbohydrate Exchange," *American Journal of Clinical Nutrition* 34, 3 (1981): 362-66.
39 There has been some debate over the efficacy of glycemic index and glycemic load as predictors of negative health outcomes, but the evidence indicating its utility is substantial. For more insight into its utility, see Janette Brand-Miller, "The Importance of Glycemic Index in Diabetes," *American Journal of Clinical Nutrition*, supplement, 59 (1994): 747S-52S; Simin Liu and Walter Willett, "Dietary Glycemic Load and Atherothromotic Risk," *Current Atherosclerosis Reports* 4 (2002): 454-61.
40 Ludwig et al., "High Glycemic Index Foods," 1. A more technical definition is that the glycemic index "is defined as the area under the glycemic response curve after consumption of 50 gm. of carbohydrate from a test food divided by the area under the curve after consumption of 50 gm of a control substance, either white bread or glucose" (ibid.).
41 Support for the hypothesis that high-glycemic foods and low-fibre intake increase the risk of type 2 diabetes was found in one large American prospective study; see J. Salmeron, J.E. Manson, M.J. Stampfer, et al., "Dietary Fiber, Glycemic Load, and Risk of Non-Insulin Dependent Diabetes Mellitus in Women," *Journal of the American Medical Association* 277 (1997): 472-77. A similar relationship was found in a large study of African American women, for instance. See Supriya Krishnan, Lynn Rosenberg, Martha Singer, Frank B. Hu, Luc Djousse, L. Adrienne Cupples, and Julie R. Palmer, "Glycemic Index, Glycemic Load, and Cereal Fiber Intake and Risk of Type 2 Diabetes in US Black Women," *Archives of Internal Medicine* 167, 21 (26 November 2007): 2304-9. High-glycemic foods have also been associated with lowering of the "good" HDL cholesterol and positively associated with fasting insulin levels and the ratio of total cholesterol to HDL, considered a key predictor of ischemic heart disease. See Huaidong Du, Daphne L. van der A., Marit M.E. van Bakel, Carla J.H. van der Kallen, Ellen E. Blaak, Marleen M.J. van Greevenbroek, Eugène H.J.M. Jansen, et al., "Glycemic Index and Glycemic Load in Relation to Food and Nutrient Intake and Metabolic Risk Factors in a Dutch Population," *American Journal of Clinical Nutrition* 87 (2008): 655-61.
42 Kaye Foster-Powell, Susanna H.A. Holt, and Janette C. Brand-Miller, "International Table of Glycemic Index and Glycemic Load Values," *American Journal of Clinical Nutrition* 76, 1 (2002): 5-56.
43 The following discussion is based on arguments and evidence provided by Cordain et al., "Origins and Evolution."
44 Janette Brand, Philip Nicholson, Anne Thorburn, and A. Stewart Truswell, "Food Processing and the Glycemic Index," *American Journal of Clinical Nutrition* 42 (December 1985): 1192-96.
45 Ibid., 1194.
46 Ibid., 1195.
47 Rosanna Mentzer Morrison, Jean Buzby, and Hodan Farah Wells, "Guess Who's Turning 100: Tracking a Century of American Eating," in *Amber Waves: The Economics of Food, Farming, Natural Resources, and Rural America* (Washington: USDA, Economic Research Service, March 2010), 17, http://www.ers.usda.gov/.
48 Laura Gabriela Sánchez-Lozada, MyPhuong Le, Mark Segal, and Richard J. Johnson, "How Safe Is Fructose for Persons with or without Diabetes?" *American Journal of Clinical Nutrition* 88 (2008): 1189.
49 See M.S. Segal, E. Gollub, and R.J. Johnson, "Is the Fructose Index More Relevant with Regards to Cardiovascular Disease Than the Glycemic Index?" *European Journal of*

Nutrition 46, 7 (2007): 406-17; C.M. Brown, A.G. Dulloo, G. Yepuri, and J.P. Montani, "Fructose Ingestion Acutely Elevates Blood Pressure in Healthy Young Humans," *American Journal of Physiology* 294, 3 (2008): 730R-7R; K.I. Stanhope, S.C. Griffen, B.R. Bair, M.M. Swarbrick, N.I. Keim, and P.J. Havel, "Twenty-Four-Hour Endocrine and Metabolic Profiles Following Consumption of High-Fructose Corn Syrup, Sucrose, Fructose, and Glucose-Sweetened Beverages with Meals," *American Journal of Clinical Nutrition* 87 (2008): 1194-203.

50 See P.J. Havel, "Dietary Fructose: Implications for Dysregulation of Energy Homeostasis and Lipid/Carbohydrate Metabolism," *Nutrition Review* 63, 5 (2005): 133-57.

51 See D.S. Ludwig, K.E. Peterson, and S.L. Gortmaker, "Relation between Consumption of Sugar-Sweetened Drinks and Childhood Obesity: A Prospective, Observational Analysis," *Lancet* 357 (2001): 505-8; J. Giamattea, "Television Watching and Soft Drink Consumption: Associations with Obesity in 11- to 13-Year-Old School Children," *Archives of Pediatric Adolescent Medicine* 157 (2003): 882-8; A.U. Makik, V.S. Schulze, and M.B. Hu, "Intake of Sugar-Sweetened Beverages and Weight Gain: A Systematic Review," *Southern American Journal of Clinical Nutrition* 84, 2 (2006): 274-88.

52 C. Cavadini, A.M. Siega-Riz, and B.M. Popkin, "US Adolescent Food Intake Trends from 1965 to 1996," *Archives of Disease in Childhood* 83 (2000): 18-24.

53 Patricia Kreutler, *Nutrition in Perspective* (Englewood Cliffs, NJ: Prentice Hall, 1980), 109.

54 Ibid., 110.

55 See Mann and Truswell, *Essentials of Human Nutrition*, 285.

56 Calculated from Statistics Canada, Agriculture Division. Derived from data estimating the disappearance of food each year, and indicates retail weight and eviscerated weight for beef and chicken respectively.

57 Ibid. for Canada. For US data, see Anthony Winson, "Bringing Political Economy into the Debate on the Obesity Epidemic," *Agriculture and Human Values* 21, 4 (Winter 2004): 303, table 2.

58 Mann and Truswell, *Essentials of Human Nutrition*, 284, fig. 20.3.

59 Ibid.

60 This difference exists even though smoking rates are higher in Japan. The difference is particularly notable with males. See H. Ueshima, A. Okayama, S. Saitoh, H. Nakagawa, B. Rodriquez, K. Sakata, N. Okuda, S.R. Choudhury, and J.D. Curb, "Differences in Cardiovascular Disease Risk Factors between Japanese in Japan and Japanese-Americans in Hawaii: The INTERLIPID Study," *Journal of Human Hypertension* 17 (2003): 631-39. As these authors note, "Among the established major risk factors, dietary lipids and the serum lipids they influence are critically important for the occurrence of epidemic CHD" (637).

61 Interview with Bruce Holub, professor emeritus, Department of Human Nutrition, University of Guelph, Guelph, ON, January 2008. See also M. Spence, J. Davignon, B. Holub, J.A. Little, and B.E. McDonald, *Report of the Ad Hoc Committee on the Composition of Special Margarines* (Ottawa: Minister of Supply and Services, Department of Health and Welfare, Bureau of Nutritional Sciences, 1980). Early concerns were also raised by Kummerow and Kritchevsky, among others. See F.A. Kummerow, "Lipids in Atherosclerosis," *Journal of Food Science* 40 (1975): 12-17; D. Kritchevsky, "Influence of Trans Unsaturated Fat on Experimental Atherosclerosis," in *Dietary Fats and Health*, ed. E.G. Perkins and W.T. Visek (Champaign, IL: American Oil Chemists' Society, 1983), 403-13.

62 Caroline M. Pond, *The Fats of Life* (Cambridge: Cambridge University Press, 1998), 101, and Jim Mann and Murray Skeaff, "Lipids," in Mann and Truswell, *Essentials of Human Nutrition*, 39.

63 Ibid.

64 For a review of some of the numerous studies concerning these issues, see Margaret Craig-Schmidt and Carmen Teodorescu, "Trans Fatty Acids in Foods," in *Fatty Acids in Foods and Their Health Implications*, ed. Chink K. Chow (Boca Raton: CRC Press, 2008), 378.

65 See Lorna R. Vanderhaeghe and Karlene Karst, *Healthy Fats for Life* (Toronto: John Wiley and Sons, 2004), 4.

66 This section draws heavily from a major 2006 review of the results of dozens of studies that have examined the relationship between trans fats and health outcomes. See Dariush Mozaffarian, Martijn B. Katan, Alberto Ascherio, Meir J. Stampfer, and Walter C. Willett, "Trans Fatty Acids and Cardiovascular Disease," *New England Journal of Medicine* 354, 15 (13 April 2006): 1601-13.

67 Ibid., 1602.

68 Ibid.

69 Ibid., 1604-5.

70 Ibid.

71 Craig-Schmidt and Tedorescu, "Trans Fatty Acids in Foods," 407.

72 Refer to the Health Canada website for further information, at http://www.hc-sc.gc.ca/fn-an/nutrition/.

73 This was claimed by a representative of Health Canada, in any case, in a presentation given to members of the Canadian Association for Food Studies, Ottawa, 25 May 2009.

74 Michael Morris, Elisa Na, and Alan Kim Johnson, "Salt Craving: The Psychobiology of Pathogenic Sodium Intake," *Physiology and Behavior* 94 (2008): 709-21.

75 Cordain et al., "Origins and Evolution."

76 Morris, Na, and Johnson, "Salt Craving," 711.

77 S.A.M. Adshead, *Salt and Civilization* (New York: St. Martin's Press, 1992), 7.

78 For a discussion of the development of commodity history, see ibid., Preface.

79 The point about the decline of salt intake stimulating an appetite for it is argued in ibid., 26.

80 An excellent discussion of this is found in Mark Kurlansky, *Salt: A World History* (New York: Penguin Books, 2002).

81 Adshead, *Salt and Civilization*, 8.

82 Ibid., 26.

83 Kurlansky, *Salt: A World History*, 41-42.

84 Ibid., 128.

85 See Graham MacGregor and Hugh de Wardener, *Salt, Diet and Health* (Cambridge: Cambridge University Press, 1998), 5.

86 Ibid.

87 Derek Denton, *The Hunger for Salt* (Berlin: Springer-Verlag, 1982), 86-87.

88 Cited in MacGregor and de Wardener, *Salt, Diet and Health*, 8.

89 See ibid., 9-10.

90 Morris, Na, and Johnson, "Salt Craving," 718.

91 MacGregor and de Wardener, *Salt, Diet and Health*, 12.

92 See F.M. Sacks, L.P. Svetkey, W.M. Vollmer, et al. "Effects on Blood Pressure of Reduced Dietary Sodium and the Dietary Approaches to Stop Hypertension (DASH) Diet," *New England Journal of Medicine* 344 (2001): 3-10.

93 This is noted in Morris, Na, and Johnson, "Salt Craving," 711.

94 MacGregor and de Wardener, *Salt, Diet and Health*, 137.

95 Shiraz I. Mishra, Charlotte Jones-Burton, Jeffrey C. Fink, Jeanine Brown, George L. Bakris, and Matthew R. Weir, "Does Dietary Salt Increase the Risk for Progression of Kidney Disease?" *Current Hypertension Reports* 7 (2005): 385-91, and Charlotte Jones-Burton, Shiraz I. Mishra, Jeffrey C. Fink, Jeanine Brown, Weyinshet Gossa, George L.

Bakris, and Matthew R. Weir, "An In-Depth Review of the Evidence Linking Dietary Salt Intake and Progression of Chronic Kidney Disease," *American Journal of Nephrology* 26 (2006): 268-75.

96 A useful discussion of these outcomes is found in MacGregor and de Wardener, *Salt, Diet and Health*, 137-51.

97 See Edward Frohlich, "The Salt Conundrum: A Hypothesis," *Hypertension* 50, 1: 161-66.

98 Norman Campbell, "Hypertension Prevention and Control in Canada," *Journal of American Society of Hypertension* 2, 2 (2008): 97-105.

99 Hillel W. Cohen, Susan M. Hailpern, Jing Fang, and Michael H. Alderman, "Sodium Intake and Mortality in the NHANES II Follow-Up Study," *American Journal of Medicine* 119 (2006): 275.e7-275.e14.

100 See Andre Picard, "Heart Disease Killing More Women," *Globe and Mail*, 23 June 2009, L1, L4.

101 See Frohlich, "The Salt Conundrum."

102 Cordain et al., "Origins and Evolution," 350.

103 Ibid.

104 See, for example, Jane E. Brody, "Exploring a Low-Acid Diet for Bone Health," *New York Times*, 23 November 2009, http://www.nytimes.com/.

105 Cordain et al., "Origins and Evolution," 342.

Chapter 3: From Neolithic to Capitalist Diets

1 John Burnett, cited in Sidney Mintz, *Sweetness and Power: The Place of Sugar in Modern History* (New York: Viking Books, 1985), 126.

2 Felipe Fernández-Armesto, *Near a Thousand Tables* (Toronto: Key Porter, 2002), 80. This author has an informative and speculative discussion about the strengths and weaknesses of several explanations of the transition to agriculture.

3 See Heather Pringle, "Neolithic Agriculture: The Slow Birth of Agriculture," *Science* 282 (1998): 1446, http://cas.bellarmine.edu/.

4 Alan H. Simmons, *The Neolithic Revolution in the Near East* (Tucson: University of Arizona Press, 2007), 4.

5 See the authoritative treatment by Daniel Zohary and Maria Hopf, *Domestication of Plants in the Old World*, 2nd ed. (Oxford: Oxford University Press, 1993). For an engaging treatment of this process, see Jared Diamond, *Guns, Germs, and Steel: The Fates of Human Societies* (New York: W.W. Norton, 1999), chaps. 5 and 10.

6 See Diamond, *Guns, Germs, and Steel*, chap. 5.

7 Pringle, "Neolithic Agriculture."

8 This discussion is largely based on the analysis provided by Marie Elaine Danforth, "Nutrition and Politics in Prehistory," *Annual Review of Anthropology* 28 (1999): 1-25. Evidence found in the National Museum of Anthropology, Mexico City, is also used here.

9 Ibid., 12.

10 Cited in ibid., 13.

11 Ibid., 9.

12 Ibid., 12, notes studies making this argument.

13 Hans J. Teuteberg, "Periods and Turning Points in the History of European Diets: A Preliminary Outline of Problems and Methods," in *Food in Change: Eating Habits from the Middle Ages to the Present Day*, ed. A. Fenton and E. Kisban (Edinburgh: John Donald Publishers, 1986), 11-23.

14 See Massimo Montanari, "Food Systems and Models of Civilization," in *Food: A Culinary History*, ed. J.L. Flandrin and M. Montanari (New York: Penguin Books, 2000), 77-78.

15 See ibid.

16 Ibid., 17.

17 Mikhail Rabinowitsch, "Eating Habits in Russian Towns in the Sixteenth to Nineteenth Centuries: The Main Phases of Development," in Fenton and Kisban, *Food in Change*, 105.

18 Alan Davidson, "Columbian Exchange," in *The Oxford Companion to Food*, ed. Alan Davidson (Oxford: Oxford University Press, 1999).

19 Alfred Crosby, *The Columbian Exchange* (Westport, CT: Greenwood Press, 1972).

20 Davidson, "Columbian Exchange," 207.

21 See Diamond, *Guns, Germs, and Steel*, 78.

22 Davidson, "Columbian Exchange."

23 Jean Louis Flandrin, "The Early Modern Period?" in Flandrin and M. Montanari, *Food*, 351.

24 For a classical treatment of the impact of the Enclosure Acts that precipitated this abrupt rural transformation, see Paul Mantoux, "Redistribution of the Land," chap. 3 in his *The Industrial Revolution in the Eighteenth Century* (New York: Harper Torchbooks, 1961). For a graphic illustration of the population shift from the rural counties to the industrializing northwest of England, see 350-53.

25 For an in-depth discussion of these developments, see, among other sources, Max Weber, "Developmental Tendencies in the Situation of East Elbian Rural Labourers," trans. K. Tribe, *Economy and Society* 8, 2 (1979), and Anthony Winson, "The 'Prussian Road' of Agrarian Development: A Reconsideration," *Economy and Society* 11, 4 (1982): 381-408.

26 See A. Gibson and T.C. Smout, "From Meat to Meal: Changes to Diet in Scotland," in *Food, Diet and Economic Change Past and Present*, ed. Catherine Geissler and Derek Oddy (Leicester, UK: University of Leicester Press, 1993), 10-34. In terms of considering the decline of animal-based proteins in the diet as a move to a poorer diet, this must be placed in its social and historical context. As these authors argue, "Such a shift can be seen as a deterioration in the quality of life, for European peoples have always shown a marked preference for meat over farinaceous food when given the option, and rises or falls in the consumption of meat are always regarded as significant evidence of alterations in the standard of living in the controversies over nineteenth-century welfare" (ibid., 11).

27 Ibid., 28-29. See also T.C. Smout, "Landowners in Scotland, Ireland and Denmark in the Age of Improvement," *Scandinavian Journal of History* 12 (1987): 79-97, and Eric Richards, *A History of the Highland Clearances*, vol. 1 (London: Croom Helm), 1982.

28 See the important study by Fraginals on the history of the sugar industry in Cuba for insights into the environmental destruction wrought by this activity. M. Fraginals, *The Sugarmill: The Socioeconomic Complex of Sugar in Cuba* (New York: Monthly Review Press, 1976), 74-76.

29 Ibid.

30 Maguelonne Toussaint-Samat, *A History of Food* (Oxford: Blackwell, 1994), 15.

31 Ibid., 21.

32 Ibid.

33 Ibid., 23.

34 Ibid., 30.

35 More is known about the medieval English diet than about those of many societies, over a long period. As Sidney Mintz notes, for the great majority, it was largely based on bread consumption, derived from wheat, and from rye, oats, and barley when wheat was scarce. This was supplemented with peas, beans, and some dairy during the good years, along with occasional meat from wild and domestic animals, and some fruits in season. See Mintz, *Sweetness and Power*, 75.

36 Ibid., 78.

37 Ibid., 85-95.

38 Ibid., 96.

39 Ibid., 67-68. The data are derived from a study by Noel Deerr, cited by Mintz.

40 Cuba's planters were able to ramp up production dramatically once the British market opened up to them. See Elizabeth Abbott, *Sugar: A Bittersweet History* (Toronto: Penguin Books, 2008), chap. 9.

41 Cordain et al., "Origins and Evolution," 343.

42 Abbott, *Sugar*, 372.

43 Ibid., 126.

44 Cordain et al., "Origins and Evolution," 343.

45 See Mintz, *Sweetness and Power*, 125-27.

46 John Burnett, cited in ibid., 129.

47 R.H. Campbell, cited in ibid., 128.

48 Ibid., 128.

49 See ibid., 130.

50 See W.J. Moore, "Dental Caries in Britain from Roman Times to the 19th Century," in Geissler and Oddy, *Food, Diet and Economic Change*. Teeth can be especially useful in the effort to infer dietary composition because of their high resistance to deterioration over time, even in comparison with bone.

51 Ibid., 55-56.

52 Ibid., 56.

PART 2: THE BEGINNINGS OF THE INDUSTRIAL DIET, 1870-1940

1 Attributed to Fran Lebowitz, in "Fran Lebowitz's Travel Hints," *Social Studies*, cited in M.J. Cohen, ed., *The Penguin Dictionary of Epigrams* (Toronto: Penguin Books, 2001).

Chapter 4: From Patent Flour to Wheaties

1 Richard Perren, "Structural Change and Market Growth in the Food Industry: Flour Milling in Britain, Europe, and America," *Economic History Review*, 2nd series, 43, 3 (1990): 423-24.

2 Elizabeth Etheridge, *The Butterfly Caste: A Social History of Pellagra in the South* (Westport, CT: Greenwood, 1972), 124-25.

3 Perren, "Structural Change and Market Growth," 430.

4 Ibid., 422.

5 As Kuhlmann notes, "The wheat berry is composed of four parts: the outer husk or bran, forming about five percent of the berry; next to this a layer of ... gluten cells, forming three or four percent of the total weight; inside this, the starchy interior, or endosperm, which makes up about eighty percent of the kernel; and, at the base of the kernel, the embryo or oily germ, forming ten or eleven percent of the berry." Charles B. Kuhlmann, *The Development of the Flour-Milling Industry in the United States* with Special Reference to the Industry in Minneapolis (New York: Houghton Mifflin, 1929), 113.

6 Ibid.

7 Ibid., 423.

8 For a brief but insightful contextual overview of the tragic and violent history of the Great Plains at this time, see Ronald Wright, *What Is America? A Short History of the New World Order* (Toronto: Vintage Canada), 2008. An excellent account of the events

of this time from an observer sympathetic to the plight of the Plains Indians and one who interviewed many of the survivors of the Indian Wars of that era is to found in Stanley Vestal, *Sitting Bull: Champion of the Sioux* (New York: Houghton Mifflin, 1932).

9 See Marvin McInnis, "Migration," ed. Donald Kerr and Deryck Hollsworth, in *The Historical Atlas of Canada*, vol. 3 (Toronto: University of Toronto Press, 1990), plate 27.

10 Perren, "Structural Change and Market Growth," 423-24.

11 Kuhlmann, *The Development of the Flour-Milling Industry*, chap. 5.

12 General Mills, "Our Origins," in *General Mills: 75 Years of Innovation, Invention, Food and Fun*, 69, http://www.generalmills.com/. As Kuhlmann explains, "Strong flour, containing much gluten, expands greatly, thereby making a light bread. It absorbs much water which is an advantage to the baker who sells his bread by weight": *The Flour-Milling Industry*, 230.

13 Kuhlmann, *The Flour-Milling Industry*, 118-19.

14 General Mills, "Our Origins," 69, 72. Interestingly, in his extensive account of the industry, Kuhlmann does not mention de la Barre but focuses on the leadership of George Christian in this regard (see ibid., chap. 4). It took some time before the new technology was a complete success, as the first rollers made of porcelain and, later, cast iron proved less than satisfactory.

15 Perren's data on the milling industry in the United Kingdom during the period when roller milling was taking root there (roughly 1880 to 1890) indicate the dramatic gains in output per worker that could be had. Perren, "Structural Change and Market Growth," 428. Kuhlmann describes the period between 1870 and 1880 as the era of "new process" milling, and the decade after the era of roller milling. Kuhlmann, *The Flour-Milling Industry*, 125.

16 See Perren, "Structural Change and Market Growth," 429.

17 Ibid., 424. The accumulation by certain millers of sufficient capital to build large mills, and some millers' buying out of other millers and centralizing production within one company, no doubt facilitated the inevitably expensive process of technological transformation.

18 As Perren notes, "The economics of roller milling encouraged this extension into new territories, known as 'overlapping'" (ibid., 433).

19 See N.L. Kent and A.D. Evers, "Nutrition," in *Technology of Cereals*, ed. N.L. Kent and A.D. Evers (Oxford: Elsevier, 1994).

20 Ibid., 236-37.

21 Ibid., 238.

22 Ibid., 236-37.

23 Glen L. Weaver, "A Miller's Perspective on the Impact of Health Claims," *Nutrition Today* 36, 3 (May/June 2001): 116.

24 See, for example, the four-part history of nutrition authored by Kenneth Carpenter. Kenneth Carpenter, "A Short History of Nutritional Science," *Journal of Nutrition* 133 (2003).

25 In fact, mandatory enrichment of wheat flour did not become mandatory until 1976, though enrichment of flour by millers was common before then. See http://www.canadianmillers.ca/flour_enrichment.htm.

26 Perren, "Structural Change and Market Growth," 430.

27 Etheridge, *Butterfly Caste*.

28 Ibid., 4, 7, 69.

29 Etheridge notes that Southern millworkers were paid approximately one-half of millworkers in the mills of the northeastern United States for the same kind of work, and had to work more hours to get it. Ibid., 195.

30 Edward Jenner Wood, *Scientific American*, Supplement, 82 (15 July 1916): 43, cited in Etheridge, 244, note 13.

31 Etheridge, *Butterfly Caste*, 124-25.
32 This account is drawn from ibid., 125-26.
33 *Northwestern Miller*, Editorial, 2 April 1946, 21.
34 Ibid.
35 Kuhlmann, *The Flour-Milling Industry*, 127-28.
36 Ibid., 130.
37 This was certainly the case in Canada; for example, see Seymour Martin Lipset, *Agrarian Socialism: The Cooperative Commonwealth Federation in Saskatchewan* (Berkeley: University of California Press, 1950), 19.
38 Ibid., 130.
39 General Mills, "Our Origins," 67.
40 Ibid., 130-34.
41 Charles Davies, *Bread Men: How the Westons Built an International Empire* (Toronto: Key Porter, 1987), 40.
42 Davies, *Bread Men*, 42-45.
43 Kuhlmann, *The Flour-Milling Industry*, 284-86. In Canada, there was a particularly dramatic expansion of chain store operation in the latter part of the 1920s; see Dominion Bureau of Statistics, "Food Chains in Canada, 1930," in *Census of Merchandising and Service Establishments* (Ottawa: Dominion Bureau of Statistics, 1933), 4.
44 See Anthony Winson, *The Intimate Commodity: Food and the Agro-Industrial Complex in Canada* (Toronto: Garamond Press, 1993), chap. 7.
45 Richard Tedlow, *New and Improved: The Story of Mass Marketing in America* (New York: Basic Books, 1990), 194.
46 The geographical scope of Bell's consolidation effort is indicated in the mills that were amalgamated, which included the Red Star Milling Company of Kansas, the Royal Milling Company of Montana, the Kalispell Flour Mills Company, and the Rocky Mountain Elevator Company. In 1929, he added the Sperry Flour Company of California, the Kell Group from the Southwest, the El Reno mill of Oklahoma, and the Larrowe Milling Company of Michigan. See General Mills, "Our Origins," 67.
47 Davies, *Bread Men*, 42.
48 Department of Justice, *Flour-Milling Industry: Investigation into an Alleged Combine in the Manufacture, Distribution and Sale of Flour and Other Grain-Mill Products*, Ottawa, Report of the Commissioner, Combines Investigation Act, 29 December 1948, 109, 118.
49 Ibid., chap. 11, 105-8.
50 Ibid., 105.

Chapter 5: Pushing Product for Profit

1 Harvey Levenstein, *Revolution at the Table: The Transformation of the American Diet* (New York: Oxford University Press, 1988), 43.
2 Nassim Nicholas Taleb, *The Bed of Procrustes* (New York: Random House, 2010), 4.
3 Levenstein, *Revolution at the Table*.
4 Paul Baran and Paul Sweezy, *Monopoly Capital: An Essay on the American Economic and Social Order* (New York: Monthly Review Press, 1966).
5 Microsoft 7 Encarta 7 2006, compact disc, s.v. "Erie Canal" (Redmond, WA: Microsoft Corporation, 2005).
6 Baran and Sweezy, *Monopoly Capital*, 116.
7 Ibid.
8 *Northwestern Miller*, 7 July 1915, 25.
9 Ibid., 118.
10 Richard Tedlow, *New and Improved: The Story of Mass Marketing in America* (New York: Basic Books, 1990), 18, table 4-1.

11 Ibid., 5-6.
12 Levenstein, *Revolution at the Table*, 37.
13 Ibid., 36.
14 *Ladies Home Journal* 13, 4 (November 1892).
15 Gregory Price, "Cereal Sales Soggy Despite Price Cuts and Reduced Couponing," *Food Review* 23, 2 (May-August 2000): 23.
16 *Ladies Home Journal* 18, 8 (July 1893): 18. A sign perhaps of the evolution of the English language, it seems highly unlikely that Post would have chosen the term "pre-digested" today to promote his innovation.
17 Price, "Cereal Sales Soggy," 23.
18 Levenstein, *Revolution at the Table*, 33.
19 These figures are carcass weight, so actual weight of meat consumed would be considerably less. See Eric Ross, "Patterns of Diet and Forces of Production: An Economic and Ecological History of the Ascendancy of Beef in the United States Diet," in *Beyond the Myths of Culture: Essays in Cultural Materialism*, ed. Eric Ross (New York: Academic Press, 1980), 191.
20 Ibid., table 7.1 and 206-7.
21 General Mills, *General Mills: 75 Years of Innovation, Invention, Food and Fun*, 32-35.
22 Ibid., 32-34.
23 Horace B. Powell, *The Original Has This Signature: W.K. Kellogg* (Englewood Cliffs, NJ: Prentice-Hall, 1956), 92-93, 98-99.
24 Ibid., 103.
25 Ibid., 104.
26 Ibid., 134-35.
27 Ibid., 135.
28 Ibid., 142.
29 John J. Riley, *A History of the American Soft Drink Industry* (New York: Arno Press, 1972), 8. Various sorts of prepared liquid refreshments were common in many societies, of course, stretching back to antiquity. In France in the seventeenth century, an association of "Limondiers" existed whose members made a commercial enterprise out of distributing a lemonade concoction from tanks carried on their backs. Ibid., 8.
30 Pendergast's book offers insight into the prominence of patent medicines in the 1800s in the United States. See Mark Pendergast, *For God, Country and Coca-Cola* (New York: Collier Books, 1993).
31 Coca extractions were hardly novel in this era, when opium was widely available and morphine widely used, and morphine addiction a common social ill. As Pendergast notes, Dr. Pemberton was likely himself a morphine addict. Ibid., chap. 2.
32 Ibid., 24.
33 Ibid., 118.
34 Ibid., chaps. 2 and 3.
35 Ibid., 101-2, 105.
36 See Riley, *History of the American Soft Drink Industry*.
37 Ibid., 135.
38 Robinson is credited by Pendergast with the insight that, instead of advertising to the few who sought medicinal relief, Coca-Cola should market to the masses who wanted a refreshing drink. Pendergast, *For God, Country and Coca-Cola*, 66.
39 Ibid., 89-90.
40 Ann Hoy, *Coca-Cola: The First Hundred Years* (Atlanta: Coca-Cola Company, 1986).
41 Ibid.
42 Pendergast, *For God, Country and Coca-Cola*, 91.

43 Timothy J. Muris, David T. Scheffman, and Pablo T. Spiller, *Strategy, Structure, and Antitrust in the Carbonated Soft-Drink Industry* (Westport, CT: Quorum Books, 1993), 12.

44 Pendergast, *For God, Country and Coca-Cola*, 91. The trial was related to a lawsuit that Candler launched against the US government after the Internal Revenue Service ruled in 1898 that Coca-Cola was a drug and therefore subject to a new tax the government had levied. The trial lasted until 1902 and was settled in Candler's favour. Ibid., 61.

45 Ibid., 64-65.

46 As Pendergast notes, however, guaranteeing a fixed price for syrup came to haunt Candler when costs for raw materials rose, and for this and other reasons, Coca-Cola – and other companies in later times – has tried to capture control of bottling operations that it gave away in the beginning, when bottling seemed like a venture likely to fail. Ibid., 84.

47 Ibid., 84.

48 See Riley, *History of the American Soft Drink Industry*, 137, 142, 148, and 275, table 1.

49 Ibid., 140-41.

PART 3: THE INTENSIFICATION OF THE INDUSTRIAL DIET, 1945-80

1 I credit the authors of a recent editorial in a leading Canadian medical journal with arguing for the designation of food products high in sodium, sugars, and fats as "pathogens" in an effort to draw attention to their substantial role in debilitating health. See Norm Campbell, Kim D. Raine, and Lindsay McLaren, "'Junk Foods,' 'Treats,' or 'Pathogenic Foods'? A Call for Changing Nomenclature to Fit the Risk of Today's Diets," *Canadian Journal of Cardiology* 28, 4 (2012): 1-2.

2 Anthony Winson, "Bringing Political Economy into the Debate on the Obesity Epidemic," *Agriculture and Human Values* 21, 4 (Winter 2004): 302-3.

3 On culinary deskilling, an especially theoretically informed treatment, see JoAnn Jaffe and Michael Gertler, "Victual Vicissitudes: Consumer Deskilling and the (Gendered) Transformation of Food Systems," *Agriculture and Human Values* 23 (2006): 143-62.

4 Harriet Friedmann and Philip McMichael, "Agriculture and the State System: The Rise and Decline of National Agricultures, 1870 to the Present," *Sociologia Ruralis* 29, 2 (1989): 104.

5 Ibid., 106.

6 For excellent discussions of the development of these processor-integrators and the mechanisms by which they subordinate farm operators in the case of poultry and hog production, see William Boyd and Michael Watts, "Agro-Industrial Just-in-Time: The Chicken Industry and Postwar American Capitalism," *Globalizing Food: Agrarian Questions and Global Restructuring* (New York: Routledge, 1997), and Alessandro Bonanno and Douglas Constance, *Stories of Globalization: Transnational Corporations, Resistance, and the State* (University Park, PA: Penn State University Press, 2008), chaps. 5 and 6.

Chapter 6: Speeding Up the Making of Food

1 David Harvey, *The Enigma of Capital* (New York: Oxford University Press, 2009), 41.

2 D.C. Rule, K.S. Broughton, S.M. Shellito, and G. Maiorano, "Comparison of Muscle Fatty Acid Profiles and Cholesterol Concentrations of Bison, Beef Cattle, Elk and Chicken," *Journal of Animal Science* 80 (2002): 1210.

3 Interest in the issue of turnover time among rural sociologists was sparked by an important article by Susan Mann and James Dickinson in the 1970s; see "Obstacles to the Development of a Capitalist Agriculture," *Journal of Peasant Studies* 5, 4 (1978): 466-81.

4 In the real world, the innovations made by a company would likely be copied by competitors, reducing its extraordinary profits over the long term. The prospects for enhanced returns over the short term, nevertheless, provide the incentive for investments to reduce the turnover time of capital.

5 I say "largely" correct because there are other dangers associated with such products, including food safety issues when unclean meat is cooked at temperatures too low to kill pathogenic bacteria.

6 Eric Ross, "Patterns of Diet and Forces of Production: An Economic and Ecological History of the Ascendancy of Beef in the United States Diet," in *Beyond the Myths of Culture: Essays in Cultural Materialism,* ed. Eric Ross (New York: Academic Press, 1980), 204.

7 See Ian MacLachlan, *Kill and Chill: Restructuring Canada's Beef Commodity Chain* (Toronto: University of Toronto Press, 2000), 69.

8 Ross, "Patterns of Diet."

9 G.M. Ward, P.L. Knox, and B.W. Hobson, "Beef Production Options and Requirements for Fossil Fuel," *Science* 198 (21 October 1977): 265.

10 US Federal Trade Commission of 1920, cited in Ross, "Patterns of Diet," 205.

11 For a comprehensive analysis of the concentration of economic power in agricultural, processing, and retailing spheres and the implications of this for smaller producers and processors in particular, see Mary Hendrikson, John Wilkinson, William Heffernan, and Robert Gronski, *The Global Food System and Nodes of Power,* report prepared for Oxfam America, 2008, http://ssrn.com/.

12 Ross, "Patterns of Diet," 205.

13 Ward, Knox, and Hobson, "Beef Production Options," 265.

14 Ross, "Patterns of Diet," 206.

15 Most notable here was the industrial invention allowing farmers to increase nitrogen in their soils with the use of synthetic nitrogen, rather than the traditional means via nitrogen-fixing plants. The Haber-Bosch process produces this nitrogen with the use of fossil fuels, typically natural gas. See Michael Pollen, *The Omnivore's Dilemma: A Natural History of Four Meals* (New York: Penguin Books, 2006), 44-47, for an informative discussion of this process and the man behind it.

16 MacLachlan, *Kill and Chill,* 312, fig. 9.1.

17 Ibid., 64-65.

18 Ibid., 67.

19 R.L. Willham, "Genetics of Fat Content in Animal Products," in *Fat Content and Composition of Animal Products* (Washington, DC: National Academy of Life Sciences, 1976), 88.

20 Ibid.

21 As MacLachlan notes, rolled barley is favoured by feedlots in Alberta, whereas, in the southern plains of the United States, sorghum is common in feeds. MacLachlan, *Kill and Chill,* 66.

22 Alessandro Bonanno and Douglas Constance, *Stories of Globalization: Transnational Corporations, Resistance, and the State* (University Park, PA: Pennsylvania State University Press, 2008), 126.

23 In *The Face on Your Plate* (New York: W.W. Norton, 2009), Jeffrey Moussaieff Mason provides an eloquent and informative investigation into confinement-animal-rearing systems and their impacts on the animals raised within them. He provides plenty of reasons to seriously rethink the eating of animals raised in this fashion.

24 See L. Cordain, S.B. Eaton, J. Brand Miller, N. Mann, and K. Hill, "The Paradoxical Nature of Hunter-Gatherer Diets: Meat-Based, yet Non-Atherogenic," *European Journal of Clinical Nutrition,* supplement 1, 56 (2002): S46.

25 See Jim Mann and A. Stewart Truswell, eds., *Essentials of Human Nutrition* (Oxford: Oxford University Press, 2007), 284-85. For more details on fats and their impact on health, see Chapter 2, this volume.
26 G.J. Miller, R.A. Field, M.L. Riley, and J.C. Williams, "Lipids in Wild Ruminant Animals and Steers," *Journal of Food Quality* 9 (1986): 331-43, esp. 336 and 341.
27 This estimate comes from S. Boyd Eaton, Marjorie Shostak, and Melvin Konner, *The Paleolithic Prescription* (New York: Harper and Row, 1988),7.
28 See Viktoria Olsson and Jana Pickova, "The Influence of Production Systems on Meat Quality, with Emphasis on Pork," *Ambio* 34, 4-5 (2005), 340. See also Cordain et al., "Paradoxical Nature," S47.
29 G.J. Miller, M.L. Masor, and Riley M.L., "Intramuscular Lipids and Triglyceride Structures in Range and Feedlot Steers," *Journal of Food Science* 46 (1981): 1333; Miller et al., "Lipids," 331-43.
30 Olsson and Pickova, "The Influence of Production Systems," 341.
31 Rule et al., "Comparison of Muscle Fatty Acid Profiles," 1202-11; J.L. Duynisveld, E. Charmley, and P. Mir, "Meat Quality and Fatty Acid Composition of Pasture Finished Beef Steers Fed Barley and Soybeans," *Canadian Journal of Animal Science* 86 (2006): 535-45.
32 Mark Bittman, "Rethinking the Meat-Guzzler," *New York Times*, 27 January 2008.
33 Rule et al., "Comparison of Muscle Fatty Acid Profiles," 1210.
34 C.J. Lopez-Bote, R. Sanz Arias, A.I. Rey, A. Castaño, B. Isabel, and J. Thos, "Effect of Free Range Feeding on n-3 Fatty Acid and α-Tocopherol Content and Oxidative Stability of Eggs," *Animal Feeding Science Technology* 72 (2002): 33-40.
35 D.B. Mutetika and D.C. Mahan, "Effect of Pasture, Confinement and Diet Fortification with Vitamin E and Selenium on Reproducing Gilts and Their Progeny," *Journal of Animal Science* 71 (1993): 3211.
36 Ibid.
37 See A. Tolan, J. Robertson, C.R. Orton, M.J. Head, A.A. Christie, and B.A. Millburn, "The Chemical Composition of Eggs Produced under the Battery, Deep Litter and Free Range Conditions," *British Journal of Nutrition* 30 (1973) (paper no. 4): 186.
38 Ibid., 191.
39 Lopez-Bote et al., "Effect of Free Range Feeding, 38.
40 Søren Krogh Jensen, Anna Kirstin Bjørnbak Johannsen, and John E. Hermansen, "Quantitative Secretion and Maximal Secretion Capacity of Retinol, b-Carotene and a-Tocopherol into Cows' Milk," *Journal of Dairy Research* 66 (1999): 511-22.
41 An informative account of the near total control of the corporate integrators in the case of the poultry industry can be found in William Boyd and Michael Watts, "Agro-Industrial Just-in-Time: The Chicken Industry and Postwar American Capitalism," *Globalizing Food: Agrarian Questions and Global Restructuring* (New York: Routledge, 1997), 192-225.
42 Bittman, "Rethinking the Meat-Guzzler."
43 An excellent documentary on this situation is *The Future of Food*, http://www.thefutureoffood.com.
44 Animal welfare issues are exposed in Michael W. Fox's classic *Inhuman Society: The American Way of Treating Animals* (New York: Macmillan, 1990).
45 See Francisco Diez-Gonzalez, Todd Callaway, Menas Kizoulis, and James Russell, "Grain Feeding and the Dissemination of Acid-Resistant Escherichia Coli from Cattle," *Science* 281, 5383 (11 September 1998): 1666-68.
46 A Canadian case in point is the listeria contamination of meat emanating from a large Maple Leaf Inc. plant in 2009. Large quantities of product were believed to be contaminated and had to be recalled, at tremendous cost to the company, the largest pork

processor in Canada. See CBC News, "Listeriosis Outbreak Timeline," 11 September 2009, http://www.cbc.ca/news/.

Chapter 7: The Simplification of Whole Food

1 This is discussed in Kafui Kwami Adom, Mark Sorrells, and Rui Hai Liu, "Phytochemicals and Antioxidant Activity of Milled Fractions of Different Wheat Varieties," *Journal of Agricultural Food Chemistry* 53, 6 (2005): 2297-306.

2 Ibid.

3 William Friedland, Amy Barton, and Robert Thomas, *Manufacturing Green Gold: Capital, Labor, and Technology in the Lettuce Industry* (New York: Cambridge University Press, 1981), chap. 2; 109, table 4.2.

4 See K. Kiple and K. Conneè Ornelas, "Potatoes (White)," in *The Cambridge World History of Food*, http://www.cambridge.org/.

5 As Schlosser notes, Ray Kroc wrote in his memoir that "the french fry [was] ... almost sacrosanct for me, its preparation a ritual to be followed religiously." See *Fast Food Nation: The Dark Side of the All-American Meal* (New York: Houghton Mifflin, 2001), 114.

6 Ibid., 117. A good part of what made fast-food french fries so appealing was the beef fat used in the frying process, and the copious amounts of salt typically added.

7 See Kathryn Munoz, Susan Krebs-Smith, Rachel Ballard-Barbash, and Linda Cleveland, "Food Intakes of US Children and Adolescents Compared with Recommendations," *Pediatrics* 100 (1997): 323-29; Statistics Canada, "Overview of Canadians' Eating Habits," *The Daily*, 6 June 2006, http://www.statcan.ca/.

8 Another finding was that student milk purchasers invariably avoided plain white cow's milk, buying sweetened chocolate milk instead. More details on findings of this exploration of school food environments can be found in Anthony Winson, "School Food Environments and the Obesity Issue: Content, Structural Determinants, and Agency in Canadian High Schools," *Agriculture and Human Values* 25 (2008): 499-511.

9 Rong Tsao, Shahrokh Khanizadeh, and Adam Dale, "Designer Fruits and Vegetables with Enriched Phytochemicals for Human Health," *Canadian Journal of Plant Science* 86 (2006): 773-86; M.V. Eberhardt, C.Y. Lee, and R.H. Liu, "Antioxidant Activity of Fresh Apples," *Nature* 405 (2000): 903-4.

10 Deanna Rosolen, "Unleashing the Power of Phytochemicals," *Food in Canada*, April 2005.

11 See "Red Delicious Apples," http://www.stemilt.com/Our_Fruit/.

12 This research did not have the advantage of testing onions from the same growing situation, as in the case of Rong Tsao's apple research, so factors such as climate, soils, and growing regimes may have influenced the results. See Jun Yang, Katherine Meyers, Jan van der Heide, and Rui Hai Liu, "Varietal Differences in Phenolic Content and Antioxidant and Antiproliferative Activities of Onions," *Journal of Agricultural and Food Chemistry* 52, 22 (2004): 6787-93.

13 Ming Liu, Xin Qi Li, Courtney Webber, Chang Yong Lee, Janice Brown, and Rui Hai Liu, "Antioxidant and Antiproliferative Activities of Raspberries," *Journal of Agricultural and Food Chemistry* 50, 10 (2002): 2926-30.

14 Rui Hai Liu, "Potential Synergy of Phytochemicals in Cancer Prevention: Mechanisms of Action," *Journal of Nutrition*, supplement 134 (2004): 3479S-85S; Cornell University, "Disease-Fighting Chemicals in Apples Could Reduce the Risk of Breast Cancer, Cornell Study in Rats Suggests," *Science Daily*, 12 March 2005, http://www.sciencedaily.com/.

15 Friedland, Barton, and Thomas, *Manufacturing Green Gold*.

16 Commissioner Public Works and Mines, "Fruit Growing in Nova Scotia," reprinted from *The Annual Report of the Secretary for Agriculture, Province of Nova Scotia for the*

Year 1916 (Halifax: Commissioner Public Works and Mines, 1917), 162. In author's collection.

17 Agriculture and Agri-Food Canada, *Canadian Apple Online: History*, http://www. atn-riae.agr.ca/.

18 Frank Browning, *Apples* (New York: North Point Press, 1998), 106.

19 Robert Alison, "Scientists Decry Genetic Similarity of Today's Apples," *Toronto Star*, 7 August 2004, http://www.ecoearth.info/.

20 Quoted in Browning, *Apples*, 143.

21 See the company website at http://www.stemilt.com.

22 See Dan Wheat, "Stemilt's Young President Eyes Future of Fruit Industry," *Agricultural News*, 21 April 2010, http://www.capitalpress.com/.

23 Quoted in Browning, *Apples*, 146-47.

Chapter 8: Adulteration and the Rise of Pseudo Foods

1 Noel Coley, "The Fight against Food Adulteration," *Education in Chemistry*, March 2005, http://www.rsc.org/.

2 David Kessler, *The End of Overeating: Taking Control of the Insatiable North American Appetite* (Toronto: McClelland and Stewart, 2009), 19.

3 See *The Canadian Encyclopedia*, s.v. "Food Legislation," http://www.thecanadian encyclopedia.com/.

4 Coley, "The Fight against Food Adulteration."

5 Ibid.

6 See G.W. Monier-Williams, "Nutrition and Pure Food Laws," *Proceedings of the Nutrition Society*, 3 March 1951: 363-64, http://journals.cambridge.org/.

7 Ibid., 364.

8 Gary Gnirss, "A History of Food Law in Canada," *Food in Canada*, May 2008, 38.

9 James Harvey Young, *Pure Food: Securing the Federal Food and Drugs Act of 1906* (Princeton, NJ: Princeton University Press, 1989), 35-39.

10 Ibid., 6.

11 Ibid., 266.

12 In China, a history of diluting infant formula had led the government to crack down on offending companies. Formula was increasingly being checked with a test that used nitrogen content as a surrogate for assessing the protein content of foods such as milk, and hence a check on whether they had been watered down. Unscrupulous processors chose to mix melamine, a cheap chemical that has a high nitrogen content, in with their watered-down milk to fool government inspectors as to the protein content of the products. Melamine ingestion, unfortunately, can have deadly toxic effects on humans and other animals if ingested in sufficient amounts. See Julie R. Ingelfinger, "Melamine and the Global Implications of Food Contamination," *New England Journal of Medicine* 359 (25 December 2008): 2745-48.

13 Monier-Williams, "Nutrition and Pure Food Laws."

14 See Anthony Winson, "Bringing Political Economy into the Debate on the Obesity Epidemic," *Agriculture and Human Values* 21, 4 (Winter 2004): 299-312.

15 See ibid. In addition to the social science literature, this study is increasingly being cited in the medical science literature.

16 *Oxford Dictionary of English*, 2nd ed., s.v. "food"; Microsoft 7 Encarta 7 2006, compact disc, s.v. "Food" (Redmond, WA: Microsoft Corporation, 2005).

17 As North Americans become increasingly obese, so too have their pets and even the ever present urban rats that feed off the edible products dominating our food environments, according to author Jerry Langton. See *Rat: How the World's Most Notorious Rodent Clawed Its Way to the Top* (New York: St. Martin's Press, 2007).

18 New legislation stipulates that from April 2007, HFSS advertisements will not be permitted during or immediately before or after radio and television programs made for children (including preschool), or during or immediately before or after programs that are likely to be of particular appeal to children aged four to nine; and as of 1 January 2008, HFSS advertisements are not permitted during or immediately before or after programs that are likely to be of particular appeal to children aged four to fifteen. See Ofcom, http://www.ofcom.org.uk/consult/. However, the Conservative government elected in the United Kingdom in 2010 has adopted a much more "business friendly" approach to food policy that may undermine these advances.

19 US Department of Agriculture, "Energy Balance and Weight Management," *Report of the Dietary Guidelines Advisory Committee on the Dietary Guidelines for Americans, 2010* (Washington, DC: Centre for Nutrition Policy and Promotion, 2010), D1-9, http://www.cnpp.usda.gov/.

20 Winson, "Bringing Political Economy into the Debate."

21 CyberSoft Inc., *The NutriBase Nutrition Facts Desk Reference*, 2nd ed. (New York: Avery, 2001), 309-12. "Light" ice creams tend to have substantially lower fat levels than regular ice cream.

22 Ibid., 460-63.

23 Eric Schlosser, *Fast Food Nation: The Dark Side of the All-American Meal* (New York: Houghton Mifflin, 2001), 121.

24 Ibid., 125-26.

25 Kessler, *End of Overeating*.

26 Howard Moskowitz, Jacqueline Beckley, and Julie Adams, "What Makes People Crave Fast Foods?" *Nutrition Today* 37, 6 (November/December 2002): 237-42, also takes a quantitative approach to "craveability."

27 Kessler, *End of Overeating*, 16.

28 Ibid., 19.

29 Ibid., 31.

30 Ibid., 32.

31 Ibid., 32-34.

32 Ibid., 49.

33 Ibid., 37.

34 Some of this more recent research is examined in Centre for Science in the Public Interest, "Food and Addiction: Can Some Foods Hijack the Brain?" *Nutrition Action Health Letter* 39, 4 (May 2012): 3-7.

Chapter 9: The Spatial Colonization of the Industrial Diet

1 J. Kahane, "Sweet Opportunities: Maximize Your Profits in Confectionery," *Canadian Grocer*, September 2000, 59.

2 Cited in Marion Nestle and Michael Jacobsen, "Halting the Obesity Epidemic: A Public Health Policy Approach," *Obesity* 115 (2000): 19.

3 Kahane, "Sweet Opportunities," 59.

4 One might expect this penetration to be greater in the United States, where a much higher proportion of these institutions are for-profit enterprises.

5 Cited in Marion Nestle and Michael Jacobsen, "Halting the Obesity Epidemic," 19.

6 This was greatly facilitated, it should be remembered, by the then-novel franchising method of handling the bottling aspect of the company, with independent bottlers rapidly being established across the United States. There were over a hundred bottlers of Coca-Cola even by 1900.

7 As Marx noted, the process of centralization "is the concentration of capitals already formed, destruction of their individual independence, expropriation of capitalist by

capitalist, [and] transformation of many small into few large capitals ... Capital grows in one place into a huge mass in a single hand, because it has in another place been lost by many. This is centralization proper, as distinct from accumulation and concentration." Karl Marx, *Capital*, vol. 1 (Moscow: Progress Publishers, 1977 (repr. of English edition, ed. Frederick Engels [London: S. Sonnenschein, Lowrey, 1887]), 586.

8   In the United States, the Sherman Antitrust Act of 1890 made illegal "every contract, combination in the form of trust or otherwise, or conspiracy, in restraint of trade or commerce among the several States, or with foreign nations." This was amended by the Clayton Antitrust Act in 1914. Antitrust legislation in Canada has historically proven to be much weaker and the opportunities for monopolizing markets that much more possible.

9   See Anthony Winson, *The Intimate Commodity: Food and the Agro-Industrial Complex in Canada* (Toronto: Garamond Press, 1993), 104-5.

10 Tillotson notes that he has surveyed the authors of the US dietary guidelines on this score. See James E. Tillotson, "The Mega-Brands That Rule Our Diet, Part 1," *Nutrition Today* 40, 6 (November/December 2005): 257-60.

11 Ibid., 21.

12 Stephen Hymer, "The Internationalization of Capital," *Journal of Economic Issues* 6, 1 (1972): 99.

13 J. Kahane, "Sweet Opportunities," 59.

14 Anonymous, "Scrutinizing Snacks," *Progressive Grocer*, Special Report, November 1998, 8-9, 10-11.

15 Cited in D. Wellman, "The Big Crunch," *Supermarket Business* 54, 3 (March 1999): 46-48.

16 John Shoesmith, "Changing the Way C-Stores Do Business," *Canadian Grocer*, October 1992, 30-34.

17 Agriculture and Agri-Food Canada, Market and Industry Services Branch, Food Bureau, *The Canadian Snack Food Manufacturing Industry* (Ottawa: Market and Industry Services Branch, 1998), http://www4.agr.gc.ca/.

18 Frederic M. Scherer, "The Breakfast Cereal Industry," in *The Structure of American Industry*, 6th ed., ed. Walter Adams (New York: Macmillan, 1982), 195.

19 Ibid., 195.

20 Ibid.

21 Ibid., 211.

22 *Consumers Report*, February 1981, 76. Fortunately for consumers, in recent years, corporate concentration in the supermarket chain store end of the food economy has opened up opportunities for the latter to market store brands of breakfast cereals that have undercut somewhat the prices established earlier by the breakfast cereal-processing giants. This retail concentration has not always had positive outcomes for consumers, however. In this regard, see Winson, *Intimate Commodity*, chap. 7.

23 Agriculture and Agri-Food Canada, *Canadian Snack Food Manufacturing Industry*.

24 For a fuller discussion of this process, see Winson, *Intimate Commodity*, 122-27.

25 John Connor, Richard T. Rogers, Bruce W. Marion, and Willard E. Mueller, *The Food Manufacturing Industries* (Toronto: Lexington Books, 1985), 79.

26 Ibid., chap. 3.

27 Ibid., 80-82.

28 J. Taylor, S. Evers, and M. McKenna, "Determinants of Healthy Eating in Children and Youth," *Canadian Journal of Public Health*, supplement 3, 96 (2005): 20S-26S.

29 Marion Nestle, *Food Politics: How the Food Industry Influences Nutrition and Health*, 1st ed. (Berkeley: University of California Press, 2002), 22.

30 Calculated from *Advertising Age*, Special Report, Profiles Supplement, 25 June 2007.

31 Standard and Poor's analyst Donald Marleau, cited in *Toronto Star*, "Biofuels Push Up Corn Prices," January 29, 2011, B1.

32 See D. Howe, "The Food Distribution Sector," in *The Food Industry: Economics and Politics*, ed. Jim Burns (London: Heinemann, 1983), 307. The leverage that retailer concentration gives them has been recognized for some time. As Howe noted in the early 1980s, "The dominance of the large food distributors vis-à-vis manufacturers is evidenced by the additional discounts these mass distributors are able to extract from processors despite the market concentration among the latter" (113).

33 Eben Shapiro, "P&G Takes on the Supermarkets with Uniform Pricing," *New York Times*, 26 April 1992, 5.

34 Robert Matas, "Stocking Shelves Has a Hidden Cost," *Globe and Mail*, 12 February 1987, 1.

35 This is true for the traditional small and medium food processors that had emerged over the course of the twentieth century. In recent years, some chains have made space for small, artisanal processors, to make their food environments more interesting, especially to those with higher disposable incomes. The bulk of processed food sold is still controlled by an ever smaller number of major players, despite the proliferation of brands that give the illusion of a competitive marketplace.

36 See Michel Chevalier, "Increase in Sales Due to In-Store Display," *Journal of Marketing Research* 12 (1975): 426-31; Keith Cox, "The Effect of Shelf Space on Sales of Branded Products," *Journal of Marketing Research* 7 (1970): 55-58.

37 This is a trend that was noted in the trade journals some time ago. See S. MacLean, "A Frozen Novelty Is No Longer Just a Summertime Treat," *Canadian Grocer*, March 1992, 15-21.

38 These cereals, a breakfast favourite of North American children and bestsellers in the prepared-cereal category, have on average between four and five teaspoons of sugar for each single-serving equivalent. Four grams of sugar are equivalent to one teaspoon of sugar. See Joanne Larsen, *Ask the Dietitian: Junk Food*, 2003, http://www.dietitian.com/.

39 D. Burn, "Thriving on Consumers Hand-to-Mouth Existence," *Food in Canada*, January-February 1999, 13.

40 Neilsen Marketing Research, *Category Management: Positioning Your Organization to Win* (Chicago: NTC Business Books, 1992), 20.

41 See Kathy Chapman, P. Nicholas, D. Banovic, and R. Supramaniam, "The Extent and Nature of Food Promotion Directed to Children in Australian Supermarkets," *Health Promotion International* 21, 4 (2006): 331-39.

42 For a discussion of "food deserts," see L.F. Alwitt and T.D. Donley, "Retail Stores in Poor Urban Neighbourhoods," *Journal of Consumer Affairs* 31, 1 (1997): 139-64; Steven Cummins and Sally MacIntyre, "Food Environments and Obesity: Neighbourhoods or Nation?" *International Journal of Epidemiology* 35 (2006): 100-4; Rodolfo Nayga and Zy Weinberg, "Supermarket Access to the Inner City," *Journal of Retailing and Consumer Services* 6, 3 (1999): 141-45.

43 Reuben Guberman, "Convenience Stores: Past and Present," *Journal of Food Distribution Research* 2, 2 (September 1971): 36.

44 *Convenience Store News*, 28 August 2006, 31-32.

45 Ibid.

46 Anthony Winson, "Bringing Political Economy into the Debate on the Obesity Epidemic," *Agriculture and Human Values* 21, 4 (Winter 2004): 307.

47 Health and Welfare Canada, *Health Promotion* (Ottawa: Supply and Services Canada, 1989).

Chapter 10: Meals Away from Home

1 J. Tillotson, "Fast Food Through the Ages – Part 1," *Nutrition Today* 43, 2 (March/April 2008): 70.

2 S. Stender, J. Dyerberg, and A. Astrup, "Fast Food: Unfriendly and Unhealthy," *International Journal of Obesity* 31 (2007): 888.

3 US Department of Agriculture, "Energy Balance and Weight Management," *Report of the Dietary Guidelines Advisory Committee on the Dietary Guidelines for Americans, 2010* (Washington, DC: Centre for Nutrition Policy and Promotion, 2010), D1-6, http://www.cnpp.usda.gov/.

4 Although I was at first concerned that the salesman was only trying to upsell me a more expensive model, a closer look at the cheaper stoves did confirm in my mind that they were not up to the rigours of regular cooking.

5 Biing-Hwan Lin, Jayachandran Variyam, Jane Allshouse, and John Cromartie, *Food and Agricultural Commodity Consumption in the United States: Looking Ahead to 2020*, Agricultural Economic Report No. 820, (Washington: USDA, 2003), 5.

6 David Shardt, "It Was 40 Years Ago Today," *Nutrition Action Health Letter*, January/February 2011, 10.

7 See Daniel Workman, "Top Fast Food Countries," 29 August 2007, http://suite101.com/.

8 "R&I Top 400 Rankings," *Restaurant and Institutions*, 1 July 2008.

9 See James Binkley, "Calorie and Gram Differences between Meals at Fast Food and Table Service Restaurants," *Review of Agricultural Economics* 30, 4 (2008): 750.

10 I can think of no more insightful analysis of the forces that actually shape dietary recommendations than Marion Nestle's *Food Politics: How the Food Industry Influences Nutrition and Health*, 1st ed. (Berkeley: University of California Press, 2002), which focuses on the American situation.

11 Various studies have linked high-sugar foods and beverages to excess weight gain and obesity. For a review of these studies, see Jim Mann, "Sugar Revisited – Again," *Bulletin of the World Health Organization* 81, 8 (2003): 552, http://www.scielosp.org/.

    More recent evidence points to a link between excess sugar consumption and heart disease. See Alice Park, "Study: Too Much Sugar Increases Heart Risks," *Time*, 21 April 2010.

12 US Department of Health and Human Services and US Department of Agriculture, *Dietary Guidelines for Americans, 2010*, http://www.cnpp.usda.gov/; World Health Organization, *Diet, Nutrition and the Prevention of Chronic Diseases*, 2002, 56, http://whqlibdoc.who.int/.

13 See US Department of Health and Human Services, *2010 Dietary Guidelines Policy Document – Executive Summary*, 2010, http://www.cnpp.usda.gov/.

14 US Department of Health and Human Services and US Department of Agriculture, *Dietary Guidelines for Americans, 2010*, http://health.gov/dietaryguidelines/.

15 Health Canada, *Trans Fat Monitoring Program: Fourth Set of Monitoring Data* (Ottawa: Health Products and Food Branch, Food Directorate, Bureau of Nutritional Sciences, 2009), http://www.hc-sc.gc.ca/.

16 Stender, Dyerberg, and Astrup, "Fast Food," 888.

17 M.A. Pereira, A.I. Kartashov, C.B. Ebbeling, L. Van Horn, M.S. Slattery, and D.R. Jacobs Jr., "Fast Food Habits, Weight Gain, and Insulin Resistance (the CARDIA Study): 15-Year Prospective Analysis," *Lancet* 365 (2005): 36-42.

18 Margaret Craig-Schmidt and Carmen Teodorescu, "Trans Fatty Acids in Foods," in *Fatty Acids in Foods and Their Health Implications*, ed. Chink K. Chow (Boca Raton: CRC Press, 2008), 377-437.

19 See, for example, Megan Ogilvie, "Vegetarian Indian Fare Has No Health Halo," *Toronto Star*, 29 April 2011.

20 Tillotson, "Fast Food Through the Ages – Part 1," 73.

21 Information available at http://www.aboutmcdonalds.com/ and James Tillotson, "Fast Food: Ray Kroc and the Dawning of the Age of McDonald's," *Nutrition Today* 43, 3 (May-June 2008): 107-13.

PART 4:
GLOBALIZATION AND RESISTANCE IN THE NEO-LIBERAL ERA

1 Larry Busch and Carmen Bain, "New! Improved? The Transformation of the Global Agrofood System," *Rural Sociology* 69, 3 (2004): 321-46.

2 Ibid., 323.

3 Norm Campbell, Kim D. Raine, and Lindsay McLaren, "'Junk Foods,' 'Treats,' or 'Pathogenic Foods'? A Call for Changing Nomenclature to Fit the Risk of Today's Diets," *Canadian Journal of Cardiology* 28, 4 (2012): 403-4.

4 Lang and Heasman, *Food Wars: The Global Battle for Mouths, Minds and Markets* (London: Earthscan, 2004), 22.

Chapter 11: The Industrial Diet Goes Global

1 See "PepsiCo India Sales to Hit $1-Billion Mark Soon," *Domain-b.com*, 26 October 2004, http://www.domain-b.com/.

2 André Picard, "What Are We Doing to Stop the World's No. 1 Killer?" *Globe and Mail*, 6 December 2007, L6-7.

3 Quoted in Philip McMichael, "The Impact of Globalization, Free Trade and Technology on Food and Nutrition in the New Millennium," *Proceedings of the Nutrition Society* 60 (2001): 219.

4 This is not to say that no opportunities for growth in this context exist, only that compared with expansion in past decades, they are much more limited. Among the few growth opportunities today are those in the areas of the so-called "functional" foods and beverages, fresh and processed organic products, new ice cream products, and various food products and retail options catering to new-immigrant populations.

5 Barry M. Popkin, "Global Nutrition Dynamics: The World Is Shifting Rapidly toward a Diet Linked with Non-Communicable Diseases," *American Journal of Clinical Nutrition* 2, 84 (2006): 289.

6 This is in part tied up with the contemporary phenomenon of "land grabbing" impacting developing countries. For a deeper discussion of this issue, see the special issue of *Journal of Peasant Studies* 38, 2 (March 2011).

7 World Health Organization, "Obesity and Overweight," in *Global Strategy on Diet, Physical Activity and Health*, 2003, http://www.who.int/dietphysicalactivity/.

8 Ibid., 291.

9 Ibid., fig. 3.

10 J. Luo and F.B. Hu, "Time Trends of Obesity in Pre-School Children in China from 1989 to 1997," *International Journal of Obesity* 26 (2002): 553-58.

11 Yangfeng Wu, "Overweight and Obesity in China," *British Medical Journal* 333 (19 August 2006): 362-63.

12 Ricardo Uauy, Cecilia Albala, and Juliana Kain, "Obesity Trends in Latin America: Transiting from Under- to Overweight," *Journal of Nutrition*, supplement, 131 (2001): 893S-99S.

13 See Shashank Joshi and Rakesh Parikh, "India: Diabetes Capital of the World – Now Heading towards Hypertension," *Journal of the Association of Physicians of India* 55 (May 2007): 223-24.

14 Picard, "What Are We Doing?" L7.

15 Paul Zimmet, K.G.M.M. Alberti, and Jonathan Shaw, "Global and Societal Implications of the Diabetes Epidemic," *Nature* 414 (13 December 2001): 782.

16 Sarah Wild, Gojka Roglic, Anders Green, Richard Sicree, and Hilary King, "Global Prevalence of Diabetes," *Diabetes Care* 27, 5 (2004): 1047-53.

17 Orit Pinhas-Hamiel and Philip Zeilter, "The Global Spread of Type II Diabetes Mellitus in Children and Adolescents," *Journal of Pediatrics* 146 (2005): 693-700.

18 Catherine Yu and Bernard Zinman, "Type 2 Diabetes and Impaired Glucose Tolerance in Aboriginal Populations: A Global Perspective," *Diabetes Research and Clinical Practice* 78 (2007): 159-70.

19 A. Ramachandran, M.V. Jali, V. Mohan, C. Snehalatha, and M. Viswanathan, "High Prevalence of Diabetes in an Urban Population in South India," *British Medical Journal* 297 (3 September 1988): 587-90.

20 Joshi and Parikh, "India – Diabetes Capital of the World," 324.

21 See Jacob Mafunda, R. Chatora, Y. Ndambakuwa, P. Nyarango, A. Kosia, J. Chifamba, A. Filipe, A. Usman, and H. Sparks, "Emerging Non-Communicable Disease Epidemic in Africa: Preventive Measures from the WHO Office for Africa," *Ethnicity and Disease* 6 (Spring 2006): 521-26.

22 See Ayesha Motala, "Diabetes Trends in Africa," *Diabetes/Metabolism Research and Reviews* 18 (2002): S14-S20.

23 I visited small supermarkets that were operating in San José, Costa Rica, in 1979 and a larger supermarket operating in a well-to-do barrio of Mexico City the same year, for example. The produce and meats they offered were generally of inferior quality compared with the main food markets, however. This was to change by the 1990s. The earliest academic treatment of supermarkets in developing countries I have found is Erdener Kaynak and Tamer Cavusgil, "The Evolution of Food Retailing Systems: Contrasting the Experience of Developed and Developing Countries," *Academy of Marketing Science* 10, 3 (Summer 1982): 249-68. They note that Latin America had the earliest development of this retail form.

24 See, for example, Thomas Reardon, Peter Timmer, Christopher Barrett, and Julio Berdegué, "The Rise of Supermarkets in Africa, Asia, and Latin America," *American Journal of Agricultural Economics* 85, 5 (2003): 1140-46; Dinghuan Hu, Thomas Reardon, Scott Rozelle, Peter Timmer, and Honglin Wang, "The Emergence of Supermarkets with Chinese Characteristics: Challenges and Opportunities for China's Agricultural Development," *Development Policy Review* 22, 5 (2004): 557-86.

25 Anthony Winson, "Bringing Political Economy into the Debate on the Obesity Epidemic," *Agriculture and Human Values* 21, 4 (Winter 2004): 299-312.

26 See ibid.

27 This was my argument in my book *The Intimate Commodity* for Canada twenty years ago. More recently, Australian food analysts are making similar arguments in that context. See G. Lawrence and D. Burch, "Understanding Supermarkets and Agri-Food Supply Chains," in *Supermarkets and Agrifood Supply Chains: Transformations in the Production and Consumption of Foods*, ed. G. Lawrence and D. Burch (Cheltenham, UK: Elgar Publishing, 2007), 1-28.

28 James Tillotson, "Trends: Global Supermarkets," *Nutrition Today* 35, 3 (May/June 2000): 85.

29 These factors are mentioned in one of a series of articles produced by a research team that has pioneered the exploration of supermarket expansion in the developing countries and considered in particular the impact of this on the supply chain, notably the different types of agriculturalists who supply these chains. See Reardon et al., "The Rise of Supermarkets."

30 See *The Manufacturing Confectioner*, June 2009, 13.

31 See Reardon et al., "The Rise of Supermarkets," 1142.

32 W. Bruce Traill cautions that Reardon and his colleagues' analysis of the present and likely spread of supermarkets in South and East Asia is somewhat exaggerated. See Traill, "The Rapid Rise of Supermarkets," *Development Policy Review* 24, 2 (2006): 163-74.

33 This is reported in 2009 in "China Fact Sheet," an online publication found at Walmartstores.com.

34 See M. Chávez, "The Transformation of Mexican Retailing with NAFTA," *Development Policy Review* 2, 4 (2002): 503-13. Chávez makes the same point regarding the class of clientele that was initially served by early supermarkets in the case of Mexico.

35 According to John Harner, "Globalization of Food Retailing in Guadalajara, Mexico: Changes in Access Equity and Social Engagement," *Journal of Latin American Geography* 6, 2 (2007): 35.

36 Ibid., 35.

37 Ibid., 1141, 1143.

38 "Brazil Fact Sheet," 2009, originally found at walmartfacts.com, accessed June 2009.

39 Ibid., 1144.

40 Jason Konefal, Michael Mascarenhas, and Maki Hatanaka, "Governance in the Global Agro-Food System: Backlighting the Role of Trans-National Supermarket Chains," *Agriculture and Human Values* 22 (2005): 294.

41 This copycat behaviour by indigenous entrepreneurs is noted in the detailed study of McDonald's penetration of Asian markets by anthropologist James Watson and others, in James Watson, ed., *Golden Arches East: McDonald's in East Asia* (Stanford, CA: Stanford University Press, 2006).

42 Ibid., 13.

43 Yunxiang Yan, "McDonald's in Beijing: The Localization of Americana," in Watson, *Golden Arches East*, 62-63.

44 Ibid., 61.

45 As Yunxiang Yan notes of one young mother interviewee, "She wants her daughter not only to learn the skills needed in a modern society but also to eat modern food so she will grow up to be a successful person who knows how to enjoy a modern way of life." Ibid., 65.

46 Ibid., 50.

47 Ibid., 54.

48 Information for this section was found in McDonald's Corporation 2007 annual report, http://www.aboutmcdonalds.com/.

49 Yum! Brands, 2005 *Annual Customer Mania Report*, 2005, http://www.yum.com/investors.

50 Ibid., 3.

51 *Burger King Corporation Annual Report*, 8-10, http://www.media.corporate-ir.net/.

52 This and subsequent information taken from the company's *Nestlé Management Report*, 2007, http://www.nestle.com/.

53 For further information on this controversy and company campaigns to discredit its critics, see Marion Nestle, *Food Politics*, 2nd ed. (Berkeley: University of California Press, 2007), chap. 6.

54 See American Academy of Pediatrics, "Policy Statement: Breast Feeding and the Use of Human Milk," *Pediatrics* 115 (2 February 2005): 496-506; Julie Smith, "The Marketed Environment," in Jane Dixon and Dorothy Broom, eds., *The Seven Deadly Sins of Obesity* (Sydney: University of New South Wales Press, 2007), 101-25.

55 I have made an estimate of this last figure based on data from Nestlé, *Nestlé Management Report*, 2007, 60. It was not possible to estimate ice cream consumption for the different geographical regions, as these were grouped with other milk products.

56 Kraft Foods Inc., *Annual Report*, 2007.

57 Ibid., 3.

58 Ibid., 14.

59 Rosenfeld quoted in Gordon Pitts, "Kraft CEO Still Digesting Cadbury Takeover," *Globe and Mail*, 7 June 2010, B8.

60 Because much of its product sales occur through independent bottlers, revenue figures are difficult to calculate precisely.

61 See http://www.pepsiindia.co.in; "PepsiCo India grows 50 percent in Q3," *New Delhi Business Standard Reporter,* 15 October 2009, http://www.business-standard.com/; "PepsiCo to Set Up 4 New Plants in India," ExpressIndia.com, 19 November 2009, http://www.expressindia.com/.

62 This quote comes from PepsiCo CEO Steven Reinemund on the occasion of his 2004 visit to the company's India operations. See "PepsiCo India Sales."

63 See interview with the PepsiCo India CEO, "Pepsi Working to Tap India's Youth," *FoxBusiness.com,* 28 July 2009, http://www.foxbusiness.com/.

64 See "Pepsi Launches New 'What's Your Way!' Campaign for 'Youngistaan,'" 1888 Press Release, 21 October 2009, http://www.1888pressrelease.com/.

65 Jonathan Birchall, "Coca-Cola Aims to Triple China Sales," *Financial Times,* 22 November 2009, http://www.ft.com/.

66 Coca-Cola Limited, press release, "Coca-Cola Accelerates Expansion in China: Two Plant Openings Mark New Wave of Investment in China," 24 June 2009, http://www.thecoca-colacompany.com/.

67 For a company history of its involvement with the Olympics over the years, see Coca-Cola, http://www.thecoca-colacompany.com/.

68 Shaun Rein, "What Coca-Cola Did Wrong, and Right, in China," 24 March 2009, http://www.forbes.com/.

69 Birchall, "Coca-Cola."

70 Ibid. Rein notes that the central government typically approves takeovers of large national companies only if there is some added benefit, such as transfer of technology, advanced management, or access to foreign markets. Although there is relatively little evidence that the rapid expansion of American drink giants PepsiCo and Coca-Cola has yet sparked much in the way of popular nutritional controversy over their growing influence in developing countries, there has been considerable debate and protests of another kind. In India, for example, following the 2003 release of a study by the New Delhi-based Centre for Science and Environment that provided data indicating that the soft drink products of these companies had high levels of pesticides, a parliamentary committee was established and its report later corroborated the findings of the New Delhi NGO. The retesting of soft drinks in 2006 again found high pesticide levels, indicating little had been done in the interim. More recently, the Indian state of Kerala established a law to secure compensation for victims of alleged ground water contamination and depletion by these same companies. See Centre for Science and Environment, "Pesticides in Soft Drinks," http://www.cseindia.org/; Centre for Science and Environment and Pollution Monitoring Laboratory, "Analysis of Pesticide Residue in Soft Drinks," 2 August 2006, http://www.indiaenvironmentportal.org.in/; Savvy Soumya Misra, "Making Coca-Cola Pay," http://www.cseindia.org/; "Pepsi and Coke in India Victory," BBC News, 22 September 2006, http://news.bbc.co.uk/.

Chapter 12: Transformative Food Movements and the Struggle for Healthy Eating

Parts of this chapter were developed in an article published in *Rural Sociology* 75, 4 (December 2010), in an issue examining alternative food movements.

1 Jane Dixon and Dorothy Broom, eds., *The Seven Deadly Sins of Obesity* (Sydney: University of New South Wales Press, 2007), 178.

2 Kevin Morgan and Roberta Sonnino, *The School Food Revolution* (London: Earthscan Books, 2008), 165.

3 Author interview with Nick Saul, 22 June 2009.

4 Wynne Wright and Gerad Middendorf, *The Fight over Food* (University Park, PA: Pennsylvania State University Press, 2008), 3. See also William Friedland, "New Ways of Working and Organization: Alternative Agrifood Movements and Agrifood Researchers," *Rural Sociology* 75, 4 (2010): 601-27.

5 The literature documenting population-wide trends in weight gain in the developing and developed world is extremely extensive, and it is not possible to reference it here in a meaningful way. See Anthony Winson, "Bringing Political Economy into the Debate on the Obesity Epidemic," *Agriculture and Human Values* 21, 4 (Winter 2004): 299-312; "School Food Environments and the Obesity Issue: Content, Structural Determinants, and Agency in Canadian High Schools," *Agriculture and Human Values* 25 (2008): 499-511; and Chapter 11 in this volume for some useful citations; see Chapter 2 for discussion and documentation of the relationship between excess weights and early mortality and disease.

6 Excellent treatments of the forces behind neo-liberal policy in Canada is to be found in John Warnock, *Free Trade and the New Right Agenda* (Vancouver: New Star Books, 1988), and Patricia Marchak, *The Integrated Circus: The New Right and the Restructuring of Global Markets* (Montreal and Kingston: McGill-Queen's University Press, 1991).

7 Marion Nestle, *Food Politics*, 2nd ed. (Berkeley: University of California Press, 2007).

8 Its official report can be found at http://www.nfu.ca/gapsreport.html. The report notes, among many things, that "both procedural and data gaps were found which fail to properly address the human safety requirements of this drug under the Food and Drugs Act and Regulations." The whistle-blowing scientists were suspended from their duties by Health Canada and eventually fired in July 2004. For further details, see Chopra, *Corrupt to the Core: Memoirs of a Health Canada Whistleblower* (Caledon, ON: KOS, 2008), and Dr. Shiv Chopra, interview by Anna Maria Tremonti, *The Current*, CBC Radio One, 22 November 2011, http://www.cbc.ca/thecurrent/.

9 The testimony of one of the scientists, Dr. Margaret Haydon, to the Senate Standing Committee on Agriculture and Forestry, noted that an "offer" of between $1 and $2 million had been made by Monsanto to Health Canada scientists in a meeting. This scientist also testified that notes and files critical of scientific data provided by Monsanto had been stolen from a locked filing cabinet in her office, and that all files pertaining to the hormone technology were being controlled by one senior manager in Health Canada's Human Safety Division. Upon hearing this testimony, Senator Whelen is reported to have remarked, "What the hell kind of a system have we got here?": J. Baxter, "Monsanto Accused of Attempt to Bribe Health Canada for rBGH (Posilac) Approval," *Ottawa Citizen*, 23 October 1998, A1.

10 Marie-Monique Robin, *Le Monde Selon Monsanto*, directed by Marie-Monique Robin (Paris: ARTE éditions/Le Découverte, 2007), DVD; Marie-Monique Robin, *The World According to Monsanto*, directed by Marie-Monique Robin (Paris: ARTE France Développement, 2008), DVD. Distributed in Canada by the National Film Board.

11 On the US context, see, for example, Samuel Epstein, "Potential Public Health Hazards of Biosynthetic Milk Hormones," *International Journal of Health Services* 20 (1990): 73-84; Appendix 12, "Cancer Risks of Hormonal Milk," in *The Politics of Cancer Revisited*, by Samuel Epstein (Fremont Center, NY: East Ridge Press, 1998), 600-27. On the French context, see Robin, *Le Monde Selon Monsanto*.

12 See the Kroger press release on this issue at http://www.thekrogerco.com/.

13 Interview with Professor Bruce Holub, professor emeritus, Department of Human Nutrition, University of Guelph, Guelph, ON, December 2008.

14 See Sheryl Ubelacker, "Ottawa Urged to Set Amount of Trans Fats Allowed in Foods," *Globe and Mail*, 13 February 2009, A1.

15 Ibid.

16 Morgan and Sonnino, *School Food Revolution*.

17 S. French, M. Story, J.A. Fulkerson, and P. Hannan, "An Environmental Intervention to Promote Lower-Fat Food Choices in Secondary Schools: Outcomes of the TACOS Study," *American Journal of Public Health* 94, 9 (2004): 1507-12; M. Story, K. Kaphingst, and S. French, "The Role of Schools in Obesity Prevention," *Future of Children* 16, 1 (2006): 109-42, http://www.futureofchildren.org.

18 Michele Simon, *Appetite for Profit: How the Food Industry Undermines Our Health and How to Fight Back* (New York: Nation Books, 2006).

19 Story, Kaphingst, and French, "Role of Schools," 113-14.

20 Janet Poppendieck, *Free for All: Fixing School Food in America* (Berkeley: University of California Press, 2010), chap. 3.

21 Morgan and Sonnino, *School Food Revolution*, chap. 5.

22 This trend to transform kitchens into reheat operations for edible commodities of dubious nutritional value was noted in my fieldwork on school food environments in Ontario; see Winson, "School Food Environments."

23 Jeanette Orrey, cited in Morgan and Sonnino, *School Food Revolution*, 93.

24 Poppendieck, *Free for All*.

25 On the lucrative youth market, see Nestle, *Food Politics*, 2nd ed., chaps. 8 and 9. On this market being pivotal, see J.E. Brody, "Schools Teach 3 C's: Candy, Cookies and Chips," *New York Times*, 24 September 2002.

26 Manitoba Council on Childhood Nutrition, *Food and Nutrition in Manitoba Schools Survey Report*, 2001, 17, http://www.mbschoolboards.ca/.

27 Winson, "School Food Environments," 501.

28 See M. Nestle, "Soft Drink Pouring Rights," *Public Health Reports* 115 (2000): 308-19, for example. Pouring rights refer to the right granted to a beverage company through a contractual agreement to exclusive access to an institutional food environment, presumably in return for some monetary or non-monetary compensation to the granting institution.

29 French et al., "Environmental Intervention," 1507-12.

30 H. Wechsler, N.D. Brener, S. Kuester, and C. Miller, "Food Service and Foods and Beverages Available at School: Results from the School Health Policies and Programs Study 2000," *Journal of School Health* 71, 7 (2001): 313-24.

31 On Scottish social policy innovations, see Morgan and Sonnino, *School Food Revolution*, 93-94.

32 School Food Trust, 2005, http://www.schoolfoodtrust.org.uk/.

33 See M. Nelson, "The School Food Trust: Transforming School Lunches in England," *Nutrition Bulletin* 36, 3 (September 2011): 381-89.

34 In comparison, one can think of the ten long years of John Howard's conservative politics in Australia predating the recent Labor Party victory; the domination of the Republican Party in the United States through the Bush years and their still powerful role under the Obama administrations; the rule of the right-wing Christian Democrats in Germany; the Sarkozy government in France; the Berlusconi reign in Italy; the long-standing rule of a right-of-centre Liberal Party, followed by minority and now majority Conservative Party governments in Canada; and so on. Nevertheless, even in Britain it is clear that without considerable pressure from civil society, Tony Blair's Labour Party of recent years would have more likely left untouched the neo-liberal status quo.

35 J.E. Fried and M. Nestle, "The Growing Political Movement against Soft Drinks in Schools," *Journal of the American Medical Association* 288, 17 (2002): 2181.

36 See US Department of Health, Human Services, *The Surgeon General's Call to Action to Prevent and Decrease Overweight and Obesity* (Washington, DC: US Government Printing Office, 2001).

37 See Simon, *Appetite for Profit*.
38 Story, Kaphingst, and French, "Role of Schools," 122-23.
39 Ontario Society of Nutrition Professionals in Public Health, School Nutrition Workgroup Steering Committee, *Call to Action: Creating a Healthy School Nutrition Environment*, 2004, http://www.osnpph.on.ca.
40 Rumours circulated for some months during the time of writing among Canadian food analysts about leading politicians in British Columbia being spurred into action by an analyst's report arguing that the costs of obesity-related diseases would soon be so large that spending on health would strip revenues from all other ministries. A conversation between the author and a policy analyst in the provincial Ministry of Agriculture and Lands in June 2007 confirmed that such a report did exist and that it had a considerable impact.
41 M. Vallianatos, R. Gottlieb, and M.A. Haase, "Farm-to-School: Strategies for Urban Health, Combating Sprawl, and Establishing a Community Food Systems Approach," *Journal of Planning Education and Research* 23 (2004): 414-23.
42 Amanda Marshall, *Best Practices in Farm to School* (Toronto: Ontario Farm to School Network, 2006), 13-14.
43 See http://www.farmtoschool.org/.
44 Author's fieldwork with the project in 2006 and 2007.
45 K. Morgan and A. Morley, *Relocalising the Food Chain: The Role of Creative Public Procurement* (Cardiff, Wales: Regeneration Institute, Cardiff University, 2002).
46 Marshall, "Best Practices," 2006, 17-18.
47 See http://www.pepsico.com/
48 See Ofcom, "Television Advertising of Food and Drink Products to Children: Statement and Further Consultation," 2006, http://www.ofcom.org.uk/.

Chapter 13: Case Studies of a Transformative Food Movement

1 See http://www.marinorganic.org.
2 See M. Hamm and A. Bellows, "Community Food Security and Nutrition Educators," *Journal of Nutrition Education and Behavior* 35, 1 (2003): 37-43.
3 Author interview with Debbie Field, executive director of *FoodShare*, Toronto, July 2009.
4 FoodShare, *FoodShare Strategic Plan*, 2009-2011 (Toronto: FoodShare, 2009).
5 Debbie Field, "As FoodShare Sees It," *FoodShare* 15, 1 (2009): 2.
6 Foodshare, *FoodShare Strategic Plan*, 1.
7 Toronto District School Board, *Nutrition Task Force Report*, April 2009, 10.
8 There appears to be little public information about this reality, but I was able to verify this by contacting the majority of Ontario school boards in 2004 and asking how cafeteria food was provisioned.
9 Author interview with Lori Nikkel, Field to Table Schools Coordinator, Toronto, July 2009.
10 See Anthony Winson, "School Food Environments and the Obesity Issue: Content, Structural Determinants, and Agency in Canadian High Schools," *Agriculture and Human Values* 25 (2008): 499-511, which also discusses the situation in other Canadian provinces.
11 As was indicated in surveys of what was available in school cafeterias in several provinces conducted at different times since 2000; see ibid.
12 Toronto District School Board, *Nutrition Task Force Report*.
13 Ibid., 8.
14 Author's interview with Nick Saul, executive director of The Stop, Toronto, 22 June 2009. This organization originated as a food bank under the leadership of Reverend

Campbell Russell in the 1970s, much like FoodShare. It had at the time of interview drop-in and breakfast programs, a food bank, a community garden, a perinatal program, and a weekend farmers' market and food literacy programs for students at a renovated facility previously used by the city's transit commission, now known as the Green Barn. Saul referred to his organization as a "community food centre."

15 This research project, titled "Building Regional Food Hubs in Ontario: Fostering Linked-Up Thinking and Practice through Sustainable Food Systems," is funded by the Social Sciences and Humanities Research Council of Canada and involves a wide diversity of researchers. It has attempted to capture the diversity of alternative food networks and activities across the province and has conducted in-depth case studies of numerous initiatives to better understand their motivating influences, limitations, and prospects for growth.

16 Reported in Morgan and Sonnino, *School Food Revolution*, 172.

17 See Winson, "School Food Environments," and S.B. Austin, S. Melly, B. Sanchez, A. Patel, S. Buka, and S. Gortmaker, "Clustering of Fast Food Restaurants around Schools: A Novel Application of Spatial Statistics to the Study of Food Environments," *American Journal of Public Health* 95, 9 (2005): 1575-81.

18 See, for example, Darren Savage, "Student Food Fight in Brampton," *Toronto Sun*, 5 May 2012, 1-3. This conservative tabloid has chosen to give front-page exposure to a small group of students protesting recent Ontario government guidelines eliminating junk foods and beverages from high school cafeterias and vending machines, guidelines that follow those of several other provincial governments.

19 Vanessa Farquharson, "Fast-Food Giant Loses Foothold at Sick Kids," *Globe and Mail*, 21 March 2011, A14.

20 See Greenbelt Fund, "New Approach Means More Ontario Food for Hospital Patients," 18 January 2012, http://bpsinvestmentfund.ca/. Local food initiatives can be seen as complementary to, although not exactly the same as, healthy-eating initiatives. They would seem to be driven more by environmental goals than health goals, although it is difficult to draw a clear dividing line between such objectives.

Chapter 14: Toward a Sustainable and Ethical Health-Based Dietary Regime

1 Mark Bittman, "How to Save a Trillion Dollars," *New York Times*, 12 April 2011.

2 Mark Bittman, "Rethinking the Meat-Guzzler," *New York Times*, 27 January 2008.

3 Lang and Heasman, *Food Wars: The Global Battle for Mouths, Minds and Markets* (London: Earthscan, 2004), 16.

4 Further discussion on the ecological consequences of a meat-intensive diet is found in Tony Weis, "Crisis in the Food System: The Environmental Crisis," in *Critical Perspectives in Food Studies*, ed. M. Koc, J. Sumner, and A. Winson (Toronto: Oxford University Press, 2012), 104-21.

5 An in-depth analysis of the costs of factory farming of animal protein is to be found in World Society for the Protection of Animals, *What's on Your Plate? The Hidden Costs of Industrial Animal Agriculture in Canada* (Toronto: WSPA, 2012), http://www.wspa.ca/food.

6 For comprehensive coverage of myriad ways in which the food industry sells its products to children and youth, see J. Michael McGinnis, Jennifer Appleton Gootman, and Vivica I. Kraak, eds., *Food Marketing to Children and Youth: Threat or Opportunity?* (Washington, DC: National Academies Press, 2006), 516, http://www.nap.edu/.

7 Numerous writers have documented the radical deterioration of working conditions under the "race to the bottom" economics in the neo-liberal era. A wide-ranging discussion of the issue and reference to the extensive literature treating it can be found in Anthony Winson and Belinda Leach, *Contingent Work, Disrupted Lives: Labour and*

Community in the New Rural Economy (Toronto: University of Toronto Press, 2002), chap. 1.

8 Examples of this view are legion, though it was especially nicely illustrated by a recent editorial in Canada's leading newspaper, the *Globe and Mail*, castigating the Canadian Medical Association for advocating strong government measures to combat obesogenic food environments, and advocating the individual's right to freedom of choice in making decisions over the food they eat, free from government interference. See Editorial, "Toward a Utopia of Apples and Nuts," *Globe and Mail*, 27 April 2011, A16.

9 See Kelly Brownell and Katherine Battle Horgen, *Food Fight: The Inside Story of the Food Industry, America's Obesity Crisis and What We Can Do about It* (New York: McGraw Hill, 2004), 268-69.

10 George Lakoff, *Don't Think Like an Elephant: Know Your Values and Frame the Debate* (White River Junction, VT: Chelsea Green, 2004), xv.

11 Cited in Brownell and Horgen, *Food Fight*, 305.

12 See Mark J. Eisenberg, Renée Atallah, Sonia M. Grandi, Sarah B. Windle, and Elliot M. Berry, "Legislative Approaches to Tackling the Obesity Epidemic," *CMAJ* 183, 13 (September 20, 2011): 1496-1500.

13 Yoni Freedhoff and Paul C. Hébert, "Partnerships between Health Organizations and the Food Industry Risk Derailing Public Health Nutrition," Editorial, *Canadian Medical Association Journal* 183, 3 (February 22, 2011): 291-92.

14 I describe the conditions that prevailed in the Canadian context that led to calls for state intervention in the grains and dairy sectors in *The Intimate Commodity: Food and the Agro-Industrial Complex in Canada* (Toronto: Garamond Press, 1993), chap. 4. The market situation was sufficiently dire in both of these cases that the banking interests, in the case of the Prairie wheat economy, and the largest processors, in the case of the dairy industry in Ontario, came to see state intervention as a necessary step to restore the health of their respective industries.

15 See Brownell and Horgen, *Food Fight*, esp. chap. 11.

16 They have, in turn, built on the work of Kersh and Morone on the conditions for social health movements to take place; see R. Kersh and J. Morone, "The Politics of Obesity: Seven Steps to Government Action," *Health Affairs* 21 (2002): 141-53.

17 These points, with the exception of the issue around animal proteins, are inspired by what Loren Cordain calls the "seven keys to the Paleo diet"; see *The Paleo Diet* (Hoboken, NJ: John Wiley and Sons, 2002).

INDEX